The JOURNAL *of*
WILLIAM MACLAY

The JOURNAL *of* WILLIAM MACLAY

UNITED STATES SENATOR FROM
PENNSYLVANIA, 1789-1791

Introduction by
CHARLES A. BEARD

NEW YORK
ALBERT & CHARLES BONI
1927

INTRODUCTION

This Journal by William Maclay, who may be called with
some justice the original Jeffersonian Democrat, is one of the
most precious human documents for the study of American
manners, morals, and intelligence, political and general. Cover-
ing the years 1789–91, it deals with the period which witnessed
the inauguration of the federal government under the Constitution. Through the burning glare of its spot light stalk, amble,
or drift all the distinguished personalities of the age, from
George Washington to Fisher Ames. It opens the doors of
private homes, reporting table talk and gossip, describing the
"intellectual climate" of the time. In one burst of illumina-
tion after another, it shoots fire-flares into the workshop behind
the splendid façade of Alexander Hamilton's public structure,
showing us the great fathers of the republic in their shirt sleeves,
planning, caucusing, cutting, fitting, compromising, and deciding. Glowing through its pages are the emotions that called into
life the popular party led to victory by Thomas Jefferson in
1800. Besides all this, the Journal has a special value for politics, because the Senate of the United States at the time sat behind closed doors, keeping from the eyes and ears of the com-
monalty the sights and sounds that accompanied Hamilton's
great economic measures on their way through that exalted legislative body, enriching thousands of private citizens while establishing national credit and firmly fixing the American republic
upon a secure foundation.

It must be conceded, of course, that William Maclay was not
a cold, judicial witness to the scenes he describes. A Scotchman
from the interior of Pennsylvania, a lawyer with a classical
training, who lived on a farm near Harrisburg, then almost a
frontier town, Maclay was a bit awkward in the presence of
grand Virginia gentlemen and plutocratic merchants from Boston or Philadelphia. Elected to the United States Senate by the
Pennsylvania legislature in 1789, he entered that small, compact

upper chamber of planters, speculators, financiers, and merchants, with a decided animus. An apostle of agrarian simplicity, he feared and disliked the party of ceremony, high tone, and strong government—the party that was striving to surround the new republican system with pomp and circumstance to dazzle the forerunners of Moronia—ancestors of the tabloid readers. Primarily concerned with the interest of the small farmers for whom he spoke—on whom most of the taxation for the support of Hamilton's system was to fall—Maclay opposed that efficient Secretary's scheme for funding the depreciated debt at face value and likewise his project for establishing a United States Bank, both measures designed to make the load for the burden-bearers as heavy as possible without spoiling the play by breaking their backs. Finding himself surrounded in Congress by men who were speculating in public securities and making money out of the very laws they were passing, the agrarian Maclay saw Jefferson's "corrupt squadron" in full operation long before the Sage of Monticello arrived on the scene to take up his duties as Secretary of State. And hearing the same pocket-filling legislators daily resorting to the rhetoric of patriotism and purity, Maclay early acquired a certain bitterness of temper, which made it impossible for him to appreciate all the humor of the situation and to appraise at full value all the splendid national services rendered by the party of Alexander Hamilton. Moreover Maclay was unacquainted with that great law of political science according to which the bee fertilizes the flower that it despoils, working wonders in destiny beyond the purposes of the hour; and being ignorant of that law, he allowed his bitterness to get the better of his discretion, filling his pages with savage comment and terrible scorchings, unrelieved by a regard for extenuating circumstance and noble motives—plus fifty per cent profit. For all these reasons and many more, Maclay's Journal is a piquant and dangerous document, to be read only by a select audience, behind closed doors, and in quiet hours when the Grand Khan for the Preservation of Public Purity is not watching.

It will, perhaps, help the reader to pick his way through the technicalities and personalities of Maclay's Journal to give a brief account of the great political measures on the carpet in the period covered by its pages and to indicate their economic significance. First among the issues before Congress, when our author took his place in the Senate, was the project for funding at face value all the continental debt of the United States and the assumption by the federal government of the revolutionary war debt incurred by the states. Combined, these two accounts amounted to about $60,000,000 in round numbers. Now during the preceding years, this paper, which had been highly inflated from the beginning, had sadly depreciated in value, until it was selling at from ten to fifteen cents on the dollar. While the public credit was in this demoralized condition, shrewd speculators sent agents around, bought up enormous quantities at low prices, and put their holdings quietly away in anticipation of a better day. As soon as the Constitution was adopted, their paper began to rise rapidly and when it was rumored that Hamilton, as Secretary of the Treasury, intended to propose that Congress should fund it all at face value, the appreciation of public securities became all the more marked. To make a long story short, by the political action of Congress during Maclay's sessions, a number of American citizens found their private estates enormously increased. Altogether perhaps $40,000,000 was transferred from the taxpayers to the security holders. Of course many of the latter, perhaps a majority, were bona fide patriots who had lent money to the government in the hour of its distress but many others were speculators who had bought up old paper from the original creditors.

In the Senate and in the House of Representatives, this security holding interest was abundantly defended. Of the twenty-six Senators who composed the upper house as fully organised, at least sixteen were security owners and of the fourteen Senators who voted in favor of the assumption bill in July, 1790, ten were security holders. In the House of Representatives, more than one-half of the members were owners of federal paper. Like the owners outside of Congress, probably a majority of them were bona fide public creditors, but beyond a question a number of them were feverish speculators enriching themselves while redeeming the faith of the republic.

Second among Hamilton's measures, which vexed the soul of Senator Maclay, was a scheme for a United States Bank, with a large capital stock, three-fourths of which was to consist of newly uttered federal paper. Thus the Bank was to draw interest on the bonds subscribed as stock, engage in a general banking business, issue notes, make discounts, and lend money, making a handsome profit on the basis of the once almost worthless revolutionary war debt. The right to buy bank stock with new bonds added of course to their value and helped to carry them higher in the stock market. Now several members of Congress were interested in the Bank as well as in raising the price of their securities.

Third among Hamilton's projects was his revenue scheme. He proposed to raise the money to meet the obligations of the new funded debt by laying customs duties which gave protection to manufacturing industries, supplemented by excises on whiskey. By one logical process or another, the spokesmen of the agricultural interest in Congress got it into their heads that these two species of taxation fell especially upon the tillers of the soil, who at the time formed about nine-tenths of the population. Through a chain of reasoning not very subtle, they arrived at the conclusion that Hamilton's party of finance, manufacturing, and merchandising was thriving at the expense of agriculture. With the correctness of that conclusion, the historian is not especially concerned, but the existence of the conviction is a prime factor of which he must take cognizance.

The situation, thus intrinsically amazing to bucolic innocence, was made all the more irritating to the agrarian school by the action of the former Tories, who had been loyal to King George during the late revolutionary war and had remained in the country. As Dr. J. Franklin Jameson points out in his little book on *The American Revolution Considered as a Social Movement,* the old Tories had numbered in their ranks perhaps a majority of the richest merchants, lawyers, and Anglican divines, and those who staid in the United States were drawn by social position and interest to the party of Hamilton rather than to the party of radicals led by Jefferson. Thus the former Tories, as well as the merchants, speculators, financiers, and manufacturers, looked to the Secretary of the Treasury as the best hope for "sound public policies." Hence the stern old Roman from his Harrisburg farm, William Maclay, on taking his bearings in

Congress, found his position almost too perplexing for endurance.

According to his own account, Maclay arrived in Congress with exalted notions of public duty and senatorial obligations, but before long "a heavy kind of melancholy" settled down upon him. On August 31, of his first year's service, he felt compelled to record: "With the Senate I am certainly disgusted. I came here expecting every man to act the part of a god; that the most delicate honor, the most exalted wisdom, the most refined generosity was to govern every act and be seen in every deed. What must my feelings be on finding rough and rude manners, glaring folly, and the basest selfishness apparent in almost every public transaction! They are not always successful it is true; but is it not dreadful to find them in such a place?" His humor was not improved when he discovered that Senator William S. Johnson, who had played the rôle of a non-resistant Tory in the Revolution and whose son was among the boldest speculators in public securities, was allowed mileage to Connecticut, although he lived in New York where he was at the time acting as the efficient president of Columbia College. (April 3, 1790.)

Maclay's difficulties were made all the more harassing because he had to find his way about in the shadows. The air was full of rumors. Speculators were buzzing around in every quarter. But as the account books of the government were safely guarded in Hamilton's department, it was impossible to discover who were bona fide patriots, interested solely in establishing a strong government and rehabilitating public credit, and who were plain gamblers using their inside information to enrich themselves in the market. Hence Maclay had to form his judgments largely on the basis of gossip, and in the natural extension of his suspicion, he became too severe in his judgments. This must be conceded even though we reject J. Franklin Jameson's harsh judgment to the effect that Maclay's mind was "sullen, mean, and envious."

Yet it would be a mistake to imply that Maclay was without humor. On the contrary, he must have had a sardonic grin on his face most of the time during the highest-toned debates. For example, on February 15, 1790, he went over to the House of

Representatives, to hear Hamilton's partisans attack James Madison's proposal to make a compromise in funding the debt, by paying part of the increased value to the original creditor who had risked his money to save his country and part to the speculator who had purchased the depreciated paper to enrich himself. In a long argument, Ames, of Massachusetts, a security holder, bitterly criticised this project, and Maclay, after listening to it, recorded in his Journal that Ames "had 'public faith,' 'public credit,' 'honor,' and above all 'justice,' as often over as an Indian would the 'Great Spirit,' and if possible with less meaning and to as little purpose. Hamilton, at the head of the speculators, with all the courtiers, are on one side. These I call the party who are actuated by interest. The opposition are governed by principle, but I fear in this case interest will outweigh principle." Anyway, Madison was beaten.

Besides the matter of "interest" which vexed Maclay's agrarian soul, there was the ceremonial business which made him endless trouble. In their anxiety to give the federal government dignity and power, the supporters of Hamilton's projects sought to surround President Washington with pomp and circumstance. Speaking on this point, the Vice-President, John Adams, the presiding officer in the Senate, said that when Washington "comes here we must have a seat for him. In England it is called a *throne*. To be sure, it is behind that seat we must seek shelter and protection." Lee, of Virginia, then proposed that they should have "a seat with a canopy for the President." But on account of objections from such radicals as Maclay, no canopied throne was provided—leading one to speculate whether later administrations, let us say, those of Harding and Coolidge, would not have been more efficient with some such ceremonial support.

The same party of prostration which wanted a throne also desired a resounding title for the President, suggesting that this great functionary should be called "his Highness the President of the United States of America and Protector of the Rights of the Same." John Adams, who, as a member of the middle class in Massachusetts, had often been snubbed by the upper class assembled around the court of the provincial governor, blazed out hotly for titles, and it looked for a while as if the President might be accorded some of the dignity of the Grand Turk; but the attempt was defeated amid much scorn from Maclay. Even the presidential message was not to be hailed as "His Most Gracious Speech."

Equally savage was Maclay's aversion for presidential levees. "Nothing is regarded, or valued at such meetings," he snapped, "but the qualifications that flow from the tailor, barber, or dancing master. To be clean shaved, shirted, and powdered, to make your bows with grace, and to be master of small chat on the weather, play, or newspaper anecdote of the day are the highest qualifications necessary. Levees may be useful in old countries where men of great fortune are collected, as it may keep the idle from being much worse employed. But here I think they are hurtful." So instead of the grand levee, with His Highness, President Coolidge and Her Highness, Lady Coolidge, standing on a raised throne under a gilt canopy, bowing coldly to admirers on the floor below, there are hand-shaking parties on New Year days.

Besides illuminating, in his way, political issues and customs, Maclay drew pictures of his great contemporaries, as he saw them through the spectacles of opposition. For Washington, he had deep respect, but as the play proceeded, he came to the conclusion that the President was being used by Hamilton's party to promote the economic measures that so sharply divided the country. On March 4, 1790, the Senators dined at the executive mansion. "The President," wrote Maclay, "seemed to bear in his countenance a settled aspect of melancholy. No cheering ray of convivial sunshine broke through the cloudy gloom of settled seriousness. At every interval of eating or drinking he played on the table with a fork or knife like a drumstick. Next to him, on his right, sat Bonny Johnny Adams, ever and anon mantling his visage with the most unmeaning simper that ever dimpled the face of folly." In a moment of bitterness, Maclay burst out on December 14, 1790, that "Republicans are borne down by fashion and a fear of being charged with a want of respect to General Washington. If there is treason in the wish I retract it, but would to God this same General Washington were in heaven! We would not then have him brought forward as the constant cover to every unconstitutional and irrepublican act."

To such a pass, had Maclay's temper brought him after a few months' service in the Congress of the United States.

Although even in the most perplexing moments, Maclay had the highest respect for President Washington's personal character and dignity, he could not find anything to praise in the Secretary of State, Thomas Jefferson, who was in due time to marshal the agrarian hosts under a Republican banner and oust the party of Hamilton from power. When on May 24, 1790, Jefferson appeared before a Senate committee of which Maclay was a member, the diarist was not favorably impressed. "Jefferson is a slender man; has rather the air of stiffness in his manner; his clothes seem too small for him; he sits in a lounging manner, on one hip commonly, and with one of his shoulders elevated much above the other; his face has a sunny aspect; his whole figure has a loose, shackling air. He had a rambling, vacant look, and nothing of that firm collected deportment which I expected would dignify the presence of a secretary or minister. I looked for gravity but a laxity of manner seemed shed about him. He spoke almost without ceasing. But even his discourse partook of his personal demeanor. It was loose and rambling and yet he scattered information wherever he went—and even some brilliant sentiments sparkled from him. The information which he gave us respecting foreign ministers, etc., was all high-spiced." Such was the man whose opinions and judgments with reference to Hamilton's economic policies and political conduct, Maclay anticipated all along the line, voicing at the national capital the sentiments of democratic-republicanism long before the sage of Monticello discovered what "game was on the carpet" or arrived at any definite theories concerning it—if indeed Jefferson ever did possess any reasoned economic system.

Descending frequently from high matters of state, Maclay made notes in his Journal on every kind of topic that interested his contemporaries. On July 12, 1789, for example, he surveyed the ways of Providence, and finding no rhyme, reason, or justice gave up the effort to "rend the impenetrable veil." Sunday, February 13, 1791, he heard a large company of neighbors discussing religion and recorded: "most unmercifully was it handled." Anticipating the modern hard-headed school, someone gave an economic interpretation of Protestantism: "The new doctrine was, faith is better than cash; only believe, and save your money." July 21, 1790, Maclay had a great laugh at England's historic pretexts for war: "balances of power, balances of trade, honor of the flag, sovereignty at sea, &c" and came to the conclusion that the British had paid dearly for such delusions. Foreign affairs, rheumatism, cures of ills, the physical effects of wines, menus at state dinners, family affairs, avarice and ambition in politics, scrambles over mileage and pay for members of Congress, in a word, everything in the pageant of life received a shrewd, and sometimes cutting, memorandum in Maclay's pages.

To crown it all, Maclay knew the English language and could write it. His style is clear, ordered, moving, and it is made rich with racy old words and ripping figures of speech. Anyone who really wants to discover the spirit that lay behind Jeffersonian democracy simply must read, nay, study, this Journal, having an eye, of course, for the bias of the author; and anyone who loves rich old lore, like old wine in dusty bottles, must make it a familiar companion.

CHARLES A. BEARD.

New Milford, Connecticut,
April 20, 1927.

PREFACE

There is a tendency, when dealing with public men of the past, to throw a glamour around their memory, and, by a systematic perversion or ignoring of facts, to lead present generations to regard them as little less than deities. The signers of the Declaration of Independence, the framers of our Constitution, and all who in any way were involved in the inception of this nation, are venerated with a childlike awe, rendering us oblivious to the motives which led to those occurrences or to the pressure of circumstances which induced many to take the course they did. The journal of William Maclay, beginning with the 24th of April, 1789, and ending on the 3d of March, 1791, gives a graphic description of the debates, ceremonies, and social life of that important period of our national existence. Some hesitancy has been felt in giving an unreserved publication of this journal to the world, owing to the severity of the criticisms made on prominent personages, which in a large degree serve to dispel the roseate illusions in reference to men of that day. It should be kept in mind, however, that the journal was strictly private in its nature, intended merely for personal reference, and that the thought of its publication seems never to have entered the mind of its author, else he undoubtedly would have smoothed over many phrases and erased entire passages, as being too forcible for public expression.

But in just this circumstance lies the great value of the work. William Maclay wrote every evening of events which took place during the day. He wrote while his mind was yet heated with the fierce debates in the Senate, and while the scenes were yet fresh in his memory, thus transmitting on paper pictures of historical events which are wonderfully vivid. Great care, therefore, has been taken to give the present publication word for word from the original manuscript, even to the spelling of proper names: Ellsworth being spelled with one "l," Read as Reed, Beckley, Clerk of the House of Representatives, as Buckley, and Carroll as Carrol.

William Maclay, like many of those who were actively engaged in the Revolution, was of Scotch descent, his father,
Charles Maclay, having sailed for America in 1734. The
brothers of William Maclay were also active in the movements
which led to the overthrow of British supremacy in America;
his brother, the Hon. John Maclay, being a member of that
conference held in "Carpenters' Hall" which declared that "they,
in behalf of the people of Pennsylvania, were willing to concur
in a vote of Congress declaring the United Colonies free and
independent States." John Maclay also served three terms in
the Pennsylvania Legislature, 1790, 1792, and 1794. Another
brother of William Maclay, the Hon. Samuel Maclay, was
chosen Speaker of the Pennsylvania State Senate, of which
body he was a member from 1797 to 1802, and resigned in 1802
in order to serve in the United States Senate, where he represented Pennsylvania from 1802 to 1809.

William Maclay was born on the 20th of July, 1737, in New
Garden Township, Pennsylvania, and was educated in the
classical school of the Rev. John Blair. He studied law, and was
admitted to practice at the York County bar, April 28, 1760.
At the close of the French and Indian War he visited England
and had an interview with Thomas Penn, one of the proprie-
taries, relative to the surveys in the middle and northern parts
of the province. In 1772 he laid out the town of Sunbury, and
erected for himself a stone house, which was standing a few
years since. He acted as the representative of the Penn family,
and took a prominent part in the so-called Pennamite war. At
the outset of the Revolution, although an officer of the pro-
prietary Government, he took an active part in favor of independence, during which struggle he held the position of assistant commissary. In 1781 he was elected to the Assembly of
Pennsylvania, and from that time filled the offices of member of
the Supreme Executive Council, Judge of the Court of Common
Pleas, deputy surveyor, and was one of the commissioners for
carrying into effect the laws respecting the navigation of the
Susquehanna. In January, 1789, he was elected to the United
States Senate. The question as to who should hold the long term
of office was decided by lot—William Maclay drawing the short
term, while Robert Morris, his colleague, drew the long term.

William Maclay began to differ with the Federalists very early in the session. He did not approve of the state ceremony attendant upon the intercourse of the President with Congress; he flatly objected to the presence of the President in the Senate while business was being transacted; and boldly spoke against his policy in the immediate presence of President Washington. He was one of the foremost in opposing the chartering of the United States Bank, even at the sacrifice of personal popularity, for the strong Democratic position he took and the stubbornness with which he maintained it in the face of overwhelming pressure cost him his re-election, he being succeeded by an ardent Federalist.

So pronounced were the Democratic views of William Maclay, and so boldly and ably did he maintain his position in the face of the opposition, that the question can well be raised if he, rather than Thomas Jefferson, was not the true founder of the Democratic party. It is well known that on the organization of the "new Government," as it was then called, April, 1789, Thomas Jefferson was in France, where he had resided since 1784, and that he did not arrive in New York, then the seat of government, until March, 1790, some eleven months after the Federal machine had been in operation. And it was some time after he took his place as Secretary of State that his influence and ability as a leader of men were felt among the elements composing the Democratic party. It was during these first months of the new Government's life that questions seriously affecting its character, whether to be monarchial or republican in its forms, were fiercely debated and decided. It was then that the foundations of the great Democracy were laid; the superstructure erected by Thomas Jefferson being in conformity with the precedents then and there irrevocably established.

Who, then, was the leader of the opposition to this strong monarchical tendency? The records of the First Congress, unfortunately, are fragmentary and meager, so that little has been known of the stirring debates that took place at that time. The Journal of William Maclay, however, throws a flood of light on this period, and establishes beyond cavil the claims of Pennsylvania to having produced the father of the Democratic party in the person of William Maclay.

For a hundred years this valuable journal has been jealously guarded from public scrutiny by the descendants of the statesman. Portions of it were privately printed in 1880, and a limited edition distributed among the members and friends of the family. Many passages, however, were suppressed, as being too caustic in their strictures on eminent personages whom we are accustomed to regard with the highest veneration. This, however, in a great measure, destroyed the complexion of the context and the value of the work. But, now that an unreserved publication is called for in the interest of history, it will be seen that William Maclay was foremost in the opposition to these extreme monarchical views of the Federalists, and that in combating and subverting their aspirations he laid the foundation of the Democratic party.

On his retirement from the Senate, William Maclay resided on his farm, adjoining Harrisburg, where he erected a stone mansion. In the year 1795 he was elected a member of the Pennsylvania House of Representatives, and was again elected in 1803. He was a presidential elector in 1796, and from 1801 to 1803 officiated as one of the Associate Judges of Dauphin County. He died on the 16th of April, 1804, in Harrisburg, and is buried in Paxtang churchyard.

He was a man of the strictest integrity, positive opinions, keen insight into the underlying motives of men, and with indomitable perseverance and tenacity of purpose in carrying out views once formed. In personal appearance he was six feet and three inches in height, light complexion, while his hair, in middle age, appears to have been brown, and was tied behind or "clubbed." Mr. Harris, of Harrisburg, narrates that he "well remembered, when a young collegian, during the summer vacation he used to watch Mr. Maclay wearing a suit of white flannel, with lace ruffles, walking up and down the river-bank in Maclayville—as it was then called—and he thought he had never seen such a dignified, majestic old gentleman: while," he added, "I was always half afraid of him—he seemed to awe me into insignificance."

EDGAR S. MACLAY.

New York, *August, 1890.*

CONTENTS

PART ONE:

FIRST SESSION
OF THE FIRST CONGRESS

CHAPTER I

ON TITLES AND CEREMONIES

New York, 24th April, 1789.—I understood that it was agreed among the Senators yesterday that they would meet at the Hall this morning and go in a body to pay their respects to General Washington. I went about ten o'clock to the Hall, accordingly; there was, however, no person there. After staying some time, Elsworth came in. I suspected how it was. I repeated the conversation of last night, and asked him whether he had been to wait on the General. *Yes, he had been, and a number more with him; some went last night and some this morning.* What a perfidious custom it is! I, however, whipped downstairs and joined the Speaker and a number more of the Pennsylvanians who were collecting for that purpose. Went, paid my respects, etc. Mind this, not to resent it, but to keep myself more out of his power. Mr. Izard had yesterday been very anxious to get a report adopted respecting the communications between the Houses. It was so, but now we hear the House laughed at it. Mr. Izard moved to have the adoption taken from the minutes. No, this could not be done.

But now a curious scene opened. Mr. Lee, being of the Title Committee of yesterday, produced a copy of the resolution for appointing that committee, and moved that the House should pass a vote for transmitting it down to the Lower House. This was truly ridiculous; but, mind, this base business had been gone into solely yesterday on the motion of our Vice-President.

This was barefaced indeed. But now Lee wanted to bring it on again when the President would not appear in it. I likewise suspect Lee's integrity in this business. He knows the giving of titles would hurt us. I showed the absurdity of his motion plain enough, but it seems to me that, by getting a division of the resolution, I could perhaps throw out the part about titles altogether. Mr. Carrol, of Maryland, showed he was against titles. I wrought it so far that I got a question whether we should throw out the part about titles altogether. We lost the question on the throwing out that part. However, I could plainly see that we had gained ground with the House.

Now a most curious question arose. The Vice-President knew not how to direct the letter to the Speaker. He called on the House to know how it should be directed. The House showed a manifest disinclination to interfere. The Vice-President urged, and ceased not until a question was pointedly put whether the Speaker should be styled *honorable*. It passed in the negative, and from this omen I think our Vice-President may go and dream about titles, for none will he get.

April 25th, Saturday.—Attended the House. Ceremonies, endless ceremonies, the whole business of the day. I did not embark warmly this day. Otis, our Secretary, makes a most miserable hand at it. The grossest mistakes made on our minutes, and it cost us an hour or two to rectify them. I was up as often I believe as was necessary, and certainly threw so much light on two subjects that the debate ended on each.

The Vice-President, as usual, made us two or three speeches from the Chair. I will endeavor to recollect one of them. It was on the reading of a report which mentioned that the President should be received in the Senate chamber and proceed thence to the House of Representatives to be sworn: "Gentlemen, I do not know whether the framers of the Constitution had in view the two kings of Sparta or the two consuls of Rome * when they formed it; one to have all the power while he held it, and the other to be nothing. Nor do I know whether the architect that formed our room and the wide chair in it (to hold two, I suppose) had the Constitution before him. Gentlemen, I feel great difficulty how to act. I am possessed of two separate powers; the one in *esse* and the other in *posse*. I am Vice-President. In this I am nothing, but I may be everything. But I am president also of the Senate. When the President comes into the Senate, what shall I be? I can not be [president] then.

---

* "Are we," Adams observed in the Senate, "the two kings of Sparta, the two consuls of Rome, or the two suffetes of Carthage?"—J. C. Hamilton's History of the United States, vol. iii, p. 560.

No, gentlemen, I can not, I can not. I wish gentlemen to think what I shall be."

Here, as if oppressed with a sense of his distressed situation, he threw himself back in his chair. A solemn silence ensued. God forgive me, for it was involuntary, but the profane muscles of my face were in tune for laughter in spite of my indisposition. Elsworth thumbed over the sheet Constitution and turned it for some time. At length he rose and addressed the Chair with the utmost gravity: "Mr. President, I have looked over the Constitution (pause), and I find, sir, it is evident and clear, sir, that wherever the Senate are to be, there, sir, you must be at the head of them. But further, sir (here he looked aghast, as if some tremendous gulf had yawned before him), I shall not pretend to say."

Thursday next is appointed for swearing in the President. I am worse of my rheumatism, but perhaps it is owing to the change of the weather, for the wind is at the northeast and cold. Gave Mr. Vandalsen an half Johannes; * he is to sell it and give me credit for the amount of his bill, 41s. 3d.

26th April, Sunday.—Went out half after nine o'clock. Visited Governor St. Clair, General Butler, Delany, McPherson, at Elsworth's. Called on Mr. Clymer and Mr. Fitzsimons. Mr. Clymer in the *exceptionables,* or peevish and fretting at everything. I know not how it is, but I can not get into these men. There is a kind of guarded distance on their parts that seems to preclude sociability. I believe I had best be guarded too. The very end of this visit was to try to concert some measures with them for the removal of Congress. But they kept me off. I mentioned a favorable disposition in some of the Maryland gentlemen to be in unison with the Pennsylvanian delegation. They seemed not to credit me. Mr. O'Brien and Mr. Hartly came in, and I took my leave. Came home, and, as the day was blustering and cold, stayed all day in my room. Wrote some letters. Mr. Wynkoop dined out, so I saw nobody.

27th April, 1789, Monday.—Tried my knee and walked a good deal. Attended the Hall. We had prayers this day by the chaplain, Dr. Provost. A new arrangement was reported from the Joint Committee of Ceremonies. This is an endless business.

---

* A Portuguese gold coin, equal to about eight dollars.

Lee offered a motion to the Chair that after the President was sworn (which now is to be in the gallery opposite the Senate chamber), the Congress should accompany him to Saint Paul's Church and attend divine service. This had been agitated in Joint Committee. But Lee said expressly *that they would not agree to it.* I opposed it as an improper business after it had been in the hands of the Joint Committee and rejected, as I thought this a certain method of creating a dissension between the Houses. Izard got up in great wrath and stuttered that *the fact was not so.* He, however, would say nothing more. I made an effort to rise. The Vice-President hurried the question, and it was put and carried by the churchman. Mr. Carrol, though he had been the first to speak against it, yet was silent on this vote. This proves him not the man of firmness which I once thought him.

I went after this to hear the debate in the House of Representatives. The duty of six cents had been reported by the Committee on Molasses. The partiality of the New England members to this article was now manifest. All from their quarter was a universal cry against it. Three o'clock came, and an adjournment was called before the matter was settled.

I took a long walk after dinner with the Speaker and General Muhlenberg, and my knees stood it very well. Hope I shall be perfectly well in a few days. God grant it!

28th April.—This day I ought to note with some extraordinary mark. I had dressed and was about to set out, when General Washington, the greatest man in the world, paid me a visit. I met him at the foot of the stairs. Mr. Wynkoop just came in. We asked him to take a seat. He excused himself on account of the number of his visits. We accompanied him to the door. He made us complaisant bows—one before he mounted and the other as he went away on horseback.

Attended at the Hall. Just nothing at all done. I, however, paid my formal visit to the Vice-President this morning, being nearly recovered of my lameness. Quitted the Hall about twelve. Called on Mr. Langdon, who has been sick some time. It began to rain, and I came home.

I may as well minute a remark here as anywhere else, and, indeed, I wish it were otherwise, not for what we have, but for what others want; but we have really more republican plainness and sincere openness of behavior in Pennsylvania than in any other place I have ever been. I was impressed with a different opinion until I have had full opportunity of observing the gentlemen of New England, and sorry indeed am I to say it, but no people in the Union dwell more on trivial distinctions and matters of mere form. They really seem to show a readiness to stand on punctilio and ceremony. A little learning is a dangerous thing ('tis said). May not the same be said of breeding? It is certainly true that people little used with company are more apt to take offense, and are less easy, than men much versant in public life. They are an unmixed people in New England, and used only to see neighbors like themselves; and when once an error of behavior has crept in among them, there is small chance of its being cured; for, should they go abroad, being early used to a ceremonious and reserved behavior, and believing that good manners consists entirely in punctilios, they only add a few more stiffened airs to their deportment, excluding good humor, affability of conversation, and accommodation of temper and sentiment as qualities too vulgar for a gentleman.

Mr. Strong gave us this morning a story which, with many others of a similar nature (which I have heard), places this in a clear point of light. By the Constitution of Massachusetts the Senate have the right of communicating bills to their Lower House. Some singular business made them [the Lower House] shut their doors. At this time called Samuel Adams of the Senate to communicate a bill. The door-keeper told him his orders. Back returned the enraged Senator; the whole Senate took flame and blazed forth in furious memorial against the Lower House for breach of privilege. A violent contest ensued, and the whole State was convulsed with litigation.

29th April.—Attended the Hall this day. A bill was read the second time respecting the administering the oath for the support of the new Government. A diversity of opinion arose whether the law should be extended so as to oblige the officers of the State governments to take the oaths. The power of Congress to do this was asserted by some and derided by others in pointed terms. I did not enter into the merits of either side, but before the question was put gave my opinion that the first step toward doing good was to be sure of doing no harm. Gentlemen had been very pointed for and against this power; if we divided here, what must we expect the people out of doors to be? That in the exercise of the powers given us by Congress we should deal in no uncertainties; that while we had the Constitution *plainly* before us all was safe and certain, but if we took on us to deal in doubtful matters we trod on hollow ground, and might be charged with an assumption of powers not delegated. I therefore on this ground was against the commitment, and with it closed the business of the day. The bill, however, was committed.

I have observed ever since we began to do business that a Jehu-like spirit has prevailed with a number of gentlemen, and with none more than with the member from the Ancient Dominion, who is said to be a notorious anti-Federalist (a most expensive and enormous machine of a Federal Judiciary, pompous titles, strong efforts after religious distinctions, coercive laws for taking the oaths, etc.). I have uniformly opposed, as far as I was able, everything of this kind, and I believe have sacrificed every chance of being popular and every grain of influence in the Senate by so doing. But be it so. I have the testimony of my own conscience that I am right. High-handed measures are at no time justifiable, but now they are highly impolitic. Never will I consent to straining the Constitution, nor never will I consent to the exercise of a doubtful power. We come here the servants, not the lords, of our constituents. The new Government, instead of being a powerful machine whose authority would support any measure, needs helps and props on all sides, and must be supported by the ablest names and the most shining characters which we can select. The President's amiable deportment, however, smooths and sweetens everything. Charles Thompson has, however, been ill used by the Committee of Arrangements of the ceremonial. This is wrong. His name has been left out of the arrangements for to-morrow.

30th April, Thursday.—This is a great, important day. Goddess of etiquette, assist me while I describe it. The Senate stood adjourned to half after eleven o'clock. About ten dressed in my best clothes; went for Mr. Morris' lodgings, but met his son, who told me that his father would not be in town until Saturday. Turned into the Hall. The crowd already great. The Senate met. The Vice-President rose in the most solemn manner. This son of *Adam* seemed impressed with deeper gravity, yet what shall I think of him? He often, in the midst of his most important airs—I believe when he is at loss for expressions (and this he often is, wrapped up, I suppose, in the contemplation of his own importance)—suffers an unmeaning kind of vacant laugh to escape him. This was the case to-day, and really to me bore the air of ridiculing the farce he was acting. "Gentlemen, I wish for the direction of the Senate. The President will, I suppose, address the Congress. How shall I behave? How shall we receive it? Shall it be standing or sitting?"

Here followed a considerable deal of talk from him which I could make nothing of. Mr. Lee began with the House of Commons (as is usual with him), then the House of Lords, then the King, and then back again. The result of his information was, that the Lords sat and the Commons stood on the delivery of the King's speech. Mr. Izard got up and told how often he had been in the Houses of Parliament. He said a great deal of what he had seen there. [He] made, however, this sagacious discovery, that the Commons stood because they had no seats to sit on, being arrived at the bar of the House of Lords. It was discovered after some time that the King sat, too, and had his robes and crown on.

Mr. Adams got up again and said he had been very often indeed at the Parliament on those occasions, but there always was such a crowd, and *ladies along,* that for his part he could not say how it was. Mr. Carrol got up to declare that he thought it of no consequence how it was in Great Britain; they were no rule to us, etc. But all at once the Secretary, who had been out, whispered to the Chair that the Clerk from the Representatives was at the door with a communication. Gentlemen of the Senate, how shall he be received? A silly kind of resolution of the committee on that business had been laid on the table some days ago. The amount of it was that each House should communicate to the other what and how they chose; it concluded, however, something in this way: That everything should be done with all the *propriety* that was *proper.* The question was, Shall this be adopted, that we may know how to receive the

Clerk? It was objected [that] this will throw no light on the subject; it will leave you where you are. Mr. Lee brought the House of Commons before us again. He reprobated the rule; declared that the Clerk should not come within the bar of the House; that the proper mode was for the Sergeant-at-Arms, with the mace on his shoulder, to meet the Clerk at the door and receive his communication; we are not, however, provided for this ceremonious way of doing business, having neither mace nor sergeant nor Masters in Chancery, who carry down bills from the English Lords.

Mr. Izard got up and labored unintelligibly to show the great distinction between a communication and a delivery of a thing, but he was not minded. Mr. Elsworth showed plainly enough that if the Clerk was not permitted to deliver the communication, the Speaker might as well send it inclosed. Repeated accounts came [that] the Speaker and Representatives were at the door. Confusion ensued; the members left their seats. Mr. Read rose and called the attention of the Senate to the neglect that had been shown Mr. Thompson, late Secretary. Mr. Lee rose to answer him, but I could not hear one word he said. The Speaker was introduced, followed by the Representatives. Here we sat an hour and ten minutes before the President arrived— this delay was owing to Lee, Izard, and Dalton, who had stayed with us while the Speaker came in, instead of going to attend the President. The President advanced between the Senate and Representatives, bowing to each. He was placed in the chair by the Vice-President; the Senate with their president on the right, the Speaker and the Representatives on his left. The Vice-President rose and addressed a short sentence to him. The import of it was that he should now take the oath of office as President. He seemed to have forgot half what he was to say, for he made a dead pause and stood for some time, to appearance, in a vacant mood. He finished with a formal bow, and the President was conducted out of the middle window into the gallery, and the oath was administered by the Chancellor. Notice that the business done was communicated to the crowd by proclamation, etc., who gave three cheers, and repeated it on the President's bowing to them.

As the company returned into the Senate chamber, the President took the chair and the Senators and Representatives their seats. He rose, and all arose also, and addressed them (see the address). This great man was agitated and embarrassed more than ever he was by the leveled cannon or pointed musket. He trembled, and several times could scarce make out to read, though it must be supposed he had often read it before. He put part of the fingers of his left hand into the side of what I think the tailors call the fall of the breeches [corresponding to the modern side-pocket], changing the paper into his left [right] hand. After some time he then did the same with some of the fingers of his right hand. When he came to the words *all the world,* he made a flourish with his right hand, which left rather an ungainly impression. I sincerely, for my part, wished all set ceremony in the hands of the dancing-masters, and that this first of men had read off his address in the plainest manner, without ever taking his eyes from the paper, for I felt hurt that he was not first in everything. He was dressed in deep brown, with metal buttons, with an eagle on them, white stockings, a bag, and sword.

From the hall there was a grand procession to Saint Paul's Church, where prayers were said by the Bishop. The procession was well conducted and without accident, as far as I have heard. The militia were all under arms, lined the street near the church, made a good figure, and behaved well.

The Senate returned to their chamber after service, formed, and took up the address. Our Vice-President called it *his most gracious speech.* I can not approve of this. A committee was appointed on it—Johnson, Carrol, Patterson. Adjourned. In the evening there were grand fireworks. The Spanish Ambassador's house was adorned with transparent paintings; the French Minister's house was illuminated, and had some transparent pieces; the Hall was grandly illuminated, and after all this the people went to bed.

May 1st.—Attended at the Hall at eleven. The prayers were over and the minutes reading. When we came to the minute of the speech it stood, *His most gracious speech.* I looked all around the Senate. Every countenance seemed to wear a blank. The Secretary was going on: I must speak or nobody would. "Mr. President, we have lately had a hard struggle for our liberty against kingly authority. The minds of men are still heated: everything related to that species of government is odious to the people. The words prefixed to the President's speech are the same that are usually placed before the speech of his Britannic Majesty. I know they will give offense. I consider them as improper. I therefore move that they be struck out, and that it stand simply address or speech, as may be judged most suitable."

Mr. Adams rose in his chair and expressed the greatest surprise that anything should be objected to on account of its being taken from the practice of that Government under which we had lived so long and happily formerly; that he was for a dignified and respectable government, and as far as he knew the sentiments of people they thought as he did; that for his part he was one of the first in the late contest [the Revolution], and, if *he could have thought of this, he never would have drawn his sword.*

Painful as it was, I had to contend with the Chair. I admitted that the people of the colonies (now States) had enjoyed formerly great happiness under that species of government, but the abuses of that Government under which they had smarted had taught them what they had to fear from that kind of government; that there had been a revolution in the sentiments of people respecting government equally great as that which had happened in the Government itself; that even the modes of it were now abhorred; that the enemies of the Constitution had objected to it the facility there would be of transition from it to kingly government and all the trappings and splendor of royalty; that if such a thing as this appeared on our minutes, they would not fail to represent it as the first step of the ladder in the ascent to royalty. The Vice-President rose a second time, and declared that he had mentioned it to the Secretary; that he could not possibly conceive that any person could take offense at it. I had to get up again and declare that, although I knew of it being mentioned from the Chair, yet my opposition did not proceed from any motive of contempt; that, although it was a painful task, it was solely a sense of duty that raised me.

The Vice-President stood during this time; said he had been long abroad, and did not know how the temper of people might be now. Up now rose Mr. Read, and declared for the paragraph. He saw no reason to object to it because the British speeches were styled *most gracious*. If we chose to object to words because they had been used in the same sense in Britain, we should soon be at a loss to do business. I had to reply. "It is time enough to submit to necessity when it exists. At present we are at no loss for words. The words speech or address without any addition will suit us well enough." The first time I was up Mr. Lee followed me with a word or two by way of seconding me; but when the Vice-President, on being last up, declared that he was the person from whom the words were taken, Mr. Lee got up and informed the Chair that he did not know that circumstance, as he had been absent when it happened. The question was put and carried for erasing the words without a division.

After the House adjourned the Vice-President took me to one side, declared how much he was for an efficient Government, how much he respected General Washington, and much of that kind. I told him I would yield to no person in respect to General Washington; that our common friends would perhaps one day inform him that I was not wanting in respect to himself [Adams]; that my wishes for an efficient Government were as high as any man's, and begged him to believe that I did myself great violence when I opposed him in the chair, and nothing but a sense of duty could force me to it. He got on the subject of checks to government and the balances of power. His tale was long. He seemed to expect some answer. I caught at the last word, and said undoubtedly without a balance there could be no equilibrium, and so left him hanging in geometry.

The unequivocal declaration that he would never have drawn his sword, etc., has drawn my mind to the following remarks: that the motives of the actors in the late Revolution were various can not be doubted. The abolishing of royalty, the extinguishment of patronage and dependencies attached to that form of government, were the exalted motives of many revolutionists, and these were the improvements meant by them to be made of the war which was forced on us by British aggression— in fine, the amelioration of government and bettering the condition of mankind. These ends and none other were publicly avowed, and all our constitutions and public acts were formed in this spirit. Yet there were not wanting a party whose motives were different. They wished for the loaves and fishes of government, and cared for nothing else but a translation of the diadem and scepter from London to Boston, New York, or Philadelphia; or, in other words, the creation of a new monarchy in America, and to form niches for themselves in the temple of royalty.

This spirit manifested itself strongly among the officers at the close of the war, and I have been afraid the army would not have been disbanded if the common soldiers could have been kept together. This spirit they developed in the Order of Cincinnati, where I trust it will spend itself in a harmless flame and soon become extinguished. That Mr. Adams should, however, so unequivocally avow this motive, at a time when a republican form of government is secured to every State in the Union, appears to me a mark of extreme folly.*

Mem., 1790.—It is worthy of remark that about this time a spirit of reformation broke out in France which finally abolished all titles and every trace of the feudal system. Strange, indeed, that in that very country [America], where the flame of freedom had been kindled, an attempt should be made to introduce these absurdities and humiliating distinctions which the hand of reason, aided by our example, was prostrating in the heart of Europe. I, however, will endeavor (as I have hitherto done) to use the resentment of the Representatives to defeat Mr. Adams and others on the subject of titles. The pompous and lordly distinctions which the Senate have manifested a disposition to establish between the two Houses have nettled the Representatives, and this business of titles may be considered as part of the same tune. While we are debating on titles I will, through the Speaker, Mr. Muhlenberg, and other friends, get the idea suggested of answering the President's address without any title, in contempt of our deliberations, which still continue on that subject. This once effected, will confound them [the Senators] completely, and establish a precedent they will not dare to violate.

---

* "John Adams was included by Jefferson among the believers in monarchy."—Randall's Life of Jefferson, vol. i, p. 586.

Let me not remember it to his disadvantage, but on Thursday, soon after I came to the Hall, the Vice-President stepped up to me; said he had called at my lodgings, but found I was abroad. I thanked him for the honor he did me, and I expressed my sorrow, in the usual way, for being abroad. I was, however, a little surprised, considering the hurry of the day, and more especially as I had but just left home. At night I asked Vandalsen whether any cards had been left for me. "No." "Did anybody call?" "Nobody." "Are you sure the Vice-President did not?" "I am very sure. I know Mr. Adams, the Vice-President, as well as I know any man. I have been at home the whole day; he did not call." From the drift of dust and feathers one finds how the wind blows. I did not minute this on Thursday, thinking that perhaps some mistake had happened which would explain itself. Perhaps it may still do so.

The President's speech is now in the hands of every one, and is received with merited applause. A thought as to the composition of it. But first I will lay down my own rules for judging in cases of this kind. When every word conveys an idea and sentiment follows expression, the composition is good; but when the words and expressions are so happily arranged that every corresponding idea and sentiment brings a kindred group in its train, the composition rises to excellent, grand, sublime. Now for the sinking scale. When the ideas follow slowly, with difficulty, or not at all, the composition may be termed heavy, dull, stupid. I will read it again, but I declare I am inclined to place it under the *heavy* head.

May 2d.—Attended Senate. This a day of no business whatever. Langdon came and shook hands very heartily with me. Some of the other New England men [were] shy. Patterson only was at the Senate chamber before me. He passed censure on the conduct of the Vice-President, said he made himself too busy. He hinted as if some of the Senate would have taken notice of the *gracious* affair if I had not. I told him I was no courtier and had no occasion to trim, but said it was a most disagreeable thing to contend with the Chair, and I had alone held that disagreeable post more than once. After Senate adjourned, I saw the Vice-President standing disengaged. I stepped up to him, asked for his health, and fell into commonplace chat. He is not well furnished with small talk more than myself, and has a very silly kind of laugh. I have often looked with the utmost attention at him to see if his aspect, air, etc., could inspire me with an opinion of his being a man of genius; but it was like repeating "Tristam, tristam." No; the thing seems impossible. It is a silly opinion of mine, but I can not get rid of it, that every man, like a labeled bottle, has his contents marked on his· visage.

May 3d, Sunday.—I did not feel very well this day. Determined to try the warm bath. Went and bespoke it to be ready at eleven. Went; continued in the water near half an hour. Had a most profuse sweat, but found a little of a headache. I wet my head as well as the rest of me. I can recollect that bathing or swimming used to give me the headache: will see how it will affect me. This day the first that seems genial and warm. It is now four o'clock, and I will take a walk.

In my walk I fell in with Mr. Sturges, Mr. Wyngate, and Mr. Goodhue. We took a circuit on the island and came into town. On the way we talked of the permanent residence. They all allowed that New York was not the place. One of them said it ought to be in Pennsylvania. I said little, but remarked that, although we could be better accommodated in Philadelphia, I thought we should think of the permanent residence where houses should be built for the members from each State, when they would not be degraded to the humiliating necessity of begging for lodgings from house to house. I, however, remarked coolly that Virginia offered a quiescence in this plan, expecting the Pennsylvanians would be fretted into an acceptance of their measure for the Potomac; that the Potomac was convenient for a great part of Pennsylvania; that, by our joining votes to those of Virginia and Maryland and the more southerly States, we could go to the Potomac any time. One of them remarked that in Senate the numerous votes of Virginia would not avail. I did not get time to answer, for another replied that we had numbers on our side in the Senate also. They asked me to go to their lodgings to drink tea. I did so. There we found Mr. Thatcher and Mr. Grout. I sat a good while. Mr. Thatcher talked most, but a good deal wildly. There was a good deal said about the different new countries. I recommended the Genesee and the heads of the Susquehanna, I really think deservedly. I, however, had no objections to drawing their attention to the Susquehanna.

4th May, Monday.—Went pretty early to the post-office to deliver letters. As I came back, met General St. Clair. He seemed desirous of speaking with me; said he had been at my lodgings, and asked me what I thought of the President's new arrangements. It was the first I had heard of them. The President is neither to entertain nor receive invitations. He is to have levee days on Tuesdays and Fridays, when only he is to be seen. I told the General that General Washington stood on as difficult ground as he ever had done in his life: that to suffer himself to be run down, on the one hand, by a crowd of visitants so as to engross his time, would never do, as it would render the doing of business impracticable; but, on the other hand, for him to be seen only in public on stated times, like an Eastern Lama, would be equally offensive. If he was not to be seen but in public, where nothing confidential could pass between him and any individual, the business would, to all appearance, be done without him, and he could not escape the charge of favoritism. All court would be paid to the supposed favorite; weakness and insignificance would be considered as characteristic of the President, and he would not escape contempt; that it was not thus the General gained the universal plaudits of his admiring fellow-citizens. I reiterated these ideas in every shape and in every different light I could place them for near half an hour that we walked in front of St. Paul's Church. The General said he wished to collect men's sentiments, and the design was to communicate them to the General [Washington]. I told him my late conduct in the Senate had been such as would render any opinion of mine very ungracious at court, and perhaps he had best never make any mention of my name. Much more was said, but not worth committing to paper.

Attended Senate. Soon after the bill prescribing the oath, etc., was taken up, and the amendments. The first amendment was on the enacting clause. It stood, *Be it enacted by the Congress of the United States;* the amendment, *by the Senate and Representatives.* It was openly avowed by Mr. Izard that the dignity and pre-eminence of the Senate was the object aimed at by the

amendment; but the words of the Constitution are, "All legislative power herein granted shall be vested in a *Congress* of the
United States." Again, section 8, the "Congress shall have
power," etc. The amount of all I said resolved itself into this:
The *legislative authority,* the *power* (of making laws in certain
cases) is given to *Congress.* Let Congress execute this trust
under the same name. In other words, it is under the *Firm* of
Congress that we have received our *authority* and *power.* Let
us execute it under the same *firm.* Elsworth, who is a vastly
better speaker than I am, was in sentiment with me this time.
He placed the subject in various lights, and said enough, I
thought, to convince any one who was not determined to be
otherwise. But the fact with us is that the point sought after is
to find out what will be most agreeable, or, in other words,
where will the majority be? for never was a text more practiced on than that "in a multitude of counselors" (say Senators)
"there is safety." Indeed, it seems the governing principle. Mr.
Izard gave us a kind of dissenting speech from both original
and amendment. He wanted the President's name in it. Our
Vice-President rose in the chair to deliver sentiments to the
same purpose, and upon this principle he was rather against
the amendment because it did not mention the President. The
amendment carried.

The next amendment was a clause obliging the officers of
the State Legislature to take the oath within a month after the
1st of August. Mr. Elsworth argued on the inaccuracies of the
language of the amendment; that it was doubtful as to the intent
of it every way. I thought he nearly exhausted the subject. Before the vote was put I chose to say something. It amounted to
this: that the subject was a doubtful one every way, that the
power of Congress at any time, or the propriety of exercising it
at this time, is admitted. The words of the amendment were also
doubtful and doubted. I would therefore deal in no doubtful
matters. Izard rose in a flame, declared he knew not what gentlemen meant by talking of doubts. He never heard of any. He was
very angry. Mr. Langdon followed him. Read the Constitution
that all *officers,* both of the *United States* and *several States,*
should be bound by oath, etc.

I had to get up in my own defense. I observed the gentleman

mistook the point. The question was not whether the officers should take the oath, but was it our business to interfere in it? It was equally clear that Senators, Representatives, and electors were to be chosen by the States, but who ever thought of a law to oblige them to do these things? The adopting States, by the terms of their adoption, had pledged themselves to conform to the Constitution, which contained these things among its fundamental rules; that among the powers delegated to Congress this was not mentioned, nor was it necessary, being already provided for in the Constitution; that as to doubts, individuals had doubted and States had doubted. Massachusetts, it appeared, considered the power of making a law to be with Congress. Connecticut thought so differently that they had passed a State law for the purpose; that, for my part, I greatly doubted at least the propriety of meddling with it unless the States should be guilty of neglect. But that I was not so uncharitable as to damn him that doubted not. Up rose Lee. He was for the amendment, but had more doubts than anybody. The rage of speaking caught hold of half the Senate at least. Some sensible things were said, but a great many foolish ones. Elsworth rose a second time. He took nearly the track I had been on, but he explained everything with a clearness and perspicuity which I was quite incapable of. I was highly pleased with him. How readily do the sentimental strings sound unison when both are touched by the same agreeable motive! But enough, the amendment was carried against us.

I learned this day that the title selected from all the potentates of the earth for our President was to have been taken from Poland, viz., *Elective Majesty*. What a royal escape! Dined this day with the French Minister, the first place I have been at since my illness. But I have minuted enough for this day, so stop.

May 5th.—The bill of yesterday [prescribing the oath] had a third reading, but now how is it to be sent to the other House? A motion was made and seconded that it go by the Secretary. From half after eleven to half after one was this important question agitated. The other House had affronted the Senate by sending up the bill in a letter, and now we would not send it down by a member. The dignity of the House was much insisted on. We were plagued again with the House of Lords and Commons, and "parliamentary" was the supplementary word to every sentence. I doubted much whether I should rise or not; however, when everybody else had something to say, I scorned to be silent. I remarked that I rose with reluctance on a subject when I had not been able to draw any information from experience, as the State I had the honor of representing had but one House; yet from what I could learn the States which had two Houses in the Union carried on their communications by members; that this I considered as the most cordial and friendly mode of intercourse, and that I would much rather take example from our own States than from Great Britain; that this intercourse, therefore, was the one which I most sincerely wished, and thought the sooner it was adopted the better; that if our members should be ill-treated below, as had been alleged by some gentlemen, the fault would not be ours, and then we would be fully justified in adopting some other mode; that a communication by our Secretary was a bad one; that it interrupted business, as we could not proceed without him. If we meant it by way of returning the affront that had been offered to us, this was wrong. We should send the bill by letter, and this would be treating them in kind.

I was answered, or at least an attempt was made, but I was not convinced. Mr. Langdon got up soon after, and seemed to adopt all I had said, but the motion was carried against us. Elsworth was with us and so was Mr. Carrol, but he concluded with saying he would this time vote for the Secretary to go down with the bill. Gave my landlord another half Johannes. He now owes me £2 1s. 10d. Paid him for some wood.

I forgot to minute a very long speech of Mr. Elsworth when the bill was on the third reading. He prefaced his discourse by saying he would make no motion, but gentlemen might do as they pleased after he had delivered his sentiments. The whole amounted to this, that the great and dignified station of the President and the conspicuous part he would act in the field of legislation, as all laws must pass in review before him, and were subject to his revision and correction, etc., entitled him to have his name or place marked in the enacting clause of all laws; or at least he should be brought into view among the component parts of Congress. Ideas of the above kind were dwelt on and varied with agreeable enough diction for nearly a quarter of an hour. I am confident Elsworth neither wished nor expected to have any serious motion made on such untenable ground. What, then, could be his motive? Solely to play the courtier? Something of this kind had been hinted from the Chair. Mr. Izard had been explicit on the subject, Mr. Elsworth now plays a middle game. He knows the thing can not take place, but he will bring it fully in view so that he can say, "It was not my fault," and thus secure his interest with the high-toned courtiers. Is such a man to be trusted? No motion was made; indeed, the spirit of his address was reducible to this: "I will make no motion; if any of you are foolish enough to do it, you may."

May 6th.—No Senate this day; there was a commencement at Saint Paul's Church; the Senate were served with tickets. Dr. Johnson, the principal of the college, could not attend with us. I had heard that Mr. Morris was come to town. I went for his lodgings. This another useless journey, for he has not come. I would have been very glad of Mr. Morris' company. It has happened otherwise. I have been a bird alone. I have had to bear the chilling cold of the North and the intemperate warmth of the South, neither of which is favorable to the Middle State from which I come. Lee and Izard, hot as the burning sands of Carolina, hate us. Adams with all his frigid friends, cool and wary, bear us no good-will. I could not find a confidant in one of them, or say to my heart, "Here is the man I can trust." What has been my conduct, then? Spirit of Rectitude, bear witness for me. Have I trimmed to one of them? Or have I withheld a single sentiment that my judgment approved of? I trust I have not. Regardless of consequences, with no eye to emolument, without desire for reappointment, I mean to act as if I were immortal, and yet I wish to give satisfaction and content to the State that sent me here. Never, however, will I purchase that with discontent in my own bosom, nor does my dear country demand such a sacrifice at my hand.

May 7th.—The bill for taking the oath for the support of the Constitution came up. The amendments all agreed to, and a small one added. The committee reported an answer to the President's speech. It was read. One part was objected to, which stated the United States to have been in *anarchy* and *confusion,* and the President stepping in and *rescuing* them.   A very long debate. The words were struck out. Mr. Lee offered part of a sentence which, I thought, filled the sentence with propriety. It was, however, lost. Mr. Patterson offered a clause, "rescued us from evils *im*pending *over* us." This was carried; but half the Senate nearly made sour faces at it. Mr. Elsworth said it was tautological, but seemed at a loss as to mending it. I rose, more in consequence of a kind of determination that I have adopted of saying something every day than from any fondness of the subject. I admitted that there appeared something tautological in the words, and it was not easy to mend them consistent with elegant diction, but, if the first syllable was taken from the word *im*pending, it would then stand, "evils pending over us." The objection would be obviated, but I would not say the language would be eloquent. But, since I was up, I could not help remarking that I thought the whole clause improper; that to state the whole Union as being in anarchy or under impending ruin was sanctifying the calumnies of our enemies, who had long labored in the foreign gazettes to represent us as a people void of government. It was fixing a stain on the annals of America, for future historians would appeal to the transactions of this very day as a proof of our disordered circumstances. I therefore was against the whole clause. Mr. Wyngate followed me, and was for having the clause struck [out]. This could not well be done consistent with order. I mentioned that, if a reconsideration was moved, I would second it. It was reconsidered and amended, and afterward recommitted to the same committee. They retired for the purpose of dressing it.

Now the Vice-President rose to draw the attention of the Senate to the manner of delivering the answer to the President. A committee was appointed to confer on this and other subjects with a committee of Representatives. "There are three ways, gentlemen" (said our Vice-President), "by which the President may communicate with us. One is personally. If he comes here, we must have a seat for him. In England it is called a *throne.* To be sure, it is behind that seat we must seek for shelter and protection. The second is by a minister of state. The third is by his chamberlain or one of his aides-de-camp, I had almost said, but that is a military phrase. It may become a great constitutional question." Seeing the House look blank, he said, "I throw these things out for gentlemen to think of." Mr. Lee got up and said something on the propriety of having a seat with a canopy for the President. Mr. Langdon said something, but did not seem well collected, and spoke so low I did not hear him.

The time was trifled till near three o'clock. The day was cold, and the members collected near the fire, leaving their seats. The committee returned with the message, and it really read vastly better, and was altered in the exceptional phrases. In one place, speaking of the Government, it mentioned "dignity and *splendor*." I submitted it to the gentlemen who had the amending of it whether "respectability" was not better than *splendor*. Mr. Carrol, of the committee, did not defend the word "splendor," but said "respectability" had been used before, if he recollected right. Mr. Patterson said it sounded much better than "respectability," and rounded the period. Dr. Johnson said "splendor" signified in this place the highest perfection of government. These were the three members of the committee. I mentioned that, if the word *respectability* had been used immediately before, it would be improper; that *dignity* alone I thought expressed all that was wanted. As to the seeking of sounding names and pompous expressions, I thought them exceptionable on that very account, and that no argument was necessary to show it; that different men had a train of different ideas raised by the same word; that "splendor," when applied to government, brought into my mind, instead of the highest perfection, all the faulty finery, brilliant scenes, and expensive trappings of royal government, and impressed my mind with an idea quite the reverse of republican respectability, which I thought consisted in firm and prudent councils, frugality, and economy.

I found I was not seconded, and concluded that my motion went to recommend a reconsideration of the word "splendor" to the committee. They did not alter it, and the answer was agreed to. The Vice-President rose in the chair and repeated twice, with more joy in his face than I had ever seen him assume before, he hoped the Government would be supported with *dignity and splendor.* I thought he did it by way of triumph over me for a former defeat I gave him, but may be I was mistaken.

May 8th.—Attended a joint committee on the papers of the old Congress. Made progress in the business. Agreed to meet at half-past ten on Monday and report. Senate formed. The Secretary, as usual, had made some mistakes, which were rectified, and now Mr. Elsworth moved for the report of the Joint Committee to be taken up on the subject of titles. It was accordingly done. Mr. Lee led the business. He took his old ground—all the world, civilized and savage, called for titles; that there must be something in human nature that occasioned this general consent; that, therefore, he conceived it was right. Here he began to enumerate many nations who gave titles—such as Venice, Genoa, and others. The Greeks and Romans, it was said, had no titles, "but" (making a profound bow to the Chair) "you were pleased to set us right in this with respect to the Conscript Fathers the other day." Here he repeated the Vice-President's speech of the 23d ultimo [April], almost verbatim all over.

Mr. Elsworth rose. He had a paper in his hat, which he looked constantly at. He repeated almost all that Mr. Lee had said, but got on the subject of kings—declared that the sentence in the primer of *fear God and honor the king* was of great importance; that kings were of divine appointment; that Saul, the head and shoulders taller than the rest of the people, was elected by God and anointed by his appointment.

I sat, after he had done, for a considerable time, to see if anybody would rise. At last I got up and first answered Lee as well as I could with nearly the same arguments, drawn from the Constitution, as I had used on the 23d ult. I mentioned that within the space of twenty years back more light had been thrown on the subject of governments and on human affairs in general than for several generations before; that this light of knowledge had diminished the veneration for titles, and that mankind now considered themselves as little bound to imitate the follies of civilized nations as the brutalities of savages; that the abuse of power and the fear of bloody masters had extorted titles as well as adoration, in some instances from the trembling crowd; that the impression now on the minds of the citizens of these States was that of horror for kingly authority.

Izard got up. He dwelt almost entirely on the antiquity of kingly government. He could not, however, well get further back than Philip of Macedon. He seemed to have forgot both Homer and the Bible. He urged for something equivalent to nobility having been common among the Romans, for they had three names that seemed to answer to honorable, or something like it, before and something behind. He did not say Esquire. Mr. Carrol rose and took my side of the question. He followed nearly the track I had been in, and dwelt much on the information that was now abroad in the world. He spoke against kings. Mr. Lee and Mr. Izard were both up again. Elsworth was up again. Langdon was up several times, but spoke short each time. Patterson was up, but there was no knowing which side he was of. Mr. Lee considered him as against him and answered him, but Patterson finally voted with Lee. The Vice-President repeatedly helped the speakers for titles. Elsworth was enumerating how common the appellation of President was. The Vice-President put him in mind that there were presidents of fire companies and of a cricket club. Mr. Lee at another time was saying he believed some of the States authorized titles by their Constitutions. The Vice-President, from the chair, told him that Connecticut did it. At sundry other times he interfered in a like manner. I had been frequently up to answer new points during the debate.

I collected myself for a last effort. I read the clause in the Constitution against titles of nobility; showed that the spirit of it was against not only granting titles by Congress, but against the permission of foreign potentates granting *any titles whatever;* that as to kingly government, it was equally out of the question, as a republican government was guaranteed to every State in the Union; that they were both equally forbidden fruit of the Constitution. I called the attention of the House to the consequences that were like to follow; that gentlemen seemed to court a rupture with the other House. The Representatives had adopted the report, and were this day acting on it, or according to the spirit of the report. We were proposing a title. Our conduct would mark us to the world as actuated by the spirit of dissension, and the characters of the Houses would be as aristocratic and democratical.

The report [of the Committee on Titles] was, however, rejected. "Excellency" was moved for as a title by Mr. Izard. It was withdrawn by Mr. Izard, and "highness" with some prefatory word, proposed by Mr. Lee. Now long harangues were made in favor of this title. "Elective" was placed before. It was insisted that such a dignified title would add greatly to the weight and authority of the Government both at home and abroad. I declared myself totally of a different opinion; that at present it was impossible to add to the respect entertained for General Washington; that if you gave him the title of any foreign prince or potentate, a belief would follow that the manners of that prince and his modes of government would be adopted by the President. (Mr. Lee had, just before I got up, read over a list of the titles of all the princes and potentates of the earth, marking where the word "highness" occurred. The Grand Turk had it, all the princes of Germany had [it], sons and daughters of crown heads, etc.) That particularly "elective highness," which sounded nearly like "electoral highness," would have a most ungrateful sound to many thousands of industrious citizens who had fled from German oppression; that "highness" was part of the title of a prince or princes of the blood, and was often given to dukes; that it was degrading our President to place him on a par with any prince of any blood in Europe, nor was there one of them that could enter the list of true glory with him.

But I will minute no more. The debate lasted till half after three o'clock, and it ended in appointing a committee to consider of a title to be given to the President. This whole silly business is the work of Mr. Adams and Mr. Lee; Izard follows Lee, and the New England men, who always herd together, follow Mr. Adams. Mr. Thompson says this used to be the case in the old Congress. I had, to be sure, the greatest share in this debate, and must now have completely sold (no, sold is a bad word, for I have got nothing for it) every particle of court favor, for a court our House seems determined on, and to run into all the fooleries, fopperies, fineries, and pomp of royal etiquette; and all this for Mr. Adams.

May 9th.—Attended the Hall at ten o'clock to go on the Judicial Committee. Met many of the members. I know not the motive, but I never was received with more familiarity, nor quite so much, before by the members. Elsworth in particular seemed to show a kind of fondness. The Judicial Committee did no business. Senate formed. It took a long time to correct the minutes. Otis keeps them miserably. At length the committee came in and reported a title—*His Highness the President of the United States of America and Protector of the Rights of the Same.* Mr. Few had spoken a word or two with me, and signified his unwillingness to do anything hastily. He got up and spoke a great deal against hasty measures. He did not pointedly move for postponement, but it amounted nearly to it. The Clerk of the other House in the mean time appeared at the bar and announced the adoption of the report of the Joint Committee (rejecting titles).

I got up and expressed my opinion that what had fallen from the honorable gentleman from Georgia amounted to a motion for postponement, and asked leave to second him. I then pointed out the rupture that was likely to ensue with the other House; that this was a matter of very serious import, and I thought it our indispensable duty to avoid any inconvenience of that kind; that by the arrangement between the Houses in case of disagreement a conference might be requested; that my intention was, if the postponement was carried, to move immediately for a committee of conference to be appointed on the difference between the Houses, and I had hopes that by these means all subject of debate would be done away. Mr. Read got up and moved that the report might be adopted. He was not seconded, but the motion was in itself idle. Mr. Strong spoke in favor of the postponement, and was interrupted from the Chair. Mr. Dalton after some time spoke in favor of it. I could now see a visible anxiety in the Chair.

I had a fine, slack, and easy time of it to-day. Friends seemed to rise in succession. Lee went over his old ground twice, but owned at last there was great difficulty every way, but said plainly the best mode was for the House to adopt the report, and then the other House would follow. He found, however, the current began to turn against him, and he laid his head on his hand as if he would have slept. Mr. Strong was up again. He said among many things that he thought the other House would follow, but there was a risk in it.

Mr. Izard got up at last. He, too, was for a postponement. I could see the Vice-President kindled at him. Mr. Izard said we knew the other House had adopted the report [rejecting titles]. The Vice-President interrupted him and said no; we had no right to know it nor could we know it until after the Clerk had this morning given official information. The members fixed themselves, and the question was called for.

Up now got the Vice-President, and for forty minutes did he harangue us from the chair. He began first on the subject of order, and found fault with everything almost, but down he came to particulars, and pointedly blamed a member for disorderly behavior. The member had mentioned the appearance of a captious disposition in the other House. This was disorderly and spoke with asperity. The member meant was Mr. Izard. All this was only prefatory. On he got to his favorite topic of titles, and over the old ground of the immense advantage of, the absolute necessity of them. When he had exhausted this subject he turned a new leaf, I believe, on the conviction that the postponement would be carried and perhaps the business lost by an attention to the other House.

"Gentlemen, I must tell you that it is you and the President that have the making of titles. Suppose the President to have the appointment of Mr. Jefferson at the court of France. Mr. Jefferson is, in virtue of that appointment, the most illustrious, the most powerful, and what not. But the President must be himself something that includes all the dignities of the diplomatic corps and something greater still. What will the common people of foreign countries, what will the sailors and the soldiers say, 'George Washington, President of the United States'? They will despise him *to all eternity*. This is all nonsense to the philosopher, but so is all government whatever."

The above I recollect with great precision, but he said fifty more things, equally injudicious, which I do not think worth minuting. It is evident that he begins to despair of getting the article of titles through the House of Representatives, and has turned his eye to get it done solely by the Senate.

Having experienced relief by the interference of sundry members, I had determined not to say another word, but his new leaf appeared so absurd I could not help some animadversions on it. I rose. Mr. President, the Constitution of the United States has designated our Chief Magistrate by the appellation of the *President of the United States of America.* This is his title of office, nor can we alter, add to, or diminish it without infringing the Constitution. In like manner persons authorized to transact business with foreign powers are styled *Ambassadors, Public Ministers,* etc. To give them any other appellation would be an equal infringement. As to grades of orders or titles of nobility, nothing of the kind can be established by Congress.

Can, then, the President and Senate do that which is prohibited to the United States at large? Certainly not. Let us read the Constitution: *No title of nobility shall be granted by the United States.* The Constitution goes further. The servants of the public are prohibited from accepting them from any foreign state, king, or prince. So that the appellations and terms given to nobility in the Old World are contraband language in the United States, nor can we apply them to our citizens consistent with the Constitution. As to what the common people, soldiers, and sailors of foreign countries may think of us, I do not think it imports us much. Perhaps the less they think, or have occasion to think of us, the better.

But suppose this a desirable point, how is it to be gained? The English excepted, foreigners do not understand our language. We must use Hohen Mogende to a Dutchman. Beylerbey to a Turk or Algerine, and so of the rest. From the English indeed we may borrow terms that would not be wholly unintelligible to our own citizens. But will they thank us for the compliment? Would not the plagiarism be more likely to be attended with contempt than respect among all of them? It has been admitted that all this is nonsense to the philosopher. I am ready to admit that every high-sounding, pompous appellation, descriptive of qualities which the object does not possess, must appear bombastic nonsense in the eye of every wise man. But I can not admit such an idea with respect to government itself. Philosophers have admitted not the utility but the necessity of it [government], and their labors have been directed to correct the vices and expose the follies which have been ingrafted upon it, and to reduce the practice of it to the principles of common sense, such as we see exemplified by the merchant, the mechanic, and the farmer, whose every act or operation tends to a productive or beneficial effect, and, above all, to illustrate this fact, that government was instituted for the benefit of the people, and that no act of government is justifiable that has not this for its object. Such has been the labor of philosophers with respect to government, and sorry indeed would I be if their labors should be in vain.

After all this he had to put the question, and the postponement was carried. I kept my word, and offered the resolution for a conference on the differences, etc. It was carried, and the committee appointed. Elsworth, the most conceited man in the world, drew up a new resolution. It was to keep the differences out of sight, and to proceed *de novo* on a title for the President. I did not enter into debate, but expressed my fear that the House of Representatives would be irritated and would not meet us on that ground. And, as if they meant to provoke the other House, they insisted that the minute of rejection should go down with the appointment of the committee. Little good can come of it thus circumstanced, more especially as the old committee were reappointed.

May 10th.—Being Sunday, bathed and stayed at home all the day after, as it was raining and I was afraid to go out, for fear of catching cold. Wrote to my family as usual. A Philadelphia merchant was in with Mr. Wynkoop. He alleged that Mr. Fitzsimons delayed the Impost bill, while his own Indiamen should arrive, for it seems he has more than one. On Friday evening Mr. Fitzsimons avowed that he had set Gerry on to bring in the Company bill. Now, it seems the Company bill must be rejected again. I asked Mr. Fitzsimons what could be the means of the bill hanging so long in the hands of the committee. He blamed Gerry; said it was left with Gerry last Saturday; that he had called this evening (Friday), and he found it still lying on Mr. Gerry's table untouched. I asked if he did not expect blame; he said he was afraid they would say of him, as he was a merchant, that he delayed it until his own vessels would arrive from the East Indies. *They do, indeed, say so;* and I say the bill is

delayed by some means to the great loss of revenue. Mr. Wynkoop remarked that Mr. Fitzsimons acted in a double capacity
—as a merchant and as a Representative. The man replied
shrewdly, *"You will always find the merchant uppermost."*

May 11th.—I have actually delayed making up my journal
for this day until the morning of the 12th. I feel how very
wrong it is. There is a bluntness over my memory already. The
first thing I did in the morning was delivering my letters at
the post-office. Called to see if Mr. Morris was come to town.
He was not. Met two committees at the hall: first on the affairs
of the Old Congress Papers. This business disposed of, the
second on the judiciary department. Senate met. Mr. Lee moved
to put off the order of the day, on the subject of titles, until
to-morrow. Agreed to. He then moved to consider the appointing of a Sergeant-at-Arms. This lost, Mr. Izard and sundry
gentlemen of the Senate [were] dissatisfied with our Vice-
President. He takes on him to school the members from the
chair. His grasping after titles has been observed by everybody.
Mr. Izard, after describing his air, manner, deportment, and
personal figure in the chair, concluded with applying the title
of *Rotundity* to him. I have really often looked at him with
surprise mingled with contempt when he is in the chair and no
business before the Senate. Instead of that sedate, easy air which
I would have him possess, he will look on one side, then on the
other, then down on the knees of his breeches, then dimple his
visage with the most silly kind of half smile which I can not
well express in English. The Scotch-Irish have a word that
hits it exactly—*smudging*. God forgive me for the vile thought,
but I can not help thinking of a monkey just put into breeches
when I saw him betray such evident marks of self-conceit. He
made us a speech this day also, but, as I did not minute the heads
of it when he spoke, I will not attempt to recollect it.

Senate adjourned, and the Judicial Committee met. Sat like
near three o'clock. Appointed a sub-committee to draft a bill.
I do not like it in any part, or rather I generally dislike it, but
we will see how it looks in form of a bill. After dinner we were
called on by the Speaker and his brother and asked to eat a
Pennsylvania dinner to-morrow. Took a walk.

I received a ticket from the President of the United States

to use his box this evening at the theatre, being the first of his appearance at the playhouse since his entering on his office. Went. The President, Governor of the State, foreign Ministers, Senators from New Hampshire, Connecticut, Pennsylvania, M. [Maryland or Massachusetts?], and South Carolina; and some ladies in the same box. I am old, and notices or attentions are lost on me. I could have wished some of my dear children in my place; they are young and would have enjoyed it. Long might they live to boast of having been seated in the same box with the first Character in the world. The play was the "School for Scandal." I never liked it; indeed, I think it an indecent representation before ladies of character and virtue. Farce, the "Old Soldier." The house greatly crowded, and I thought the players acted well; but I wish we had seen the *Conscious Lovers,* or some one that inculcated more prudential manners.

May 12th.—Went early this morning to wait on Mr. Fitzsimons. Was informed that Mr. Morris had called to see him this morning. Took no notice of this, but went in quest of Mr. Morris. Found him at the door where he kept his office. Took a long walk with him, and gave him a detail of all that had happened in the Senate since he left it, as exactly as I could. He seemed to listen to me in a friendly way. Came to the Hall at eleven. Senate met, but there really was nothing happened worth mentioning. The business of considering the title, which was laid on the table, was postponed to see what would be the result of the conference of the joint committee on that business. Adjourned.

Went to hear the debates of the House of Representatives from the gallery. From thence went with Mr. Morris to the President's levee. Stayed until the company began to withdraw. Felt, I believe, a little awkward, for my knee pained me, and this business of standing was not very agreeable to me. Left Mr. Morris at the levee; came home. Stayed till four o'clock, and went and dined with the Speaker of the House.

This day the Vice-President gave us no set speech from the chair, but I know not whether it was want of memory or design, but a motion made by me and seconded by Lee was passed by him and a second motion put. He [Mr. Adams], however, seemed confused. The speech which he made yesterday was on the subject of our having a Sergeant-at-Arms. He seemed to wish that the officer should be _Usher of the Black Rod_. He described this office as appurtenant to the House of Lords, and concluded by telling us that Sir Francis Mollineaux was the officer, _and that he had the honor of being introduced to the House of Lords._

My business with Mr. Fitzsimons this morning was to inform him how much I feared the cabal of the New England members in the Senate; and that, if they were not gratified in some measure on their favorite article of molasses, they would join with every member who objected to any single article, and promise him gratification in his particular humor if he would join them. By these means, all the discontents being united, and indulgence given even to caprice and whim, the bill would be lost. He laughed at my fears. The molasses affair was to be called up again. I asked him if he was sure of [a] majority in the House for continuing the duty at six cents. "Very confident of it"; yet he was mistaken, and it was reduced to five.

I felt a great joy on the coming of Mr. Morris to town, for now I shall have one in whom I can confide.

May 13th.—Paid some visits this morning. Senate met. The Vice-President put us in mind that the report for the President's title lay on the table. Mr. Lee informed the House that the committee on that business had met, but being in the Senate chamber were dispersed on the meeting of the Senate, and had agreed to meet to-morrow morning. Report for classing the Senate permitted to lie on the table. Moved, and a committee appointed to confer on the subject of newspapers. A committee of nine appointed for the penal Federal laws. I can observe total change of behavior, or at least a considerable one, in our Vice-President. Instead of directing two Senators to read the ballots for committee-men, as he did heretofore, he this day read them aloud from the chair, and the Clerk tallied. This is the first step toward reformation, and I hope it will be _progressive_.

May 14th.—This a most stormy day, with rain. Went to the Hall half after nine. Met Mr. Ellicott and took him with me to the Board of Treasury. He left his papers. I met the committee for the dividing of the rooms. I told Few and the committee in general that I had heard there were designs on foot to saddle Congress with the expenses of the City Hall. He did not give a word of answer. L'Enfant was with us, and, like most Frenchmen, was so talkative that scarce a word could be said. Adjourned, to meet to-morrow at ten o'clock. Senate met. The Vice-President reminded us of the title report. The committee was out on that business. Classing report adopted. A motion of yesterday was on the table for the regulating joint committees. Elsworth, according to his custom, drew another one. Mr. Langdon withdrew his complaisance to Mr. Elsworth. Lee moved to strike out the latter part of Elsworth's. Elsworth, in complaisance to Lee, seconded him. This spoiled the motion, and, all complaisance being at an end, the rest was rejected by the House.

It was here the Vice-President made us his speech for the day. He said parliamentary customs, when found convenient, should be followed as good examples (this is the first time I ever heard him guard his parliamentary lessons, but I observed yesterday that there was a change) ; that conferences were very seldom used by the Houses in Great Britain; that little benefit was obtained from them; that there could be but little use only in case of difference of opinion with respect to bills. The whole seemed to aim at lessening the intercourse between the two Houses. I could not help thinking of his speech of the 9th instant. It seemed the second part of it.

Now rose Mr. Lee to report on titles from the Joint Committee. He reported that the committee from the other House had adhered in the strictest manner to their former resolution. He moved that the report, which had been laid on the table, in favor of titles, should be entered on the files of the House, and that a motion which he had in his hand should be adopted. The spirit of the motion was that, to keep up a proper respect for our Chief Magistrate, attention should be paid to the customs of civilized nations; that the appearance of the affectation of simplicity would be injurious; that the Senate had decided in favor of titles from these motives; but that, in conformity to the practice of the other House, for the present, they resolved to address the President without title.

Yesterday Mr. Muhlenberg accosted me with *Your High-*

ness of the Senate. On my pausing, he said Mr. Wynkoop
had been christened by them "His Highness of the Lower
House," and he thought I was entitled to the same distinction
in the Senate. As we had the business all over again to-day, I
determined to try what ridicule could do. Mr. President, if
all men were of one stature, there would be neither high nor
low. Highness, when applied to an individual, must naturally
denote the excess of stature which he possesses over other men.
An honorable member told us the other day of a certain king
[Saul] who was head and shoulders taller than anybody else.
This, more especially when he was gloriously greased with a
great horn of oil, must render him *highly* conspicuous. History,
too, if I mistake not, will furnish us with an example where
a great Thracian obtained the empire of the world from no
other circumstance. But, if this antiquated principle is to be
adopted, give us fair play. Let America be searched, and it is
most probable that the honor will be found to belong to some
huge Patagonian. This, indeed, is putting one sadly over the
head of another. True, but Nature has done it, and men should
see where she leads before they adopt her as a guide.

It may be said that this business is metaphorical, and the
high station of the President entitled him to it. Nothing can
be true metaphorically which is not so naturally, and under
this view of the proposed title it belongs with more propriety
to the man in the moon than anybody else, as his station (when
we have the honor of seeing him) is certainly the most exalted
of any that we know of. Gentlemen may say this is fanciful.
Would they wish to see the subject in the most serious point of
view that it is possible to place? Rome, after being benighted
for ages in the darkest gloom of ecclesiastic and aristocratic tyranny, beheld a reformer [Rienzi] in the fourteenth century, who,
preaching from stocks and stones and the busts and fragments
of ancient heroes, lighted up the lamp of liberty to meridian
splendor. Intoxicated with success, he assumed a string of titles,
none of which, in my recollection, was equally absurd with the
one before you; in consequence of which, and of his aping
some other symbols of nobility and royalty, he fell and pulled
down the whole republican structure along with him, marking
particularly the subject of titles as one of the principal rocks

on which he was shipwrecked. As to the latter part of the title,
I would only observe that the power of war is the organ of protection. This is placed in Congress by the Constitution. Any attempt to divest them of it and place it elsewhere, even with
George Washington, is treason against the United States, or,
at least, a violation of the Constitution.

In order to get out of the kind of puzzle which Lee had
engaged us in, we moved a general postponement of the report
on the title, hoping this would cut up the whole matter by the
roots. It was carried. And even after this Lee hung with obstinacy to the idea of putting it on the files of the House.

Through the whole of this base business I have endeavored
to mark the conduct of General Washington. I have no clew
that will lead me fairly to any just conclusion as to his sentiments. I think it scarce possible, but he must have dropped
something on the subject which has excited so much warmth.
If he did, it was not on our side, or I would have heard it.
But no matter. I have, by plowing with the heifer of the other
House, completely defeated them.

Mr. Carrol rose and opposed the imperfect resolution being
put on the files by order of the House. I seconded him in opposing this, as putting such a thing on the files by special order of
the House was giving it an authority which no postponed paper
should have, and carried the air of adoption. Papers were never
specially ordered on the files but with a view of perpetuating
information. A special order for putting on the files would hereafter be considered as an adoption, this part of this motion
being lost by a general postponement of the report.

Mr. Morris rose after the question had been carried, and
expressed his dislike of the title, viz., *Highness and Protector
of the Rights of America.* He said the protection lay with the
whole Congress. He was right in his remarks, but he was told
the question was carried. Mr. Carrol expressed great dislike at
the fore part of the motion, which stated the acts of the Senate
to be in favor of titles, when, in fact, no such resolution ever
had passed the Senate. I rose and moved a division of the
motion. Was immediately seconded by Mr. Carrol. Now a long
debate ensued. Mr. Elsworth traversed the field of titles over
again. Dr. Johnson spoke much more to the point. Mr. Patter-

son, after reading over the motion, was of opinion that a division should take place at the word "Senate." I was also, with Mr. Morris, of opinion that the division would stand best at this place. I withdrew my motion and seconded his for the division from the word "Senate." The division was full enough to answer all the purposes which they avowed, taking it at this place. But it is evident they have not given up the idea of titles, and seem insultingly to say so to the House of Representatives. Affectation of simplicity is directly charged on the other House. This they amended by putting in the word *appearance.*

I had endeavored to draw my principal argument, when last up, from the unfairness of the fore part. It expressly recited a determination of the Senate to grant titles. No such resolution had ever passed. It might be implied that the Senate were in favor of titles, but why refer to a resolution that did not exist? Accommodation was the principle held out. But was ever [a] thing done with so ill grace? It was saying, "We meet you on the principles of accommodation, but you are completely wrong, and we are perfectly right." Can any good come of such accommodation? Mr. Carrol declared that the idea held forth was that the Senate were for titles, but it was well known they were not all for titles. He was opposed, and so were sundry other gentlemen. He wished only for a fair question, that it might be seen who were for them and who were not. He wished the yeas and nays, and let the world judge. Mr. Few declared the gentleman had missed the opportunity of the yeas and nays. They should have been called when the report against titles was rejected. Mr. Few was much out in this, for there were but three of us, and he need not have made his remarks. It was evident that they wished to prevent the yeas and nays. The question was put. The House divided. Eight with us; ten against us. Mr. Carrol called for the yeas and nays. None rose with him but Mr. Henry and myself, and for want of another man we lost them.

The committee was now ordered to wait on the President to know the time when he will be pleased to receive the address of the Senate. The report of the joint committee on the enrollment of papers was read, and the House adjourned.

And now I hope we have disposed of a business [relating to titles] which in one shape or other has engaged almost the

whole time of the Senate from the 23d of April, the day that
our Vice-President began it. Had it not been for Mr. Lee I am
firmly convinced no other man would have ventured to follow
our Vice-President. But Lee led, Elsworth seconded him, the
New England men followed, and Mr. Izard joined them, but
really *haud passibus æquis,* for he was only for the title of
"Excellency," which had been sanctioned by use. Lee has a cul-
tivated understanding, a great practice in public business, with
a factious, restless disposition. He has acted as a high priest
through the whole of this idolatrous business.

It is easy to see what his aim is. By flattering the President
of the Senate he hopes to govern all the members from New
England and, with a little assistance from Carolina or Georgia,
to be absolute in the Senate. Elsworth, and some more of the
New England men, flatter him in turn, expecting he will be with
them on the question of residence [of Congress]. Had it not
been for our Vice-President and Lee, I am convinced the Senate
would have been as averse to titles as the House of Representatives. The game that our Vice-President and Mr. Lee appear
to have now in view is to separate the Senate as much as possible from the House of Representatives. Our Vice-President's
doctrine is that all honors and titles should flow from the President [of the United States] and Senate only. But, once more,
subject of titles, farewell; may I never hear motion or debate on
thee more!

Memorandum: The fall of Rienzi, the Roman reformer, who
split on the rock of titles, was completely in point.

May 15th.—Called early this morning on Mr. Scott. I know
not where he was, but I did not find him until the fourth time
of my calling. It was to guard him on the subject of appropriating the rooms of the City Hall. This is a deceitful business.
I put into his hands a form of a report. But he does not seem
to be the right stuff to work with; but I have got the business
in a good train, and Mr. White, of Virginia, is to draw a report.

Senate met. On the reading of the minutes Mr. Few got up
and moved warmly that the minute of yesterday on the division
of Mr. Lee's motion should be struck out. Lee was for it in
a moment. By these means the vote of yesterday, which respected
titles, would have the appearance of unanimity. It was opposed

by Mr. Carrol, Elsworth, and myself. The minute, however, remained. The committee reported that the President of the United States would receive our address a quarter after twelve on Monday. It was said we should go in carriages.

The classing report was called for; the ballots were drawn. I fell in the first class.*

The Vice-President now informed the Senate that a letter had come to his hand which he supposed was intended for him, but it was most improperly directed. It was directed to "His Excellency the Vice-President." He asked the opinion of the Senate, laughingly, and concluded it was against all rule. I said that until we had a rule obliging people to be regular we must submit to their irregularities, more especially of this kind. Mr. Morris said the majesty of the people would do as they pleased. All this I considered as sportive. But he [Mr. Adams] put a serious question, Should the letter, so directed, be read? Langdon and sundry others said yes; and read it was, from Loudon, the printer, offering to print for us. Adjourned.

I can not help here noting a trait of insolence in Lee, Elsworth, and Johnson. This committee [of titles] take on them to inform the committee of the Representatives *that the Senate would, for the present, address the President under the same style and title as the House of Representatives had given him.* This, in fact, was saying the Senate will do what we please. Insolence, indeed, but the fact justifies it. But, with all their art, I have balked them for once.

May 16th.—Settled all accounts with Mr. Vandalsen, and he owes me twelve shillings and sixpence. Visited Mr. Dalton and Mr. Langdon. Attended the committee on the dividing the rooms; declared my sentiments plainly, with all respect to the residence of Congress. It was brought in view by talk of this kind: that from here we would go; that I scorned all private trick and cabal about it, and would openly, at all times, declare for a departure from this place. Committee to meet on Monday at ten.

Senate met. A message came from the House of Repre-

---

* The short term of two years in the Senate (which were decided by lot), with Mr. Dalton, Mr. Elsworth, Mr. Elmer, Mr. Carrol, and Mr. Grayson.

sentatives. It was on the affair of a joint committee on newspapers and employing printers. Sundry petitions had come in from different printers. One was just now read from one Fenno. I moved that Fenno's, and all petitions of a similar nature, should be referred, for information, to the Committee on Newspapers and Employing Printers. It was seconded. Elsworth rose in great warmth and opposed it violently. Some more of the New England men joined him. It really seemed to me as if he wished to try whether he could not carry anything. He was, however, disappointed. A report of a committee for revising the minutes was read. The petition of one Duncan Campbell was read, and occasioned sundry remarks. Laid on the table.

The address to the President was now produced engrossed. The word "to" disobliged Elsworth, and a long debate ensued about it. I did not touch the trite subject. But it was to be signed, and here a mighty difficulty was signified from the Chair, and the wisdom of the House called on to determine if the Chair had done right. Every act had been signed "J. A., Vice-President." The Vice-President gave this information in such a way as left nobody in doubt that his opinion went with the practice. Mr. Carrol got up and said he thought it a matter of indifference, and concluded that he agreed it should be signed "Vice-President." His looks, I thought, betrayed dissent. But the goddess of good nature will apologize for this slight aberration from sentimental rectitude. He has for some time past been equally with myself opposed to the opinions of the Chair, and this was his peace-offering. About two weeks ago I was with Mr. Read, of the Delaware State, in the upper gallery of the House of Representatives. A message came from the Senate. The signature was read aloud: "John Adams, Vice-President." Mr. Read turned to me and said, "This is wrong." Yet Mr. Read now made a very long speech, declaring there was no impropriety in it. Mr. Lee hinted, very diffidently, his disapprobation of it. Mr. Morris said our acts should be signed by our Vice-President. Mr. Elsworth showed some inconvenience that would attend this practice.

I rose. Said the very term Vice-President carried on the

face of it the idea of holding the place of the President in his absence; that every act done by the Vice-President as such implied that when so acting he held the place of the President. In this point of view nothing could be more improper than the Vice-President signing an address to the President. It was like a man signing an address to himself. That the business of the Vice-President was when he acted exactly the same with that of President, and could not mix itself with us as a Senate.

Here the Vice-President tried very hard to raise a laugh. Seeing him willing to bear me down, I continued: "Sir, we know you not as Vice-President within this House. As President of the Senate only do we know you. As President of the Senate only can you sign or authenticate any act of that body." He said after I sat down that he believed he need not put the question; a majority of those who had spoken seemed to be in favor of his signing as President of the Senate. Mr. Carrol said he need not put the question, and none was put. Adjourned.

May 17th, Sunday.—Stayed at home all this day and bathed. Wrote letters to sundry persons. Did not go out until four o'clock, when I thought it warm enough. Called at the lodging of Mr. Fitzsimons and Clymer. They had gone to Brunswick. Walked to the Speaker's house. We walked to Cuyler's Hook. The east wind blew raw and cold. I left them and came home. Found myself rather indisposed. Caught some cold in my walk and was the worse for it. I never had been in a place remarkable for such variable weather. Set out when one will, with ever such agreeable sunshine, I never have been able to go two miles and return without a change of air. The wind which crosses the North [Hudson] River is cold. But there is a rawness in the east wind that, with me, seems to clog the springs of life. Mr. Scott, however, from Washington County [Pennsylvania], has experienced a favorable revolution in his health since he came here.

May 18th, Monday.—Attended the Hall at ten o'clock on what was called the arrangement committee, but they did not meet, and nothing was done; general discourse only obtained among [the members], principally on the necessity of our removal to the permanent residence. White, Sturges, and Scott were with me.

Senate met. The address [to the President] was read over, and we proceeded in carriages to the President's to present it. Having no part to act but that of a mute, I had nothing to embarrass me. We were received in an antechamber. Had some little difficulty about seats, as there were several wanting, from whence may be inferred that the President's major-domo is not the most provident, as our numbers were well enough known. We had not been seated more than three minutes when it was signified to us to wait on the President in his levee-room. The Vice-President went foremost, and the Senators followed without any particular order. We made our bows as we entered, and the Vice-President, having made a bow, began to read an address. He was much confused. The paper trembled in his hand, though he had the aid of both by resting it on his hat, which he held in his left hand. He read very badly all that was on the front pages. The turning of the page seemed to restore him, and he read the rest with more propriety. This agitation was the more remarkable, as there were but twenty-two persons present and none of them strangers.

The President took his reply out of his coat-pocket. He had his spectacles in his jacket-pocket, having his hat in his left hand and the paper in his right. He had too many objects for his hands. He shifted his hat between his forearm and the left side of his breast. But taking his spectacles from the case embarrassed him. He got rid of this small distress by laying the spectacle-case on the chimney-piece. Colonel Humphreys stood on his right, Mr. Lear on his left. Having adjusted his spectacles, which was not very easy, considering the engagements on his hands, he read the reply with tolerable exactness and without much emotion. I thought he should have received us with his spectacles on, which would have saved the making of some uncouth motions. Yet, on the whole, he did nearly as well as anybody could have done the same motions. Could the laws of etiquette have permitted him to have been disencumbered of his hat, it would have relieved him much.

After having read his reply, he delivered the paper to the

Vice-President with an easy inclination, bowed around to the company, and desired them to be seated. This politeness seems founded on reason, for men, after standing quite still some time, want to sit, if it were for only a minute or two. The Vice-President did not comply, nor did he refuse, but stood so long that the President repeated the request. He declined it by making a low bow, and retired. We made our bows, came out to the door, and waited till our carriages took us up. Colonel Humphreys waited on us to the door.

Returned [to the Hall]. Senate formed. The address and reply were ordered on the minutes. The Clerk of the House of Representatives brought up the Impost bill. Thursday was assigned for it. Some petitions were read, and the House adjourned.

May 19th.—Paid visits to ten o'clock. Attended at the City Hall, but the arranging committee did not meet. Senate met at eleven. A report was taken up regulating the mode of keeping the journals, and directing them to be published monthly. Agreed to, and the committee appointed to prepare them for the press. Adjourned. I was not of any committee, so went into the House of Representatives to hear the debates. The House was in committee of the whole on the establishment of the great departments. Stayed until after two o'clock.

Had agreed with sundry of our Pennsylvania friends to go to the levee. General Muhlenberg came to me and told me they would meet me in the committee-room. We did so, and went to the levee. I went foremost, and left them to follow and do as well as they could. Indeed, they had no great thing of a pattern, for I am but a poor courtier. The company was large for the room. The foreign Ministers were there, Van Berkel, the Dutch Minister (for the first time, I suppose), gaudy as a peacock. Our Pennsylvanians withdrew before me. The President honored me with a particular *tête-à-tête.* "How will this weather suit your farming?" "Poorly, sir; the season is the most backward I have ever known. It is remarkably so here, but by letters from Pennsylvania vegetation is slow in proportion there." "The fruit, it is to be expected, will be safe; backward seasons are in favor of it, but in Virginia it was lost before I left that place." "Much depends on the exposure of the orchard. Those with a northern aspect have been found by us [in Pennsylvania] to be the most certain in producing fruit." "Yes, that is a good observation and should be attended to." Made my bow and retired.

May 20th.—I attended at the Hall about half after ten o'clock. The committee did not meet me. Senate met, but there was no business done. Adjourned, that the committee might go to work. I thought I got cold yesterday in the House of Representatives, and set off to come home. Colonel Few overtook me, and we took a long walk to view the gardens of a Dutchman who lives beyond the Bowery. Spent some time, with a degree of satisfaction, viewing his harmless and silent little beauties of the garden. On the road Mr. Few threw out many generous sentiments on the subject of the temporary residence. The general belief is, however, that he is favorable to this place [New York]. Returned and felt nothing the better for my walk. Stayed at home the residue of the day. Mr. Clymer and Mr. Fitzsimons called to see us. Nothing remarkable.

CHAPTER II

THE FIRST TARIFF DEBATE

May 21st.—Went about half after nine to Mr. Morris' lodgings. He was out, but was expected in. Stayed until ten, then went to the Hall and stayed until the Senate met. Our Vice-President is progressive in reformation. He used to keep us until half after eleven, or a quarter at least. He was here this day at eight or ten minutes before eleven, and, strange to tell, he was without a sword.

The Impost bill, being the order of the day, was taken up and postponed until Monday. A resolution was handed to the Chair by Elsworth. It was for the Senate forming something like a committee of the whole. However, it seemed to amount to nothing more than a suspension of our rules for the time mentioned or alluded to in it. Adjourned. I returned home to write letters.

An idea has gone abroad that the mercantile interest has been exerted to delay this [impost] bill. The merchants have undoubtedly regulated the prices of their goods agreeable to the proposed duties, so that the consumers of dutied articles really pay the whole of the impost; and whatever the proposed duties exceed the State duties now paid is clear gain to the merchant. Some of them, indeed, dispute the payment of the State impost. The interim collection bill is rejected in the Lower House, and the reason given is the most loose I ever heard assigned, viz., "It was said a better one was forming." Surely this was no parliamentary reason. Had any new bill been offered to the House, had any been in the hands of a committee, the reason would have justified the measure; but because it is said Mr. Williams, of Baltimore, is making one of his own motion, and without any order of the House, it is not so proper. Perhaps it may turn out best.

May 22d.—Attended at the Hall at ten o'clock, and waited

a whole hour for the committee for arranging the rooms. They did not meet. The Senate met. Soon after, the Clerk of the Lower House attended with the bill for taking the oaths, which was presented to the Chair. The Vice-President rose and addressed the House: "I have, since the other day, when the matter of my signing was talked of in the Senate, examined the Constitution. I am placed here by the people. To part with the style given me is a dereliction of my right. It is being false to my trust. Vice-President is my title, and it is a point I will insist upon." He said several other things, then paused and looked over the bill. He then addressed the Senate again, and with great positiveness told them that he would sign it as Vice-President of the United States and President of the Senate. He asked Mr. Lee if it had been compared, and handed it to Mr. Lee. I can not say whether he signed it before he spoke to Mr. Lee or after, but it was not read nor was any question whatever put upon it—whether it should be read, whether it should be signed, or any other motion whatever. Mr. Elsworth got up and declared himself satisfied with that way of signing it. Mr. Strong got up and thought it should be Vice-President alone. This certainly is a most egregious insult to any deliberative body, but, as Patterson told me a day or two after the *gracious affair* * that if I had not opposed that measure somebody else would, I determined to see who would oppose this—and all was silence.

Adjourned till Monday at eleven o'clock.

Called on Mr. Morris this afternoon. Told him that murmurs were abroad against the conduct of the Congress; that, although the duty was not collected for the use of the public, yet, as the rates were in the possession of everybody, the merchants had raised their goods in proportion; that the public was now in the act of paying, and the merchants gainers, for the public treasury got nothing; that commercial influence was blamed for the delay. He replied, "I suppose they blame me." I answered, "These things were said before he came to town." I desired him to appoint some time when I could wait on him in order to examine the Impost bill, that we might be prepared with any amendments which we would offer. He appointed Sunday at

---

* See under date May 1, 1789.

9 A. M. I asked his opinion as to the height of the duties generally. He said he wished to see the bill for collection, and to know
under what penalties smuggling would be prohibited, that from
them he could form an opinion whether they were too high or
not. I replied that they would not be too high with regard to the
amount of the revenue raised, and I would have the penalties
and prohibitions against smuggling as severe as possible; and if,
under the circumstances, the depravity and villainy of people
would render the impost unproductive, it would, at least, demonstrate the necessity of adopting some other mode of supply-
ing the treasury.

May 23, Saturday.—This a fine day and all the world are
run a-gadding. Mr. Dennis called this morning. He says the
ship Chesapeake from Bengal is unloading at Amboy. The duties
on this ship would, by this act, have been about eight thousand
pounds; some say ten. I am much distressed with the delays of
Congress. The reputation of our Administration will be ruined.
The merchants have already added the amount of the duties to
the price of goods. In this point of view the impost is levied,
but not a farthing goes into the Treasury of the United States;
and all the difference between the State duties levied and the
proposed duties is clear gain to the merchants. In the Jerseys
it is all clear gain, for they have no duties, and vessels are daily
crowding there to store their goods until the impost takes place.
Delany's estimate of the impost for Pennsylvania for the year
was $863,623—323,858: 12: 6. Half of this taken for the spring
importation is $161,929: 6: 6; as Pennsylvania is supposed one
eighth of the Union, if we were adopting States, the loss would
be $1,295,434: 10; and the devil of it is that the sum will actually
be paid by the consumers.

I could not bear my own thoughts on this subject any longer.
I considered it as my duty to go and rouse our Pennsylvania
members. I called on the Speaker and his brother first. They
admitted all I said. From there I went to Mr. Scott. He said
it was undeniable. I endeavored to rouse all of them. From there
I went to the lodgings of Mr. Fitzsimons and Mr. Elsworth;
found Mr. Fitzsimons, declared my mind with great freedom,
and he heard me with more patience than ever I remember.
He said he wished he had stuck to this business from the

beginning; that he had brought this draft of a bill which was committed to Gerry, Lawrence, and himself. He left it with Lawrence, being an official man, to correct; that Lawrence kept it three weeks and did nothing; that Gerry then took it, and kept it two weeks, and put it in the hands of Mr. Williams, of Baltimore, who had kept it until within three or four days; that it came from Williams a most voluminous thing of more than forty pages; that he would now stick to it until it was finished.

There could not have been selected within the walls of the House two such improper characters as Gerry and Lawrence: Gerry highly anti-Federal, married, and intimately connected with the trade of this place; Lawrence, of New York, a mere tool for British agents and factors. Nothing else could have been expected. The foregoing calculation, founded on Delany's estimate, is certainly much too high. But if we suppose the port of Philadelphia to receive one fifth only of the importations, and throw one half off for errors and accidents, yet still the loss sustained will be near a million and a half of dollars, and the greater part of this sum actually remains as profit to the merchant. Mr. Fitzsimons has promised that the bill shall be reported on Monday. The Speaker has promised to go among the members and rouse them all in his power. For my part, think what they will of me, I will not be silent.

May 24th.—Being Sunday, I attended Mr. Morris, agreeable to appointment. We did not perfectly agree about the preamble of the bill, but there was no difference of consequence. It was verbal only. We came to the discrimination between nations in treaty and those not. Here we differed. He was totally against it. He used arguments. I made some reply, but each retained his opinion. Mr. Morris said the teas would bear more. He said double, and I agreed to it. I alleged that all seven and a half *ad valorem* articles should be raised at least to ten per cent. Mr. Morris seemed of the same way of thinking. Mr. Morris, however, suddenly exclaimed: "Let us go to Fitzsimons, he knows all about it; he has been thinking on the subject. I want to go and take a stroll somewhere." I thought by this he did not like close thinking. I have been of this opinion before now. He has, however, a strong and vigorous mind when it does act. To Fitzsimons we went and found him very busy at the bill. Mr. Carrol, of the Representatives, came in. We got on the discrimination. We were all of a different opinion from Mr. Morris. We asked Mr. Fitzsimons the reason of so many articles being at seven and a half, which we thought should be ten, along with glass and china. He said there really was no reason for it, but the House would not agree to it.

Mr. Morris proposed a jaunt to the Narrows, but no boat could be got. We then walked up the North River to one Brannan's, who has the greenhouse and gardens. Here we dined. Mr. Morris often touched me on the subject of my dislike to the Vice-President. We got on the subject of their salaries. Mr. Morris mentioned $20,000 for the President and $8,000 for the Vice-President. I opposed both, but it was in the funny way, all of it. At one time, however, when Mr. Morris was absent, I spoke seriously to Fitzsimons, saying the old proverb must be reversed. Here it was, "Be no service, but salary." Mr. Morris had alleged that the Vice-President must see the foreign ministers, etc., as the President could not, and the salary was to enable him to do so. And what obligation is he under to do so? Some of the Presidents of Pennsylvania have had £1,250 to enable them to see strangers. Some have not spent £10 per annum in that way. They had hinted so often at my dislike of the Vice-President that after dinner I gave them one of his speeches in the Senate. Was this prudent? No. But I never was a prudent man.

Strolled after dinner about the house taken by the Vice-President. Sat in the shade. Crossed through the fields and came at length to Baron Polnitz. This man we found sensible and well informed. He had studied agriculture, and has more machines in that way than I have seen before. I have heard him spoken rather disrespectfully of. This, however, I suppose, flowed from the force of our old habits, derived from the English, who seldom speak well of a foreigner. I will see him again. It is said he has moved in the higher stations of life and seen much. But I intend to hear from him, and perhaps will hear more of him in the mean time.

May 25th.—Wrote letters to my family. Went early this morning to the Hall. The Senate met. The Impost bill was taken, and, according to Elsworth's resolution, we were to act as if in a committee of the whole. But the Vice-President kept the chair, and I thought it made Mr. Elsworth look foolish. A message was announced from the President by General Knox. According to the resolution we were in committee, but the Vice-President kept the chair, and the General Knox advanced and laid the papers—being very bulky—on the table. The Vice-President had given us a speech before the minutes were read, on the subject of receiving a message from the President. His supreme delight seems to be in etiquette. But I really believe he had a further view in it. The entry on the minutes for Friday did not appear to me to correspond with the facts. There was something that imported the bill being reported by the committee that composed it, and the minute read that the *Vice-President* signed it. I determined I would not imbroil myself with him if possible, and nobody made any observation. By making his observations at this time, he diverted the attention of the Senate from the minutes.

We sat on the Impost bill, and debated long on the style of the enacting clause. It was an old field, and the same arguments were used which had fomerly been advanced; but the style of the law which had already passed was adopted. Now came the first duty of twelve cents on spirits of Jamaica proof. We debated until quarter past three, and it was reduced to eight. Adjourned.

When I came home in the evening I told Mr. Wynkoop the business of the day. He said things of this kind made him think whether our style of government in Pennsylvania was not best. Certain it is that a government with so many branches affords a larger field for caballing; first in the Lower House, and the moment a party finds a measure lost or likely to be lost, all engines are set to work in the Upper House. If they are likely to fail here, the last attempt is made with the President, and, as most pains are always taken by bad men and to support bad measures, the calculation seems in favor of the exertions and endeavors that are used more than in the justness of the measure. On the other hand, a fuller field is open for investigation, but, unfortunately, intrigue and cabal take place of fair inquiry. Here an observation forces itself upon me: that, in general, the further any measure is carried from the people, the less their interests are attended to.

I fear that our impost will be rendered in a great measure unproductive. This business is the work of the New England men. They want the article of molasses quite struck out, or, at least, greatly reduced; therefore they will strike at everything, or, to place it in a different point of view, almost every part will be proscribed either by one or other of those who choose to be opponents, for every conspirator must be indulged in the sacrifice of his particular enemy. I called on Mr. Fitzsimons some time ago to express my fears on this very head, and I wished him to consent to a reduction of the molasses duty to four cents, to avoid a thing of this kind; but I was not attended to. Indeed, I thought he had the best right to know. I felt too much confidence about that time in the return of Mr. Morris.

May 26th.—Attended the Hall early. Was the first. Mr. Morris came next, the Vice-President next. I made an apology to the Vice-President for the absence of our chaplain, Mr. Linn. There had been some conversation yesterday in the Senate about the style of the Bishop. It had been entered on the minutes *right reverend*. The Vice-President revived the discourse; got at me about titles. I really never had opened my mouth on the affair of yesterday. He, however, addressed to me all he said, concluding: "You are against titles. But there are no people in the world so much in favor of titles as the people of America; and the Government never will be properly administered until they are adopted in the fullest manner." "We think differently, indeed, on the same subject. I am convinced that were we to adopt them in the fashion of Europe, we would ruin all. You have told us, sir, that they are idle in a philosophic point of view. Governments have been long at odds with common sense. I hope the conduct of America will reconcile them. Instead of adding respect to government, I consider that they would bring the personages who assume them into contempt and ridicule."

Senate met. After some motions as to the business which should be taken up, and the appointment of a committee of conference on the mode of receiving communications from the President, the impost was taken up. There was a discrimination

of five cents in favor of nations having commercial treaties
with us per gallon on Jamaica spirits. Then rose against all
discrimination, Mr. Lee, Mr. Dalton, Mr. Izard, Mr. Morris,
Mr. Wingate, and Mr. Strong. At first they rather gave opinions
than any arguments. I declared for the discrimination; that if
commercial treaties were of any use at all, nations in treaty
should stand on better terms than those who kept at a sulky
distance; but, if we now treated all alike, we need never hereafter propose a commercial treaty. I asked if we were not called
on by gratitude to treat with discrimination those nations who
had given us a helping hand in the time of distress. Mr. Carrol
rose on the same side with me. I was, however, answered from
all sides. All commercial treaties were condemned. It was echoed
from all parts of the House that nothing but interest governed
all nations. My very words were repeated and contradicted in
the most pointed terms. I never had delivered anything in the
speaking way on which I was so hard run. Mr. Strong, who is
but a poor speaker, showed ill-nature; said nothing like reason
or argument had been offered. It was insisted that this discrimination was showing an inimical disposition to Great Britain;
it was declaring commercial war with her.

I had to reply as well as I could. I alleged that these arguments were against the whole system of administration under
the old Congress, and, in some measure, against the engagements entered into by that body, although these engagements
were sanctified by the Constitution; that Great Britain had
nothing to do in this business; that nations in treaty were on
terms of friendship; that strangers had no right to be offended
at acts of kindness between friends. She might be a friend, if
she pleased, and enjoy these favors. On the contrary, I thought
our friends were the people, who had a right to be offended
if no discrimination took place. It had been asserted that interest
solely governed nations. I was sorry it was so much the case,
but I hoped we would not in every point be governed by that
principle. The conduct of France to us in our distress, I thought,
was founded, in part, on more generous principles. Had the
principle of interest solely governed, she would have taken
advantage of our distress when we were in abject circumstances
and would have imposed hard terms on us, instead of treating on

the terms of mutual reciprocity. She likewise remitted large sums
of money. Was this from the principle of interest only? What
had been the conduct of the two nations since the peace? Civility
on the part of the French, and very different treatment by the
British. Our newspapers teem with these accounts. Elsworth
had said, it has been asked if we were not called on by gratitude,
etc. I answer no. The answer "no" has been given to the calls
of gratitude in this business, but the great voice of the people
at large would give a very different answer. So far as my sphere
of knowledge extended I had a right to say so; but the sense
of the people at large, expressed by their representatives in the
clause before us, holds a different language.

Mr. Langdon spoke, and seemed to be of our opinion. I did
not hear a "no," however, on the question but Mr. Carrol's
and my own.

All ran smooth now till we came to the molasses. Till quarter
after three did the New England members beat this ground,
even to the baiting of the hook that caught the fish that went
to buy the molasses. The motion was to reduce it to four cents
from five. I had prepared notes, but there was such an eagerness
to speak, and, finding that we should carry it, I let them fight
it out. The votes for four [cents] carried. All the arguments
of the other House were repeated over and over.

May 27th.—I spent this morning in writing letters to my
family, to go by General Butler, who sets off this day and will
pass by Harrisburg. Attended Senate. The minutes were read. I
was astonished to hear Strong immediately get up and begin a
long harangue on the subject of molasses. One looked at another.
Mr. Carrol had taken his seat next to me. Several of the gentlemen murmured. At last Mr. Carrol rose and asked pardon for
interrupting any gentleman, but said that matter had been
determined yesterday. The Vice-President said the question had
been taken on four cents being put instead of five, but no question had been taken on the paragraph after it was amended. The
whole sentence was on molasses per gallon, four cents; that a
second should be put on it was idle; but it was plain that this
matter had been agreed on between the Vice-President and the
New England men, and in all probability they have got some
people who voted for four yesterday to promise to vote for less

to-day. Dalton, however, got up and made a long speech that some of the gentlemen are absent, and particularly the gentlemen who moved for the four cents, and desired it might be put off till to-morrow. I must declare this the most uncandid piece of proceeding that I have ever seen in the Senate.

Now came wine of Madeira. All arguments of yesterday were had over again, and it was voted at eighteen cents. When we came to loaf-sugar, it was postponed. When we came to cables, the New England men moved to postpone everything of that kind (Mr. Langdon being absent) until we came to steel. I then moved an adjournment, as it was near the time, for I wished Mr. Morris to be here, as I expected a pointed opposition on that business, and as he has all the information on the most of subjects. I have been as attentive as possible to get information, as far as my sphere of influence extended, but the private communications of the citizens of Philadelphia have generally been by letter to Mr. Morris, Mr. Fitzsimons, or Mr. Clymer. I regret that they furnish me with none of this information. I must, however, serve my country as well as I can. The collection bill is at last reported. I can not think but that there has been a studied delay in this business. The bill itself is said to be a volume. It is ordered to be printed.

May 28th.—Having found the opposition to run hard yesterday against the impost, I determined to go this morning among all my Pennsylvania friends, and call on them for any information which they could give me in the way of their private letters or otherwise. I got an account of all the sugar-houses in Philadelphia from the Speaker. Called on Mr. Morris. Told him the war on molasses was to be waged again. Called on Mr. Clymer and Mr. Fitzsimons. Got from Mr. Fitzsimons a list of the Pennsylvania protecting duties. Then went to the Hall. I was here near an hour before any person came. Langdon, Carrol, and the Vice-President came. The discourse was general on the subject of government. "If our new Government does well," said our Vice-President, "I shall be more surprised than ever I was in my life." Mr. Carrol said he hoped well of it; it would be sufficiently powerful. "If it is," said Mr. Adams, "I know not from whence it is to arise. It can not have energy. It has neither rewards nor pun-

ishments." Mr. Carrol replied the people of America were enlightened. Information and knowledge would be the support
of it. Mr. Adams replied, information and knowledge were
not the sources of obedience; that ignorance was a much better
source. Somebody replied that it had formerly been considered
as the mother of devotion, but the doctrine of late was considered as rather stale. I began now to think of what Mr. Morris
had told me, that it was necessary to make Mr. Adams Vice-
President to keep him quiet. He is anti-Federal, but one of a
very different turn from the general cast. A mark may be
missed as well above as below, and he is a high flier.

Senate met. Cables, cordage, etc., came up. They stood at
seventy-five cents. Mr. Langdon spoke warmly against this.
Mr. Morris moved a reduction to fifty cents. I urged him so
much that he said sixty. This was seconded. I had to show
some pointed reason why I urged sixty. Indeed, it was much
against my will that any reduction took place. The protecting
duties of Pennsylvania were 4s. 2d., about fifty-six cents. To
place the manufacturers of Pennsylvania, who had a claim on
the faith of the State, on a worse ground than they stood before, would be injurious in a degree to their private property,
and break the engagement the State had made with them.
This argument went to all the protecting duties of Pennsylvania. Gentlemen had complained that they had no hemp in
the Western States. This was the case of Pennsylvania. At
the close of the war the protecting duties on cordage called for
the manufacturing of it. The manufacture called for the hemp.
It was, in fact, a bounty on the raising of that article. The
effect of the protecting duty in Pennsylvania was at first felt by
the importers. It was for a time an unproductive expense. It
is thus almost with every distant prospect. He that plants an
orchard can not immediately eat the fruit of it; but the fruit
had already ripened in Pennsylvania, and so it would in other
places. I was up four times in all. We carried it, however, at
sixty.

We passed on with little interruption until we got to twine.
Mr. Lee kept us an hour and a quarter on this business, because
the Virginians had hitherto imported their nets from Britain.
Once for all I may remark of him [Mr. Lee] that he has given

opposition to every article, especially the protecting duties. He declares openly against the principle of them. Mr. Grayson declares against all impost as the most unjust and oppressive mode of taxation. It was in vain Lee was told he could be supplied with all the nets Virginia wanted from any part of New England; that what could be supplied from any one part of the Union should be protected by duties on the importation of the same articles from foreign parts. It was lowered to one dollar and fifty cents.

And now for the article of molasses. Lee, who is a perfect Ishmael, declared the second question totally out of order. It is true, parliamentary precedent might be alleged in favor of such second question; but in the present case it was evidently a trick, and I guessed some parties had changed sides. From the discourse it appeared to me that Mr. Few, of Georgia, had changed. The Vice-President made a harangue on the subject of order. The facts were all agreed to, viz.: that it was agreed to strike out five cents; that the first motion seconded was to insert two cents. The second motion seconded was for three cents. The third motion seconded was for four cents. That a very long and tedious discussion took place with all the three motions before the Chair; that an adjournment had been called for, and negatived expressly on the avowed reason that the committee would first get rid of the article; that the Vice-President mentioned from the chair that he would put the question on four first, that being the highest sum. The question was put and carried, and the Senate afterward adjourned.

The Vice-President made a speech, which really was to me unintelligible. He seemed willing to persuade the members that the above was a very unfair mode of doing business, and that they had not an opportunity of declaring their sentiments freely in the above way. He concluded, however, *that after the four*[cents] *had been carried it was in order to move for any lower sum.* Somebody whispered that he ought to get his wig dressed. Mr. Morris rose and declared it was with reluctance that he differed with the Chair on a question of order, and was beginning to argue on the subject, but the New England men, seeing their darling Vice-President likely to be involved in embarrassment for the unguarded steps he had taken in their favor, with one consent declared they were satisfied to pass the article at present and take it up in the Senate.

Now came the postponed article of loaf-sugar. Lee labored with spite and acrimony in this business. He said the loaf-sugar of America was bad. It was lime and other vile compositions. He had broken a spoon in trying to dissolve and separate it, and so I must go on breaking my spoons and three millions of people must be taxed to support half a dozen people in Philadelphia. He pronounced this sentence, especially the part about the spoon, with so tremulous an accent and so forlorn an aspect as would have excited even Stoics to laughter. There was a laugh, but no retort on him. I supported the motion by showing that the sugar-baking business was of importance, as it gave employment to many other artificers—the mason, bricklayer, carpenter, and all the artificers employed in building, for they had to build largely. The coppersmith, potter, and cooper were in much employ with them. The business was in a declining state, and some sugar-houses discontinued; that in Pennsylvania the old protecting duty was 9/10 per hundred-weight, and the raw sugar was one per cent; that now there was no protecting duty whatever, for one cent on the pound of brown sugar was in proportion to three on the loaf; that the sugar-baker of Pennsylvania was therefore undeniably on a worse footing than formerly, at least by the whole amount of the Pennsylvania protecting duty, as he paid 6/6 per hundred-weight more on the importation of the raw material. The British, too, aimed at a monopoly of this business, and gave a bounty of 26s. sterling on exportation; so that it became us to counteract them or lose the manufacture. Mr. Morris and Mr. Dalton satisfied some gentlemen as to the manner of importing sugars. I thought this as plain a subject as could come before the House, and yet we divided, and the Vice-President gave us the casting vote. He desired leave to give us the reason of his vote. This seemed to imply a degree of vanity, as if among us all we had not placed the matter in a right point of view. For my part I was *satisfied* with his vote. It was near four o'clock. Adjourned.

May 29th.—The Senate met. The article of steel was passed over with little difficulty, and here I confess I expected con-

siderable opposition. Nails and spikes came next. Here an opposition from the Carolina and Georgia members led to an
increase of the duty. Now came salt. Up rose Mr. Lee, of the
Ancient Dominion. He gave us an account of the great revenue
derived from salt in France, England, and all the world. Condemned the general system of the bill. Said this was almost
the only article in it that would reach the interior parts of the
State. The interior parts of the country with their new lands
could much better afford to pay high taxes than the settlers of
the exhausted lands; that the carriage of it was nothing, for
they all had teams and fine horses. He concluded a lengthy
harangue with a motion for twelve cents, which, in his opinion,
was vastly too low. He was seconded by Mr. Carrol, of Maryland. Elsworth rose for an augmentation, but said if twelve was
lost he would move for nine. Lee, Carrol, Elsworth, and Mr.
Morris, speakers in favor of the augumentation. Any reduction
seemed out of the question with everybody. Against the augmentation [were the] speakers Izard, Few, and self.

I thought my friends on our side of the question were rather
warm, and used some arguments that did not apply well. They,
perhaps, with equal justice, thought the same of me. I advocated
the new settlers; endeavored to show that their superior crops
were justly due to superior labor; that every acre of new land
cost from five to ten dollars per acre, clearing and fencing. The
expenses of new buildings were immense. Men spent an active
life on a farm, and died with the farm in debt to them; that
new settlers labored for posterity—for the public. They were
the real benefactors to the community, and deserved exemption
if any. It had been said it was their choice. No. Necessity, dire
necessity, compelled many. But were they exempted from the
effects of the other part of the bill? No. They could raise no
sheep, of course no wool, coarse duffels,* blankets, swan-skins
—in a word, all their woolens were imported, and they would
of course pay the imposts on these articles from *necessity,*
which was not the case in general with other citizens, who might
either manufacture or buy as they had the materials.

But, over and above this, luxuries would find their way among
them. All people, down to the savage, were fond of finery, the

---

* A coarse woolen cloth, having a thick nap.

rudest the most so. And I was convinced that the poor, the amount of their several stocks taken into consideration, spent more in superfluities than the rich; that, all these arguments apart, the article of salt was the most necessary of any in the bill, and in proportion to the original cost was the highest taxed; that it was a new and an untried source of revenue in many of the States; that it ought, therefore, to be touched with a gentle hand, if at all; that I knew not whether the discontents would follow that had been predicted, and I hoped they would not, but wished we could avoid giving occasion for any; that for these reasons I should at present be for leaving it where the wisdom of the other House had placed it. The question was put. The House divided, and the Vice-President gave it in our favor.

In the course of the debate it came out that Mr. Fitzsimons had furnished Mr. Carrol with all his remarks and the documents which he had collected on the subject of revenue, as well respecting Pennsylvania as the Union in general. I do think that as an individual I have taken as much pains to collect information as any of them. But I am much less known, and of course information by letter from individuals has generally fallen to the share of Mr. Fitzsimons, Mr. Morris, and Mr. Clymer. The information from the Collector's office I never could get at, although Mr. Fitzsimons told me in Philadelphia that Mr. Delany had furnished him (*but voluntarily*) with. Mr. Morris has a statement of the Custom-House in Philadelphia, or some such paper. He used it this day as he sat beside me. I asked him to let me see the article of salt in it. He said it was not there.

What shall I think of Lee, this Ishmael of the House? He labored [on] the subject of titles with a diligence worthy of a better cause. He seemed disposed to destroy the whole effect of the Impost bill on every other article. The tax on salt he knows must be odious, and this he is for doubling at the first word. He is a great advocate for an excise. If I really wished to destroy the new Constitution, to injure it to the utmost of my power, I would follow exactly the line of conduct which he has pursued. Far be it, however, from me to say this of him. People employ the same means for very different ends, and such is the vanity of human opinion that the same object is often aimed at by means directly opposite. Adjourned to Monday.

May 30th.—The Speaker called. He dined yesterday with the President. A number of the Senators were present. The Pennsylvanians had agreed to call on Mrs. Morris between ten and eleven. Mr. Morris had yesterday mentioned that time as convenient time to her. The gentlemen of Congress have, it seems, called on Mrs. Washington and all the congressional ladies. Speaker Wynkoop and self called on Mrs. Morris half after ten. Not at home. Left our cards. Being in the lady way, we called to see Mrs. Langdon and Mrs. Dalton. Found Mr. Langdon; the ladies abroad. This finished the visiting tour. Came home; felt uncommonly heavy this day. It was warm. Never wished so much for home; think I must absolutely set off for home about this day week. The Collection bill is reported, and I will do all I can to inspire my acquaintances with a spirit of expedition in both Houses.

May 31.—Being Sunday, was called on this morning by General St. Clair. He desired my commands for Philadelphia. Wrote by him to Mr. Peters and Mr. Harris. I find going out hurts me. I come home almost from every walk with a sore throat, complaint in my breast, or something of that kind. I therefore determined to stay at home more. Read and kept my room.

June 1st, Monday.—Called this morning on Mr. Clymer and Mr. Fitzsimons. I wished for a general abstract of the trade of the United States; Mr. Fitzsimons had such a paper, for he one day gave us some business from it. He, however, put Sheffield's pamphlet into my hand. I had never read Sheffield's work, and therefore received it with pleasure. Came to the Hall and was soon delighted with the reception of letters from my family, who were all well, and my dear little son Billy recovered of the small-pox, for which he has been inoculated.

The Impost bill was taken up, and a number of articles passed over. When we came to tea, the impost proceeded on a discrimination in favor of our own ships. Here a motion was made by Elsworth, seconded by Lee, that went against all discrimination in favor of our own shipping, or, in other words, against any protecting duty for the East India trade;

and, indeed, the argument went against the East India trade altogether. I got up early in this business. I laid it down that the use of tea was now so general that any interdiction of it was impossible; that have it the people would. If this, then, was the case, common prudence told us to get it from the first hand; that it was evident teas were now obtained vastly cheaper than before our merchants traded to China. This difference had been stated at fifty per cent on some teas. It had been alleged against this trade that it destroyed the lives of seamen. The fact had been represented to me differently by those who made the voyage; that it was the practice of all nations to encourage their own trade, but our permitting the British to supplant us in this trade was suffering them to encourage their trade at our expense.

It had been said the British would take raw materials from us and give us teas. I was well informed that the Chinese took many articles from us, and some that no other people would take. A detail of these articles I had no doubt would be more fully entered into by some of the gentlemen who would follow me. To talk of not protecting a trade sought after by all the world was a phenomenon in a national council. I therefore was clearly for the discrimination. Mr. Morris followed. He went most minutely into the India trade; showed that ginseng was a considerable article in that trade, anchors, iron, spars, masts, naval stores of all kinds. He, in fact, made it clear that a dollar sent to Europe for East India goods would not import more than half a dollar sent to the East Indies. The debate was amazingly lengthy. Both Few and Elsworth said the trade had been represented as flourishing; this it had obtained without any protecting duties; why, then, give any now?

I rose to information, and mentioned that the protecting duty of Pennsylvania was twopence per pound and the protecting duty of New York twopence, and that the ill policy of withdrawing these duties now, when the trade to the East Indies was threatened with combination against it, was evident. We got the discrimination carried by nine votes to eight.

Now for the duty. Mr. Morris moved to raise all the tea-duties. This was lost. But I wish we had uniformly moved

to raise, for by this means we secured it at the rate in the bill.
When we came to the real discrimination, now a great debate
arose. Four cents was the difference on Boheas, and so, nearly
in proportion. Mr. Lee moved for eight, avowedly on this
principle that the four cents were more than the old protecting duty under which the trade had flourished. This debate
was mostly conducted on our side by Mr. Morris. I only showed
that, though the difference between six and ten cents was more
than the old protecting duties, the difference between six and
eight was less, and that the gentlemen, on their own principle,
should have moved for more than eight. But in the critical situation of the trade to the East, with combinations in India contracts and ships fitted out at Ostend, and the increasing endeavors of the English to engross the whole trade of the East,
the discrimination of four was not too much. Carried at four
o'clock—at nine to eight.

In the first argument I mentioned that, if there had been
any exclusive company engrossing the India trade, there might
be something in the arguments. This, however, was not the
case, nor could it be.

June 2d.—Had an excellent opportunity of writing home
by the person who brought my letters yesterday. This employed me to near eleven o'clock. Attended at the Hall. After
some preliminary business, proceeded on the Impost bill without
much opposition till we came to an enumeration of fifteen or
sixteen articles which all stood at seven and a half per cent.
The most of these articles stood, in the old protecting duties
of Pennsylvania, at twelve and a half per cent. I feared much
the spirit of reduction would get into the opposers of the impost,
and that they would be for lowering everything. From this sole
motive I would have an augmentation, by way of securing the
duty where it was. However, I had better ground. I set out
with naming over the greater part of the articles on which the
protecting duties of Pennsylvania were over twelve and a half
per cent and thirteen per cent in New York. I reasoned from
the effect of these duties on the promoting the manufacture.
But by the present duties the manufactures would stand on
worse ground by five per cent than they had done under the
State laws; that although the United States were not absolutely

obliged to make good the engagements of the State to individuals, yet, as individuals had embarked their property in these manufactures, depending on the State laws, I thought it wrong to violate those laws without absolute necessity.

I was, as usual, opposed by the Southern people. Before I rose I spoke to Mr. Morris to rise and move an augmentation. He said *no*. Mr. Few, of Georgia, asserted that the manufactures of Pennsylvania would be better off under the seven and a half than they had been under the twelve and a half per cent. Mr. Morris got up and asserted the same thing. I declare I could not believe either of them. Mr. Morris, however, stated the manufacture of paper to be in the most flourishing condition imaginable in Pennsylvania; said he was afraid to mention the amount of paper that had been exported last year lest he might not be believed; that it had been stated to him at not less than £80,000. He went through the business down to gathering the rags in the street. After this it was in vain to say anything more, but the effect was that it stood at seven and a half.

A number of articles were now raised to ten per cent. But what surprised me was that Mr. Morris was against raising leather and leather manufactures, canes, walking-sticks, whips, ready-made clothing, brushes, gold, silver, and plated ware, jewelry and paste-work, wrought tin and pewter ware. He gave no reason for this, which is not usual with him. Some of the articles were, notwithstanding, placed at ten without him. His weight in our Senate is great on commercial subjects. Mr. Morris moved, at my request, to have cotton exempted for some time from duty. This was carried by a kind of compromise. We proceeded smoothly till we came to the drawback on fish, etc., and New England rum. Long conversations on this subject; but agreed to. We expected a sharp debate on the drawback or discount on American vessels, but it was passed *nem. con.* The last clause Mr. Morris moved to expunge, but it was carried, and I heard not a "No" but his own. It was now late, and we adjourned.

I omitted to mention in its proper place that Mr. Morris moved for ten per cent on a long list of scythes, sickles, axes, spades, shovels, locks, hinges, etc., down to plow-irons, but none of them were carried, and, of course, stood in the mass of five per cent.

June 3d.—In rather a disagreeable situation with my swelled knee. This vile rheumatism seems determined to torment me while I stay here. Attended at the Hall at ten; read the newspaper. At eleven the Senate met. The Clerk from the House of Representatives came with a message and brought up the law about the oaths. The impost was taken up; the title and preamble debated, and altered a little. And now a lengthy debate took place on a motion of Mr. Lee to put off the consideration of the bill until Monday next. I spoke first against the motion. I was for proceeding immediately. The bill had been very long under consideration. The public expectation had been tired. A million of dollars had been lost to the treasury, and, what was still worse, the people had paid the money; for the merchants had raised their goods, and the impost was in actual collection on all the spring importations; that I wished the new Government might stand fair with the public and give them no just cause of censure at so early a period. After very considerable debate, Mr. Morris moved that to-morrow be assigned for the second reading in the Senate. This was agreed to.

Now a very long debate took place about the newspapers. All the printers in the city crowd their papers into the hands of the members. The bulk of the papers consist of advertisements. Useful information ought not to be excluded; but this is overdone. The real mean appears to me to be the taking of one or two papers by each member. But one part of the House struggled for taking all, the other for taking none. No vote could be carried for either, and, of course, the printers will continue their old practice of sending and expecting payment.

Mr. Morris some time ago promised the London prices current. His words were, "I will give you one." They are of no use in the world to anybody further than all the duties are marked in them, and on the business of the impost they may be useful. I thought he was long in performing his promise, and this day asked him for it. He said he had one and would let me see it, but he had it not here; perhaps I was mistaken in this business.

June 4th.—Went to the Hall at ten, but found the members

occupied by two committees. Sauntered about till eleven; rather disagreeable. Senate was formed. The minutes were read. They stood: Mr. Langdon administered the oath to the *Vice-President;* the *Vice-President* administered, etc. The law is, the oath, etc., shall be administered *by any* one member of the Senate *to the President of the Senate,* and by him to all the members. And again: *The President of the Senate for the time being.* The minutes are totally under the direction of our Vice-President, or rather Otis is his creature. I told Patterson that I would not get up again, but let them be as they would.

But now a discourse was raised again whether the members should be styled honorable on the minutes. The Vice-President declared from the chair that it was a most serious affair, and a vote of the House should be taken on it. He gave us a touch again on the subject; was against using the word unless "right" was added to it. He said a good deal to this purpose. Lee was up in a moment for it. The Vice-President made us a second speech. He said it was of great importance. If we took the title "honorable," it was a colonial appellation, and we should disgrace ourselves forever by it; that it was applied to the justices of every court. Up now rose Grayson, of Virginia, and gave us volley after volley against all kinds of titles whatever. Louder and louder did he inveigh against them. Lee looked like madness. Carrol and myself exchanged looks and laughs of congratulation. Even the Vice-President himself seemed struck in a heap—Izard would have said *rotundity.* Grayson mentioned the Doge of Venice in his harangue, as he was mentioning all the great names in the world. "Pray, do you know his title?" said the Vice-President from the chair. "No," says Grayson, smartly, "I am not very well acquainted with him."

We now took up the Impost bill, and proceeded smoothly till we came to the article of molasses. It was the wish of the majority of the Senate to have the question without any debate; but now Mr. Dalton rose, and we were obliged to hear everything over again which had been formerly advanced. It was long and tedious. Some observations were just and pertinent, but many were quite foreign to the purpose. Dr. Johnson rose on the same side. Dalton was for lowering it to three cents, but Dr. Johnson said he had been convinced that it ought to be but two, or rather none at all. The drift of the doctor's argument was: Molasses, imported, is either distilled, and then as a raw material it ought not to be taxed, or it is consumed by the poor as food, and so ought not to be taxed. So it ought not to be taxed at all.

Up rose Strong, and, facing himself to the right where Mr. Morris and myself sat, fell violently on the members from Pennsylvania, with insinuations that seemed to import that we wished to overcharge New England with an undue proportion of the impost. What was the most remarkable, Mr. Morris had whispered to me that he would not get up on this business, but would attend with the utmost attention to all their arguments, fully determined to give them their utmost weight. But when this attack was begun, I could see his nostrils widen and his nose flatten like the head of a viper. Elsworth, however, got up before him, and this gave him time to recollect himself. He rose after Elsworth, and charmingly did he unravel all their windings. It is too long to set down, but he was clear and conclusive.

I, in the mean while, busied myself in examining the abstract of the importations into Philadelphia given me by Delany. In this place I can not help remarking that there is something of a singularity in my disposition. Although I was equally concerned, I really felt joy on this attack, and the more so when I saw Mr. Morris was moved. The buffetings that I used to get from some of these people in his absence, and the sentimental insults that I received, seemed now to say, "Take you, too, a part."

When he had done, I rose and repeated from their own observations that the whole of the molasses imported into Massachusetts was three million gallons. Two millions they distilled and had the drawback, if they chose to export it, so that this was totally out of the question. That consumed in the State, in substance, was the remaining million. But we imported last year so much molasses into Pennsylvania that, making sufficient allowance for two distilleries that were worked, the remainder for consumption, in substance, was half a million. Was this the object to make such a stir about? It was said that some of the New England rum was drunk in the State. Be it so. Take any given quantity, be it what it may, it is consumed under a duty of four cents per gallon; for the gallon of molasses yields in distillation rather a larger than a less quantity than gallon for gallon. But we import near one million of gallons of spirits into Pennsylvania, and this is consumed under a duty of from eight to ten cents per gallon. We imported also five million gallons of raw sugar; above one million of coffee, which was said to be half of the coffee used in the United States; besides a full proportion of all other goods. I spoke not at random nor without book. Here was the abstract in the hand-writing of Sharp Delany, the collector. Were we, then, the people for imposing unequal burdens? No. We were imposing no burdens of which we were not about to bear a share—a great, perhaps the greatest, share.

Dalton rose and remarked on the great uncertainty of all calculations. He was, however, modest. A variety of people spoke. Some heat seemed at one time to rise between Lee and Langdon. There was a considerable shifting about the question. It was at last settled that the question should be to reduce the duty to three cents, expressly on the condition of taking away the drawback. Mr. Morris and myself voted against it. Izard, Gunn, and some others voted expressly on the condition of the drawback being taken away. The others joined, but with a design of retaining the drawback. So stands this curious affair till to-morrow. Past three, and adjourned. I must not omit that Carrol got up and spoke well on our side. He stated the inequality of duty on molasses and sugar as sweets; that a gallon of molasses was equal, as a sweet, to seven pounds of good brown sugar. Seven cents on one, four on the other.

June 5th, Friday.—Came with my swelled knee. Called this morning on Mr. Fitzsimons, and got from him a list of the imports into Pennsylvania and into Virginia. Went to the Hall, and waited until the meeting of the Senate. We now fell to the imposts, and proceeded to the article of loaf-sugar; and here they directly moved a reduction of one cent. Lee and Elsworth spoke against it, as formerly. I rose and repeated the sum of the old arguments. Dr. Johnson, who was with us before, now fell off. Dalton changed. It was reduced to three. We swam on smoothly to teas, imported from any other country than China. This clause admitted all foreigners to come directly to America from China and India. Dalton moved an amendment that should confine the direct trade from India and China to the United

States to our own vessels. Mr. Morris got up and said that although he was in sentiment with the gentleman, yet, as he believed it would not meet the approbation of gentlemen, he would not second the motion, but leave the matter until experience would fully show the necessity of it.

Mr. Carrol got up, said if the matter was right it should be tried now and not wait for experiment, which might be attended with detriment, and seconded the motion. And now, strange to tell, both Lee and Elsworth rose and supported the motion. I listened with astonishment when I recollected the debates on this very subject on Monday last. The whole trade to India was then inveighed against, condemned, and almost execrated, and now the very men declared for it and for securing it exclusively to ourselves. This change I can not account for. If there was any preconcerted measure, Mr. Morris certainly knew nothing of it. One inference, however, follows clearly from the conduct of Lee and Elsworth, that they are governed by conveniency or cabal. Had judgment been the rule of their conduct, their behavior on Monday would not have been so inconsistent with that of to-day. I was content with the bill as it stood. The difference of duty and the discount of ten per cent in favor of our own vessels I thought pretty well for protecting our trade without absolutely excluding all the world. But I had another reason. I doubt much whether the House of Representatives will agree to our amendments. Every new one will or may be a source of dissension or delay. I have labored with all the diligence in my power to hasten on the impost, but I am counteracted; for what can one man do? It now seems evident that remarkable influence is exerted to delay the impost until they get in all their summer goods. This is detestable; this is— But I have not a name for it. I wish we were out of this base, bad place.

Yesterday was the anniversary of his Britannic Majesty's birth. It was a high day, and celebrated with great festivity on that account. The old leaven anti-revolutionism has leavened the whole lump, nor can we keep the Congress free from the influence of it.

People may act as they think proper in their elections, and they will still do so. Lawyers and merchants are generally their choice. But it seems as difficult to restrain a merchant from striking at gain as to prevent the keen spaniel from springing at game that he has been trained to pursue. Habit with them has become a second nature. Indeed, the strongest propensities of nature are often postponed to it. Lawyers have keenness and a fondness for disputation. Wrangling is their business. But long practice in supporting any cause that offers has obliterated regard to right and wrong. The question only is, Which is my side? And this, the slightest circumstance, a word, a hint, a nod, a whim, or silly conceit, often determines with them. Who are above pressing influence, treats, dinners, attentions, etc? And whenever the digit is made, whenever the part is chosen, all that follows is a contest for victory. O candor and integrity! jewel of the human soul, where are ye to be found? Seldom in professional men; often in the plain and sober countryman; never, however, in the sordid clown.

About two o'clock the words "levee" and "adjourn" were repeated from sundry quarters of the House. Adjourn to Monday? The Vice-President caught hold of the last. "Is it the pleasure of the House that the adjournment be to Monday?" A single "No" would not be heard among the prevailing ayes. Here are the most important bills before us, and yet we shall throw all by for empty ceremony, for attending the levee is little more. Nothing is regarded or valued at such meetings but the qualifications that flow from the tailor, barber, or dancing-master. To be clean shaved, shirted, and powdered, to make your bows with grace, and to be master of small chat on the weather, play, or newspaper anecdote of the day, are the highest qualifications necessary. Levees may be extremely useful in old countries where men of great fortune are collected, as it may keep the idle from being much worse employed. But here I think they are hurtful. They interfere with the business of the public, and, instead of employing only the idle, have a tendency to make men idle who should be better employed. Indeed, from these small beginnings I fear we shall follow on nor cease till we have reached the summit of court etiquette, and all the frivolities, fopperies, and expense practiced in European governments. I grieve to think that many individuals among us are aiming at these objects with unceasing diligence.

Settled with Mr. Vandalsen, and he owes me 11s. 6d.

June 6th.—It was half-past ten when Mr. Bell called on me.
He represented Mrs. Baxter's situation to be so low that I
might never see her if I did not do it soon. He seemed so
earnest that I should go with him that I agreed to meet him
in half an hour at the ferry-house and accompany him home.
The wind was high and direct ahead. It was five when we
reached Elizabethtown Point. Here was Governor Livingston
and a dinner party. They had eaten their fish, and were saun-
tering on the porch. Mr. Bell introduced me to the Governor
—a man plain and rather rustic in his dress and appearance.
I had often heard of his being a man of uncommon abilities,
and was all attention; but the occasion offered nothing but
remarks of the convivial kind. But we learned that the old
gentleman, in returning late, was overturned in his [sedan]
chair and much bruised.

'Twas near night when we came to Mr. Bell's. Poor Mrs.
Baxter lay a skeleton indeed. I can not say but she may recover,
but much, indeed, does it seem against her. She, too, was gay,
and she yet is young. Useful lesson to the fluttering females
of the neighborhood, if lesson were of any service in these giddy
times. I soon found I was not the only member of Congress
in this quarter. Most of the Representatives from South Carolina
were floating in this neighborhood this evening and all Sunday.
The house was filled with decent visitants, mostly, however,
females, and charmingly did they chat it. The almost only subject was the measures that were pursued to detain Congress in
New York. There is in this vicinity a Mrs. Ricketts. This lady
leads the business in this quarter. She enters into it with a spirit
that risks reputation and sets censure at defiance; indeed, the
volumes of conversation poured out on this subject might be
styled with propriety the "Campaigns of Mrs. Ricketts." But,
while she is characterized as the mere flash of frivolity, her
husband is represented as a pattern of industry and economy,
and that he indulges his *cara sposa* in her utmost extravagance,
not from a sheepish or sneaking disposition, but from the purest
motives of benevolence and a sincere desire of making her
happy. This character made a deep impression on my milky
temper, and I sincerely wished to have seen him somewhere in

a field by himself that I might have chatted with and learned
something more of him.

June 8th.—Wrote letters to my family and Mr. Harris. Set
off in a frail [sedan] chair for the Point with a lady, but the
chair had like to have broke down, and I quitted it to her. Came
to the Point [Elizabethtown Point] a few minutes too late for
the first boat; left it at a quarter after ten in a second boat,
but it was half after two before I reached New York, sweated
and almost boiled in a burning sun. Upon the whole the jaunt
was a disagreeable one, but it was right to see the poor, languid,
perhaps dying Mrs. Baxter. How lately was she as gay as the
summer insect, and how soon may any of us be as she is!

Heard, on my coming to my lodgings, of the arrival of two
Indiamen at Philadelphia, under command of Barry and Trux-
ton, who report all the rest to be on their way. And now perhaps
we shall get the Impost and Collection bills passed.

June 9th.—Although I was not present yesterday, nevertheless they were busy at the impost. The affair of confining
the East India trade to the citizens of America had been negatived, and a committee had been appointed to report on this
business. The report came in with very high duties, amounting to a prohibition. But a new phenomenon had made its
appearance in the House since Friday. Pierce Butler, from
Carolina, had taken his seat and flamed like a meteor. He
arraigned the whole Impost law, and then charged (indirectly)
the whole Congress with a design of oppressing South Carolina.
He cried out for encouraging the Danes and Swedes and foreigners of every kind to come and take away our produce.
In fact, he was for a Navigation act reversed. Elsworth, Morris,
Carrol, Dalton, Langdon, for the report; Few, Izard, Butler,
Lee, against it. And until four o'clock was it battled with less
order, less sense, and less decency, too, than any question I
have ever yet heard debated in the Senate.

I did not like the report well, but concluded to vote for it,
all things considered, rather than, by rejecting it, to have all
set afloat on that subject again. Butler's party had conducted
themselves with so little decorum that any effect their arguments might have had was lost by their manner; and nobody
rose but themselves. This was really the most misspent day

that I remember in Congress. I did not rise once, but often called for the question. To-morrow is assigned for the third reading of the bill, and I hope we will finish it, or at least send it down to the other House. If I had stood in need of any proof of the instability of Lee's political character, this day gave me a fresh instance of it. Now again he has vilified and traduced the India trade.

June 10th.—Attended at the Hall at the usual time, and the Impost bill was taken up for a third reading. I will not enter into any detail of the speeches and arguments entered into. We once believed that Lee was the worst of men, but I think we have a much worse than he in our lately arrived Mr. Butler. This is the most eccentric of creatures. He moved to strike out the article of indigo. "Carolina was not obliged to us for taking notice of her affairs"; ever and anon crying out against local views and partial proceedings; and that the most local and partial creature I ever heard open a mouth. All the Impost bill was calculated to ruin South Carolina. He has words at will, but scatters them the most at random of any man I ever heard pretend to speak. He seems to have a particular antipathy to Mr. Morris. Izard has often manifested something of a similar disposition. We sat until four o'clock, but did not get quite through it.

June 11th.—Attended the Hall as usual. Mr. Izard and Mr. Butler opposed the whole of the drawbacks in every shape whatever. Mr. Grayson, of Virginia, warm on this subject, said we were not ripe for such a thing. We were a new nation, and had no business for any such regulation—a nation *sui generis.* Mr. Lee said drawbacks were right, but would be so much abused he could not think of admitting them. Mr. Elsworth said New England rum would be exported instead of West India to obtain the drawback.

I thought it best to say a few words in reply to each. We were a new nation, it was true, but we were not a new people. We were composed of individuals of like manners, habits, and customs with the European nations. What, therefore, had been found useful among them came well recommended by experience to us. Drawbacks stood as an example in this point of view to us; but, if the thing was right in itself, there could be no just argument drawn against the use of a thing from the abuse of it. It would be the duty of the Government to guard against abuses by prudent appointments and watchful attention to officers; that, as to changing the kind of rum, I thought the Collection bill would provide for this by limiting the exportation to the original casks and packages. I said a good deal more, but really did not feel much interested either way. But the debate was very lengthy. Butler flamed away, and threatened a dissolution of the Union with regard to his State, *as sure as God was in the firmament!* He scattered his remarks over the whole Impost bill, calling it partial, oppressive, etc., and solely calculated to oppress South Carolina; and yet ever and anon declaring how clear of local views, how candid and dispassionate he was! He degenerated into mere declamation. His State would live or die glorious, etc. We, however, got through by three o'clock.

I will now memorandum one remark. The Senators from Jersey, Pennsylvania, Delaware, and Maryland, in every act, seemed desirous of making the impost productive both as to revenue and effective for the encouragement of manufactures, and seemed to consider the whole of the imposts (salt excepted) much too low. Articles of luxury many of them would have raised one half. But the members, both from the North, and still more particularly from the South, were ever in a flame when any articles were brought forward that were in any considerable use among them.

Dined this day with Mr. Morris. Mr. Fitzsimons and Mr. Clymer, all the company, except Mrs. Morris and three children. Mrs. Morris talked a great deal after dinner. She did it gracefully enough, this being a gayer place, and she being here considered as at least the second female character at court. As to taste, etiquette, etc., she is certainly first. I thought she discovered a predilection for New York, but perhaps she was only doing it justice, while my extreme aversion, like a jealous sentinel, is for giving no quarter. I, however, happened to mention that they were ill supplied with the article of cream. Mrs. Morris had much to say on this subject; declared they had done all they could, and even sent to the country all about, but that they could not be supplied. She told many anecdotes on this subject; particularly how two days ago she dined at the President's. A large, fine-looking trifle was brought to table, and appeared exceedingly well indeed. She was helped by the President, but on taking some of it she had to pass her handkerchief to her mouth and rid herself of the morsel; on which she whispered the President. The cream of which it is made had been unusually stale and rancid; on which the General changed his plate immediately. "But," she added with a titter, "Mrs. Washington ate a whole heap of it."

But where in the world has this trifle led me? I have ever been very attentive to discover, if possible, General Washington's private opinions on the pompous part of government. His address of "fellow-citizens" to the two Houses of Congress seems quite republican. Mrs. Morris, however, gave us something on this subject. General Washington, on a visit to her, *had declared himself in the most pointed manner for generous salaries; and added that, without large salaries, proper persons could never be got to fill the offices of government with propriety.* He might deliver something of this kind with propriety enough without using the word "large." However, if he lives with the pompous people of New York, he must be something more than human if their high-toned manners have not some effect on him. On going first among Indians, I have observed decent white people view them with a kind of disgust; but, when the Indians were by far the most numerous, the disgust would, by degrees, wear off, indifference follows, and by degrees attachment and even fondness. How much more likely are the arts of attention and obsequiousness to make an imitative impression!

June 12th.—Attended the Judicial Committee and had the bill read over. It was long and somewhat confused. I was called out; they, however, reported it soon after the Senate met, and a number of copies were ordered to be struck off. Monday sennight appointed for it. The Indian treaties were now taken up and referred to a committee of three to report. Mr. Butler made a most flaming speech against the Judicial bill. He was called to order from the Chair, and was not a little angry about it. The French Convention was called up and read respecting the privileges of consuls, vice-consuls, etc., but was postponed.

We now adjourned, and I went to the levee. I was rather

late. Most of the company were coming [away]. I felt easier than I used to do, and I believe I had better attend every day until I finish the affair of Davy Harris. I spoke to Colonel Humphreys, and desired to know when I should call on him. He said nine o'clock. I believe I will go at that hour to-morrow. In the evening, Mr. White, of Virginia, called on me. We walked after tea; had much discourse on the subject of removing Congress. I have not been mistaken in my opinion of the Virginians. He declared for staying here, rather than agree to the Falls of the Delaware. As we came home, the Speaker overtook us on horseback.

June 13th.—Being Saturday, and having no party made to go anywhere, went to the House of Representatives to hear the debates. They were on the Collection bill. I stayed two hours. They were in committee, and really made but small progress. There was not one debate worth committing to paper.

Settled with my landlord. He owes me £1 10s. 2d.

June 14th.—Wrote this day two sets of letters home—one to Mr. Harris, inclosing one to Mrs. Maclay, to go by a Mrs. Ofsay, of Harrisburg; the other set to go by the post. Oh, this was a dreary, joyless day! I think I shall long remember it. I was ill with my sore knee; went to the bathing-house and bathed; did not go to any place of worship; could not engage myself to reading; had, indeed, no book of an engaging nature. I will leave a blank here, which I can fill up at my leisure if I choose.

My mind revolts, in many instances, against the Constitution of the United States. Indeed, I am afraid it will turn out the vilest of all traps that ever was set to ensnare the freedom of an unsuspecting people. Treaties formed by the Executive of the United States are to be the law of the land. To cloak the Executive with legislative authority is setting aside our modern and much-boasted distribution of power into legislative, judicial, and executive—discoveries unknown to Locke and Montesquieu, and all the ancient writers. It certainly contradicts all the modern theory of government, and in practice must be tyranny.

Memorandum: Get, if I can, The Federalist without buying it. It is not worth it. But, being a lost book, Izard, or some

one else, will give it to me. It certainly was instrumental in
procuring the adoption of the Constitution. This is merely a
point of curiosity and amusement to see how wide of its
explanations and conjectures the stream of business has taken
its course.

June 15th, Monday.—Attended at the Hall, and the Tonnage
Act was taken up. We got about half-way through the first
clause of it by four o'clock. A clause stood, "On all ships or
vessels within the United States, *and belonging wholly to citizens
thereof.*" Izard moved to have the latter part struck out, the
effect of which would have been that no discrimination would
have been made between our own citizens and foreigners. Lee,
Butler, Grayson, Izard, and Few argued in the most unceasing
manner, and, I thought, most absurdly, on this business. The
first time I made a short remark that the foreigner and citizen
must both build their ships in America, and then evidently, for
everything that followed, they stood alike; that the superior
capital of the foreigners would enable them to build ships lower
than us, and would in time give them the whole of our trade;
that the bill bore on the face of it a discrimination in favor of
our merchants, but the fact would turn out otherwise, and therefore I was for continuing the clause as it stood.

A little before the question was put, I rose a second time;
said no former transaction was so likely to throw light on this
subject as a short history of the British Navigation Act. Cromwell originated it in a spleen against the Dutch, but the effects
were seen before the Restoration [1660], and it was then re-
enacted. Great murmurs arose. The Scotch thought themselves
ruined, and sent their peers up to remonstrate against it. The
tonnage of Great Britain then stood 95,266. In fifteen years it
was 190,533; in twenty years more it was 273,693. The present
tonnage of Massachusetts alone is now 100,000.

It has been urged that it would be time enough, half a century
hence, to talk of measures for a navy. A single State was in a
better condition now, in point of shipping, than the British
nations at the Restoration. Therefore, delay was the worst policy.
It was generally allowed that the spirit of the Navigation Act
was to give a monopoly of the trade of the British nation to
their own shipping and sailors. In a view solely mercantile,

this was perhaps wrong, as by these means our foreign articles would be dearer and our home produce cheaper. But the object was a national one. Shipping and sailors were the objects; and, though the landed part of the community was not perhaps so rich, yet the nation was safe, for national power is of more consequence than individual wealth. The suspension of the Navigation Act, it was believed, would be productive of a great flow of wealth to the British nation, or at least the manufacturing and agricultural parts of it, but the purchase would cost them their shipping and sailors. And, finally, the foreigners would have a monopoly of the whole traffic, one of the worst of evils, provided they conducted their navigation on terms of more economy, as was generally believed of the Dutch. But what are we doing? Were we passing a Navigation Act? No. A slight discrimination was all that was aimed at, and if the motion was adopted the discrimination would operate against us. The question was put and the clause remained.

Near four o'clock, and adjourned.

June 16th.—This day passed the residue of the Tonnage bill, with much debate. Broke up early, and went to hear the debates in the House of Representatives. After dinner went and walked a considerable time to try to gain strength in my knee. Some observations having called me up this day, I endeavored to comprise all I had to say in as little bounds as possible, by observing that there were two extremes in commercial relations equally to be avoided. The principle of the Navigation Act might be carried so far as to exclude all foreigners from our ports. The consequences would be a monopoly in favor of the mercantile interest. The other was an unlimited license in favor of foreigners, the consequence of which would be a monopoly in favor of the cheapest carriers, and in time a total dependence on them. Both extremes ought to be avoided, by giving certain indulgences to our own trade and that of our friends, in such degree as will secure them the ascendency, without hazarding the expulsion of foreigners from our ports.

June 17th.—The balloting business prevented my mentioning in order the more important debate on the Tonnage Act. The villainous amendments (for which we may thank the influence of this city) for doing away with the discrimination between foreigners in and out of treaty with us have been carried. It was in vain that I gave them every opposition in my power. I laid down a marked difference between impost and tonnage. The former imposition is paid by the consumer of the goods; the latter rests on the owner of the ship, at least in the first instance; that sound policy dictated the principle of encouraging the shipping of our friends; that nations not in treaty would not be considered as the most friendly. I read the fifth article of the commercial treaty with France, and denied that we had power of imposing any tonnage on her shipping, save an equivalent to the one hundred sols on coasters. I gave my unequivocal opinion that a want of discrimination in her favor was contrary to the spirit of the treaty, and expressed fears of her resentment. Elsworth answered me, but the most that he said was that our interests called for it, and he pledged himself that we would never hear from France about it. But speaking was in vain. I never saw the Senate more listless nor inattentive, nor more determined.

Inclosed copies of the Judicial bill to Lewis, Peters, Tench Coxe, and Myers Fisher. Called on Mr. Morris, and signed with him jointly letters to the President and the Chief Justice inclosing copies. From here called on Mr. Scott. Told him of the request of the arrangement committee. Met and made a short report. The Senate formed, passed the residue of the Impost bill without much debate.

In now came Mr. Jay to give information respecting Mr. Short, who was nominated to supply the place of Mr. Jefferson at the court of France while Mr. Jefferson returned home. And now the Vice-President rose to give us a discourse on the subject of form; how we should give our *advice* and *consent*. I rose, perhaps more early than might have been wished by some, and stated that this business was in the nature of an election; that the spirit of the Constitution was clearly in favor of ballot; that this mode could be applied without difficulty; that, when the person was put up in nomination, the favorable tickets should have a yea and the others should be blanks. Few, of Georgia, rose and seconded me. Izard made a long speech against it. Mr. Carrol spoke against it, Mr. Langdon, and Mr.

Morris; but Lee, Elsworth, and Butler for it. Mr. Morris' speech turned principally on its being below the dignity of the Senate, who should be open, bold, and unawed by any consideration whatever.

I rose at last and spoke perhaps longer than I had done on any former occasion. It had been considered as unworthy of a Senator to conceal any vote. The good of the public, however, required secrecy in many things, but the ballot did not take away the right of open conduct. On the contrary, it was the duty of every Senator to disclose the defects of any candidate where they were great or might be attended with danger to the public. But as the nominations came from the President, it was not to be expected that characters notoriously flagitious would ever be put in nomination. Every Senator when voting openly would feel inconvenience from two quarters, or at least he was subjected to it. I would not say, in European language, that there would be court favor and court resentment, but there would be about the President a kind of sunshine that people in general would be well pleased to enjoy the warmth of. Openly voting against the nominations of the President would be the sure mode of losing this sunshine. This was applicable to all Senators in all cases. But there was more. A Senator, like another man, would have the interests of his friends to promote. The cause of a son or brother might be lodged in his hands. Will such a one, in such a case, wish openly to oppose the President's judgment?

But there are other inconveniences. The disappointed candidate will retaliate the injury which he feels against the Senator. It may be said the Senator's station will protect him. This can only extend to the time of his being in office, and he, too, must return to private life, where, as a private man, he must answer for the offenses given by the Senator. The ballot left the judgment equally free, and none of the above inconveniences followed. When, then, equal advantages flowed, without any of the disadvantages, the mode least subject to inconvenience was preferable. Many gentlemen had declared how perfectly indifferent it was to them. I believe the same thing of every Senator in the present House. But was this always to continue? No. We must expect men of every class and every description within these walls. The present character of our President was no security that we should always have men equally eminent; that in those places where elections were conducted *viva voce* the hopes and fears of electors were so wrought on by the wealthy, powerful, and bold, that few votes were given entirely free from influence, unless it was by the happy few who were independent in spirit as well as in fortune; that we need not expect the Senate would always be composed of such desirable characters. It had been clearly stated and admitted that the mode by ballot was equally applicable to the present case as that by *viva voce,* and, being free from any inconveniences that the other was subject to, ought undoubtedly to be adopted.

June 18th.—And now the mode of approving or disapproving of the nomination. I did not minute it yesterday, but our Vice-President rose in the chair and delivered his opinion how the business ought to be done. He read the Constitution, argued, and concluded: "I would rise in the chair, and put the question individually to the Senators: Do you advise and consent that Mr. Short be appointed *chargé d'affaires* at the court of France? Do you and do you?" Mr. Carrol spoke long for the *viva voce* mode. He said the ballot was productive of caballing and bargaining for votes. He then wandered so wide of the subject as to need no attention. Mr. Elsworth made a most elaborate harangue. A great part of it was, however, about the duty of our Vice-President, and inventing a mode how he also might ballot in the case of a division. He, however, toward the close of it made a strange distinction, that voting by ballot suited bashful men best, but was the worst way for bad and un-principled men. I wished to repeat nothing of what had been said yesterday, but replied that, so far from balloting being productive of caballing, it was the very bane and antidote against it; that men made bargains for certainties, but it was in vain to purchase or bargain for a vote by ballot, which there was no certainty of the party ever obtaining, as he had no method of securing the performance of a promise or of knowing whether he was deceived or not; that as to the distinction of balloting being the worst way for bad men, I thought differently. The worst of men were known to respect virtue. The ballot removed all extrinsic force or obligation. It was the only chance of making a bad man act justly; the matter was left to his own conscience; there were no witnesses. If he did wrong, it was because he loved vice more than virtue, which I believe, even among bad men, was not the fact in one case out of ten. The question was at last taken, and carried by eleven votes, seven against it. Izard was so crooked he voted against us, though he had spoken for us, and quoted Harrington to show his reading.

The people who lost this question manifested much uneasiness, particularly the Vice-President and Langdon. Langdon was even fretful. The Vice-President threw difficulties in our way. The Senate had decreed their advice and consent by ballot. "Nothing like this in history had ever been heard before. But what rank was Mr. Short to hold in the diplomatic corps? What kind of commission was he to have? This must be settled by ballot." He [Adams] set us afloat by these kinds of queries, and an hour and a quarter was lost in the most idle discourse imaginable. He seemed willing to entangle the Senate, or rather some of them were entangled about the Secretary of the Legation and the *chargé d'affaires,* not knowing the distinction. We, however, got through it by a resolution declaring our advice and consent in favor of Mr. Short.

After having again explained the manner of concurring or rejecting a nomination by ballot in a manner so plain as did not admit of contradiction, I replied to the observation that "no example of anything of the kind could be found in history," that in the old kingdom of Aragon, where, though the executive was monarchical, yet that republican provisions had been attended with unexampled attention. The court appointed by the Justiza gave their sentence by ballot, and [I] offered to produce history to the point, but was not contradicted. Took up the impost and talked idly to pass the usual time of adjournment. An adjournment was called for and took place.

I have ever been as attentive as I possibly could be to discover the real disposition of President Washington. He has been very cautious hitherto, or rather inactive, or shall I say like a pupil in the hands of his governor or a child in the arms of his nurse? The message about Mr. Short touches a matter that may be drawn into precedent. It states the desire of Mr.

Jefferson to return for some time, and nominates Mr. Short to supply his place during such absence. The leave for return, etc., is not laid before the Senate. Granting this power to be solely with the President, the power of dismissing ambassadors seems to follow, and some of the courtiers in the Senate fairly admit it. I chose to give the matter a different turn, and delivered my opinion: That our concurring in the appointment of Mr. Short fully implied the consent of the return of Mr. Jefferson; that if we chose to prevent the return of Mr. Jefferson, it was only to negative the nomination of Mr. Short or any other one to fill his place. It is the fault of the best governors, when they are placed over a people, to endeavor to enlarge their powers by applying to public stations what would be laudable in private individuals, a desire of bettering their stations. Thus the farmer acts well who by industry adds field to field, and so would the governor who would add to the public wealth or happiness; but adding to the personality, if I may so speak, or to the personal power of the governor, is a faulty industry. A question has been agitated with great warmth in the House of Representatives whether the sole power of displacing officers, or, to speak strictly, the Secretary of Foreign Affairs, shall remain with the President. From the small beginning in the case of Mr. Short, it is easy to see what the court opinion will be with respect to this point. Indeed, I entertain no doubt but that many people are aiming with all their force to establish a splendid court with all the pomp of majesty. Alas! poor Washington, if you are taken in this snare! How will the gold become dim! How will the fine gold be changed! How will your glory fade!

Neutrality, the point of profit, the grand desideratum of a wise nation, among contending powers. Multiplied engagements and contradictory treaties go to prevent this blessing and invite a nation in foreign quarrels. China, geographically speaking, may be called the counterpart to our American world. Oh, that we could make her policy the political model of our conduct with respect to other nations—ready to dispose of her superfluities to all the world! She stands committed by no engagement to any foreign part of it; dealing with every comer, she seems to say, "We trade with you and you with us, while common interest sanctifies the connection; but, that dissolved, we know no other engagement."

June 19th, Friday.—And now the Impost bill, as sent back from the House of Representatives with an almost total rejection of our amendments, was taken up. There was but little speaking. Mr. Lee made a distinction, in his parliamentary way, between the word "insist" and "adhere," and it was carried to use the word "insist." After the first two articles were insisted on, Mr. Morris moved that one question should be taken on all the other disagreements. "Saving time" was his object, but we only lost by it. He did not seem to have been well understood. I rose and explained his motion, and to his satisfaction, as he said. The result of the whole was that we insisted on nearly all our amendments, and I suppose they [the Representatives] will adhere to the original bill. This really seems like playing at cross-purposes or differing for the sake of sport. I voted on the principles of accommodation throughout the whole. Indeed, this was but repeating my former vote. Indeed, there was nothing to differ about; only opinion founded on conjecture. One imagined a thing was too high; another thought it too low; my opinion was they were all too low to raise the money which we wanted; others wished them low on purpose that the deficiency might be so great that we would be forced into an excise. I abhorred this principle, though my colleague is fond of it. Adjourned over to eleven o'clock on Monday.

And now I will endeavor to use this interval in riding, to try to drive this vile rheumatism out of my knee. I have never been perfectly recovered of it, and my right knee is still much swelled. Went to hire a horse after dinner. Could not get a very indifferent one with saddle and bridle under two shillings per hour; thought this extravagant, and would not pay it. Spent [until] night trying to get one. Vandalsen hired one for me at a dollar per day or half for half a day. Saturday was on horseback at five o'clock and rode to near eight; came home; breakfasted; rested one hour and a half; rode to twelve asked what I had to pay, and was obliged to pay six shillings. The horse would not have sold for more than six or seven pounds. Was exceedingly fatigued; bathed; rested to near four, and joined the Speaker and a party to drink tea at one Lephers, where we were civilly treated. Think my knee is not the worse of the riding. The day excessively hot.

June 21st.—Rode till eight o'clock; very warm; think I never felt the heat more oppressive in my life. Stayed at home and wrote to my family. In the evening Clymer and Fitzsimons passed; walked a short way with them. I gave my opinion in plain language that the confidence of the people was departing from us, owing to our unreasonable delays; asked them, "Have you received any letters showing signs of such a temper?" Fitzsimons said no, but the thing told for itself, and could not be otherwise.

£1 7s. 8d. due by my landlord.

CHAPTER III

THE JUDICIARY BILL

June 22d.—Attended the Senate. The bill for settling the new judiciary was taken up. Much discourse about the mode of doing business. We were in committee. The first and second clauses postponed. A question was taken whether there should be district courts. Much wrangling about words. This was carried. But now Mr. Lee brought forward a motion nearly in the words of the Virginia amendment, viz., "That the jurisdiction of the Federal courts should be confined to cases of admiralty and maritime jurisdiction." Lee and Grayson supported this position. Elsworth answered them, and the ball was kept up until past three o'clock. The question was going to be put. I rose and begged to make a remark or two. The effect of the motion was to exclude the Federal jurisdiction from each of the States except in admiralty and maritime cases. But the Constitution expressly extended it to all cases, in law and equity, under the Constitution and laws of the United States; treaties made or to be made, etc. We already had existing treaties, and were about making many laws. These must be executed by the Federal judiciary. The arguments which had been used would apply well if amendments to the Constitution were under consideration, but certainly were inapplicable here. I sat down; some called for the question and some for an adjournment. The adjournment carried.

Strong this day mentioned in conversation that the President *would continue no longer in office than [when] he saw matters fairly set going,* and then Mr. Adams will begin his reign. This no doubt is a desirable era for the New England men. The very principles which actuated Dr. Rush and myself when we puffed John Adams in the papers and brought him forward for Vice-President will probably make him President. We knew his vanity, and hoped by laying hold of it to render him useful

83

among the New England men in our scheme of bringing Congress to Pennsylvania. But his pride, obstinacy, and folly are equal to his vanity, and, although it is a common observation that fools are the tools of knaves—and I am certain weak men are often brought forward with such views—yet John Adams has served to illustrate two points at least with me, viz., that a fool is the most unmanageable of all brutes, and that flattery is the most irksome of all service.

June 23d.—Attended at the Hall a little after ten. Came into the Senate chamber. There was nobody here but Mr. Adams. He was in the great chair. When I came in he left it; came and sat near me until he read a newspaper; shifted to the chair next to me; began a discourse on the subject of Pennsylvania. Said they were "the best republicans in the Union. Their adoption was unequivocal. This could not be said of Boston, New York, or Virginia." *Surely* there was a meaning in this. I replied that we had, no doubt, our faults; but certainly the virtues of plainness, industry, and frugality would be allowed to us in some degree; that Federalism was general, but there was a general abhorrence of the pomp and splendid expense of government, especially everything which bordered on royalty. Several members came in and joined us.

Senate formed and the business of yesterday was taken up just where we left it. The discourses of yesterday were all repeated. Mr. Lee endeavored to give the whole business a new turn, to elude the force of what I had said yesterday. According to his explanation on admiralty and maritime jurisdiction he would have taken in a vast field. I rose and read over from the Constitution a number of the powers of Congress—viz., collecting taxes, duties, imposts, naturalization of foreigners, laws respecting the coinage, punishing the counterfeiting of the coin, treason against the United States, etc.; declared that no force of construction could bring these cases within admiralty or maritime jurisdiction, and yet all these cases were most expressly the province of the Federal Judiciary. So that the question expressly turned on this point, "Shall we follow the Constitution or not?" I said a good deal more, but this was the substance. Mr. Lee, after some time, opposed me with a very singular argument. He rose and urged that the State judges would be all sworn to support the Constitution; that they must obey their oath and, of course, execute the Federal laws. He varied this idea in sundry shapes. I rose and opposed to this that the oath taken by the State judges would produce quite a contrary effect; that they would swear to support the Constitution; that the Constitution placed the judicial power of the Union in one Supreme Court, and such inferior courts as should be appointed; and, of course, the State judges, in virtue of their oaths, would abstain from every judicial act under the Federal laws, and would refer all such business to the Federal courts; that if any matter made cognizable in a Federal court should be agitated in a State court, a plea to the jurisdiction would immediately be put in and proceedings would be stayed. No reply was made; the question was soon taken and the motion was rejected.

The first clause of the bill was now called for. Grayson made a long harangue. I mentioned that I thought this an improper time to decide absolutely on this part of the bill. If the bill stood in its present form and the Circuit Courts were continued, six judges appeared to be too few. If the Circuit Courts were struck out, they were too many; that it would have pleased me better; but as we were in committee I would not consider myself as absolutely bound by anything that happened now, but would reserve myself until the second reading in the Senate. Mr. Elsworth rose and made a most elaborate harangue on the necessity of a numerous bench of judges. He enlarged on the importance of the causes that would come before them, of the dignity it was necessary to support, and the twelve judges of England in the Exchequer Chamber were held up to view during the whole harangue, and he seemed to draw conclusions that twelve were few enough. I readily admitted that the information respecting the English courts was fairly stated. But in England the whole mass of litigation in the kingdom came before these judges, the whole suits arising from eight or nine millions of people. Here it was totally different. The mass of causes would remain with the State judges. Those only arising from Federal laws would come before the Federal judges, and these would be comparatively few indeed. When they became numerous it would be time enough to increase the judges.

Mr. Grayson rose again and repeated his opinion that numbers were necessary to procure respectable decisions. I replied that, in my opinion, the way to secure respectable decisions was to choose eminent characters for judges; that numbers rather lessened responsibility, and, unless they were all eminent, tended to obscure the decisions. The clause, however, was passed. Adjourned at the usual hour.

June 24th.—Rode out early this morning, but returned before eight. Attended [Senate] at the usual time. The bill for the judiciary was taken up. The first debate that arose was whether there should be Circuit Courts or courts of *nisi prius.* This distinction was started by Mr. Johnson, from Connecticut. Was adopted, and spoke long to by Mr. Butler. This kept us most of the day. I did not give a vote either way—indeed, I do not like the bill. The vote was for district courts. We proceeded to a clause about Quakers taking an affirmation. I moved an amendment that all persons conscientiously scrupulous of taking an oath should take the affirmation. Great opposition to this. The Quakers abused by Izard. Mr. Morris and myself defended them. I read the Constitution by which the affirmation is left open to every one, and called this whole clause unconstitutional. The President himself may qualify by affirmation—the Constitution does not narrow the ground of conscience. I was up and down often in this business; but the grand procession of the Freemasons came by with much noise of music a little after three, and the House adjourned.

Had a very long walk this afternoon with Mr. Contee and Mr. Seney, of Maryland. They seem agreeable and accommodating men. They were very willing to remove Congress from this place. They named Harrisburg, I believe to try me. I said little in favor of it, but assured them that of two hundred acres which I had adjoining that town they should have one [hundred] if they went there.

My memory certainly fails me of late. I had this day some conversation of importance with some person which I had determined to note down, but it has escaped from my memory, and I can neither recollect person, place, nor subject, only that I had determined to minute it.

June 25th.—Mr. Wynkoop came to town last night. I went

this morning with him to visit Mr. Partridge and Mr. Sedgwick, who had been polite enough to leave cards at my lodgings. Found their lodging with some difficulty. This business over, attended at the Hall. First business was to take up the Impost bill. Concurred with the Lower House about the style of the enacting clause. But a spirit of great obstinacy was manifested with regard to the fourth and fifth clauses. Mr. Morris most pointedly against discrimination, etc., between nations in treaty and others. Lee and Elsworth same. The Tonnage bill was read. The same difference occurred. Managers of conference [were] chosen on both bills—Mr. Morris, Mr. Lee, and Mr. Elsworth. Read the bill for the Department of Foreign Affairs. Laid on the table. And now took up the judiciary and the affair of the affirmations. Ran Elsworth so hard and the other anti-affirmants on the anti-constitutionalism of the clause that they at last consented to have a question taken whether the clause should not be expunged, and expunged it was. Labored in the judiciary till three, and adjourned.

June 26th.—Attended the Hall at the usual time. The managers were met and the conference begun. The Senate formed, but the managers were absent at the conference. Some were for proceeding and others were for waiting. The members strayed to and from the conference chamber. An adjournment was often spoken of; at last moved and carried. Well may it be said that men are but children of a larger growth, for on this question being carried there was the same flutter of joy among the members that I have seen among children in a school on giving leave; and away all hurried, except a few that remained a little to see if the conference would finish. Among them I was one who wished to know the results of the conference.

June 27th, Saturday.—Went a little before ten to deliver a letter to Mr. Morris in favor of Mr. Harris from a Mr. Ridley. Mr. Morris read the letter and only remarked, "Mr. Harris' friends are much in earnest." I mentioned the petition which I held in my hand from Mr. Harris. The point I wished to bring matters to was for him to deliver it in. He was guarded, and threw out such sentiments as showed me he would not move in the matter; said the petition had best be inclosed in a cover and directed to the President. I held it up; said it was directed already; that Mr. Harris wished it might be put into the hands of Colonel Humphreys; that I thought I had best follow his directions. I went with my lame knees, first to visit Colonel Butler, who had been thrown from a [sedan] chair with Mr. Huger and was hurt. Mr. Morris went with me. He has never asked me to his house save once, and I shall not go much.

From visiting Mr. Butler I went to the President's. The day was now hot, the walk was long, I was lame, and the streets were ripped up a great part of the way to be paved anew; all these things made the journey one of consequence. Some years ago ten times as far would have been nothing. I saw Colonel Humphreys; inquired for the President's health, and delivered Mr. Harris' petition. Humphreys was cold. I can not say what will come of it, but my hopes are not high. I am an ill courtier. The part I have taken in Senate has marked me as no courtier, and I fear will mark poor Davy as a man not to be brought forward. Returned to the Hall very much fatigued.

The Senate met. The managers of the conference reported an agreement of a number of articles. But the bill was not in the Senate. It seems when the conference was agreed to by the Senate, and notice of such concurrence sent down to the House of Representatives, our wise Secretary sent down the bills along with the communication. I was for insisting that in parliamentary language the bills were still before the Senate; they had been there when the conference was appointed; no vote of the Senate had been passed to send them down; the conference was appointed only on the disagreement. There was a great deal said, the amount of which resolved itself into this —that a mistake had been committed. Mr. Morris said if the bills had been fairly in his possession he would have brought them back to the Senate. He actually went to try to get them from the managers on the part of the House of Representatives.

There seemed to be a jealousy between the two Houses who should act first, as the one which acted last would reject the bill, or at least have the blame of rejection if the bill was lost. Gentlemen could not reconcile themselves to act without the bills, for there were two of them, one on impost and the other the Tonnage Act. Some moved to act on the report of the managers. After, however, much desultory conversation, it was agreed to take up the bill for the judiciary.

We were proceeding on this when a message was announced. Sundry communications were brought by the Clerk, and the amendments of the Senate were all adopted on the Impost bill save on the articles of porter and coal. Such was the haste of the Vice-President that he put one question on both these articles at once, and both agreed to. But the Tonnage bill was retained, and the principle of discrimination between nations in treaty and those not was still adhered to by the House of Representatives on this bill. Made some further progress in the judiciary, and adjourned about two o'clock.

June 28th, Sunday.—Spent this day, except a small ride in the morning, at home, and wrote to my dear family. How can I answer it to myself that I stay so long from them? How happy will my return make all their little hearts, and yet I stay here wrangling vile politics in a contentious Senate, where there is no harmony of soul, no wish to communicate a happy sensation; where all is snipsnap and contradiction short; where it is a source of joy to place the speech of a fellow-Senator in a distorted or ridiculous point of view; where you may search the whole Union and can not say that you can find the man of your heart! But away with them, and let me think of my dear family. Sent a set of letters by Dr. Ruston for my family.

June 29th, Monday.—Attended at the Hall early. Sent my letters to the post-office; and now for the judiciary. I made a remark where Elsworth in his diction had varied from the Constitution. This vile bill is a child of his, and he defends it with the care of a parent, even with wrath and anger. He kindled, as he always does, when it is meddled with. Lee, however, after some time joined me. Although the Vice-President showed himself against us, we carried the amendment.

We got on to the clause where a *defendant was required, on oath, to disclose his or her knowledge in the cause,* etc. I rose and declared that I wished not to take up the time of the committee, as, perhaps, few would think with me (this I said in allusion to what had happened in the committee when I had exerted myself in vain against this clause), but that I could not pass in silence a clause which carried such inquisitorial powers with it, and which was so contrary to the sentiments of my constituents; that extorting evidence from any person was a species of torture, and inconsistent with the spirit of freedom. But perhaps I should say something more pointed when the matter came before the House in Senate. (My reason of acting thus was: I had spoken to Mr. Morris and found he would not second me in it, as Myers Fisher had not taken notice of this matter in his letter.) Patterson, however, of the Jerseys, sprang up; declared he disliked the clause, and having spoken a while moved to strike it out. I then rose and declared, since one man was found in the Senate for striking it out, I would second him.

Up now rose Elsworth, and in a most elaborate harangue supported the clause; now in chancery, now in common law, and now common law again, with a chancery side. He brought forward Judge Blackstone, and read much out of him. Patterson rose in reply, and followed him through these thorny paths, as I thought, with good success. He showed, justly enough, that Blackstone cut both ways, and nothing could be inferred from him but his ridiculing the diversity of practice between chancery practice and that of common law. Elsworth heard him with apparent composure. He rose with an air of triumph on Patterson's sitting down. "Now," said he, "everything is said that can possibly be said to support this motion. The very most is made of it that ingenuity can perform"; and he entered again the thorny thicket of law forms, and seemed to batter down all his antagonist had said by referring all that was advanced to the forms of law, with which everything had been shackled under the British Government. He really displayed ingenuity in his defense. He made repeated use of the term "shackled," and how we were now free, and he hoped we would continue so.

I determined to have a word or two at the subject. Said I was happy to hear that the world was unshackled from the customs of ancient tyranny; that there was a time when evidence in criminal cases was extorted from the carcass of the wretched culprit by torture. Happily we were unshackled from this, but here was an attempt to exercise a tyranny of the same kind over the mind. The conscience was to be put on the rack; that forcing oaths or evidence from men, I considered as equally tyrannical as extorting evidence by torture; and of consequence had only the difference between excusable lies and willful perjury. I hoped never to see shackles of this kind imposed. Chancery had been quoted; common law had been quoted as practiced in England, but neither would apply to the present case. The party was to answer in chancery, but it was to the judge, and his questions were in writing; but here, by the clause, he must be examined in the open court before the bench and jury and cross-examined and tortured by all the address and malice of the bar. I had further to add that, by the Bill of Rights of the State that I had the honor to represent, *no person could be compelled to give evidence against himself;* that I knew this clause would give offense to my constituents.

Elsworth rose and admitted that three new points had been started. He aimed a reply, but I thought he missed the mark in every one. The rage of speaking now seemed to catch the House. Bassett was up; Read and Strong [were] at it. We sat till half after three; and an adjournment was called before the question was put. Elsworth moved an amendment that the plaintiff, too, should swear at the request of the defendant, just before the House adjourned.

June 30th.—I am still miserably lame with the rheumatism. Attended at the Hall at the usual time. The clause with Elsworth's amendment was taken up. I rose first. Said that, instead of the clause being amended, I thought it much worse; that it was alleged with justice against the clause, as it stood before, that great opportunities and temptations to perjury were held out, but this was setting the door fairly open. The contest now would be, who would swear most home to the point. If I was against it before, I was much more so now. Mr. Lee rose, and seemed to mistake the matter. I rose and endeavored to do the business justice.

Up rose Elsworth and threw the common law back all the way to the wager of law, which he asserted was still in force. Strong rose and took the other side in a long harangue. He went back to the ancient trial by battle, which, he said, was yet unrepealed, but said repeatedly there was no such case as the present. Elsworth's temper forsook him. He contradicted Strong with rudeness; said what the gentleman asserted was not fact; that defendants were admitted as witnesses; that all might be witnesses against themselves. Got Blackstone; but nothing could be inferred from Blackstone but such a thing by consent. Patterson got up, and back he went to the feudal system. He pointedly denied Elsworth's position. Bassett rose. Read rose, and we had to listen to them all. The question was, however, put first on Elsworth's amendment, and was lost; next on striking out, and it was carried.

The Tonnage bill was taken up. We concurred in one clause, but adhered in the next. And now back to the judiciary. Mr. Lee moved that the postponed clause about the ambassadors, consuls, etc., should be taken up. It was so. I saw Mr. Adams begin to fidget with a kind of eagerness or restlessness, as if a nettle had been in his breeches. He could not restrain himself long, and up he got to tell us all about ambassadors, other Ministers, and consuls; and what he did with his Majesty here and his Majesty there; and how he got an answer in this case, and how he never got an answer in that; and how he had, with Mr. Jefferson, appointed Mr. Barclay to the Emperor of Morocco; and how the Parliament of Bordeaux mistook the matter and dismisses Mr. Barclay from an arrest, etc. I could not help admiring the happiness of the man. When he had occasion to refer to something said by Elsworth, he called him "the *right* honorable gentleman."

July 1.—Very lame, particularly in my right knee. Attended at the Hall at the usual time. The clause was taken up of the Judiciary bill "that suits in equity shall not be sustained in either of the courts of the United States in any case where a remedy may be had at law." Dr. Johnson rose first against the clause. Elsworth answered him, and the following gentlemen all in turn: Lee, Read, Bassett, Patterson, and Grayson. Strong spoke in favor of the clause. The lawyers were in a rage for speaking. Many things were said in favor of chancery that I knew to be wrong. Never was there a field more beaten, from the first Chancellor down. The lawyers seemed all prepared to show their extensive reading.

It was near three, and I determined to say something. A case was often put of a man covenanting to convey land and dying before performance; that there was no relief without chancery. I, however, rose, said much information had been given on this important subject, but I wished for a great deal more. For instance, I desired to know the number of attorneys and persons employed in the law department in England, and the millions (for it was said to amount to several annually) extorted by the law department from that nation; particularly whether the sum so extracted did not exceed the aggregate of the sums in dispute before the courts. Whether any nation in the world, besides the English, would pay their taxes and support any such expensive judiciary; that these points being settled would afford matter of important advice to us, whether it was prudent to imitate the famous English jurisprudence in all its parts; that the advantages of chancery were to my certain knowledge overstated; that the famous case of the bond performance gave little trouble in Pennsylvania; that the person having paid his bond, brought his suit, and the parties generally consented to a judgment and the sale of the lands, and the sheriff made title; that I thought the clause a good one, and wished it to be more effectual to prevent the flow of causes into that tedious court.

Up rose George Read in angry mood. Said he had a cause of that kind in Pennsylvania; that he had consulted the ablest men there and received for answer [that] there was no remedy in Pennsylvania, and asserted that the people of Pennsylvania wished for chancery, and many of them lamented the want of it.

I got up; declared, as far as I knew the sentiments of the people of Pennsylvania, they disliked a chancery, but that many of them knew not even the name. I never heard any people speak in favor of it, but some gentlemen of the bar, and even among them some doubted whether it would do most harm or good; that in the general it was considered by those who knew anything of the matter, as the field where the gentlemen of the bar would reap the fullest harvest, and it was considered that they enjoyed a plentiful crop as matters stood now. I stated the affair of the bond over again so plainly that Read called out, "In case of consent, I grant it." I had only to add, in case they do not consent, twelve honest jurors are good chancellors, if not to give the land, at least to give the value of it. The clause stood on the question. The gentlemen of the bar in the House seem to have made common cause of it, to push the power of chancery as far as possible. Mr. Morris seemed almost disposed to join them. As we rose he said, "If I had spoken, I believe I should have differed with you about chancery." I know not what put it there, but it was in my head in a moment that he has two sons studying for the law.

This day the discrimination between the ships of nations in treaty and those not, on the Tonnage bill, was rejected in the House of Representatives also, and, of course, the Tonnage bill now passes. When this doctrine was first broached in the House of Representatives, of no discrimination, it was called "Tory-ism," and there were but eight votes for it on a division. But mark the influence of the city of New York, or let me call it British influence. To work they set in the Senate, and, before the Impost bill got up, they had secured a majority to reject the discrimination. But some pretext was necessary even in the Senate. The discriminations in the Impost and Tonnage bills were said to be arrant trifles; no compensation for the injuries our trade received; that a deeper mode of retaliation should be entered on —such as would effectually cure all disadvantages and carry the remedy to every particular disease and retaliate on every nation, exactly in kind; and where a disadvantage was imposed a cor-responding one should be imposed by us, and not chastise all nations out of treaty with the same punishment. As to gratitude or national friendship, they were held not to exist, and all that was to be done with nations in treaty was to observe the terms of those treaties. A committee, therefore, of Mr. Morris, Mr. Langdon [names left blank], was appointed to examine the state of our commerce, and to bring in a bill for the protection of our commerce. But the discriminations are now struck out of both bills, and I do not expect to hear anything more about the protecting of our commerce unless it should be taken up in the House of Representatives.

Madison, too, is charged with having labored [for] the whole business of discrimination in order to pay court to the French nation through Mr. Jefferson, our Minister to Paris. I feel much readier to believe him guilty of another charge—viz., his urging the doctrine of taking away the right of removals of officers from the Senate in order to pay his court to the President, whom, I am told, he already affects to govern. Time will, however, throw light on both these subjects. *Mem.* It has done so in a remarkable manner in one of them. *Vide* 14th February, 1791.

July 2d.—Went this day to the Hall at the usual time. The bill for the judiciary was taken up. I really dislike the whole of this bill, but I endeavored to mend it in several places and make it as perfect as possible, if it is to be the law of the land. But it was fabricated by a knot of lawyers, who joined hue and cry to run down any person who will venture to say one word about it. This I have repeatedly experienced, and when I am certain (for a man may sometimes be certain of being right) of having made obvious and proper amendments, I have been pushed at from both right and left by them, and not a man to second me. Be it so, however; this is no reason that I should be silent. I ran Elsworth hard on the uselessness of part of this bill to-day, and thought I had the advantage in some of the answers I gave. But it was of little avail. Grayson, though a lawyer, told me yesterday that it was in vain to attempt anything. The people who were not lawyers, on a supposition that lawyers knew best, would follow the lawyers, and a party were determined to push it. I needed no information from him on this head.

We. however, came to a clause, the import of which was that on bonds, articles of agreement, covenants, etc., the jury should find the breach and the judges assess the damages. I attacked this mixed, half-common law, half-chancery proceeding; accused the bill of inconsistency; that a clause had already been adopted which excluded chancery where common law would afford a remedy. Here we had a jury and common law acting with the cause, and we flew from it to chancery powers. This was inconsistency. The jury were the proper chancellors in such a case to assess the damages; and I liked them much better than the judges. They were from the vicinity, and best acquainted with the parties and their circumstances. When the judgment was by default or entered up, a jury of inquiry of damages should ascertain the sum.

Strong made a long speech how this could not be done on the principles of common law and chancery principles, and seemed willing to show his accurate reading on these points, and con-

cluded by saying either he or the gentleman last up did not understand the principles of these courts, for the gentleman was
for doing what he thought could not be done. I rose quick to reply. Said the clause was before us—the clause was in our power
—what I wanted done was clearly expressed [in the clause]. I
hoped we were not always to be trammeled with the fetters of
English jurisprudence; that we would show [that] we had judgment and would act for ourselves, independent of any forms,
and concluded with a question whether we were always to be
considered as empty bottles, that could contain nothing but what
was poured into them. Several gentlemen now rose and agreed
with me in objecting to the clause. But there seemed some difficulty in amending, and it was postponed for amendment.

July 3d.—This [day] was warm; quite as much so, I thought,
as any day I remember in Pennsylvania. Attended at the Hall.
Business went on at the usual time. It was the judiciary which
we were upon. Light and very trifling debates in general. Mr.
Read got up and kept "hammering" for a long time (as Mr.
Morris termed it), and really it was difficult to say what he
would be at.

I did not embark in any debate until we came to the clause
empowering the judges, either on their own knowledge or
complaint of others, to apprehend, bail, commit, etc. I alleged
that the judges would be men of like passions and resentments
as other men; that they should not be both witnesses and judges,
accusers and all; that the complaint also should be on oath. I
moved, therefore, to strike out those words and insert "upon
oath or affirmation made and reduced to writing and signed by
the party, stating sufficient reason in law." Lee, of Virginia,
seconded me this time. But, according to custom, I had Elsworth and the gentlemen of the bar up against it. It was insisted
that this was agreeable to the laws of England; that the oath of
the judge would bind him to all this; that a judge had a right
to use his private judgment, just as a juryman had a right to
act on his private knowledge. Elsworth, Strong, Bassett, Grayson, and others, all up, and volumes did they pour out.

I could not get speaking for a long time. I, however, made a
short reply; said we were now framing the law which would be
the rule of conduct for the judges; that practice, such as the

gentlemen insisted on, had been used by judges; and, from experience, we had learned the danger of it. Cases were known
where the resentment of a judge was the accusing spirit and
prejudice pronounced judgment. Every part of English jurisprudence was not unexceptional, nor would I blindly follow
them in everything; that the case adduced of a juryman using
private knowledge would not apply. A juryman, legally speaking,
had no private knowledge, or at least none that he ought to keep
private. If he knew anything pertinent to the issue, he ought to
disclose it upon oath to his fellows in court; and this was the
law in daily practice upon it. If a judge happened to be the only
person having knowledge of the commission of a crime, let him
apply to some other justice. This I had known done. The case of
a forcible entry did not apply to common practice, and yet in
this case the justices would generally bind over witnesses to
prosecute. I hinted at some other points of the clause as imperfect, and said much more before I sat down, particularly as to
the dangerous ground on which we trod, considering the interference, or the very probable interference, of the Federal and
State Legislatures, and the giving more power over the liberty
of the citizen to the former than was usually practiced by the
latter would not fail to sow the seeds of dissension.

I had showed this clause to Mr. Morris before I moved for
the alteration. He approved of it, but he went out and stayed
away until all was over. He asked when he came in if his
presence would have altered the vote. I told him I supposed not;
we had lost it. I know nothing of the reason of his absence.
Charity and good humor will say it was accidental. He has been
—at least I thought so—rather distant with me. He has showed
me none of the communications which he has received respecting the judiciary. This has not been my conduct with regard to
him, and I know he has showed our Attorney-General's remarks
to Lee, Carrol, and Elsworth. I likewise know he has remarks
from Judge Hopkinson. Nothing shall be wanting on my part to
act in harmony with him. I whispered him at a leisure time,
"We should have a meeting and compare all the remarks we
have received, and make up our minds as to the amendments
which we will move." I paused; he did not reply; continued: "I
am quite disengaged; I will call on you at any time when it

is convenient." [He] replied: "It must be here. I have all my papers here." "Agreed, I will meet you at any time." Nothing more [said].

Settled with my landlord; he owes me fifteen shillings and eightpence. Mr. Morris had a set of remarks from Wilson and a set drawn up by Wallace which I never saw.

July 4th.—This is the anniversary of American Independence. The day was celebrated with much pomp. The Cincinnati assembled at Saint Paul's Church, where an oration was pronounced by Colonel Hamilton in honor of General Greene. The church was crowded. The Cincinnati had seats allotted for themselves; wore their eagles at their button-holes, and were preceded by a flag. The oration was well delivered; the composition appeared good, but I thought he should have given us some account of his virtues as a citizen as well as a warrior, for I supposed he possessed them, and he lived some time after the war, and, I believe, commenced farming.

Excepting my attendance at Saint Paul's Church, I kept [the] house all day, as I find going out only hurts my knees, both of which are still affected by the rheumatism.

July 5th, Sunday.—Was a rainy day; stayed at home all day, my thoughts chiefly employed about my family. How much of the sweets of life do I lose in being separated from them! After, however, having stayed so long, I had better give my attention a week or two longer.

July 6th, Monday.—Came early to the Hall in order to send my letters to the post-office. Dr. Johnson and some other members came in; familiar chat to the time of the meeting of the Senate. The judiciary was taken up and the residue of it passed without any interesting debate. Our Vice-President called for the sense of the House when it should be read the third time. The members showed plainly that they considered it as not having been touched in Senate on second reading; all that had passed having only been in committee. The Vice-President insisted that the bill had been twice read. So it certainly had, but the second reading was in a committee of the whole Senate. He said former bills had been treated just as he wanted this one treated. We knew, or at least I knew, that this was not the case. He showed a peevish obstinacy, as I thought. He does not like the doctrine of a committee of the Senate; nor has he ever submitted to it, for he ought to leave the chair. To-morrow, however, was assigned for the third reading, with a kind of saving privilege to make amendments.

Mr. Morris came in a little before we broke up. He put into my hands the letter and remarks of our Chief-Justice on the judiciary, directed to us jointly. But the Attorney-General's remarks and Judge Hopkinson's I have not yet had the opportunity of perusing. Thursday [is] assigned for the bill for Foreign Affairs, Friday for the Department of War, and Monday next for the Treasury Department.

July 7th.—Attended the Hall at the usual time. The judiciary was taken up for a third reading. I can scarcely account for my dislike for this bill, but I really fear it will be the gunpowder-plot of the Constitution. So confused and so obscure, it will not fail to give a general alarm. Elsworth has led in this business, backed with Strong, Patterson, Read often, Bassett seldom. We came to the clause which allowed the District Judges to sit on the hearing of appeals from themselves. I did not rise to oppose this. Grayson, however, got hold of it, and hammered hard at it. Bassett rose, and took partly the same side. Now I thought the matter in a hopeful way. Elsworth immediately drew an amendment, as he said, to cure their objections, though it was nothing like the matter. I drew a clause nearly in these words: "Provided that no District Judge shall sit on the re-hearing of any case formerly adjudged by him." We got Elsworth's motion postponed to put a question on it. It was agreed that the sense of the House should be taken on this. We carried it, and I rose and said, since the sense of the House was declared on this subject, I wished some of the gentlemen of the bar to frame a clause in the spirit of the determination; that the effect of the determination would reach further than the present clause, for it would prevent the Circuit Judge from sitting in the Supreme Court on an appeal where he had given original judgment. This was agreed to, so we killed two birds with one stone. The most trifling word-catching employed us till after three o'clock.

I can not help observing, under this day's head, that Mr. Phils, the late Naval Officer of Philadelphia, brought this morning most ample extracts of the trade of that port for the last year. He said there were copies sent him for his own use, but that at an early period he made out a set and delivered them to the President of the State to be forwarded to Congress, and he said they were actually forwarded. I could only say I never saw them, although I used all diligence to possess myself of every paper that could give me the smallest information.

Received letters this day from Harrisburg, and from Baltimore all well.

July 8th.—Attended the Hall this day as usual. The judiciary was taken up. Elsworth by far more accommodating this day than I ever knew him. We sat the usual time, but the debate was very trifling, indeed, and not one worth committing to paper. The Chief-Justice of Pennsylvania, Mr. Wilson, Myers Fisher, the Speaker, Mr. Peters, Tench Coxe, and sundry others have in their letters approved of the general outlines of the bill. Any amendments which they have offered have been of a lesser nature. I own [that] the appropriation of so many men of character for abilities has lessened my dislike of it, yet I can not think of the expense attending it, which I now consider as useless, without a kind of sickly qualm overshadowing me. Bradford's and Judge Hopkinson's remarks I have not yet seen, nor need I now care for them, as we will probably finish it to-morrow. Would that I had finished business so far as to be able to return home to-morrow! I find, however, I must stay yet a little longer. This is painful, but, all things considered, I can not help it.

Warm plaster for obstinate, fixed rheumatic pains, made by melting over a pan an ounce of gum plaster and two drachms of blistering plaster, spread on soft leather and applied to the part affected; taken off and wiped once in three or four days, and renewed once a fortnight.

July 9th.—Still much afflicted with rheumatism. Attended this day the usual time at the Hall. A great part of this day was taken up with light debates, chiefly conducted by the lawyers on both sides, and the object seemed to be the increasing the powers of chancery. Mr. Read, a man of obstructed elocutions, was excessively tedious. Elsworth has credit with me. I know not, however, whether it be the effect of judgment, whim, or caprice, but he is generally for limiting the chancery powers. Mr. Morris and myself differed in every vote this day. We always have differed on the subject of chancery.

This day I got copies of the three bills for the great departments. Besides being calculated on a scale of great expense, two grand objections offer themselves on these bills—the lessening of the power of the Senate, taking away from them any vote in the removal of officers, and the power of advising and consenting in one case of the first consequence; and the other the placing the President above business and beyond the power of responsibility, putting into the hands of his officers the duties required of him by the Constitution. Indeed, these appear to me to have been the moving reasons for bringing forward the bill at all. Nor do I see the necessity of having made this business a subject of legislation. The point of view in which it has presented itself to me was that the President should signify to the Senate his desire of appointing a Minister of Foreign Affairs, and nominate the man. And so of the other necessary departments. If the Senate agreed to the necessity of the office and the men, they would concur; if not, they would negative, etc. The House would get the business before them when salaries came to be appointed, and could thus give their opinion by providing for the officers or not. I see this mode might be abused. But for the House of Representatives, by a side-wind, to exalt the President above the Constitution, and depress the Senate below it, is—but I will leave it without name. They know the veneration entertained for General Washington, and believe the people will be ready to join in the cry against the Senate, in his favor, when they endeavor to make him a party. They think they have fast hold of us, and that we dare not refuse our assent to these bills, and so several of them have not failed to declare.

July 10, 1789.—This day the lawyers showed plainly the cloven foot of their intentions in the House [Senate]. Read, Bassett, Patterson, Johnson, Grayson, and others, had got a hasty kind of amendment passed late yesterday. The amount of it was that in the Circuit Courts, under the name of equity, they should have all the depositions copied and sent up on an appeal to the Supreme Court, as evidence on the rehearing of facts, or

words to that import. I had some conversation with Elsworth in the morning about it, and offered to him to move for a reconsideration of the matter. He wished to reserve this business for himself, however. He accordingly moved the reconsideration in a lengthy speech, and was seconded by Strong. At it now they went, and until after three scarce a word could be got in edgewise, for the lawyers. Butler, though lame, bounced up twice. I wished to speak, but could not get leave. The Vice-President got up in his chair. I rose and told him I wished to say a word or two:

"Sir, I am no professed admirer of the judicial system before you, but the best part of it is the Circuit Courts. These, sir, the amendment of yesterday will render abortive. The seeds of appeal, and the materials, too, provide for every cause. The system of delay is so firmly established, and the certainty of procrastination such, that justice can never be obtained in it. Let us follow the scheme a moment: The dispositions are taken and carried up six hundred or seven hundred miles to a Federal court. But, by the law, they can not be used, if the party is able to attend. The witness is subpœnaed, but does not attend. An attachment issues, but the party will kill the messenger, run to the woods, fly to the Indians, rather than attend. Well, but the court can issue a *dedimus potestatem,* and commissioners may be appointed; and in three or four years the testimony may be collected. Well, and what now? Is the fact to be tried by chancery powers? I am bold to say that no issue of fact was ever tried or found, for or against, in chancery. Facts often were carried into chancery, as evidence, but if they were doubted of, issue was joined on them, and directed to be tried by a jury. But now the business unfolds itself. Now we see what gentlemen would be at. It is to try facts on civil-law principles, without the aid of a jury, and this, I promise you, never will be submitted to." The question was put, and we carried it. But the House seemed rather to break up in a storm.

[Here a leaf of the Maclay journal, under the date of Saturday, July 10th, has been destroyed. The next entry is made under date of July 11, 1789, as follows:]

"Should go to the nearest stack of wheat, rye, hay, straw, or such like material, and draw out two stems, one in the name of each party, and the longest should win the cause." He showed it to me. I gave him a hearty laugh of approbation. Not, indeed, that I admired either the wit or novelty of it; but I considered it as the index of a sure vote. But I was mistaken. He voted against us, and the clause was lost.

I could see an air of triumph in the visages of gentlemen of the bar, Elsworth excepted, who has really credit with me on the whole of this business. The part he has acted in it I consider as candid (bating his caballing with Johnson), and disinterested. Mr. Lee, of Virginia, was for the clause, and spoke well. As we came down the stairs, Dr. Johnson was by my side. "Doctor," said I, "I wish you would leave off using these side-winds, and boldly, at once, bring in a clause for deciding all causes on civil-law principles, without the aid of a jury." "No, no," said he, "the civil law is a name I am not very fond of." I replied, "You need not care about the name, since you have got the thing."

July 12th, Sunday.—I was ill last night. My swelled knee gave me great pain, and prevented my rest. Put on flannels, and stayed at home all day. Had no book but Buchan's Family Physician. Read a good deal in it. What a lazar-house the world is! Surely the pleasures of life are as chaff, in the balance against ponderous lead, compared with the ills and dolors of the human race. Infinite Wisdom surely shows us but a small part of her works. There must be a balance somewhere. Or shall we view it in another light—that the only good we enjoy is the effect of prudence? Alas! she does not always command it. It is vain, however, to rend the impenetrable veil that conceals the mysterious ways of Providence. My dear family, I wish I were with you.

July 13th.—I forgot to minute yesterday that, late in the afternoon, Charles Thompson visited me. We had much chat of the political kind. He showed a great disposition to go into the field of the President's power. He was clearly of opinion that the President ought to remove all officers, etc. Indeed, he said so much on this subject that I had like to have entertained a suspicion that he came on purpose to sound, or rather prepare, me on the subject. I agreed to sundry of his observations, at the same time dissented, in plain but not pointed terms, from some other things. Perhaps this is the best way, on the whole, for an independent man to act. Honesty, on the whole, is the best policy. I really feel for Mr. Thompson's situation. A man who has been the graphic faculty of the old Congress, the hand and pen of that body from their first organization, and who—I feel a kind of certainty of the fact—wishes to die in an eminent office, would not suffer his friends to continue him Secretary of the Senate, and his enemies have taken advantage of it and declared him out of office, and mean to keep him so. It was certainly bad policy of him to refuse the offer of his friends. The political door is harder to be opened than any other if once it is thrown in a man's face.

The Senate met, and Mr. Bassett's motion with respect to the effect of a writ of error as a *supersedeas* to an execution was taken up. Mr. Read spoke long in support of the motion. Mr. Elsworth equally long against it. I rose and made sundry remarks, and the amendment was carried. It was not a material one in the bill, however. While the minutes were reading, I stepped to Elsworth and asked if he would not join me in an attempt to regain the clause we had lost on Saturday. He paused a little and said he would.

Mr. Elsworth rose and spoke long on the subject of the necessity of a discrimination or some boundary-line between the courts of chancery and common law. He concluded with a motion nearly in the words of the clause we had lost. Mr. Lee and myself both rose to second the motion. Mr. Lee, however, sat down and left me up. I therefore determined to avail myself of my situation and say something. Declared my concurrence of sentiment for limited chancery strictly. As the bill stood, chancery was open to receive everything. In England, where by the letter of the law no suit could be brought in chancery if the common law afforded a remedy, yet such was the nature of that court, and so advantageous had it been found to the practitioners, that it had encroached greatly on the common law. Gentlemen would not consider this as an inconvenience. So high were their ideas of English jurisprudence they said all the world admired it, and every member of this House must admire it. (This was Dr. Johnson's language on Saturday.) I was ready to admire it too, but I would first endeavor to describe it.

It [English jurisprudence] consisted of a great number of grades of courts rising in succession over each other, Common Pleas, King's Bench, Exchequer, Chancery, etc., so admirably organized and connected that the one was generally ready to begin where the other ended, and so formed that as long as a client had money he might purchase, delay, or, in other words, get law for it; that in England at this time it·was rather a trial of the depth of purse than right, and, accordingly, nothing was more common than for a man who was going to law to calculate and compare his pecuniary resources with his adversary's. The cost, however, being fairly counted, and neither party afraid, at it the angry men go. As they are eager, and bleed freely, they mount, perhaps, with tolerable rapidity, until they arrive in the regions of chancery. But here their bills are filed and all their facts collected, and in some half-dozen years, it may be, a judgment is given. But mark, the first judgment is seldom or never final. Here, then, a number of facts must be adjusted, and some ten or twenty issues in feigned wagers must be tried in the King's Bench. In some three or four years a new cargo of facts is furnished. The examiner goes to work and spends some two or three years. The Chancellor, too, perhaps, must have the opinion of the Judges of the King's Bench. Here is a new trial. But at last he gives a judgment. But two of the counsel sign a petition for a rehearing, and the whole business must be gone over again. But is the business done? No such thing. Another petition comes in for a "review," and the whole business must be gone over a third time.

Here I was interrupted by the Vice-President, who said there was an instance of a cause being finished by the present Chancellor in his lifetime. I answered quick, One swallow does not make a summer, Mr. President, and went on. But are they done yet? No such thing. The House of Lords is before them, and by the time they get out of the far end of it one or both are completely ruined. This is the progress of your wealthy parties, where plum is matched to plum. But what of your unequal matches—your poor and rich parties? Why, sir, if the relative wealth of one is to that of the other as four to one, the poor man will get about one fourth part of the way. If as two to one, half-way; if as three to four, three fourths of the way before the exhausted party drops off into ruin. (Here, by way of illustration, I repeated the Annesley cause.) For never was so admirable a machine contrived by the art of man to use men's passions for the picking of their pockets and to bring their justice into trade. The present bill before you has been considered as enjoying perfection in proportion as it approaches the British system. Sir, I have given you the opinion which I know many sensible Americans entertain of the system of English jurisprudence. With such people, English features will be no recommendation of the bill. Sir, I can not boast a general knowledge of the sentiments of men in the Union. From what I know of my own State, I am confident a great majority abhor chancery. Those whom I have generally heard advocate the chancery were professional men. I really believe that this was the case generally over the Union. I know many people complained of chancery in the Jerseys. One hundred and twenty-six pounds had been paid lately for taking the testimony only in a chancery suit in that State. Suits had been pending thirty years in their chancery, and had cost thousands; that I was clearly of opinion that everything after the verdict of a jury was a mere trap to catch fees, and might be styled the toils of the law, added to perplex the truth. The bill, however, before you, as it now stands, is not chancery. It is something much worse. The line between chancery and common law is broken down. All actions may now be tried in the Federal courts by the judges without the intervention of a jury. The trial by jury is considered as the birthright of every American. It is a privilege they are fond of, and, let me add, it is a privilege they will not part with.

This day the committee for considering our commercial injuries reported. I do not like it. The end is answered, perhaps, for which the stir was made, when this committee was appointed, and now the business ends in a bubble. I will, however, get a copy of the report before I pronounce on it.

July 14th.—The Senate met, and one of the bills for organizing one of the public departments—that of Foreign Affairs—was taken up. After being read, I begged leave of the Chair to submit some general observations, which, though apparently diffuse, I considered as pertinent to the bill before us, the first clause of which was, "There shall be an Executive Department," etc. There are a number of such bills, and may be many more, tending to direct the most minute particle of the President's conduct. If he is to be directed, how he shall do everything, it follows he must do nothing without direction. To what purpose, then, is the executive power lodged with the President, if he can do nothing without a law directing the mode, manner, and, of course, the thing to be done? May not the two Houses of Congress, on this principle, pass a law depriving him of all powers? You may say it will not get his approbation. But two thirds of both Houses will make it a law without him, and the Constitution is undone at once.

Gentlemen may say, How is the Government then to proceed on these points? The simplest in the world. The President communicates to the Senate that he finds such and such officers necessary in the execution of the Government, and nominates the man. If the Senate approve, they will concur in the measure; if not, refuse their consent, etc., when the appointments are made. The President, in like manner, communicates to the House of Representatives that such appointments have taken place, and require adequate salaries. Then the House of Representatives might show their concurrence or disapprobation, by providing for the officer or not. I thought it my duty to mention these things, though I had not the vanity to think that I would make any proselytes in this stage of the business; and, perhaps, the best apology I could make was not to detain them long. I likewise said that, if the Senate were generally of my mind, a conference between the Houses should take place. But the sense of the House would appear on taking the question upon the first clause. The first clause was carried.

Now came the second clause. It was for the appointment of a chief clerk by the Secretary, who, in fact, was to be the principal, *"whenever the said principal officer shall be removed from office by the President of the United States."* There was a blank pause at the end of it. I was not in haste, but rose first: Mr. President, whoever attends strictly to the Constitution of the United States, will readily observe that the part assigned to the Senate was an important one—no less than that of being the great check, the regulator and corrector, or, if I may so speak, the balance of this Government. In their legislative capacity they not only have the concoction of all bills, orders, votes, or resolutions, but may originate any of them, save money bills. In the executive branch they have likewise power to check and regulate the proceedings of the President. Thus treaties, the highest and most important part of the Executive Department, must have a concurrence of two thirds of them. All appointments under the President and Vice-President, must be by their advice and consent, unless they concur in passing a law divesting themselves of this power. By the checks which are intrusted with them upon both the Executive and the other branch of the Legislature, the stability of the Government is evidently placed in their hands.

The approbation of the Senate was certainly meant to guard against the mistakes of the President in his appointments to office. I do not admit the doctrine of holding commissions 'during pleasure' as constitutional, and shall speak to that point presently. But, supposing for a moment, that to be the case, is not the same guard equally necessary to prevent improper steps in removals as in appointments? Certainly, common inference or induction can mean nothing short of this. It is a maxim in legislation as well as reason, and applies well in the present case, that it requires the same power to repeal as to enact. The depriving power should be the same as the appointing power.

But was this a point left at large by the Constitution? Certainly otherwise. Five or six times in our short Constitution is the trial by impeachment mentioned. In one place, the House of Representatives shall have the sole power of impeachment. In another, the Senate shall have the sole power to try impeachments. In a third, judgment shall not extend further than to removal from office, and disqualification to hold or enjoy offices, etc. The President shall not pardon in cases of impeachment. The President, Vice-President, and *all civil officers* of the United States, shall be removed from office on impeachment, etc. No part of the Constitution is so fully guarded as or more clearly expressed than this part of it. And most justly, too, for every good Government guards the reputation of her citizens as well as their life and property. Every turning out of office is attended with reproach, and the person so turned out is stigmatized with infamy. By means of impeachment a fair hearing and trial are secured to the party. Without this, what man of independent spirit would accept of such an office? Of what service can his abilities be to the community if afraid of the nod or beck of a superior? He must consult his will in every matter. Abject servility is most apt to mark the line of his conduct, and this on the one hand will not fail to be productive of despotism and tyranny on the other; for I consider mankind composed nearly of the same materials in America as in Asia, in the United States as in the East Indies. The Constitution certainly never contemplated any other mode of removing from office. The case is not omitted here; the most ample provision is made. If gentlemen do not like it, let them obtain an alteration of the Constitution; but this can not be done by law.

If the virtues of the present Chief Magistrate are brought forward as a reason for vesting him with extraordinary powers, no nation ever trod more dangerous ground. His virtues will depart with him, but the powers which you give him will remain, and if not properly guarded will be abused by future Presidents if they are men. This, however, is not the whole of the objection I have to the clause. A chief clerk is to be appointed, and this without any advice or consent of the Senate. This chief clerk, on the removal of the Secretary, will become the principal in the office, and so may remain during the presidency, for the Senate can not force the President into a nomination for a new officer. This is a direct stroke at the power of the Senate. Sir, I consider the clause as exceptional every way, and therefore move you to strike it out.

Langdon jumped up in haste; hoped the whole would not be struck out, but moved that the clause only of the President's removing should be struck out. Up rose Elsworth, and a most elaborate speech indeed did he make, but it was all drawn from writers on the distribution of government. The President was the executive officer. He was interfered with in the appointment, it is true, but not in the removal. The Constitution had taken one, but not the other, from him. Therefore, removal remained to him entire. He carefully avoided the subject of impeachment. He absolutely used the following expressions with regard to the President: *"It is sacrilege to touch a hair of his head,* and *we may as well lay the President's head on the block and strike it off with one blow.*" The way he came to use these words was after having asserted that removing from office was his (the President's) privilege, we might as well do this as to deprive him of it. He [Elsworth] had sore eyes, and had a green silk over them. On pronouncing the last of the two sentences, he paused, put his handkerchief to his face, and either shed tears or affected to do so.

When he sat down both Butler and Izard sprang up. Butler, however, continued up. He began with a declaration that he came into the House in the most perfect state of indifference, and rather disposed to give the power in question to the President. But the arguments of the honorable gentleman from Connecticut [Elsworth], in endeavoring to support the clause, had convinced him, in the clearest manner, that the clause was highly improper, and he would vote against it. Izard now got at it, and spoke very long against the clause. Strong got up for the clause, and a most confused speech he made, indeed. I have notes of it, but think it really not worth answering, unless to show the folly of some things that he said. Dr. Johnson rose and told us twice before he proceeded far that he would not give an opinion on the power of the President. This man's conscience would not let him; he is a thorough-paced courtier, yet he wishes not to lose his interest with the President. However, his whole argument went against the clause, and at last he declared he was against the whole of it. Mr. Lee rose. He spoke long and pointedly against the clause. He repeated many of my arguments, but always was polite enough to acknowledge the mention I had made of them. He spoke from a paper which he held in his hand. He continued until it was past three o'clock, and an adjournment was called for and took place.

In looking over my notes I find I omitted to set down sundry arguments which I used. But no matter; I will not do it now.

July 15th.—Senate met. Mr. Carrol showed impatience to be up first. He got up and spoke a considerable length of time. The burden of his discourse seemed to be the want of power in the President, and a desire of increasing it. Great complaints of what is called the *atrocious assumption of power in the States.* Many allusions to the power of the British kings. *The*

king can do no wrong. If anything improper is done, it should
be the Ministers that should answer. How strangely this man
has changed!

The Collection bill was called for and read for the first time.
Now Elsworth rose with a most lengthy debate. The first
words he said were, "In this case the Constitution is our only
rule, for we are sworn to support it." But [he] neither quoted
it nor ever named it afterward except as follows. He said by
allusion, "I buy a square acre of land. I buy the trees, water,
and everything belonging to it. The executive power belongs
to the President. The removing of officers is a tree on this
acre. The power of removing is, therefore, his. It is in him.
It is nowhere else. Thus we are under the necessity of ascertaining by implication where the power is." He called Dr.
Johnson Thomas Aquinas by implication, too, and said things
rather uncivil to some other of his opponents. Most carefully
did he avoid entering on the subject of impeachment. After
some time, however, he got fairly on new ground. Lamented
the want of power in the President. Asked, Did we *ever quarrel*
with the power of the Crown of Great Britain? No, we contended with the power of the Parliament. No one ever thought
the power of the Crown too great. [He] said he was growing
infirm, should die, and should not see it, but the Government
would fail for want of power in the President. He would have
power as far as he would be seen in his coach-and-six. "We
must extend the executive arm." (Mr. Lee yesterday had said
something about the Dutch.) "If we must have examples," said
he, "let us draw them from the people whom we used always
to imitate; from the nation who have made all others bow
before them, and not from the Dutch, who are divided and
factious." He said a great deal more, but the above is all I
minuted down at the time. Mr. Izard rose and answered. Mr.
Butler rose and spoke. It was after three. Mr. Lee rose; said he
had much to say, but would now only move an adjournment.
As it was late, the House accordingly adjourned.

I have seen more caballing and meeting of members in knots
this day than I ever observed before. As I came upstairs, Elsworth, Ames, and Mr. Morris stood in a knot. Soon afterward
Elsworth, Carrol, and Strong got together. As soon as the

House adjourned, Carrol took Patterson aside, and there seemed a general hunt and bustle among the members. I see plainly public speaking on this subject is now useless, and we may put the question where we please. It seems as if a court party was forming; indeed, I believe it was formed long ago.

July 16th.—Attended pretty early this morning. Many were, however, there before me. It was all huddling away in small parties. Our Vice-President was very busy indeed; running to every one. He openly attacked Mr. Lee before me on the subject in debate, and they were very loud on the business. I began to suspect that the court party had prevailed. Senate, however, met, and at it they went. Mr. Lee began, but I really believe the altercation, though not a violent one, which he had with the Vice-President had hurt him, for he was languid and much shorter than ever I had heard him on almost any subject. Mr. Patterson got up. For a long time you could not know what he would be at. After, however, he had warmed himself with his own discourse, as the Indians do with their war-songs, he said he was for the clause continuing. He had no sooner said so than he assumed a bolder tone of voice; flew over to England; extolled its Government; wished, in the most unequivocal language, that our President had the same powers; said, let us take a second view of England; repeating nearly the same thing. Let us take a third view of it, said he. And then he abused Parliament for having made themselves first triennial and lastly septennial. Speaking of the Constitution, he said expressly these words, speaking of the removing of officers: "There is not a word of removability in it." His argument was that the Executive held this as a matter of course.

Mr. Wyngate got up and said something for striking out. Mr. Read rose, and was swinging on his legs for an hour. He had to talk a great deal before he could bring himself to declare against the motion. But now a most curious scene opened. Dalton rose and said a number of things in the most hesitating and embarrassed manner. It was his recantation; [he] had just now altered his mind. From what had been said by the honorable gentleman from Jersey, he was now for the clause. Mr. Izard was so provoked that he jumped up; declared nothing had fallen from that gentleman that could possibly convince any man; that men might pretend so, but the thing was impossible.

Mr. Morris' face had reddened for some time. He rose hastily, threw censure on Mr. Izard; declared that the canting man behaved like a man of honor; that Patterson's arguments were good and sufficient to convince any man. The truth, however, was that everybody believed that John Adams was the great converter.

But now recantation was in fashion. Mr. Bassett recanted, too, though he said he had prepared himself on the other side. We now saw how it would go, and I could not help admiring the frugality of the court party in procuring recantations, or votes, which you please. After all the arguments were ended and the question taken the Senate was ten to ten, and the Vice-President with joy cried out, "It is not a vote!" without giving himself time to declare the division of the House and give his vote in order. Every man of our side, in giving his sentiments, spoke with great freedom, and seemed willing to avow his opinion in the openest manner. Not a man of the others who had made any speech to the merits of the matter, but went about it and about it. I called this singing the war-song, and I told Mr. Morris I would give him every one whom I heard sing the war-song; or, in other words, those who could not avow the vote they were fully minded to give until they had raised spirits enough by their own talk to enable them to do it. Grayson made a speech. It was not long, but he had in it this remarkable sentence: "The matter predicted by Mr. Henry is now coming to pass: consolidation is the object of the new Government, and the first attempt will be to destroy the Senate, as they are the representatives of the State Legislatures."

It has long been a maxim with me that no frame of government whatever would secure liberty or equal administration of justice to a people unless virtuous citizens were the legislators and Governors. I live not a day without finding new reason to subscribe to this doctrine. What avowed and repeated attempts have I seen to place the President above the powers stipulated for him by the Constitution!

The vote stood: For striking out—Butler, Izard, Langdon, Johnson, Wyngate, Few, Gunn, Grayson, Lee, Maclay—ten.

Against striking out: Read, Bassett, Elsworth, Strong, Dalton, Patterson, Elmer, Morris, Henry, Carrol—ten; and John Adams.

I replied to a number of their arguments, and the substance of it is on the adjoining loose sheet. Of all the members of the House, the conduct of Patterson surprised me most. He has been characterized to me as a stanch Revolution man and genuine Whig; yet he has in every republican question deserted and in some instances betrayed us. I know not that there is such a thing as buying members, but, if there is, he is certainly sold.

I never was treated with less respect than this day. Adams behaved with studied inattention. He was snuffling up his nose, kicking his heels, or talking and sniggering with Otis the whole time I was up. Butler—though no man bears a thing of this kind with less temper—engaged Wyngate, Izard, and his end of the table in earnest conversation. Elsworth, Bassett, and Read formed another knot. Mr. Morris went out. The door-keeper was kept on a continual trot, calling out Strong, Patterson, Henry, Carrol, etc. I might have said more, but it was useless.

July 17th.—Attended at the Hall half after nine o'clock. We read and corrected the long judiciary. The Senate met at the usual time. This same judiciary was taken up and went over. And now Mr. Butler rose against it; Mr. Grayson spoke against it, and Mr. Lee was more pointed than any of them. Had Mr. Lee joined us in my objections against it at an early period, perhaps we might have now had it in better form. Mr. Butler offered a motion for leave for any member to enter his dissent on the minutes. This proved a most lengthy debate. It was four o'clock before it was decided. He lost his motion. I thought it right. And now Mr. Lee, Mr. Grayson, Mr. Butler, and Mr. Wyngate rose for the yeas and nays on the Judiciary bill. They were given; I was in the negative.

I opposed this bill from the beginning. It certainly is a vile law system, calculated for expense and with a design to draw by degrees all law business into the Federal courts. The Constitution is meant to swallow all the State Constitutions by degrees, and thus to swallow, by degrees, all the State judiciaries. This, at least, is the design some gentlemen seem driving at. O sweet Candor, when wilt thou quit the cottage and the lisping infant's lips and shed thy glory round the statesman's head? Is it inscribed on human fate that man must grow wicked to seem wise; and must the path of politics be forever encumbered with briers and thorns?

I had been much pressed to dine with the Speaker in a company of Pennsylvanians. I went there and sat till six. I am a poor string in a convivial concert. My lame knee will neither let me eat nor drink. I am old, and ought to know it. I became quite tired with the voluble tattle of the table. I never had much, but now much less, taste for convivial joys. Some of the company grew very talkative before I left them, particularly the Governor of the Western Territory. He must soon sink in the public opinion if he conducts himself as he did this evening. He was tediously talkative, and dwelt much on the fooleries of Scottish antiquity, and, what was worse, showed ill-nature when he was laughed at.

July 18th.—We had some debate yesterday about the adjournment. It was agreed to sit this day expressly with a design to take up the Collection bill. As soon as the minutes were read, Mr. Morris called for it and I seconded it. But Elsworth called for the bill on foreign affairs (as he was sick and wanted a few days' absence, and Bassett, who had stayed over the time he expected, was likewise going out of town). We had now much curious conversation. Mr. Grayson made some remarks on our mode of doing business. Our doors were shut, and a member was debarred the privilege of a protest. We were shut up in conclave. We, however, have often had this business before us. The Vice-President, however, took occasion to get up and gave us his history of protests. He said the House of Lords only had that right; they had it in the feudal right. They were originally an armed militia for the defense of the country, and were supposed to be possessed of everything honorable. But, as to the Scotch peers, that was a piece of patchwork. The Senate were an elective body, and their motives would be to preserve their popularity in order to secure their elections, and therefore they ought not to have any power of protesting.

Elsworth made a second motion that the bill for foreign affairs should be postponed till Wednesday fortnight. Langdon seconded this. Sundry gentlemen, however, called for the bill. The Vice-President put the question on the bill and it was taken up. The gentlemen against the bill, [were] Mr. Izard, Langdon, and Johnson, declared all they wished was the yeas and nays in the same form as they had passed yesterday, the Vice-President giving the casting vote. Elsworth proposed that Bassett should withdraw, and then there would be a tie. Bassett did not like it.

Elsworth proposed to withdraw, and actually did so. All this was occasioned by the absence of Butler. And now the yeas and nays were taken on the words, "by the President." Our Vice-President gave the casting vote. Mr. Lee moved an amendment in the fore part of the bill which did not seem well digested. It was lost, of course. The amount of it was that the officer should be responsible. I arose and said I could not consent to it, for by the third clause of the bill the officer was made such an abject creature, so dependent on the nod of a superior, I thought it cruel to make him in any degree responsible for measures in which he could have no free agency. He had been called servant. He was more—he was the creature of the President. The President was the responsible officer by the Constitution. It had been said no use would be made of this. I hoped there never would be any occasion; but *respondeat superior* was a maxim in law, and I supposed we would have to trust to it. Mr. Langdon moved to strike out "to be appointed by the said principal officer." I could not see what he aimed at. Dr. Johnson got up and complained of the approbation of the President in the last part of the clause as reflecting on the Senate, to whom the Constitution had given the power of approving.

I doubted whether I should rise or no, thinking all opposition vain. I determined, however, to speak: Mr. President, this clause calls the chief clerk an inferior officer. I think differently of him. This, sir, will be the man who will do the business. In England, sir—that country from which we are so fond of taking examples—the chief clerks do the business; so much so that, on an eminent character being told by a person who seemed in concern on the occasion that the Ministry were changed, asked gravely if the clerks in the office were changed; being answered no. Give yourself no further uneasiness, then; the business will meet with no interruption. So will it be here. The calling him an inferior officer, however, paves the way for his appointment by the head of the department. But what is the use of the clause here? I think freely and freely will I speak. The Secretary appoints his clerk, of course, and the clerk, of course, will take care of the office records, books, and papers, even if the principal should be removed. They are to be under oath or affirmation faithfully to execute the trust committed to them. It is not to be presumed that they will abandon the papers to the winds. What, then, is the use of the clause? Clearly to put it into the power of a President, if so minded, to exercise this office without the advice or consent of the Senate as to the affair. The consent of the President at the end of the clause points out this clearly. This is a kind of a consent unwarranted by the Constitution. The President removes the principal—the clerk pleases him well, being a man of his approbation. The Senate can not force him to a nomination, and the business may proceed during his presidency. The objects ostensibly held out by the bill are nugatory. The design is but illy concealed. It was for these reasons I formerly moved to strike out this clause, and I am still averse to the whole of it.

Patterson got up, said the latter part of the clause, perhaps, was exceptionable, and he would have no objection to strike it out. Mr. Morris rose and said something to the same import; but as Dr. Johnson had glanced somewhat at the conduct of the other House, and as what I had said leaned the same way, Mr. Morris said whatever the particular view might be of the member who brought in this clause, he acquitted the House, in general, of any design against the Senate. Mr. Elsworth rose and said much more on the same subject. I rose and said I thought nothing on this subject which I would not avow. The House of Representatives had debated four days on a direct clause for vesting the President with this power; and, after having carried it with an open face, they dropped and threw out the clause, and have produced the same thing, cloaked and modified in a different manner by a side-wind. I liked, for my part, plain dealing, and there was something that bore a very different aspect in this business.

July 19th, Sunday.—Determined to set off home, come what would. Went for Mr. Morris' lodgings; he was out of town. Visited Mr. Butler, who lives just by him. Visited Mr. Clymer, who was just returned from Philadelphia. Called on Mr. Izard on my way home. He was most violent on the subject of our late measures. He abhors our Vice-President. Came home. Read mostly in the afternoon. Visited by the Speaker, General St. Clair, Delany, Macpherson, and sundry other gentlemen. My health requires a journey home. But I this day read the story of Father Nicholas in The Lounger. I am no St. Hubert, no sinner known, no Delasmus or Turnvilles. But this story had an effect on me. I will go and see my family.

July 20th, Monday.—Asked leave of absence for three weeks on account of my health. Obtained it without difficulty. I remained some time in my place after business was over, to give an opportunity to any of the members who chose it to wish me a good journey, or to speak to me on business if they had any. Henry, of Maryland, and a group soon gathered about me. They seemed to think that my going was owing to disaffection to public measures as much as to indisposition. This I would not own but in [a] qualified sense; that my disappointment with respect to public measures and constant vexation had perhaps aggravated my indisposition.

Fun now let loose her frolics upon me, and who of all the human race will thank you for that? Not one in a thousand will believe a word of it, and if any do they will call you a fool for your pains. "Gratitude no governing principle among the *humanum pecus.* Fear only the parent of obedience among the herd of mankind. The hangman in this world and the devil in the next. Republican theories well enough in times of public commotion or at elections; but all sensible men once in power know that force is the only effectual means to secure obedience. Hence has flowed, and forever will flow, the failure of republican government. Oligarchies and aristocracies follow till monarchy tops the system, and will continue till some unskillful driver overloads the ass, and then the restive beast throws both itself and the rider in the mire, and the old process begins." "A Senator will be elected in your place before long," said one. "Your patriotism will be of great service to you then. A single dinner given by a speculator (people who do not like you) will procure ten votes where your disinterestedness has not procured you one. And you must intrigue and cabal as deep as, and deeper too, than your adversaries, or we will not see you here again. Is there a single one of the majestic mob who will not belie, defraud, deceive, and cheat you for the smallest interest? Health is too great a sacrifice for such a herd."

The whole was delivered with so comic an air that a serious answer seemed improper, and yet I wished to say something, and, for the sake of harmony, if possible in the same key: Gentlemen, I have at home good neighbors. Good—

[Here a leaf from the journal has been torn out. The next entry is made on the return of Senator Maclay to New York, August 16th.]

August 16th, Sunday.—Came to New York at ten o'clock at night, greatly fatigued with my journey. Went after breakfast to Mr. Morris' lodgings. He was abroad. Called on Mr. Clymer at his lodgings, and left his and Mr. Fitzsimons' letters. Called to see Mr. Scott and Ellicott; both abroad. Called on Mr. Izard. He gave me a short history of the court party which (as might be expected) is gaining ground. A conference has been held with the President, in which Mr. Izard declares that the President owned he had consulted the members of the House of Representatives as to his nominations, but likewise said he had not acted so with the Senators, as they could have an opportunity of giving their advice and consent afterward.

This small anecdote serves to divulge his [Washington's] conduct, or rather to fix my opinion of his conduct, for some time past, to wit, a courtship of and attention to the House of Representatives, that by their weight he may depress the Senate and exalt [his] prerogatives on the ruins. Mr. Izard was clearly of opinion that all the late measures flowed from the President. Mr. Madison, in his opinion, was deep in this business. The President showed great want of temper (as Izard said) when one of his nominations was rejected. The President may, however, be considered as in a great measure passive in the business. The creatures that surround him would place a crown on his head, that they may have the handling of its jewels.

Mr. Izard informed me of the attempt of Gorham to get the land commonly called the triangle [now Erie County] from Pennsylvania, or at least to delay the business until he could get a number of New England men to settle on it, so as to hold it by force and make a second Wyoming of it. He said Mr. Morris had got the business put off until Wednesday, expecting my coming to town. By his account a strong party is forming by Gorham, and they expect to carry it against Pennsylvania. I immediately left him, Sunday as it was, to call on Scott and Ellicott to prepare for this business. Could find none of them.

My haste and agitation on hearing of Gorham's affair prevented my noting all Mr. Izard's communications. He said all your measures are reprobated and will be rejected. Your voting by ballot, in agreeing to nominations, and so on. We have all been to dine with the great man. It's all disagreeable to him, and will be altered, etc. He gave clear hints of my loss of character at court, and in the direct influence of the President with the members of Congress, etc. For some time past (as the Indian said) I could see how the watches went, but I did not know before the way they were wound up. It was to counteract a growing influence which I observed to gain ground daily that I moved the consent to appointments to be given by ballot. The having carried this matter was passing the Rubicon in transgression, as it went to pluck up patronage by the roots, and to undo this is, it seems, a knot worthy of presidential interference.

A thought here on the subject of influence. Stripped of its courtly coloring, and it is neither more nor less than corruption. When Walpole debauched the British Senate (House of Lords), was it either morally or politically different whether he did it by court favor, loans, jobs, lottery-tickets, contracts, offices, or expectancy of them, or with the clinking guinea? The motive and effect were certainly the same. But Walpole was a villain. What, then, must be the man that follows his footsteps?

August 17, Monday.—Went out, although I was not very

well, It was near nine o'clock before I could see Mr. Scott, and he was then in bed. I saw Mr. Morris, who had just received all the papers from Mr. Ellicott about the triangle [Erie County, Pennsylvania]. Not one of them had ever thought that Pennsylvania had actually purchased this land from the Indians. I called on General St. Clair, who will set this in a clear point of view, if they will not give us time to send to Philadelphia for the deed, etc.

Attended the Senate at the usual hour. The business agitated this day in the Senate was the bill for regulating the coasting trade. Some progress was made in it, when it was postponed, and the affairs of Georgia, with respect to the Indians, were taken up. Some warmth on this business. Sat until after four and adjourned.

August 18th, Tuesday.—Busy preparing for the debate on the triangle, which is to come on to-morrow. Senate met at the usual time. The bill for the Indian treaties was taken up, and considerable debate. I asked for information—for some estimate of the expense, but it seems none had been furnished. A motion was made for reducing the sum appropriated from forty to twenty thousand dollars, but no estimate appeared for either. I lamented my want of information, but declared I hoped the House of Representatives had some just grounds to go on when they voted the forty [thousand dollars] ; that I would for once trust to them, since I must vote in the dark. But the twenty was carried. We then read over the penal law for the second time, and debated on it until the hour of adjournment.

August 19th, Wednesday.—Senate met, and went on the appointment of an officer to run the line of the triangle. I will not attempt a detail of the arguments, maps, resolves of Congress, contracts, etc., that were produced by us, which those who voted for us declared carried demonstration with them. We had every man east of the Hudson against us, and most of them speakers. Dr. Johnson, in particular, was very uncandid. Elsworth voted against us, but spoke but little. King and Schuyler managed the debate principally. Langdon was very often up. Every point on the paper annexed was canvassed, and a vast many more. I can not pretend to say how often I was up, but my throat was really sore with speaking. So plain a case I never before saw cost so much trouble. Under my present impression I am ready to vote every man void of principle who voted against this measure. At a quarter past three we got the resolve passed. I can not help writing that senatorial honor dwells not east of the Hudson. Strong was most uncandid and selfish, and often up. I wish I may soon have occasion to retract my above opinion; it is painful to think so badly of one's fellow-members.

The annexed paper: "An Act of Cession by the State of New York to the United States on the 1st March, 1781. Accepted by Congress on the 29th October, 1782."

Here showed that the cession was made on geographical principles by the map, and explain how the northwest corner of Pennsylvania came to be placed fifty (say fifty-four and a half) miles farther west, and how this company and the State of New York wish to avail themselves of that circumstance.

On the 18th of April, 1785, a cession of the same territory was accepted by Congress from the State of Massachusetts in the same words, only the Pennsylvania line was not mentioned, on a supposition that there was a vacancy of two minutes of a degree between them.

A meridian passing through the westerly bend of Lake Erie, or through a point twenty miles west of the most westerly bend of the Niagara River, one or the other must be the western limit of the State of New York, as the boundary is to be a meridian and must pass through one or other of these points.

On the 6th of June, 1788, Congress ordered the geographer of the United States to run the boundary-line, giving notice to the Executives of the States of New York and Massachusetts, and to make an accurate survey of the land lying west of the meridian between Lake Erie and the State of Pennsylvania, that the same might be sold. (Read the resolution.)

On the 16th of June, 1788, the geographer instructed Andrew Ellicott, Esq., to perform this service.

On the 7th of July, 1788, the State of Pennsylvania offered, by William Bingham and James Reed, three fourths of a dollar per acre for this land. (Read the offer.)

On the 28th of August, 1782, the Pennsylvania proposals

were accepted and the bargain closed by the Board of Treasury. (Read the acceptance.)

On the 4th of September, 1788, Congress vested the right of jurisdiction over the said tract in the State of Pennsylvania. (Read the resolution.)

Pennsylvania, thus vested with the right both to soil and jurisdiction, pursued her usual system with regard to new lands; and, although it was said that Congress ought to quiet the claims of the Indians with respect to lands sold by them, she chose, in conformity to ancient usage, to purchase of the natives. General Butler and Colonel Gibson were appointed agents at the treaty of Muskingum, and the purchase of these lands was made. We have not the deeds and other documents to produce. If they are required, we will send for them. But General St. Clair, now in town, was present at making the contract, present at obtaining the deed, and present at the payment of the consideration at Fort Pitt.

The delay of making the survey keeps out of the Treasury of the United States about six hundred and twenty-five thousand dollars, the interest of which is about nine thousand dollars, specie, per annum; and the State of Pennsylvania is retarded in the settlement of the country. If Mr. Gorham or any individual is injured, a Federal court will soon be opened. But delays are attended with national as well as State disadvantages, and ought not to be protracted. Mr. Morris will vote with and support me. But it is strange that Gorham should be so often calling him out and holding conversations with him.

August 20th, Thursday.—This was a dull day in the Senate, and might be said to make amends for the bustle of yesterday. The Coasting Trade bill engaged us all day in a round of dullness. Not one member seemed to understand the whole of it, so much had it been postponed and amended. It really rather seems a system for tolerating and countenancing smuggling than otherwise. I told them so, though I did not choose to embark much in it.

Mr. Lear has for two days past been introduced quite up to the Vice-President's table to deliver messages. Mr. Izard rose to know the reason of this. Our Vice-President said he had directed it to be so, and alleged, in a silly kind of manner, that he understood the House so. There was some talk about it a few days ago; but I understood the sense of the Senate to be that the "head of a department," if he came to deliver a message from the President, should be admitted to the table; but a private secretary received at the bar. It is not one farthing matter; but the Clerk of the Representatives is received at the bar, and I think him a more respectable character than any domestic of the President. Our Vice-President, however, never seems pleased but when he is concerned in some trifling affair of etiquette or ceremony. Trifles seem his favorite object, and his whole desire to be *totas in illis*.

August 21st, Friday.—The report of the committee that had conferred with the President was taken up. The most of it was where the President should sit on his being introduced into our chamber, and where our Vice-President should sit, etc. A second resolution was added, declaring that the Senate should give their advice and consent in all cases [to presidential nominations] *viva voce* vote. This being directly contrary to a former resolution which I had moved for, I rose and remarked that this matter had been solemnly debated formerly and decided in favor of a ballot when it came to the single point of consenting to a man's nomination; that I was still of the same opinion, and would vote against the resolution. Izard rose and said it was true that the present resolution would repeal the former one, and it was so intended, as he apprehended there was a change in the sentiments of the Senate on that subject. Mr. Morris rose and said there was a change in the sentiments of the Senate, and he hoped his honorable colleague would change his sentiments for *his own sake*.

I rose and said it was a matter in which I was not in any degree personally concerned, and if I even were, nothing would make me *for my own sake* change my vote while my judgment remained unaltered. It could not, so far as I knew, affect me personally, but even if it did it should make no odds. On the question I gave my "No" in a voice sufficiently audible. One other faint "No" only issued from the opposite side of the House. So that now the court party triumphs at large.

The words *for his own sake* were not without a meaning. I have never been at the table of the President or the Vice-

President, or [been] taken the least notice of, for a considerable time, by the diplomatic corps or the people of *ton* in the city. But I care not a fig for it. Davy Harris, too, has lost his nomination for an office in Baltimore; but be it so. I have done what is right; I followed my judgment, and rejoice in it.

Notice was given just before we broke up that the President would be in the Senate chamber at half after eleven to-morrow to take the advice and consent of the Senate on some matters of consequence; but nothing communicated.

August 22d, Saturday.—Senate met, and went on the Coasting bill. The doorkeeper soon told us of the arrival of the President. The President was introduced, and took our Vice-President's chair. He rose and told us bluntly that he had called on us for our advice and consent to some propositions respecting the treaty to be held with the Southern Indians. Said he had brought General Knox with him, who was well acquainted with the business. He then turned to General Knox, who was seated on the left of the chair. General Knox handed him a paper, which he handed to the President of the Senate, who was seated on a chair on the floor to his right. Our Vice-President hurried over the paper. Carriages were driving past, and such a noise, I could tell it was something about "Indians," but was not master of one sentence of it. Signs were made to the door-keeper to shut down the sashes. Seven heads, as we have since learned, were stated at the end of the paper which the Senate were to give their advice and consent to. They were so framed that this could not be done by aye or no.

The President told us that a paper from an agent of the Cherokees was given to him just as he was coming to the Hall. He motioned to General Knox for it, and handed it to the President of the Senate. It was read. It complained hard of the unjust treatment of the people of North Carolina, etc., their violation of treaties, etc. Our Vice-President now read off the first article, to which our advice and consent were requested. It referred back principally to some statements in the body of the writing which had been read.

Mr. Morris rose. Said the noise of carriages had been so great that he really could not say that he had heard the body of the paper which had been read, and prayed that it might be read again. It was so [read]. It was no sooner read than our Vice-President immediately read the first head over again, and put the question: Do you advise and consent, etc? There was a dead pause. Mr. Morris whispered me, "We will see who will venture to break silence first." Our Vice-President was proceeding, "As many as—"

I rose reluctantly, indeed, and, from the length of the pause, the hint given by Mr. Morris, and the proceeding of our Vice-President, it appeared to me that if I did not no other one would, and we should have these advices and consents ravished, in a degree, from us.

Mr. President: The paper which you have now read to us appears to have for its basis sundry treaties and public transactions between the Southern Indians and the United States and the States of Georgia, North Carolina, and South Carolina. The business is new to the Senate. It is of importance. It is our duty to inform ourselves as well as possible on the subject. I therefore call for the reading of the treaties and other documents alluded to in the paper before us.

I cast an eye at the President of the United States. I saw he wore an aspect of stern displeasure. General Knox turned up some of the acts of Congress and the protest of one Blount, agent for North Carolina. Mr. Lee rose and named a particular treaty which he wished read. The business labored with the Senate. There appeared an evident reluctance to proceed. The first article was about the Cherokees. It was hinted that the person just come from there might have more information. The President of the United States rose; said he had no objection to that article being postponed, and in the mean time he would see the messenger.

The second article, which was about the Chickasaws and Choctaws, was likewise postponed. The third article more immediately concerned Georgia and the Creeks. Mr. Gunn, from Georgia, moved that this be postponed till Monday. He was seconded by Mr. Few. General Knox was asked when General Lincoln would be here on his way to Georgia. He answered *not till Saturday next*. The whole House seemed against Gunn and Few. I rose and said, when I considered the newness and im-

portance of the subject, that one article had already been postponed; that General Lincoln, the first named of the commissioners, would not be here for a week; the deep interest Georgia
had in this affair—I could not think it improper that the
Senators from that State should be indulged in a postponement
until Monday; and more especially as I had not heard any inconvenience pointed out that could possibly flow from it.

The question was put and actually carried; but Elsworth
immediately began a long discourse on the merits of the business.
He was answered by Lee, who appealed to the Constitution
with regard to the power of making war. Butler and Izard
answered, and Mr. Morris at last informed the disputants that
they were debating on a subject that was actually postponed.
Mr. Adams denied, in the face of the House, that it had been
postponed. This very trick has been played by him and his New
England men more than once. The question was, however, put a
second time and carried.

I had at an early stage of the business whispered Mr. Morris
that I thought the best way to conduct the business was to have
all the papers committed. My reasons were, that I saw no
chance of a fair investigation of subjects while the President
of the United States sat there, with his Secretary of War, to
support his opinions and overawe the timid and neutral part of
the Senate. Mr. Morris hastily rose and moved that the papers
communicated to the Senate by the President of the United
states should be referred to a committee of five, to report as
soon as might be on them. He was seconded by Mr. Gunn.
Several members grumbled some objections. Mr. Butler rose;
made a lengthy speech against commitment; said we were acting
as a council. No council ever committed anything. Committees
were an improper mode of doing business; it threw business out
of the hands of the many into the hands of the few, etc.

I rose and supported the mode of doing business by committees; that committees were used in all public deliberative
bodies, etc. I thought I did the subject justice, but concluded
the commitment can not be attended with any possible inconvenience. Some articles are already postponed until Monday.
Whoever the committee are, if committed, they must make their

report on Monday morning. I spoke through the whole in a low tone of voice. Peevishness itself, I think, could not have taken offense at anything I said.

As I sat down, the President of the United States started up in a violent fret. *"This defeats every purpose of my coming here,"* were the first words that he said. He then went on that he had brought his Secretary of War with him to give every necessary information; that the Secretary knew all about the business, and yet he was delayed and could not go on with the matter. He cooled, however, by degrees. Said he had no objection to putting off this matter until Monday, but declared he did not understand the matter of commitment. He might be delayed; he could not tell how long. He rose a second time, and said he had no objection to postponement until Monday at ten o'clock. By the looks of the Senate this seemed agreed to. A pause for some time ensued. We waited for him to withdraw. He did so with a discontented air. Had it been any other man than the man whom I wish to regard as the first character in the world, I would have said, with sullen dignity.

I can not now be mistaken. The President wishes to tread on the necks of the Senate. Commitment will bring the matter to discussion, at least in the committee, where he is not present. He wishes us to see with the eyes and hear with the ears of his Secretary only. The Secretary to advance the premises, the President to draw the conclusions, and to bear down our deliberations with his personal authority and presence. Form only will be left to us. This will not do with Americans. But let the matter work; it will soon cure itself.

August 24th, Monday.—The Senate met. The President of the United States soon took his seat, and the business began. The President wore a different aspect from what he did Saturday. He was placid and serene, and manifested a spirit of accommodation; declared his consent that his questions should be amended. A tedious debate took place on the third article. I was called on by Mr. Lee, of Virginia, to state something respecting the treaty held by Pennsylvania. This brought me up. I did not speak long, but endeavored to be as pointed as possible. The third article consisted of two questions. The first I was for. I disliked the second, but both were carried.

The fourth article consisted of sundry questions. I moved pointedly for a division. Got it. Voted for the first and opposed the second part. A long debate ensued, which was likely to end only in words. I moved to have the words "in failure thereof by the United States" struck out, and, although Elsworth, Wyngate, and Dalton had spoken on the same side with me, yet I was not seconded. My colleague had in private declared himself of my opinion also. It was an engagement that the United States would pay the stipulated purchase money for Georgia in case Georgia did not. The arguments I used on this subject were so plain I need not set them down. Yet a shamefacedness, or I know not what, flowing from the presence of the President, kept everybody silent.

The next clause was for a free port on the Altamaha or Saint Mary's River. This produced some debate, and the President proposed "secure" port in place of "free" port. Agreed to. Now followed something of giving the Indians commissions on their taking the oaths to Government. It was a silly affair, but it was carried without any debate. Now followed a clause whether the cession of lands should be made an ultimatum with the Creeks. There was an alternative in case should this be negatived; but, strange to tell, the Senate negatived both, when it was plain one only should have been so. A boundary was named by a following clause which the commissioners were to adhere to. Money and honorary commissions were to be given to the Indians. The old treaties with the Creeks, Choctaws, and Chickasaws were made the basis of future treaty, though none of them were read to us nor a single principle of them explained (but it was late). The twenty thousand dollars applied to this treaty, if necessary. This closed the business. The President of the United States withdrew, and the Senate adjourned.

I told Mr. Morris, on Saturday, that I would get a copy of the queries or articles to be answered to, and call on him, that we might make up our minds. He appointed this morning, and I called accordingly. We talked and talked, but concluded nothing. I have several times called on him for similar purpose, and thus always the matter has ended.

Just as the Senate had fairly entered on business, I was

called out by the doorkeeper to speak to Colonel Humphreys. It was to invite me to dinner with the President, on Thursday next, at four o'clock. I really was surprised at the invitation. It will be my duty to go; however, I will make no inferences whatever. I am convinced all the dinners he can now give or ever could will make no difference in my conduct. Perhaps he knew not of my being in town; perhaps he has changed his mind of me. I was long enough in town, however, before my going home. It is a thing of course, and of no consequence; nor shall it have any with me.

CHAPTER IV

August 25th, Tuesday.—Attended at the usual hour. On Saturday I had proposed to Mr. Morris to bring forward all the places which had been mentioned for the permanent residence of Congress, at one time. He answered rather roughly: *"Let those that are fond of them bring them forward; I will bring forward the Falls of the Delaware."* Accordingly, although the President was every moment looked for, he presented the draught of the Falls to the Chair. Yesterday I could do nothing, for the attendance of the President. This morning, however, I took the first opportunity, and presented the draught with the description of Lancaster. I nominated Wright's Ferry, Yorktown, Carlisle, Harrisburg, Reading, and Germantown, giving a short description of each. After this, the Coasting bill was taken up and read the third time. Then the resolution for adjourning the 22d of September. A debate ensued, but was carried; after this the amendments to the Constitution sent from the House of Representatives. They were treated contemptuously by Izard, Langdon, and Mr. Morris. Izard moved that they should be postponed till next session. Langdon seconded, and Mr. Morris got up and spoke angrily but not well. They, however, lost their motion, and Monday was assigned for taking them up. I could not help observing the six year-class [of Senators] hung together on this business, or the most of them.

Now came the Compensation bill. I moved the wages to be five dollars per day. I was seconded by Elmer; but on the question only he, Wyngate, and myself rose. Mr. Morris almost raged, and in his reply to me said he cared not for the arts people used to ingratiate themselves with the public. In reply I answered that I had avowed all my motives. I knew the public mind was discontented. I thought it our duty to attend to the voice of the public. I had been informed that the average of the wages of the old members of Congress was a little better than five dollars per diem. I wished to establish this as a principle. I would then have data to fix a price on, as the old wages were never complained of. Morris, Izard, and Butler were in a violent chaff. Mr. Morris moved that the pay of the Senators should be eight dollars per day.

Up now rose Izard; said that the members of the Senate went to boarding-houses, lodged in holes and corners, associated with improper company, and conversed improperly, so as to lower their dignity and character; that the delegates from South Carolina used to have £600 per year, and could live like gentlemen, etc. Butler rose; said a great deal of stuff of the same kind; that a member of the Senate should not only have a handsome income, but should spend it all. He was happy enough to look down on these things; he could despise them, but it was scandalous for a member of Congress to take any of his wages home; he should rather give it to the poor, etc. Mr. Morris likewise paid himself some compliments on his manner and conduct in life, his disregard of money, and the little respect he paid to the common opinions of people. Mr. King got up, said the matter seemed of a delicate nature, and moved for a committee to whom the bill might be referred. This obtained, and a committee of five were appointed. By the complexion of the committee it would seem the Senate want their wages enlarged. I answered Mr. Morris in a way that gave him a bone to chaw, but I believe it is as well forgot.

August 26th.—Attended the Senate. The minutes were lengthy, but I was surprised to find no notice taken of my presenting the draft of Lancaster, the letter, and my nomination of the other places in Pennsylvania, although I had put in writing the whole matter and given it to the Secretary. When he had read about half-way of his minutes, I rose and called on him to know why he had not inserted them. He said he was not come to them, but seemed much confused. He, however, got the letter and handed it to the Vice-President, and it was read. After this the nomination was read, and Butler opposed their being put on the minutes; I, however, had a vote for their going on. Mr. Morris was all this while

out. He was of the committee on the Compensation bill. When
he came in, Otis, the Secretary, came to him and whispered
something to him. God forgive me if I heard wrong or apprehended wrong, but I thought he said, "Maclay has got that
put on the minutes." Mr. Morris went out and stayed out until
Senate adjourned, leaving his hat and stick (perhaps he was
writing letters in the adjoining room). He called in as the
Senate rose, and seemed unwilling to leave me in the room with
Otis. I went with him to the door, but returned and spoke to
Otis. All this is, perhaps, the effect of over-observation; I, however, care not.

The penal law was taken up. Elsworth had a string of amendments. For a while he was listened to, but he wrought himself
so deep in his niceties and distinctions as to be absolutely in-
comprehensible. He fairly tired the Senate, and was laughed at.
I think he may well be styled the "Endless Elsworth." I forgot to
minute yesterday that the Treasury bill was taken up. A number
of the Senate had recanted again on this bill, and were against
the power of the President's removing, and had answered accordingly. The House of Representatives sent us up an adherence, and now Mr. Morris proposed to me to leave the
House. I would neither do this nor change my mind, and he was
angry. This was before we had the difference on the Compensation bill.

Last night there was a meeting of the Pennsylvania delegation on the subject of fixing the permanent residence. There
was little of consequence said. They mentioned their former
agreement to vote for every place that should be nominated in
Pennsylvania. Clymer said some things that savored more of
independence than any of them. Mr. Scott declared he would
put himself entirely in their hands, and move anything that
should be agreed upon. Mr. Clymer declared for the Potomac
rather than stay here. I understood him that he thought this
politically right. Fitzsimons and the Speaker seemed to second
everything that Mr. Morris said. Hartley was for Susquehanna
and Yorktown. But, indeed, I think the whole measure likely to
be abortive. They have brought the whole matter forward, but
have no system. I saw this, but did not hazard a single sentiment
on the subject; indeed, I could not without implying some kind

of censure. I called this morning and endeavored to put Mr. Scott on tenable ground on the affair of removal, and left him in a proper way of thinking; at least, if he should be defeated, to advance nothing but what is defensible.

August 27th, Thursday.—The business in the Senate was the third reading of the Penal bill. We had but little debate until we came to a clause making it highly criminal to defame a foreign Minister. Here Izard, King, and Johnson made a great noise for the paragraph. Mr. Adams could not sit still in his chair. It was a subject of etiquette and ceremony. Two or three times did his impatience raise him to talk in a most trifling manner. However, it did not avail; the paragraph was lost.

Mr. Morris could not sit one moment with us (the subject of the permanent residence was in agitation in the other House). To tell the truth, Mr. Morris' whole attention seems bent to one object, to get the Federal residence to Trenton. Mr. Scott (agreeable to what had been settled this morning) brought in a motion to the following effect: "That a place ought to be fixed for the permanent residence of the General Government as near the center of population, wealth, and extent of territory as is consistent with the convenience of the Atlantic navigation, *having also due regard to the Western Territory";* and concluded that Thursday next be assigned for taking it up. This was carried.

Senate adjourned early. At a little after four I called on Mr. Bassett, of the Delaware State. We went to the President's to dinner. The company were: President and Mrs. Washington, Vice-President and Mrs. Adams, the Governor and his wife, Mr. Jay and wife, Mr. Langdon and wife, Mr. Dalton and a lady (perhaps his wife), and a Mr. Smith, Mr. Bassett, myself, Lear, Lewis, the President's two secretaries. The President and Mrs. Washington sat opposite each other in the middle of the table; the two secretaries, one at each end. It was a great dinner, and the best of the kind I ever was at. The room, however, was disagreeably warm.

First was the soup; fish roasted and boiled; meats, gammon, fowls, etc. This was the dinner. The middle of the table was garnished in the usual tasty way, with small images, flowers (artificial), etc. The dessert was, first apple-pies, pudding, etc.; then iced creams, jellies, etc.; then water-melons, musk-melons, apples, peaches, nuts.

It was the most solemn dinner ever I sat at. Not a health drank; scarce a word said until the cloth was taken away. Then the President, filling a glass of wine, with great formality drank to the health of every individual by name round the table. Everybody imitated him, charged glasses, and such a buzz of "health, sir," and "health, madam," and "thank you, sir," and "thank you, madam," never had I heard before. Indeed, I had liked to have been thrown out in the hurry; but I got a little wine in my glass, and passed the ceremony. The ladies sat a good while, and the bottles passed about; but there was a dead silence almost. Mrs. Washington at last withdrew with the ladies.

I expected the men would now begin, but the same stillness remained. The President told of a New England clergyman who had lost a hat and wig in passing a river called the Brunks. He smiled, and everybody else laughed. He now and then said a sentence or two on some common subject, and what he said was not amiss. Mr. Jay tried to make a laugh by mentioning the circumstance of the Duchess of Devonshire leaving no stone unturned to carry Fox's election. There was a Mr. Smith, who mentioned how *Homer* described *Æneas* leaving his wife and carrying his father out of flaming Troy. He had heard somebody (I suppose) witty on the occasion; but if he had ever read it he would have said *Virgil*. The President kept a fork in his hand, when the cloth was taken away, I thought for the purpose of picking nuts. He ate no nuts, however, but played with the fork, striking on the edge of the table with it. We did not sit long after the ladies retired. The President rose, went up-stairs to drink coffee; the company followed. I took my hat and came home.

August 28th.—There was a meeting of the Pennsylvania delegation at the lodgings of Mr. Clymer and Mr. Fitzsimons. I did not hear of it until I came to the Hall; but I hastened there. The Chief Justice of Pennsylvania and Mr. Pettitt attended with a memorial from the public creditors. Their business was soon done, as we promised to present it in both Houses.

But it seems there was a further design in this meeting. Mr. Morris attended to deliver proposals from Mr. Hamilton on the part of the New England men, etc. Now, after the Eastern members have in the basest manner deserted the Pennsylvanians, they would come forward with proposals through Mr. Hamilton. This same Mr. Morris is as easily duped as another.

I spoke early, and declared that now the New England men find their deceitfulness has not availed them, and yet they wish to try their arts a second time; that their only view was to get a negotiation on foot between them and the Pennsylvanians that they might break the connection that is begun between the Pennsylvanians and the Southern people. I was extremely happy to find this sentiment pervade the Pennsylvanians. Mr. Morris labored in vain, and his chagrin was visible. We came for the Hall. In coming up Broad Street, Mr. Morris declared he would oppose the Susquehanna as the permanent residence, for it was unfavorable to commerce. He observed me, and added, as far as he could consistent with the engagements he had come under to the delegation. I need no such declaration of his to fix my opinion of his conduct; he has had no other object in view but the Falls of the Delaware since he has been Senator; at least, this has been his governing object.

Attended at the Hall. And now the report of the committee on the Compensation bill was taken up. As I knew there was a dead majority against everything I could propose, I had determined not to say a word; but flesh and blood could not bear them. The doctrine seemed to be that all worth was wealth, and all dignity of character consisted in expensive living. Izard, Butler, King, Morris, led boldly. They were followed by the bulk of the Senate, at least in the way of voting. Mr. Carrol, of Maryland, though the richest man in the Union, was not with them. I did not speak long, and, enraged as I was at such doctrines, I am sure I did not speak well. I endeavored to show what the true dignity of character of individuals consisted in; as well as of the assembled Senate. And then, turning, showed that extravagant expense, haughty and distant carriage, with contemptuous behavior to the mass of mankind, had a direct contrary effect; that, in short, mankind were not esteemed in the ratio of their wealth, and that it was in vain for the Senate to attempt acquiring dignity or consequence in that way; that I was totally against all discrimination; * that we were all equally servants of the public; that if there really was any difference in dignity, as some contended, it could not be increased by any act or assumption of ours—it must be derived from the Constitution, which afforded, in my opinion, no authority for such distinction.

Elsworth seemed to aim at a kind of middle course; said he agreed there was a difference in dignity, etc., but at present was against any difference in pay. Mr. Adams was too impatient to keep his seat. Dignities, distinctions, titles, etc., are his hobbyhorses, and the creature must ride. Three times did he interrupt Elsworth. Asked him if the dignity of the Senate was to be settled by the people? If the old Congress had not degenerated for want of sufficient pay? When Elsworth said the House of Lords in Britain had no pay, he [Adams] hastily rose and said a seat in the House of Lords was worth £60,000 sterling, per annum. Elsworth laid a trap for himself.

Up rose Izard, Lee, and others, and called for the sense of the House on the principle whether there should be a discrimination or not. It was in vain to urge that this was out of order. Lee said it was a division of the clause. I mentioned that if they must have such a question they should move a postponement. It was in vain, either way they would have this question, which was a leading one. Elsworth and sundry others, who had occasionally hinted something of the superior standing of the Senate, voted with it. The yeas and nays were called. Mr. Elsworth now took the back scent. He had voted for a discrimination, but had repeatedly, in his former arguments, mentioned six dollars as enough for the Senate. To be consistent, he moved the pay of the Representatives should be five dollars, and mentioned my principle of an average of the pay which, he said, applied well to the Representatives. I rose and mentioned that this was the sum I aimed at for both Houses; but if this was carried and the Senate stood at six [dollars], we who had voted against a discrimination, if there was no division of the House, might stand in an odd light on the minutes. There was really

---

* Meaning between the Senators and Representatives as to pay.

nothing of consequence in the last observation, and it was not very well founded; but when the question on the five dollars was taken and lost, King and sundry others called for the yeas and nays with an avidity that I had never observed before. I voted against the clause, as I did against every other clause of the bill.

When the pay of the Senators came forward in the next clause at six dollars, I rose and declared I did not wish to detain the Senate, but I had voted against a discrimination when the yeas and nays were taken. I had voted a pay of five dollars per day to the Representatives. This, in my opinion, was sufficient pay for the members of either House. The yeas and nays were likewise taken on this question. I therefore moved that six dollars should be struck out and five inserted, and concluded that there would be consistency in my votes. I had voted no discrimination; I had voted for five dollars to the Representatives; I now wished to have my vote for five dollars to the Senators on the minutes.

Such a storm of abuse never, perhaps, fell on any member. "It was nonsense, stupidity." "It was a misfortune to have men void of understanding in the House." Izard, King, and Mr. Morris said every rude thing they could. I did not retort their abuse, but still explained the consistency of my motion. I stood the rage and insult of the bulk of the House, for what appeared to me an hour and a half, but it was not half so much perhaps. Izard was most vehement that no such motion should be admitted. It was foolish; it was nonsense; it was against all rule, etc. And all this, although there never was a fairer or plainer motion before the House. It was in vain that I declared I did not begin the business of the yeas and nays. It was in vain that I offered to withdraw the present motion if all the yeas and nays were taken off [the minutes]. Izard moved for the previous question. He was replied to that this would not smother the motion. When abuse and insult would not do, then followed entreaty. We adhered to the motion, and had the yeas and nays. General Schuyler joined us, so that we had four. Now some other business was done; it was past four o'clock, and we adjourned.

It is the agreement of the world that dreams are perfectly

idle, but I can not help remembering that all last night I was perplexed in my sleep with angry ideas and fretful omens. Unluckily, these preadmonitions, if they are such, never act as preventives with me.

August 29, 1789.—The House having adjourned over to Monday, I had nothing to do. I felt myself worse of my complaint; both knees swelled with the rheumatism. I, however, wished to see the Pennsylvania Representatives, and went to the Hall. I saw Hartley, and exhorted him against entering into any cabal with regard to the residence; that the line was now marked out, and the principles laid down for fixing the Federal residence were broad, open, and honorable, such as any man might avow, and, above all, cautioned him to beware of the arts and devices of the New England men. He took it kindly, but did not seem to stand in need of any such caution. A moment after I met Mr. Smith, of Maryland. He had a terrible story, and *from the most undoubted authority.* A contract was entered into by the Virginians and Pennsylvanians to fix the permanent residence on the Potomac, right or wrong, and the temporary residence was to be in Philadelphia; and Clymer and Fitzsimons were gone to Philadelphia to reconcile the citizens of that place to it. I answered, I knew nothing of all this. I doubted it. I really do not believe it. So far as respects myself, if I am considered as included, I knew it to be false. He adhered to it with a firmness that surprised me. I called on almost all the Pennsylvanians during the day, and informed them of the tale. They all disowned every communication whatever in the way of a contract with the representation of any State. I called on Mr. Smith in the evening; told him he must be misinformed. He declared he had it through one person only—from one of the Pennsylvanians themselves. He, however, would give no names. I told him, be that as it might, I believed the matter to be groundless. He seemed afraid that I would suspect Mr. Morris, but did not acquit him of it. I left him, having paid more attention to this business than perhaps it merited.

Had a card to dine with the Vice-President on Friday. Excused myself on account of my health.

On motion to amend the report as it regards the pay of the Senators by striking out six dollars and inserting five dollars.

Passed in the negative. I know what a wretch Otis is. I therefore called on him to see how he had made up the minutes of
yesterday on the three sets of yeas and nays. All was right.
I thought this necessary.

I am not well in health, but this is not all. I have a heavy
kind of melancholy hang on me, as if I was disgusted with the
world. I do not know that; with the Senate I am certainly
disgusted. I came here expecting every man to act the part
of a god; that the most delicate honor, the most exalted wisdom, the most refined generosity, was to govern every act and
be seen in every deed. What must my feelings be on finding
rough and rude manners, glaring folly, and the basest selfishness apparent in almost every public transaction! They are
not always successful, it is true; but is it not dreadful to find
them in such a place?

August 30th.—Being Sunday, found myself really ill and
a fever on me. Was ill all last night. I had an invitation to
dine with the Speaker, but was obliged to decline it. Stayed
at home all day and wrote to my dear family. Was not able
to venture out; was worse after dinner and had to go to bed.
Had a sleep and a gentle sweat, and found myself something
better after it.

August 31st.—Found myself very ill this morning; a most
acute pain settled in my left hip. I, however, dressed and
went to the Hall. After what had passed with Otis, notwithstanding I before knew him to be a villain, I scarce could suspect him of practicing anything now. When [in reading the
minutes] he came to the motion, however, he read it, "That
the pay of the Senators should be five dollars and that the pay
of the Representatives should be six." I heard him with astonishment, but there was no time to be lost. I moved the necessary
alteration and had it inserted. Izard attempted to support the
Secretary. I stayed awhile, but found myself too sick to attend.
I came out of a window and found Otis in the corner room.
I called on him to explain this business. He hummed, hawed;
said his memory was bad. I put him in mind of my having
called on him Saturday, and that it then stood right. I made
him, however, copy it on a piece of paper. He said it was so in
the other book; went to fetch it, but did not return.

Sick and came home.

September 1st.—Exceedingly ill, with a settled and acute pain in my loins, particularly on my left side or hip. Dressed, however, and went to the Hall. The Salary bill was taken up. There seemed a disposition in a number of the Senators to give princely incomes to all the Federal officers. I really was astonished. Can it be that they wish to surround the President with a set of lordly and pompous officers, and thus having provided the furniture of a court, nothing but the name of majesty, highness, or some such title will be wanted to step into all the forms of royalty? My honorable colleague seemed particularly attached to all the officers of the Treasury. He either moved or seconded motions for augmenting the salaries of every one of them. I can not, however, blame him in particular. He was more decent than many of them. The avowed object of these proposed augmentations was to enable the officers to live in style, to keep public tables, etc.

I was not able to rise against this principle, but Mr. Elsworth and others did the subject justice. I found the parties so nearly balanced that my vote generally decided in favor of the lowest sum. This made me sit in extreme pain until we got over the bill. I then withdrew, and it was really with difficulty that I got to my lodging. Almost every motion for increasing the salaries was accompanied with a declaration how vastly the salary was below the dignity of the office, and that they moved such small additions, despairing of obtaining greater from the House. The citizens of New York, where it is expected their salaries will be spent (and, I really believe, the candidates themselves), are busy, and perhaps others too, who expect favors from the officers.

September 2d.—It is vain; pain and sickness is my lot. I can not attend the Hall. Mr. Morris called late in the evening. By him I find advantage was taken of my absence, and a reconsideration was moved and an addition carried to some of the salaries. Bonny Johney Adams giving the casting vote. The moderate part of the House exclaimed violently against the taking of this advantage of my absence, and obtained a postponement of the bill until to-morrow; but, alas, I can not attend if the whole Union were at stake. I lie here fixed with so acute a pain through my loins that I can not move more than if I were impaled.

To give me any information on this subject was not, however, Mr. Morris' object. There has been a violent schism between him and the Pennsylvania delegation, or at least a part of them. He begged leave to give me the whole detail of it. It was long, containing the first engagements at the City Tavern—viz., that whatever place (for residence of Congress) in Pennsylvania the New England men should name, the Pennsylvanians should vote for it; that every place named in Pennsylvania should be voted for by the whole delegation. These things I knew not, they having been transacted while I was absent. But what I well knew was that when Scott's motion came forward the New England men, instead of naming the Falls of the Delaware, as Mr. Morris expected (this being the point to which all his negotiations with Jay, Hamilton, etc., tended), they came prepared to expose the Pennsylvanians and ridicule the whole. In this critical moment the Virginians stepped in to the support of Scott's motion, rescued the Pennsylvanians from ridicule, and gave the whole a serious face. In this state were matters on the 28th ultimo [August, 1789], and I thought then that all negotiation with the New England men was at an end. Indeed, I was not for entering into any private engagements with any of them. My constant language to the delegation was: "You are on tenable ground. Now keep yourselves there." Something was, however, said as we parted on the 28th. If the New England men have anything to say, it must come from them. Mr. Morris caught at this, and opened a negotiation with them, and carried matters so far that a meeting was appointed by Mr. Morris of the Pennsylvania delegation at Clymer's and Fitzsimons's lodgings at five o'clock yesterday evening. Mr. Morris whispered me in the Senate, "The whole business is settled, and you must come to Clymer's and Fitzsimons's lodgings at five o'clock.

On quitting the Senate chamber I called Mr. Scott out of the Representative chamber to tell him to apologize to the meeting for my absence, as I found myself scarcely able to move one step. All this was new to him. He said if any agreement was made it must be with the Virginians. I saw a cloud of mystery in the business, wished to attend, and parted with Scott, telling him if I can not attend I will send an apology by Mr. Wynkoop. I could not attend, but so nobly was the matter managed that, while Mr. Morris was introducing Mr. Goodhue and Mr. King on the part of the Eastern States, Mr. Madison was introduced on the part of the Virginians, or introduced himself. There, however, he was, and occupied a room down-stairs, while Goodhue and King sat with Mr. Morris up-stairs. Messages were exchanged. The result was, that Messrs. Clymer, Fitzsimons, Heister, Scott, and the Speaker declared totally against any treaty with the New England men. Hartley and Wynkoop declared themselves disengaged; and all parties departed. What Mr. Morris complains most bitterly of is that Fitzsimons should permit him to bring the New England men to his lodging on the terms of treaty, when he was determined against treating with them, and that there should be any terms of communicating with Mr. Madison to which he was a stranger.

Mr. Morris, however, has not quitted the game. He told me that all the New England men and [New] York delegation were now met, and they would, on the terms of the original proposals, name a place in Pennsylvania, for they had actually agreed on one, which he had no doubt was the Falls of [the] Delaware (by the by, I doubt it), and then we would see how the delegation would answer it to their constituents to negative a place in Pennsylvania. He then said something to me as to our conduct in the Senate. I said I thought we had better come under no engagements to any of them, but regulate our conduct on the principles of the interest of our State, subordinate to the great good of the Union. He agreed to this, and took his leave.

And now we shall see what a day will bring forth. The Virginia terms seem to be, "Give us the permanent residence, and we will give Philadelphia the temporary residence." Mr. Morris declared a vote could not be obtained in the Senate for an adjournment to Philadelphia.

September 3d.—Mr. Wynkoop went early to a meeting of the Pennsylvania delegation. They were staggered at the thought of voting, in the first instance, for a place out of the State.

The business came on in the House of Representatives. Goodhue took the lead. And here I could give an advantageous lecture on scheming. The mariner's compass has thirty-two points; the political one, perhaps, as many hundreds, and the schemers an indefinite number. And yet there is but one of them that will answer. It is true there were not so many points in the present case, but the wind came from an unexpected quarter. All Mr. Morris' expectations were blasted in a moment, for Goodhue moved a resolution for the Susquehanna, as the sense of the Eastern States, exclusive of New York. The debate was long and tedious, and the business of this day ended with carrying Scott's motion. Goodhue's stands until to-morrow.

Mr. Elsworth popped in this morning to see if I could not possibly attend on the Salary bill; but I could not. Mr. Elmer called in the evening. I know not in the Senate a man, if I were to choose a friend, on whom I would cast the eye of confidence as soon as on this little doctor. He does not always vote right, and so I think of every man who differs from me, but I never yet saw him give a vote but I thought I could observe disinterestedness in his countenance. If such a one errs it is the sin of ignorance, and I think Heaven has pardons ready sealed for every one of them. "Behold, O God," can such a one say, "the machine which thou hast given me to work with; faithfully have I played its powers. If the result has been error, intentional criminality was not with me."

He was very urgent for my attendance on the Salary bill, but, on seeing the state of my knee, readily admitted there could be no expectation of it. He told me Mr. Morris was exerting his utmost address in engaging votes against the Susquehanna; he had influence with the Jersey members. The argument was, that they had been treated with disrespect in not having been consulted when the [New] York and Eastern members fixed on the Susquehanna. If Mr. Morris really expects to obtain a vote for the Delaware, after what has happened, it is a proof how far interest will blind a man. But I do not believe he has any such expectations. His design must be to ruin the Susquehanna scheme, and, in fact, keep Congress in New York. I have heard him declare it ought never to be anywhere but in Philadelphia or New York. Those places suit his plans of commerce. Nor do I believe he ever will consent to its being anywhere else, unless it be on his own grounds at the Falls of the Delaware.

September 4th.—Goodhue's motion was carried. Mr. Morris called in the evening. He sat a long time. I never saw chagrin more visible on the human countenance. "Well," said he, "I suppose you are gratified." I really was vexed to see him so deeply affected. I said coolly, I could not be dissatisfied. He repeatedly declared he would vote for the Susquehanna because he had said so, but he would do everything in his power against it. This he called candor, but I think he can not call it consistency. It has long been alleged in this place that Mr. Morris governed the Pennsylvania delegation, and I believe this idea has procured Mr. Morris uncommon attention. This delusion must now vanish. He made a long visit. Mr. Wynkoop and myself said everything in our power to soften him, and we seemed to gain upon him. He mentioned with apparent regret some rich lands in the Conestoga manor which he had exchanged with John Musser for lands on the Delaware.

Still confined, and in a miserable way with my swelled knee.

September 5th.—Worse. Confined mostly to bed. Visited by sundry gentlemen. Scott, Heister, Fitzsimons called in the evening. The Susquehanna, Potomac, and Delaware in every mouth. I find Mr. Wynkoop has revived his hopes of the Delaware. He said, "If we lose the Susquehanna, then it will be fixed at the Delaware." I looked hard at him, and asked if he had seen Mr. Morris. He answered "No," hesitatingly. I find by several hints this day that there is some new scheme on foot.

Mr. Wynkoop urged me so incessantly about a doctor that I unfortunately said yes. He asked who I knew. I said Dr. Treat. He was gone in a moment, and soon after Treat and Rodgers called, very well dressed. The sole point I wished them to attend to was my left knee. I could hardly get them to look at it. They said it was immaterial. Aren't you a good hand at taking medicine? No (faintly). You are all over indisposed; you must undergo a course of physic; you must take a course of antimonials to alter your blood. A vomit, said the other, to clean your stomach. I begged leave to observe that I was well circumstanced in my body, both as to urine and blood; had not a high fever. My knee, gentlemen; my knee. And I showed it to them, flayed as it was with blistering. Here is my great pain. "Poultice it with Indian mush, and we will send you some stuff to put on the poultice; and the antimonial wine, etc., the drops and the laudanum," etc. They seemed to me like storekeepers, with their country customers; won't you take this, and this? You must take this, and this, etc.

September 6th.—Very ill, and close confined. Izard called to see me. The moment I saw him I understood that he came on a scrutinizing errand. I made no mystery of anything I knew; told him that the certain effect of any new scheme in the Yorkers or New England men would most infallibly place us at the Potomac. He repeatedly mentioned a new scheme being on foot, but I could not learn what it was. Mr. Morris is in close connection with the Yorkers, and communicates everything to them. Mr. Clymer called on me. He spoke highly in favor of the Susquehanna as being the most favorable position in the State for the benefit of Pennsylvania; blamed Mr. Morris much; said *he would yet ruin all.* In the evening the Speaker called. He speaks more confidently of the Susquehanna than any of them. I told him I did not like the adjournment when the question was ready to be put yesterday. He endeavored to account for this, but I think it bids ill.

The doctor's stuff on the blister spoiled all. It stopped the discharge, and I was much worse. They called to persuade me to take the antimony, etc.

September 7th, Monday.—I am still very ill. This day was the trial of shift, evasion, and subterfuge in the House of Representatives; but the Susquehanna vote was carried by a majority of seven, and Ames, Lawrence, and Clymer appointed a committee to bring in a bill.

Close confined, and very ill. Unable to get information, or to minute it down if I had it. I am still ill. This day the doctors called and vexed me again.

[September], Tuesday 8th.—Still close confined, and in very bad health. The Speaker called and gave us an anecdote of Mr. Madison, which seems to discover some traits of the less amiable in his character. While the salary of the Governor

of the Western Territory [General St. Clair] was before the House, in the first stage of the business, Madison had supported it at twenty-five hundred dollars. But during the Susquehanna debate, Mr. Clymer, seeing Governor St. Clair in the gallery, addressed a note to him for information. The Governor sent back an answer in writing which contradicted the position of the friends of the Potomac. This day Madison moved a reduction of five hundred dollars from his salary.

The doctors did not call to-day, and it seems like delivering me from half of my misery.

Wednesday, Thursday, Friday, and Saturday confined, but find myself much better, and now begin to think confidently of seeing my family in health on my part. The relief which I have experienced has been from the application of blisters and cupping. This week has been one of hard jockeying between the Senate and House of Representatives. The Senate insisted, and adhered, too, for a mark of superiority in their pay. It was a trial who should hold out longest. The House of Representatives gave way, more especially after the Senators told them that if you want your pay send us a bill for yourselves and we will pass it. I really wonder, in the temper the House is in, that they had not done it; but they were aware that the majority of the Senate would fly from this proposal, as I believe many of them need money as much as any of the Representatives can do. It was a trial of skill in the way of starvation, and the dignity or precedence, or call it what you will, which could not be gained from the understanding of the House of Representatives, was extorted from their purses.

I have been visited this week by all the Pennsylvanians and by Dr. Elmer and Mr. Wyngate of the Senate. I will venture but one remark on the business of the permanent residence. It will, however, be rather a series of remarks. Neither New England men nor Yorkers are sincere about moving from this place, and they firmly believe the whole will end in vapor. Mr. Morris is to destroy the Susquehanna scheme in the Senate, if not sooner, in order to bring forward the Delaware. This he will do, with small assistance from the Yorkers, by engaging the Senators of Jersey and Delaware; and, this being done,

the Delaware destroys itself, for the New England men fall to
pieces, their engagements having been only for the Susquehanna.
These arts are likely enough to succeed.

[*September*] *13th, Sunday.*—Wrote my letters for home. Sat
up a good deal, and found myself much better. In the evening
Mr. Morris, Mr. Clymer, and Mr. Fitzsimons called on me.
I thought that the Susquehanna had not got justice done in
the arguments; spoke long on this subject to possess them of my
ideas of it. All the talk and speculation about the Western
country is visionary. Nothing will come on to the Atlantic
rivers from the Western waters. If it should, the Susquehanna
has the advantage in the doubt connection by Juniata and the
West Branch. I was listened to throughout with apathy, however.

[*September 14th*], *Monday.*—About twelve Mr. Clymer
called in; said he had a letter from Reading Howell, with important information. He read a part of it, and desired I would
draw up the thoughts I had expressed last night, that a publication might be prepared against the time of taking up the bill.
Dr. Johnson and Mr. Carrol, of Carrolton, called while he was
in, and interrupted us a little. He stayed a moment after them,
and said he would call early to-morrow morning, that we might
settle on something for publication. I expressed plainly to him
the same thoughts which I minuted on Saturday; but he said
Mr. Morris was now contented. I was so unwell that I had to
go to bed; and here, leaning on my elbow, I arranged something,
but was greatly at a loss for maps and for the distances on the
Susquehanna and Potomac, beginning at tide-water, to Fort
Pitt. I sent Mr. Wynkoop to call on Mr. Smith, of Maryland,
for them. [He] was abroad. I sent a note to Mr. Smith, begging
that he would call on me with them, but he did not; so that
what I composed was with blanks.

Tuesday, 15th.—Between ten and eleven Mr. Clymer, Mr.
Fitzsimons, and Governor St. Clair called. I read what I had
prepared, and it seemed to give satisfaction, but I took notes
of sundry matters from them to be inserted. The blanks were,
however, still open. They promised to furnish these distances
from Mr. Ames. This was done after I had finished the composition, and the putting them in could not be done but clumsily.

I hastened to get over the business, expecting they would call soon, but night came without my hearing from them. I can not go out, and there is a listlessness in all our Pennsylvanians on this subject. I can think of many things which I would have done could I go about, which must now remain undone.

Wednesday, 16th.—To-morrow the bill for the permanent residence is to be taken up, and yet all is quiet on our part. Mr. Wynkoop told me he had walked a long time opposite Trinity Church with Mr. Clymer and Mr. Fitzsimons, and that they had spoken of me, and nothing more. He offered to do anything. I thought of Hartley. He is active, and will be in earnest. Mr. Wynkoop went for him. He came, and I put the paper in his hands. Mr. Wynkoop returned before the House met; told me Child was to print it, and they would send the proof-sheet to me for correction.

About two o'clock Mr. Morris, Mr. King, and Mr. Butler called on me. The talk was only about the judiciary. Mr. Morris said he had followed Elsworth in everything; if it was wrong, he would blame Elsworth. King said he had never had an opportunity of judging of it. I censured it as freely as ever.

There was a meeting of the Pennsylvania delegation this evening to regulate their conduct respecting the part they would act about the opening of the Susquehanna. They agreed to wait on Smith and Seney in the morning. I had begged Mr. Wynkoop that they should get the proof-sheet and correct it; but it is likely they would not send for it. The printer's boy, however, called on me and I corrected it. I can find that Germantown is the place that is to be played against the Susquehanna. I had hopes this opposition was dropped. I believe they are not as active as some days ago, but lie by fully bent to take all advantages. We will see what they will do. But I have laid it down as the only sure ground to adhere to the Susquehanna.

Thursday, 17th.—Some people are so hardy as to deny that the Susquehanna affords any navigation at all. Boudinot is one of them. It really would be of service to him if he could be made to blush. I wrote to Mr. Burrell to furnish an extract of the stores forwarded on the Susquehanna in the year 1779, and the usual load of a river boat. Mr. Wynkoop went to him with the letter. He said he would do what he could, but rather excused himself. I sent some information to Mr. Ames by Mr. Wynkoop, and now we must see what they will do.

The day is rainy and nobody has called. About dark Parson Lynn came in. Joy was in his countenance. He told me the Maryland condition was carried, and, of course, there would be schism among the Pennsylvanians; that Mr. Gerry had moved for the Falls of the Delaware instead of the Susquehanna. The whole of what he said convinced me that I was not in the least mistaken as to the measures they were carrying on. The Pennsylvanians will divide; the New England men and Yorkers both will come off with apparent honor, and Congress remain where it is. Late at night in comes Mr. Wynkoop, in higher spirits than ever I saw him. "It's all over with the Susquehanna. We must vote against it now. I have just come from Clymer and Fitzsimons's lodgings; they are of the same opinion; and now for the Falls of the Delaware. The Marylanders have carried a clause that Pennsylvania and Maryland shall consent, to the satisfaction of the resident, that the navigation of the Susquehanna shall be cleared, but not at their expense. We will never consent to lay our State under any restrictions." The only reply I made was: "So, then, rather than consent that the navigation of the Susquehanna should be open, you will drive Congress away from its banks. This is the point of view in which it will be considered, and in which you must expect to answer for it."

[September] 18th.—I wished to see some of our Pennsylvanians. Clymer and Fitzsimons had called a meeting last night in order to make them change their ground and vote for the Falls of the Delaware. This was the intention of the meeting, from what Wynkoop clearly enough expressed. I wrote a note to Hartley, but he came in just as I was sealing it. He was in a high rage at the Philadelphians, and declared they had been insincere from the beginning. He seemed to want my opinion. I gave it freely; to adhere firmly to the ground that had been taken, and support the bill at all events. I had written a note to the Speaker but he came in immediately after I had sent it away. He seemed clearly in sentiment with Hartley, and gave substantial reasons for it. He said an absolute agreement had been made between the Pennsylvanians on one part, and Smith and Seney, of Maryland, on the other, that the Maryland condition should not be "Pennsylvania would throw no impediment in the way of clearing the Susquehanna." This gave entire satisfaction to Smith and Seney; was to have been brought forward by the friends of the Susquehanna, and Smith and Seney by voting for it would have carried this and rejected the other Maryland condition.

But Mr. Fitzsimons broke the agreement and flew off yesterday morning. This, of course, fixed Smith and Seney to the exceptionable condition which was carried by means of their votes. So that it seems as if Mr. Fitzsimons wished some vote to be carried that would furnish him and others with a pretext for breaking off from the Susquehanna; for they could have prevented this Maryland condition if they had chosen so to do. He further said that his partner in Philadelphia mixes with all classes of people; that the common people were well satisfied with Congress being on the Susquehanna; but of late he could hear among the leading men about the bank, etc., many opinions and predictions that it never would be on the Susquehanna, etc. I think it no unfair conclusion to say that Philadelphia spite hath done this, although it be the act of but a few individuals in that place. I can now clearly account for the listlessness and apathy of some persons respecting the Susquehanna. Indeed, it is questionable whether the late application to me was anything more than a blind to cover their intended defection.

By this and yesterday's papers France seems travailing in the birth of freedom. Her throes and pangs of labor are violent. God give her a happy delivery! Royalty, nobility, and vile pageantry, by which a few of the human race lord it over and tread on the necks of their fellow-mortals, seem likely to be demolished with their kindred Bastile, which is said to be laid in ashes. Ye gods, with what indignation do I review the late attempt of some creatures among us to revive the vile machinery! O Adams, Adams, what a wretch art thou!

This evening the Speaker called. He repeated the whole of what he had told me in the morning in the presence of Mr. Wynkoop. Said he did not know what to make of men who agreed to a thing overnight and denied it in the morning. Fitzsimons and Clymer were tired of the Susquehanna, etc.

September 19th.—This morning Colonel Hartley's son called

on me with a note and showed the copy of a letter which the Colonel had written to Clymer and Fitzsimons. He called on them for an adherence to their former tenor of conduct respecting the Susquehanna, and plainly declared that their defection now would be considered as a proof of their insincerity from the beginning. I am unwilling there should be any schism among the Pennsylvania Representatives. Perhaps this letter may lay the foundation of it. Perhaps it may have the contrary effect at the present moment. It is, however, done without the advice of any person, and we are left to attend to the event. I have wished much to have seen Clymer and Fitzsimons for some days past. I dropped distant hints of this often to Mr. Wynkoop. This had no effect; I could not justify myself in sending for them. However, I know not if I could have any influence with them, and I know that Wynkoop carries faithfully every word which I say to them. Dr. Franklin says, "The world will do its own business." I must let it do so on this occasion, for my lame knees will not let me help it. Mr. Wynkoop left the House, came home, and went on a party of pleasure.

Had a note from Colonel Hartley. The permanent [residence] business is put off until Wednesday next on account of the indisposition of some of the members. The House, by a joint resolution with the Senate, are to break up on Tuesday. Appointing Wednesday [for the permanent residence business] seems like the oblivion committee in the British Parliament on the American petitions before the Revolution. But we will see what will come of it.*

In the evening Mr. Dalton called to see me. Soon after Mr. Morris and Mr. Fitzsimons came in. Soon after Mr. Scott and Parson Lynn. The Parson went away. Mr. Dalton went away. Mr. Scott said: "What shall we do with the residence? I believe we must vote for it." "I don't know," said Fitzsimons, "if the condition had only been *that we should not prevent the clearing of the Susquehanna,* I should not have cared." Scott said, "In fact, it amounts to no more now." "I don't know," said Fitzsimons. Mr. Morris said abruptly: "The contract is broken; we were to have this thing free of any condition. I have, however, a letter from Peters on this subject." He got out the letter,

---

* Hartley was mistaken when he wrote this note.

but did not read it. Mr. Scott was on his feet and went away. The others soon followed.

When Mr. Morris talked of the contract being broke, I asked: "Have any of the Eastern people given way? Have any of them voted against the Susquehanna?" Mr. Fitzsimons said none. I can readily guess what Mr. Morris means by saying the contract is broken. Need his vote be expected?

September 20th.—Being Sunday, I wrote letters to my family. The day was fine. I got a hackney-coach and rode out about an hour and a half; felt the worse for it. Perhaps it was only the fatigue. Colonel Hartley called in the morning; says the business of the permanent residence will come on to-morrow. Mr. Wyngate and General Irwin called to see me. Mr. Wyngate went yesterday evening to Newark; came home late. He soon asked me, "What news of the Federal residence?" I had no news on the subject. He talked himself a good deal on the subject. I thought I could clearly gather from what he said that the effort would be to throw off the whole business for this session, for, from what I can learn, they are not able to engage the New England men for the Delaware; therefore, postpone and wait for the chapter of chances.

Monday, 21st.—Dressed myself; weak and languid, but went to the Hall. Thought I would not be able to stay long, but when the business began I seemed amused and grew better. I stayed it out until after three o'clock. The judges' salaries were taken up. That of the Chief-Justice had been settled before at four thousand dollars; that of the *puisne* judges was put at three thousand dollars. Mr. Morris moved for five hundred dollars more, seconded by Izard; a division—nine to nine.

The Vice-President had to give the casting vote, and had the yeas and nays called on him. He, however, made a speech: "Somebody had said judges could be had for less. That people must be abandoned and forsaken by God who could speak of buying a judge as you would a horse. Judges should portion their children, bring them up, provide for them, etc. Many families in New England had suffered by the head of it being a judge." Motions were made for increasing everything almost. None, however, carried until they came to the Attorney-General. Mr. Morris moved it should be two thousand dollars. King seconded. A division—nine and nine; and the Vice-President voted for it. Wyngate called for the yeas and nays. Adams looked pitiful; said he would be made the scapegoat for everything. A member got up to have the yeas and nays retracted. Grayson, who had been with us before, spoke against having them now. So they were not called. The House of Representatives threw out this amendment, and it was reduced to fifteen hundred dollars.

Hartley called me out to tell me that the Susquehanna bill was carried [in the House of Representatives]. Mr. Morris was all day calling out members. Grayson, Gunn, King, Read, and Butler were some of them that I saw him take aside. The citizens and Wynkoop dared not vote against it. It would have had no effect if they had. Mr. Morris, being a six-years man, considers himself as independent, and he is to destroy it in the Senate. The others think to escape censure by this shift. But we know them. When I consider how agreeable it will be to the Eastern members and to the Yorkers to destroy all this business, I really fear Mr. Morris. It is so easy persuading men to do what they wish for. We must, however, wait the event.

September 22d.—Dressed and went to the Hall. Resolution came up from the other House rescinding the resolution of adjournment on this day and for adjournment on Saturday. Concurred. Bill for the permanent residence read the first time. Butler moved to postpone till next session. Seconded by Grayson. Lee, Butler, and Grayson spent about an hour. They had only Izard and Gunn to join them on this business—five in all. From hence, I think, we may prognosticate that the bill will pass in some shape or other. Mr. Morris in the deepest chagrin. Did not speak to me in the morning. Left his usual seat to avoid me. First went and sat beside Mr. Dalton, then rose and took out Mr. Read, came in again and went and took a seat beside Grayson; Bland called out Grayson; Mr. Morris followed; came in again and went and took a seat beside Elsworth. Never spoke until we were coming out of the Senate chamber. He then asked if I continued to grow better. I answered in the affirmative, but he could not talk to me.

I met Governor St. Clair at the Hall. If I had no better clew, I could tell how the Philadelphians stood by him. He was all

full of doubts; the bill would never do; the President would
never act on it; the river might not admit of navigation, etc.
The bill, however, passed, thirty-one to seventeen, in the House
of Representatives. Wynkoop can not sit with me this evening;
he is chatting down-stairs. Mr. Lynn called; told me the design
of the Virginians and the Carolina gentlemen was to talk away
the time, so that we could not get the bill passed.

September 23d.—Went to the Hall early. Mr. Carrol came
in; told me Mr. Morris was against the bill and wanted to
bring forward "Germantown" and the "Falls of the Delaware."
The Senate met, and every endeavor was made to waste time.
Lee, Butler, Grayson, refused to·go on with the business, as
Gunn was absent. Gunn came, and then they wanted to go
and see the balloon let off. But at last the bill was read over.
I was called out. There was Mr. Morris, Mr. Fitzsimons, and
Colonel Hartley. Fitzsimons began telling me what the Pennsylvanians had agreed to do. First, strike out the proviso clause.
If this could be done, then agree to the bill; but if this could
not be done, then abandon·the Susquehanna and try for the
Falls of the Delaware and Germantown. As he stated it to me,
I understood that all the Pennsylvanians but myself had agreed
to this. I told him it was a late moment to call on me when the
bill had actually been read over and the first clause taken up;
that the proviso had nothing so terrible in it as to make me
abandon the bill rather than consent to it; that I saw no safety
in anything but adhering to the bill, and if we lost the bill we
must go on to the Potomac.

Mr. Morris raged out something against the proviso, as to
the advantage the State would lose by such a proviso being
adopted, and concluded with a tremendous oath, "By God, I
never will vote for the bill unless the proviso is thrown out!"
I said, slowly, he would act as he pleased. He knows as well
as I do that the Senate never will reject the proviso. Fitzsimons and Morris, however, said, "Let us call King out."
King came. Fitzsimons said, "The Pennsylvania delegates were
against the proviso, and in case the proviso was continued, five
were for trying the Falls of the Delaware and Germantown."
Colonel Hartley corrected him and told him "only four." As
I had nothing to do with their bargain, I turned on my heel

and left them. I thought it strange conduct of our delegates, after they had all voted for the bill, to be making such offers. If the proviso is struck out, the two Marylanders will vote against us. If in, Mr. Morris has sworn he will vote against it. I have expected nothing else of him for some time.

Mr. Morris moved that the first and second clauses should be postponed, so as to come at the proviso. This brought on a lengthy debate. Butler was severe on Mr. Morris. Said his views were totally local. "Let us keep the Federal town on the Susquehanna, and let there be no navigation out of it, and then you must come to Philadelphia. But, rather than have the Susquehanna opened, which will take some of our trade away, we will not let you put the Federal town there." Morris replied with apparent heat. The other retorted. Grayson and Lee were both up. Izard was up, and long speeches were made. The question was, however, put and carried. And now Mr. Morris moved to strike out the proviso. I forgot who seconded him. The reason he gave was that the State of Pennsylvania had a bargain on hand with Maryland about this matter, and commissioners were appointed to negotiate it. Pennsylvania would suffer the Susquehanna to be opened if Maryland would suffer a canal to be dug between the bays of Chesapeake and Delaware; that he would be betraying the interest of the State in so eminent a degree that he dared not go home to Pennsylvania if such a clause was in the bill. I hinted to Mr. Morris that the last law for clearing the Susquehanna had no condition; but he answered the Marylanders thought it had. It was now that the most unbounded abuse was thrown on the State of Pennsylvania. Lee, Grayson, Butler, and Izard struggled who should be up to rail at the Government.

Mr. Carrol got up and answered Mr. Morris mildly. I whipped out and sent for Colonel Hartley and got from him the late law for clearing the Susquehanna. So great was the rage for speaking that I could scarce get a word said. I endeavored to be up first on the sitting down of Butler, but Lee was up with me. I begged for indulgence, as I had information to give which I thought very material. I stated the importance of the question, and declared it my duty to give all the information in my power; that the State of Pennsylvania deserved none of the illiberal abuse that had been bestowed on it; that no such design as shutting up the Susquehanna could be charged on the Government. I then read several clauses of the act declaring the Susquehanna and its branches highways to the Maryland line. I declared I did not think there was a single Pennsylvanian of character that could be so base as to wish the shutting up the mouth of that river; that for my part I considered the proviso as harmless, and if it tended to give satisfaction to the public at large or any individuals I had no objection to it; that I thought the business on the part of Pennsylvania done already; but if any more was wanted, I had no doubt of their doing it. I could for my part apprehend no danger from the proviso. Much, it was said, was put by it in the President's power; but he had his honor to support. I was convinced he would neither traffic with his own character nor the public expectation; and I was convinced no defect would be experienced on the part of the State of Pennsylvania.

The rage for speaking did not subside, but it took a different turn. Mr. Morris said he did not know of that law. The question, however, was put, and five only rose for rejecting the proviso— Morris, King, Schuyler, Johnson, and Dalton. There was now a cry for adjournment to see the balloon, and the Senate rose.

Mr. Clymer called about eight o'clock. Began to speak against the Susquehanna. Said there was an old interest and a new interest starting up to destroy it in Pennsylvania, by sending the trade into the new interest; that he would not for a thousand guineas the law would pass; that the old commercial interest had nourished Philadelphia; it was an ornament to the State. He seemed willing to persuade me that I should vote against the bill. I asked him how he thought it would look for me to vote against it when they had all voted for it on Monday last? He said he was induced to do so, expecting a change in the Senate; that he would not for half his estate he had done so; that he was duped into it. I told him that was not my case, for I had followed my judgment hitherto, and would continue to do so; that if we changed our ground in the Senate, and could insert any other place than the Susquehanna, we lost our hold of the Eastern people, and the whole fell to the ground, agreeable to what I had told him on Monday week, and that at the next session Virginia would come forward with five members from North Carolina, and be joined by two or three from Pennsylvania, and we should infallibly go to the Potomac— and, for my part, I would rather stay on the Susquehanna. He declared for his part he would not.

Mr. Clymer used to extol the advantages of the Susquehanna, and declared, as he sat at my bedside about a fortnight ago, that no position in Pennsylvania was equal to the Susquehanna. All this change has taken place since General Irwin came to town and declared there was a contract on foot for clearing the Conewago Falls for four thousand pounds. Now what am I to think of the citizens of Philadelphia and some others of the Pennsylvania delegation? Can I help concluding, on the most undeniable data, as well from what I have heard from circumstances and their own declarations, that they ever have been opposed to the Susquehanna, and voted for it purely to save their popularity in the State, and trusted to Morris, who is a six-years man, and who on all occasions despises the voice of the people, to destroy the bill in the Senate? Have I a name for such conduct? Thus barefacedly to drive away Congress from the State, rather than a few barrels of flour shall pass by the Philadelphia market in descending the Susquehanna, and rather than the inhabitants of this river should enjoy the natural advantages of opening the navigation of it! I think it probable these arts will prevail.

September 24th.—This day marked the perfidy of Mr. Morris in the most glaring colors. Notwithstanding his engagement entered into at the City Tavern, notwithstanding his promises repeated in many companies afterward, he openly voted against the Susquehanna. King, Schuyler, and all the New England men except Dr. Johnson, voted against it. Mr. Morris' vote alone would have fixed us on the Susquehanna forever. The affair has taken the very turn I predicted. Our ruin is plotted, contrived, and carried on in conjunction with the Yorkers. I gave an account of the center of population being in Pennsylvania—the center of wealth and the geographical center. Went at large into all the detail of the Potomac and the Susquehanna. When the Potomac was voted for, I was long on my legs—or

I shall say my knees—and they grew weary. We easily threw out the Potomac, but I well knew all this was in vain.

This whole morning and for half an hour after the Senate met, the York Senators and Representatives were in the committee room, and Mr. Morris running backward and forward, like a boy, taking out one Senator after another to them, and Adams delaying business for them. No business was ever treated with more barefaced partiality. Mr. Morris moved that the words "at some convenient place on the banks of the Susquehanna," etc., should be struck out, and that it might remain a blank for any gentleman that pleased to name a place. I objected to this as unfair, for by this means the banks of the Susquehanna would be thrown out, when in fact that place might have more friends than any other individual place, for all those who wished a different place would unite on this vote, however different their views might otherwise be; and thus the place rejected in the first instance would be laid under an unfavorable impression; that I saw no reason to deviate from the common mode, which had always been to move to strike out certain words in order to insert certain other words, and thus men would plainly see their way clear and the intention of the mover.

Mr. Adams answered me from the chair—said it was all fair. It was in vain to argue. The question was put, and seven only rose. Up got Mr. Morris; said the question was not understood, and began his explanations. He said he had often wished to explain himself on the subject of the residence, but was always prevented; that Pennsylvania was averse to the Susquehanna and would give one hundred thousand dollars to place it at Germantown. I rose to the point of order; declared that no motion or application for reconsideration could be received from a member "in the minority." Quoted parliamentary practice and appealed to the Chair. Mr. Adams now made one of his speeches. Unfortunately, it seems none of our rules reached the point. New matter had been alleged in argument, etc. It was in vain that I alleged that no business ever could have a decision if minority members were permitted to move reconsiderations under every pretense of new argument. Adams gave it against me.

Mr. Morris now assumed a bolder tone; flamed away in favor of Germantown; repeated his offers in the name of the State, etc. I declared I considered myself to enjoy the confidence of Pennsylvania in as unlimited a manner as my honorable colleague; that I firmly believed the general sense of the State was more in favor of the Susquehanna than Germantown, and that, if money was to be given, the Susquehanna was most likely to obtain it. I, however, denied that any State money was appropriated to any such purpose, and called on my colleague to produce the authority on which he made the offer. He now came forward, the great man and the merchant—pledged himself that, if the State would not, he would find the money.

A vacant stare, on this, seemed to occupy the faces of the Senate. But the New England men helped him out. It was proposed that the validity of the law should depend on the payment of the money, and that a clause for this purpose should now be inserted in the bill. And to work some of them went in fabricating such a clause. Mr. Morris had not yet been regularly seconded; but I began to see when it was too late that I had committed a mistake in not appealing to the House from the decision of the Chair.

Bassett got up and recanted; said he had not understood the question. This is usual with him. This man has repeatedly, of his own accord, told me that the Susquehanna was the only proper place. It was in vain that we urged that the question was fairly put. A reconsideration was called for. There is really such a thing as worrying weak or indifferent men into a vote. Urging that the matter had not been sufficiently explained and understood, how fair and inoffensive the measure, etc.—all these arts were played off with the utmost address on this occasion, and the weight of John Adams succeeded. It was reconsidered, and eleven voted for this "fair and inoffensive" measure.

In a moment, by way of fixing themselves against the Susquehanna, although it was still called, we will take a vote on the Susquehanna. The yeas and nays were called. And now Grayson and Lee moved for the Potomac. They had moved for striking out the word Pennsylvania so as to leave the whole banks of the Susquehanna open, and lost it. Now a most lengthy debate, in which I supported the Susquehanna; but it is too much to insert what I said. The Potomac lost it, and the blank now remained. Mr. Butler now rose and moved to fill the blank with the words "banks of Susquehanna," etc., the same words which had been struck out. I seconded the motion. Up got Mr. Morris and opposed this with warmth. He allowed that there might be a question taken on the Susquehanna, but he would have a vote taken on his place first. Butler insisted that, as his motion was fairly before the House and seconded, it must be disposed of. Morris replied without any reason on his side, indeed; but he had no need of reason when he had votes enough at hand. King got up and said he had no objection to a vote being taken on the Susquehanna, but it ought to be the last place. However, for the sake of order, they had to move a postponement of the motion on the Susquehanna. The postponement was carried.

Mr. Morris then came forward with an amendment for locating, ten miles square, adjoining the city of Philadelphia, in the counties of Philadelphia, Chester, and Bucks, including Germantown, with a proviso that the act should not be in force until one hundred thousand dollars should be secured to the United States by Pennsylvania, etc. I could not abandon the Susquehanna, at any rate in the present stage of the business; but for me to enter into a proviso which would operate as an engagement on the State without the least authority for so doing, appeared to me highly improper. I, therefore, under every view of the matter, concluded in a moment to vote against the motion.

The Susquehanna bill placed the Federal town in the heart of Pennsylvania, provided for purchasing the land, erecting buildings, etc., without one farthing expense to the State, to say nothing of the most important object of clearing the Susquehanna, which would be done by Federal and Maryland money, in case of Congress being placed on its banks. I therefore reserved my vote for the Susquehanna. The House divided on Mr. Morris' motion—nine and nine. The President rose to give the casting vote. He spoke well of the Potomac (to gratify the Virginians), slightly of the Susquehanna (which had but few friends), highly of Philadelphia and New York, in each of which places, he said, Congress ought to stay alternately four years at a time; said if the question were to reject the whole business, he could have no doubt, but, as Pennsylvania had offered the money, he would vote for Germantown. Thus fell our hopes. This unwarranted offer of money knocked down the Susquehanna. It was now near four o'clock, and an adjournment was called for and took place.

September 25th.—A good deal unwell, but attended the Hall. The Secretary had omitted the first question on the striking out of the Susquehanna and the reconsideration. He, however, corrected it himself afterward, with the leave of the House. The affair of one Brown Glassbrock took up some time, but was postponed. Carrol now moved to strike out the residence being in New York until the Federal building should be erected. I determined to leave myself free from any obligation to stay in New York, and voted with him, more especially as I was free from all obligation whatever. Mr. Morris now began to dress the bill, but seemed slack about the one hundred thousand dollars. He was called on from the Chair, however, and sundry parts of the House to bring it forward. I was very unwell, and left him to dress his own child as he pleased, and came home.

This evening Mr. Scott called to see me. He said Mr. Morris, Mr. Clymer, and Mr. Fitzsimons assured him that the Yorkers and the New England men would pass the bill, and that the Pennsylvanians, Mr. Clymer and Mr. Fitzsimons had promised that Congress should stay three years in New York. Mr. Wynkoop then said that they had made such a bargain. I told them that was the first account I had heard of the matter. I expressed my doubts of their sincerity. Wynkoop was sure of them, and that he could depend on them, etc.

September 26th.—Very unwell this day, but dressed and went to the Hall. Sat some time. The Appropriation bill was taken up. And now Colonel Schuyler brought forward an account of eight thousand dollars expended by Mr. Osgood in repairing and furnishing at the house which the President lives in. This was a great surprise to me, although a vote had originated in the House of Representatives for furnishing the house, yet I considered that allowance for all this had been made in the President's salary. I was, however, taken so unwell that I had to come home.

When I first went into the Senate chamber this morning, the Vice-President, Elsworth, and Ames stood together, railing against the vote of adherence in the House of Representatives on throwing out the words "the President" in the beginning of the Federal writs. I really thought them wrong, but, as they seemed very opinionated, I did not contradict them. This is only a part of their old system of giving the President as far as possible every appendage of royalty. The original reason of the English writs running in the King's name was his being personally in court, and English jurisprudence still supposes him to be so. But with us it seems rather confounding the executive and judicial branches. Ames left them, and they seemed rather to advance afterward. Said the President, personally, was not the subject to any process whatever; could have no action whatever brought against him; was above the power of all judges, justices, etc. For what, said they, would you put it in the power of a common justice to exercise any authority over him and stop the whole machine of Government? I said that, although President, he is not above the laws. Both of them declared you could only impeach him, and no other process whatever lay against him.

I put the case: "Suppose the President committed murder in the street. Impeach him? But you can only remove him from office on impeachment. Why, when he is no longer President you can indict him. But in the mean time he runs away. But I will put up another case. Suppose he continues his murders daily, and neither House is sitting to impeach him. Oh, the people would rise and restrain him. Very well, you will allow the mob to do what legal justice must abstain from." Mr. Adams said I was arguing from cases nearly impossible. There had been some hundreds of crowned heads within these two centuries in Europe, and there was no instance of any of them having committed murder. Very true, in the retail way, Charles IX of France excepted. They generally do these things on a great scale. I am, however, certainly within the bounds of possibility, though it may be improbable. General Schuyler joined

us. "What think you, General?" said I, by way of giving the
matter a different turn. "I am not a good civilian, but I think
the President a kind of sacred person." Bravo, my *"jure divino"*
man! Not a word of the above is worth minuting, but it shows
clearly how amazingly fond of the old leaven many people are.
I needed no index, however, of this kind with respect to John
Adams.

September 27th.—Being Sunday and a very stormy day, I
stayed at home all day. Did nothing but write letters to my
family. Exceedingly tired of this place, but the day of my
departure draws nigh, and I am much better than I have been,
and hope I shall be able to travel well enough. Saw no person
whatever save Mr. Wynkoop, who returned from an excursion
he made over the river.

September 28th.—Felt pretty well in the morning. Dressed
and went to the Hall; sat a little while, but had to get up and
walk in the machinery-room. Viewed the pendulum mill—a
model of which stands there. It really seems adapted to do
business. Returned and sat awhile with the Senate, but retired
and came home to my lodgings. Sincerely hope an adjournment will take place to-morrow. The pay list is making out,
which seems likely to finish the business. Left the old acts of
Congress, in thirteen volumes, with Mr. Vandalsen, and one
small writing-desk.

Mr. Wynkoop came in in the highest joy. All was well.
Germantown—happy Germantown—has got the Congress! He
ravished up his dinner, got his trunk and boots, and away with
him to tell the glorious news. I can not help having a despicable opinion of this man. It would not be easy to find a more
useless member. He never speaks, never acts in Congress, but
implicitly follows the two city members. He does not seem
formed to act alone even in the most trifling affair. Well it is
for him that he is not a woman and handsome, or every fellow
would debauch him.

I have just been thinking how impossible it is for the Yorkers
to be so blind as to let Congress go away in the manner Wynkoop says they have done. If the lower House have really passed
the bill, the Yorkers have no resource but in the President. I
am greatly surprised at this day's work. I have opened the book

and taken up my pen to wipe away all the surprise above mentioned. Parson Lynn has just told me that some trifling amendment was tacked to the bill, just sufficient to send it up to the Senate, and the Senate have thrown it out; and with the consent of the Philadelphians, too, I suppose.

Just as I was leaving the Hall, Izard took me aside, asked me to stay; said a trifling amendment will be made in the lower House, just enough to bring it up here, and we will throw it out. I told him I wished nothing so much as to see an end of the business. I was not able to attend, but, if I was, could not be with him on this question. Well, then you must not tell Morris of this. I was just going away, and said I will not.

[*September*] *29th.*—Came to the Hall. Saw Mr. Morris. I did not envy him his feelings. I might be mistaken, but he looked as if he feared me. I determined not to say a word to him save the salutation of good-morning, which passed mutually between us. To praise his management was impossible, and I really felt such contempt for his conduct as placed me far above the thoughts of any reproaches. He came to me after some time and desired me to walk into the committee-room. He there told me that Grayson would be absent on account of his health; that Dr. Johnson had said he would be absent, and now let us play the Yorkers a trick. Let us call a reconsideration, and perhaps we may carry it. I objected to that mode of doing business; and, besides, counted the votes and showed him that the attempt was vain, even if John Adams was in favor of the bill, which we well knew he was not. In the mean time, White and Dr. Johnson came in. By way of concluding the business of the *tête-à-tête*, I said there was no better method than leaving the business with a philosophic face. We returned to the Senate, and I have my doubts whether he meant anything more than an essay to talk me into good humor, on a supposition that I was soured at his conduct.

I could not sit in the Senate; came out and reclined as well as I could in the little committee-room. Elsworth came out in a little time. I asked him if the business was got through in the Senate. He said yes. I then went to the treasury, drew my pay, discharged my lodgings, took a place in the stage, and set off for Philadelphia.

PART TWO:

SECOND SESSION

OF THE FIRST CONGRESS

CHAPTER V

January 5th [*1790*].—Arrived at New York late on the 5th and went to lodge at the same house with the Speaker of the House of Representatives and Peter Muhlenberg, his brother, at Dr. Kuntz's.

[*January*] *6th.*—Attended at the Hall, and my presence completed a quorum. A letter from the President of the United States was received, desiring to be informed of the time a quorum would be formed, etc. Was committed to Izard and Strong. Nothing else of any consequence. Adjourned.

[*January*] *7th.*—Attended as usual. When the minutes were read, Mr. King rose and made a motion to amend the journals of yesterday with respect to the President's letter by striking out all that part and inserting a clause which he held in his hand. I saw the thing was preconcerted, and therefore did not choose to waste time. The thing was done, though contrary to all rule. Strong and Dalton moved to have the word "honorable" struck out from before the names of the members. Lost. Motion for leave to protest by Butler not seconded.

Strong and Izard reported that the President would attend in the Senate chamber at eleven o'clock to-morrow. A resolution of the Representatives for appointing of a chaplain was concurred in, and the Bishop appointed on the part of the Senate.

This day, at and after dinner, I thought uncommon pains were taken to draw from me some information as to the part I would act respecting the Federal residence. The whole world is a shell, and we tread on hollow ground at every step. I repeatedly said, I have marked out no ground for myself. My object shall be the interest of Pennsylvania, subordinate to the good of the Union. Mr. Wynkoop called in the evening. He was directly on the subject of the permanent residence. The

169

Susquehanna must never be thought of. He repeated this sentiment more than once. To have been silent would have implied consent to it. I said, for my part, I should think of the Susquehanna, and I considered Mr. Morris' conduct in destroying the bill for that place as the greatest political misfortune that ever befell that State.

January 8th.—All this morning nothing but bustle about the Senate chamber in hauling chairs and removing tables. The President was dressed in a second mourning, and read his speech well. The Senate, headed by their Vice-President, were on his right. The House of Representatives, with their Speaker, were on his left. His family with the heads of departments attended. The business was soon over and the Senate were left alone. The speech was committed rather too hastily, as Mr. Butler thought, who made some remarks on it, and was called to order by the Chair. He resented the call, and some altercation ensued. Adjourned till Monday.

January 9th.—Spent this forenoon in paying visits, and in the afternoon wrote to my family.

January 10th.—Being Sunday, stayed at home all day, as it was very cold. Read, etc. The Speaker told me this day what I have been no stranger to for a considerable time past; that a certain set in Philadelphia were determined to have me out of the Senate; that Armstrong was brought forward for that purpose, etc. A small concern, indeed, and I am happy that it did not hurt me.

January 11th.—The Senate received from General Knox the proceedings of the commissioners on the embassy to the Southern Indians. A considerable part of the day spent in reading them. 'Tis a spoiled piece of business; and, by way of justification of their conduct in not having made peace, they seem disposed to precipitate the United States into war; the not uncommon fruits of employing military men. This, however, is but my first idea of the business. Wish I may have occasion to alter it. Mr. Lear brought in a ratification from the State of North Carolina, or rather a copy of it, from the President.

And now the committee reported an answer to the President's speech. The most servile echo I ever heard. There was, however, no mending it. One part of it seemed like pledging the Senate to pay the whole amount of the public debt. This was, however, altered. Many of the clauses were passed, without either aye or no, in silent disapprobation. I told both King and Patterson that I had never heard so good an echo, for it repeated all the words entire. They both denied that they had anything to do with it, and said it was Izard's work.

January 12th.—Visited from breakfast-time to eleven with the Speaker and General Muhlenberg. On reading the minutes it was plain that our Secretary had neither system nor integrity in keeping the journal. It is not, however, worth while to blot paper with his blunders. In now came General Knox with a bundle of communications. I thought the act was a mad one, when a Secretary of War was appointed in time of peace. I can not blame him. The man wants to labor in his vocation. Here is a fine scheme on paper: To raise 5,040 officers, non-commissioned officers, and privates, at the charge of $1,152,000 for a year, to go to war with the Creeks because the commissioners, being ignorant of Indian affairs, failed of making a treaty after having spent $15,000 to no manner of purpose. But we will see what will become of it.

I made an unsuccessful motion when it was proposed that the whole Senate should wait on the President with answer to the speech. First I wished for delay, that we might see the conduct adopted by the House of Representatives. I thought it likely they would do the business by a committee. In that case I wished to imitate them; and as a committee with us had done all the business so far, I wished it to continue in their hands, that they might have exclusively all the *honors attendant on the performance;* that I, as a republican, ·was, however, opposed to the whole business of echoing speeches. It was a stale ministerial trick in Britain to get the Houses of Parliament to chime in with the speech, and then consider them as pledged to support any measure which could be grafted on the speech. It was the Socratic mode of argument introduced into politics to entrap men into measures they were not aware of. I wished to treat the speech in quite a different manner. I would commit it for the purposes of examining whether the subjects recommended in it were proper for the Senate to act upon. If they were found to be so, I would have committees appointed to bring forward the necessary bills. But we seem to neglect the useful and content ourselves with compliments only, and dangerous ones, too. But for my part I would not consider myself as committed by anything contained in the answer.

January 13th.—This was a day of small importance in the Senate. Mr. Hawkins, a Senator from North Carolina, took his seat. The silliest kind of application came from our Vice-President that the Senate should direct him to sign some bills for furniture got for Mr. Otis. I opposed it, as I know Otis. There is, in all probability, some roguery in it. It was, however, dropped, and the Senate, after sitting idle for a considerable time, adjourned.

January 14th.—This was the day devoted to ceremony by both Houses of Congress. At eleven o'clock the Senate attended at the President's to deliver their answer. At twelve o'clock the House of Representatives attended. It is not worth while minuting a word about it. We went in coaches. Got our answer, which was short. Returned in coaches. Sauntered an hour in the Senate chamber and adjourned. Every error in government will work its own remedy among a free people. I think both Senators and Representatives are tired of making themselves the gazing-stock of the crowd and the subject of remark by the sycophantic circle that surround the President in stringing to his quarters; and I trust the next session will either do without this business altogether, or do it by a small committee that need not interrupt the business of either House. I have aimed at this point all along. It is evident from the President's speech that he wishes everything to fall into the British mode of business. "I have directed the proper officers to lay before you," etc. Compliments for him and business for them. He is but a man, but really a good one, and we can have nothing to fear from him, but much from the precedents he may establish.

Dined this day with the President. It was a great dinner— all in the taste of high life. I considered it as a part of my duty as a Senator to submit to it, and am glad it is over. The President is a cold, formal man; but I must declare that he treated me with great attention. I was the first person with whom he drank a glass of wine. I was often spoken to by him. Yet he

knows how rigid a republican I am. I can not think that he
considers it worth while to soften me. It is not worth his while.
I am not an object if he should gain me, and I trust he can not
do it by any improper means.

This day the "budget," as it is called, was opened in the
House of Representatives. An extraordinary rise of certificates * has been remarked for some time past. This could not
be accounted for, neither in Philadelphia nor elsewhere. But
the report from the Treasury explained all. He [Secretary Ham-
ilton] recommends indiscriminate funding, and, in the style
of a British minister, has sent down his bill. 'Tis said a committee of speculators in certificates could not have formed it
more for their advantage. It has occasioned many serious faces.
I feel so struck of an heap, I can make no remark on the matter.

January 15th.—Attended at the Hall. A committee was appointed to bring in a bill for extending the judiciary of the
United States to North Carolina, and the Senate adjourned.
The business of yesterday [recommendation for funding certificates of the public debt] will, I think in all probability,
damn the character of Hamilton as a minister forever. It appears that a system of speculation for the engrossing certificates has been carrying on for some time. Whispers of this kind
come from every quarter. Dr. Elmer told me that Mr. Morris
must be deep in it, for his partner, Mr. Constable, of this place,
had one contract for forty thousand dollars' worth. The Speaker
hinted to me that General Heister had brought over a sum of
money from Mr. Morris for this business; he said the Boston
people were concerned in it. Indeed, there is no room to doubt
but a connection is spread over the whole continent on this
villainous business. I pray God they may not prosper.

I walked out this evening. I call not at a single house or go
into any company but traces of speculation in certificates appear.
Mr. Langdon, the old and intimate friend of Mr. Morris, lodges

---

* These were certificates of the public debt, which were issued in place
of the paper money of the old Congress, and bore interest for their face
value. They had depreciated to twenty, fifteen, twelve, and even as low as
seven cents on the dollar. It was the plan of speculators to get Congress
to redeem these certificates of the public debt at their face value, so for
what they bought at seven or fifteen cents on a dollar they would realize
a dollar on the dollar.

with Mr. Hazard. Mr. Hazard has followed buying certificates for some time past. He told me he had made a business of it; it is easy to guess for whom. I told him, "You are, then, among the happy few who have been let into the secret." He seemed abashed, and I checked by my forwardness much more information which he seemed disposed to give.

The Speaker gives me this day his opinion that Mr. Fitzsimons was concerned in this business as well as Mr. Morris, and that they stayed away [from Congress] for the double purpose of pursuing their speculation and remaining unsuspected. I have one criticism with respect to Mr. Fitzsimons. I have heretofore heard him declare himself in the most unequivocal manner in favor of a discrimination.* Mark the event.

January 16th.—As the Senate stood adjourned over to Monday, I had nothing to do, and stayed at home all day. Wrote letters to my family. The speculations in certificates in the mouth of every one.

January 17th.—Being Sunday, stayed at home all day. Have a return of the rheumatism; am afraid that the cold bath has hurt me; believe I had better abstain from it for a while. I have attended in the minutest manner to the motions of Hamilton and the Yorkers. Sincerity is not with them. They never will consent to part with Congress. Advances to them are vain. One session or two more here will fix us irremovably. We can move from here only by means of the Virginians. The fact is indubitable. I could write a little volume to illustrate it. Buckley is very intimate with the Speaker on one hand and Madison on the other. I can, through this channel, communicate what I please to Madison; and I think I know him. But if he is led, it must be without letting him know that he is so; in other words, he must not see the string.

January 18th.—Attended at the Hall at the usual time. The Senate met, but there was no business before them, and adjourned. Hawkins, of North Carolina, said as he came up he passed two expresses with very large sums of money on their way to North Carolina for purposes of speculation in certificates. Wadsworth has sent off two small vessels for the

* Not to pay the face value of all the certificates, but to grade the payment in proportion to their depreciations.

Southern States, on the errand of buying up certificates. I really fear the members of Congress are deeper in this business than any others. Nobody doubts but all commotion originated from the Treasury; but the fault is laid on Duer but *respondent superior*.

January 19, 1790.—Senate met at the usual hour. I had observed Elsworth busy for some time. There had been some intercourse between him and Izard. He rose with a motion in his hand which he read in his place. The amount of it was that a committee should be appointed to bring in a bill defining crimes and punishments under the Federal judiciary. He did not affect to conceal that a bill of this nature had been left pending before the Representatives at the end of the last session, but declared he wished to settle an important point in practice: "whether all business should not originate *de novo* with every session." He then labored long to show that this was a new session, and concluded, as the session was new, everything else should be new. Mr. Izard seconded him in a speech which I thought contained nothing new.

Bassett got up and declared that he had just taken his seat; that everything was new to him; that he could not determine in such haste, and moved a postponement. I rose, seconded Bassett, and gave as additional reasons that the matter had been acknowledged to be of great importance; that I therefore trusted it would not be gone into with so thin a representation of the Southern States; that the most respectable State was not represented at all; that I thought it improper to attempt deciding on a matter which would go to regulate the future proceedings of Congress in both Houses, as it would be fixing a precedent without some communication with the House of Representatives; that they had appointed a committee to bring forward the unfinished business which had a very different appearance from being *de novo*. Gentlemen had argued much to show this was a new session. But granting this, I could not see that the inference they wished to draw from it would follow. They need not fear a deficiency of business. There would be enough to do without rejecting the progress we had made in the former session, etc., for I was up a good while.

King got up. He labored to support Elsworth, and to show

from parliamentary proceedings that new sessions originated new business after every prorogation of Parliament. He was long. I rose, however, and took him on his own ground with regard to the prorogation of Parliaments; showed that it was a prerogative of the Crown to prorogue the Parliament; that the British Crown generally exercised this power when the Parliament was on what was considered as forbidden ground; that the Parliaments were forced into this mode of procedure, for when any Parliament had been prorogued for handling disagreeable subjects, to attempt to take them up in the same stage would inevitably be followed by the same fate. They were, therefore, obliged to begin de novo, at least with every subject the least disagreeable to the court; and, indeed, it was the best policy to begin all de novo, thus affecting to conceal their knowledge of the offensive subjects. But these were reasons of conduct which had no existence here. The President had no proroguing power. He could not check our deliberations. I had no objection to adopt rules similar to those of the Parliament of Great Britain when they would apply—not because they were in use there, but on the principle of their utility. But when a direct inconvenience attended them, as in the present case, where the deliberations of the former session on the subject before us would be lost, they ought to be rejected with scorn.

Elsworth found it would go against him. He then moved the postponement should be until to-morrow. It was lost. Moved it should be to Monday. It was lost. General postponement took place. Wyngate now rose and made a singular motion. It was that the bills formerly before the Senate for regulating the process in the Federal courts should be taken up. A pause ensued, as this was certainly unfinished business of the former session, the bill in question having been postponed on the bringing forward a temporary law. Langdon said he would have seconded the gentleman, but he considered this bill as involved in the matter which had just been postponed. Elsworth, who sometimes contradicts Langdon for the sake of contradiction, said it was not involved in it, and seconded Wyngate for bringing it on, and it was brought. The Secretary served the members of the Senate with copies of it. Wyngate put it into the hands of the Vice-President, and he read it all over, and was returning to the first paragraph, when Elsworth, finding where he was, got up, said his intention was to second the gentleman to have a committee appointed to bring in a bill for regulating processes, etc. Adams attended to him, and, without any question how to get rid of the bill, Adams put a question for a committee, and a committee was accordingly appointed. And now we will see what a figure Otis will make of the minutes in the morning. I do not want to be captious, but I must not let them draw this into precedent.

January 20th.—I am not disappointed in Otis. Every word respecting the bill was suppressed. In journals read this morning the entry stood, "Ordered that Mr. King, Mr. Strong, etc., be a committee to report a bill to regulate processes, etc." It would have been considered as manifesting a spirit of contention if I had attacked the minutes, and I let it pass, but if they endeavor to make any use of it I will then be at liberty to act and make the most of circumstances. I came early to the Senate chamber, but found our Vice-President and Elsworth both there before me. I concluded that they had come on the errand of making or correcting the journals, so as to cover Elsworth's hairbreadth escape of yesterday. They were in close consultation. I passed them, and took no further notice. Izard, Few, and Schuyler were all in conference with Elsworth.

The minutes were no sooner finished than Elsworth rose and called for the motion of yesterday, and made a speech in support of his motion. It could not be said to be very long, though he said a great deal. "To do business," "to prevent idleness," "to satisfy their constituents," "to prevent loss of time," etc., were the subjects of it.

I began with declaring that the gentleman's ardor to do business was highly laudable, but there was such a thing as making more haste than good speed; that if economy and to prevent loss of time were his objects, I thought he missed the mark by attempting to take up everything *de novo,* for thus all the time spent on the unfinished business in the former session would be lost; that I thought the present motion scarce in order. It had been moved yesterday that the motion should be taken up this day and negatived. Monday next had also been negatived. But there was a reason of much more consequence, which, though it had occurred to me yesterday, I had forborne to mention; but had since inquired of sundry members of the House of Representatives, and was assured that the very bill in question was reported by the committee for unfinished business, and the report remained on the Speaker's table unacted upon; that for us to decide on a business actually before the Representatives, I considered as highly improper, and would not fail of giving offense.

After I had done speaking I left the Senate chamber, came down-stairs, called on General Muhlenberg, gave notice by him to the Speaker how much I wanted the report of the committee. Mr. Buckley was good enough to send up by the doorkeeper the original report. I got it; found the bill reported as I had mentioned. Returned and read in my place the part I had alluded to. The affair now took a new turn, and a motion was made to appoint a committee to confer on the subject with a committee of the other House. I rose and enforced this with all the energy I was master of. It was carried, and the committee were Langdon, Henry, and myself. The Yorkers lost countenance when they saw the committee, but now they brought forward a curious motion. It was to take the sense of the Senate, in order that it might stand as a rule of conduct for the committee.

I rose against this with all my might. I have not time to set down my arguments; they are obvious. Several followed me. I had, however, concluded with a motion for postponement, which was seconded. They saw how it would go, and withdrew their motion. I consider Mr. Morris as highly blameworthy in his non-attendance [at the Senate]. He expects that the bill will be destroyed, and he wishes it may be done in his absence, that the blame may be laid on me by the citizens of Philadelphia. I wish that I could believe him incapable of this kind of conduct. I have, however, kept its head above water so far.

January 21st.—I am disappointed (strange, but can not help it) in the committee. It is Elsworth, myself, and Henry, and Henry has recanted; told me he would be of the same opinion with Elsworth. Mr. Morris took his seat this day. He took pains, pointedly, to be against me on a motion which [was] offered to the Chair; that we should take only two of the many [news] papers which are published here. It is in vain. All confidence between him and me is at an end. There, indeed, never was any between me and any of the Philadelphians.* I must look to myself and do my own conscience justice, and act independent. The Muhlenbergs are friendly, and they will be my company. The members of the committee on the part of the Representatives are Sherman, Thatcher, Hartley, Jackson, and White, to meet to-morrow at ten o'clock.

January 22d.—I met the committee a few minutes after ten. Elsworth began a long discourse, and concluded for all business which had passed between the Houses to begin *de novo.* He, Jackson, and White had much parliamentary stuff; but Hartley had some books, and the precedents were undoubtedly against them. Elsworth made room for Henry to speak by desiring him, in plain words, to do so, from which it was plain enough that they had communicated. He seemed willing that I should not speak; I, however, made way for myself, and reprobated every idea of precedent drawn from England, though I declared if notice were to be taken of them I thought they were made for us. I read from the journals the postponement of the bill, which I told them plainly had given rise to the present contest. On motion that the further consideration of the bill be *postponed to the next session of Congress,* it passed in the affirmative.

By the minutes on the journals, the bill must be taken up in the present session. Any proceeding of a contrary nature must depend on an *ex post facto* principle. We may enter into rules for the future government of our conduct, but the past is out of our power, constitutionally speaking. The general practice of all the Legislatures is in favor of taking up the unfinished business in the state it was left. So far is this from being considered as improper, that the Constitutions of some of the States enjoin it as a principle that no bill, unless in case of necessity, shall be enacted into a law in the same session in which it is originated. It is the common practice in all the arrangements of life. It stands highly recommended by economy, which is certainly a republican virtue. I considered it undeniably certain that a particular fact had given rise to this whole business. Here, then, to control a single incident, we are attempting

---

* William Maclay representing western Pennsylvania.

to establish a general rule. This is inverting the general order of business with a witness; and, to get rid of a particular bill, must involve ourselves in perpetual inconvenience.

Mr. White alleged the opinion was not new. I appealed to the minutes of both Houses where bills had been postponed to this session—in the Senate, the bill for the permanent residence; in the chamber of Representatives, the bills on crimes and punishments. It was in vain to argue. The vote went against us, and a report agreed to that the bills which had been in passage between the two Houses should be regarded as if nothing had passed in either respecting them, or words to amount to that. After the report was made in the Senate, our Vice-President wanted us to proceed immediately on it. I moved some delay, and it was postponed to Monday.

January 23d, Saturday.—This a most delightful day. There was no Senate, and as the trifling business of visiting must be got over, I set about it in good earnest. The Speaker, General Muhlenberg, and General Heister were the party with myself. We run off most of the business, and of course have nearly done with it. There was something happened to me lately which I will not minute, but let it serve as a caution to me to observe as much as possible independence of character and conduct. This is a vile world when a man must walk among his friends and fellow-mortals as if they were briers and thorns; afraid to touch or be touched by them. And yet the older I grow the more I see the necessity of it.

January 24th, Sunday.—This was a dull day every way. A small snow fell all day, and melted as it fell on the pavement. The ground whitened toward evening. 'Twas such a day as I have seen early in April, when the robins first come, and the southwest winds labor to push back the chilling air of the northeast. I stayed at home all day and wrote letters to my family. I now proposed the scheme of their writing to me every Sunday, that thus each party might act under the sentiment of reciprocity and enjoy the pleasing sensation that, while they were writing to and thinking of the object of their most tender affection, the beloved object was employed in the same sympathetic correspondence, and that our kindred hearts and affections beat unisons at the same instant, though separated as far as New York and Harrisburg.

January 25th.—The Senate met, and the Vice-President informed the House of the order of the day, to take up the report of the joint committee. I rose and observed that I saw many empty seats; the Senate was thin. I therefore wished for a little delay until the members were collected. After the House filled, the business was entered on. Mr. Morris showed a disinclination to rise. Mr. Bassett was up, and after he sat down I hinted to Mr. Morris a point that I thought might be proper in support of Bassett. I said he had better rise; if he did not, I would. He said he thought *I had better not.* I thought his conduct mysterious, though perhaps I was wrong. I rose, however, and one word brought on another. All the arguments of the committee were had over again, much enlarged and amplified. I was four times up in all; for the last two times I asked leave. I really thought I had the advantage over both Elsworth and Henry, but when is it that I do not think well of my own arguments? I found that I had made some impression on Izard. He was up, and concluded with saying something that seemed like a wish for further time to deliberate. I rose; said I considered what the honorable gentleman had said as amounting to a motion for postponement, and I begged leave to second him. He said he wished it postponed.

But now Patterson rose on our side, but he displeased Izard, and the question on the postponement was put; but we lost it after I had been twice up. But it was all in vain. Cicero, with all the powers of Apollo, could not have turned the vote in our favor. I had a small scheme in protracting the time until the other House would break up, that the example of our House might not add any weight to their scale of [the] deliberation; and I hoped that in the mean time they might, perhaps, pass on the business. Mr. Morris stuck fast to his seat, nor did he rise or say a word during the whole time. Eight voted for us and ten against us. The yeas and nays were called. The vote was hurried down into the chamber of the Representatives, and they adopted it almost without a division.

January 26th.—This a most unimportant day in the Senate.

A committee was moved for to bring in a bill for the ascertaining crimes and punishments under the Federal Legislature. The committee were appointed, withdrew for a few moments into the Secretary's office, returned with the *old bill* which had been before us last session, and reported it. This was really ridiculous, but the vote of yesterday seemed to call for it. Butler moved that a letter from some foreigner should be sent to the chamber of Representatives. The letter had been read formerly, but in so low a voice that I could not tell a word of it. It was not read now. Mr. Morris left his seat and went and looked at it; came back and said nothing about it. I was silent on Butler's motion. But when I came home, the Speaker immediately attacked me for the absurdity of our conduct in sending them a letter of much importance, touching proposals of a treaty with the republic of Genoa. I really knew nothing of the letter, but it was my own fault; and it really ought to be a lesson to me and every Senator to attend well to what is done at our Chair. There is really no dependence to be placed neither on our Vice-President nor Secretary.

January 27th.—The bill of yesterday was read by paragraphs. It was curious to see the whole Senate sitting silent and smiling at each other, and not a word of remark made or making on the bill. Elsworth rose to inform the Senate that it was the bill which had been gone through all the forms in the last session. Strong moved an amendment, however, that the judges should issue the warrants for execution of criminals. I rose and showed from the Constitution that the President of the United States had the power of granting pardons in all cases except those of impeachment; that by the judges taking on them to issue the warrants, the opportunity of his granting pardons was taken away. Elsworth, according to custom, supported his bill through thick and thin. There was a great deal said, and I was up three or four times. I moved a postponement of the clause, and it was carried.

Hawkins, the new member from North Carolina, rose and objected to the clause respecting the benefit of clergy. He was not very clear. I, however, rose—really from motives of friendship. I will not say compassion, for a stranger. I stated that, as far as I could collect the sentiments of the honorable gentle-

of Virginia. Madison and Buckley govern them. Madison's mark is the Treasury; to be our Secretary is Buckley's bait. The changes would be great political amendments.

February 1st.—This was an unimportant day in the Senate. The North Carolina members produced an act of session, which was committed. But Mr. Ellicott sent in for me, and I chatted with him in the committee-room until the Senate was about to adjourn, which was early. Mr. Hamilton is very uneasy, as far as I can learn, about his funding system. He was here early to wait on the Speaker, and I believe spent most of his time in running from place to place among the members.

Mr. Ellicott's accounts of Niagara Falls are amazing indeed. I communicated to him my scheme of an attempt to account for the age of the world, or at least to fix the period when the water began to cut the ledge of rock over which it falls. The distance from the present pitch to where the falls originally were, is now seven miles. For this space a tremendous channel is cut in a solid limestone rock, in all parts one hundred and fifty feet deep, but near two hundred and fifty at the mouth or part where the attrition began. People who have known the place since Sir William Johnson took possession of it, about thirty years ago, give out that there is an attrition of twenty feet in that time. Now, if 20 feet = 30 years = 7 miles, or 36,-960 feet; answer, 55,440 years.

February 2d.—This an unimportant day, and remarkable for nothing so much as the submission of Mr. A. Brown, of Philadelphia, printer, to the Secretary of the Treasury, who acknowledges the receipt of sundry news against the Secretary's report, but *conceives* the Secretary has refuted every argument, etc., and will publish nothing against him. This wretch is here looking for an office, and the public will certainly believe that Hamilton has bought him. These acknowledgments appeared in Mr. Lear's paper. Hard to say which is the baser creature, the buyer or seller.

February 3d.—This day nothing of importance was transacted in Senate, and the House adjourned early. The Speaker and General Muhlenberg made a point of my going with them to dine with Mr. Fitzsimons and Clymer. I would not go until they declared that they had authority to invite me. I went. The company were Pennsylvanians. No discourse happened until after the bottle had circulated pretty freely. Mr. Scott joined us. He declared it was in vain to think of any place but the Potomac. Mr. Wynkoop declared the utmost readiness to go to the Potomac. Mr. Fitzsimons seemed to bark in for some time. Clymer declared, over and over, he was ready to go to the Potomac. After some time I spoke most decidedly and plainly. I will not go to the Potomac. If we once vote for the Potomac the die is cast, Pennsylvania has lost it, and we can never return. I will bear the inconveniences of New York much longer rather than do it. Fitzsimons is an arrant fox; I could feel him trim around. Upon the whole, I am quite as well pleased that I went to this dinner; and yet they liked my company but little, if I was not much mistaken. At one time, when they were regretting the influence of New York in keeping us here, I said: "Gentlemen, we once had it in our power to fix ourselves elsewhere. As the Scotchman said in his prayers, we were left to the freedom of our own will, and a pretty hand we have made of it."

February 4th.—This a most unimportant day in the Senate. The bill for extending the impost to North Carolina was brought in to be signed. The Vice-President got up, and had a good deal to say; that a question was put in the House of Representatives, and if gentlemen wished any other method they should say so. Elsworth was immediately up; said all was perfectly right. The House had passed the bill; they had nothing more to do with it. Strong got up; had some sleeveless things to say about the practice of Parliament, but concluded all was right. I got up and declared, since gentlemen were speaking their minds, I would declare that I thought the business wrong; that, after both Houses had elaborately argued and passed a bill, it was referred to a committee of one from the Senate and two from the House of Representatives; that it was then in their power to alter the bill. If they were bad men, there was no check on them. If even a member knew of a bill to be vitiated, he would not correct it. An "if" or an "and" might most materially affect the bill. The changes of the tense of a verb might alter a whole sentence. I was clearly of opinion every bill ought to be compared at the table; and, as the Vice-President when he signed a bill, did it for and in the name of the Senate, the question should be put, "Shall it be signed or no?" It was, however, of no avail; nor, indeed, did I conclude with any motion, but meant my observations to open the way for taking up the business some other time.

This was a public day with the Speaker. All the company were Pennsylvanians except Judge Livermore. He soon went away. We had a great many clever things from Mr. Morris and Clymer on the good of the State, the clearing the Susquehanna, the Tulpachocking Canal, etc. I will vote for the Susquehanna *now,* says Mr. Morris. Even Clymer was condescending, but it was like grinning a smile. Hints were thrown out about uniting the delegation, and much could be done by their effort. I wonder if they are silly enough to think that their arts can not be seen through? The government of Pennsylvania is the object. The Speaker mentioned Charles Thompson as having been spoken of. Clymer said in such a tone of voice as he did not expect me to hear, "He will make a good Senator." I know Clymer well. Perhaps if I were to consult my own feelings and general interest, I would wish Charles Thompson or any other person in my room.

Mr. Morris threw a paper on the table before the Speaker. The Speaker took it up. Clymer muttered something. Fitzsimons looked confused and went away. I will know what this paper was. Mr. Morris said "I am quite off with the Yorkers; I will have nothing more to do with them." I can not penetrate the scheme of the Philadelphia junto as to the person they contemplate for Governor. A man who will be their tool is the design; but they have not yet fixed on the particular object.

February 5th.—This morning at breakfast the Speaker told me what the paper was. The Yorkers had stipulated, under their hands, to go to the Susquehanna, and the Pennsylvania delegation, myself excepted (who, by-the-by, was the moving spirit of the business), had agreed, under their hands, to stay two years in New York. This engagement of the Pennsylvanians had been in the hands of the Yorkers until now; that Mr. Morris had possessed himself of it; had crossed the names, and now showed it at the same time that he made the declaration against having anything to do with the Yorkers. Well might I say, "A pretty hand we have made of it!"

Attended this day at the Hall. The minutes were read, and just nothing at all more. done.

February 6th.—The Senate stood adjourned over to Monday. I had a card above a week ago to dine this day with Mr. Otto, the *chargé d'affaires* of France. It was very cold, and I sent an excuse, and stayed at home. Amused myself in writing a paper tending to show the use of the State Legislatures, maintaining their consequence in the arrangement of the empire. It was an idle day with me. Read the Roman Antiquities in an old author. I am really much better of my rheumatism since I took to keeping myself warm. Rest and warmth are, perhaps, the best applications I can make. I have drunk Madeira wines for the past three days in moderate quantities, and really think I feel better for it.

February 7th, Sunday.—This was a cold day, and I stayed at home. My employment—the writing of letters to my family. Mr. Bingham called to see us yesterday. He had much to say of the affairs of Pennsylvania. Upon some person remarking that the parties of Republican and Constitutionalists would be done away, he said the party would but take a new name; it would henceforth be the eastern and western interest of the State. I said had Congress been on the Susquehanna, such a party would never have been known. Sent a piece to Mr. Nicholson for publication, with a design to spirit up the State Legislatures to attend to their own importance and instruct their Senators on all important questions.

February 8th.—Attended Senate. The first business that presented itself was a letter from R. Morris to the Vice-President, inclosing a long memorial, praying commissioners to be appointed to inquire into his conduct while financier, and mentioning his unsettled accounts as a partner in the house of Willing & Morris, which were in train of settlement. He requested the memorial might stand on our minutes. Some little objection was made. No particular vote was taken, and it went on, of course. I am really puzzled with this conduct of my honorable colleague. The charges against him are not as financier, but as chairman of the secret committee of Congress, and for money received as a merchant in the beginning of the business. It seems admitted that he rendered important service as a financier, and if I can penetrate his design it is to cloak his faults in the secret committee with his meritorious conduct as financier. [I] must mark the end of it.

This day the report of the Secretary was taken up in the House of Representatives. I have heard Fitzsimons reprobate the funding law of Pennsylvania; heard him condemn the doctrine of an indiscriminate funding, etc. Yet this day he laid on the Speaker's table a string of resolutions merely echoed from the Secretary's report.

February 9th.—Mr. Morris' memorial was committed this day to Izard, Henry, and Elsworth. I am still more and more at a loss [to know] what he would be at. It seems as if he wanted to make a noise, to get commissioners appointed on that part of his conduct which he can defend, and thus mislead the public. I find the old resolve of Congress, the 20th June, 1785, was brought in by a committee appointed on a letter of his own. He represented this resolve of Congress to have been the act of his malevolent enemies and persecutors.

We had a message from the House of Representatives by Buckley with the Enumeration [census] bill. A message also from the President of the United States on the difference of limits between the United States and Nova Scotia, with a number of nominations.

Hamilton, literally speaking, is moving heaven and earth in favor of his [funding] system. The Rev. Dr. Rodgers called on me and General Muhlenberg this evening. He owed no visit, for that he had paid a day or two ago. Directly he began to extol Hamilton's system, and argued with it as if he had been in the pulpit. I checked him; he made his visit short. The Cincinnati is another of his [Hamilton's] machines and the whole city of New York. He is attacked, however, in this day's paper pretty smartly by Governor Clarton, as I take it, for the writer seems to aim personally at him.

February 10th.—Attended the Hall, but soon left the Senate to attend the debate in the Representatives' chamber. Stayed with them until near three o'clock, but the debates were not entertaining. It all turned on an amendment offered by Mr. Scott, the amount of which was that debts should be ascertained before provision was made for them. The committee rose without any division.

February 11th.—Attended the Senate. The committee reported yesterday, while I was out, on Mr. Morris' memorial, that the prayer of it should be granted. There was no order of the day. I wished to hear the debates of the House of Representatives and went down and found Madison up. He had got through the introductory part of his speech, which was said to be elegant. The ground I found him on was the equity power of the Government in regulating of property, which he admitted in the fullest manner, with this exception, when the State was no party. The United States owe justly and fairly the whole amount of the Federal debt. The question then is, to whom do they owe it? In this question they are not interested, as the amount is the same, let who will receive it. The case of original holder [of certificates] admits of no doubt. But what of the speculator who paid only a trifle for the evidences of the debt? The end, however, of his speech produced a revolution to the following effect: That the whole should be funded, but that in the hands of speculators at the highest market price only; and the surplus to the original holder, who performed the service. The debate lasted to the hour of adjournment, and they rose without deciding.

Dined this day with General Knox. The company large and splendid, consisting of the diplomatic corps, members of Congress, etc.

February 12th.—Attended at the Hall. The order of the day was to take up the Enumeration bill. I objected to the whole of a lengthy schedule, and moved a commitment. I was seconded, but some gentlemen wishing to proceed on the bill till they came to the clause, I withdrew my motion. Elsworth came forward with a motion to strike out the clause about the marshal, and insert one to do it by a commissioner. I opposed him; was joined by Patterson. The debate was scarce worth mentioning, but it let me into the character of Governor Johnston. He had said something for the bill as it stood, but when Elsworth made his motion, he got up to tell how convincing the gentleman's arguments were and that they had fully convinced him. This I considered as something in the taste of *esprit de corps,* for he is a lawyer. But both he and his colleague looked foolish when they took it.

I got a hard hit at Elsworth. He felt it and did not reply. The bill was immediately afterward committed and the Senate adjourned. Elsworth came laughing to me; said he could have distinguished with respect to the point I brought forward. I said: "Elsworth, the man must knit his net close that can catch you; but you trip sometimes." So we had a laugh and parted. Went immediately into the Representative chamber, but the whole day was spent on the Quaker memorial for the abolition of slavery.

February 13th.—This a vacant day. I went to the Hall to meet with Mr. R. Harris; he did not meet. We went to seek for him at Dr. McKnight's. Could not find him. Called Mr. Scott and endeavored to give him every argument in my power against Hamilton's report. I shall not minute them here. I wish, however, to arm him and every friend to discrimination with every possible argument, as I fear, if the business is lost with them, there will be small chance with us.

Dined this day in an agreeable way with Dr. Johnson, the principal of the college. The company was not large. There were three Senators, the Speaker of the House of Representatives, General Muhlenberg, and some strangers.

February 14th.—Being Sunday, wrote home to my family, to my brother, and to Mr. Nicholson, inclosing him strictures on the conduct of the secretary and O—— respecting the eleven thousand dollars paid for furniture under the resolve of April 15th last, in the character of a distressed woman complaining of her servants.

February 15th.—Attended in Senate. Our Vice-President produced the petitions and memorials of the Abolition Society. He did it rather with a sneer, saying he had been honored with a visit from a society, a self-constituted one, he supposed. He proceeded to read the petitions and memorials. Izard and Butler had prepared themselves with long speeches on the occasion. Izard, in particular, railed at the society; called them fanatics, etc. Butler made a personal attack on Dr. Franklin,

and charged the whole proceeding to anti-Federal motives:
that the Doctor, when member of convention, had consented
to the Fereral compact. Here he was acting in direct violation
of it. The whole business was designed to overturn the Constitution. I was twice up. The first time I spoke generally as
to the benevolent intentions of the society, etc. Upon Butler's
attack I requested Mr. Morris to rise and defend him [Dr.
Franklin]. King was up, speaking in favor of the Carolina
gentleman. I remarked, "King is courting them." "Yes," said
he [Morris], "and I will be silent from the same motive that
makes him speak." He then bade me rise. I did so. Showed
that the Doctor was at the head of the society, which was not
of yesterday; that he could not strictly have the acts of the
society charged to his personal account; that the society had
persevered in the same line of conduct long before the Constitution was formed; that there was nothing strictly novel in
their conduct, etc. Nothing was done or moved to be done, as
the matter is in commitment with the Representatives, where
the measure has many friends.

Adjourned, and went to hear the debates in the lower House.
Sedgwick, Lawrence, Smith, and Ames took the whole day.
They seemed to aim all at one point, to make Madison ridiculous.
Ames delivered a long string of studied sentences, but he did
not use a single argument that seemed to leave an impression.
He had "public faith," "public credit," "honor, and above all
justice," as often over as an Indian would the "Great Spirit,"
and, if possible, with less meaning and to as little purpose.
Hamilton, at the head of the speculators, with all the courtiers,
are on one side. These I call the party who are actuated by
interest. The opposition are governed by principle, but I fear
in this case interest will outweigh principle. I drank this day
at dinner two glasses of wine with the Speaker. I will continue
this practice for a week and observe the effect.

February 16th.—This day not remarkable much either way
in the Senate, except that Mr. Morris gave the clearest proof
of a disposition always to abandon me on every motion which
I make. The Enumeration [census] bill was before us. The
point at which I aimed was to begin the enumeration in April,
so that the census might be taken before our election, and the

universal belief is that Pennsylvania would be a gainer. Butler moved to have the time extended one year from the first of August next. Here I threw in the most pointed opposition, and laid down the principles of the amendment which I proposed. Elsworth said he would be for extending the time to nine months, and Mr. Morris, to my astonishment, rose and supported Elsworth for the nine months. So Butler's motion was carried. The arguments I used were that every measure tending to give the people confidence in our Government should be adopted without delay. The present representation was on a supposititious enumeration and was believed to be erroneous. A second election, therefore, ought not to proceed on such uncertain ground, etc.

February 17th.—The business done this morning was receiving the report of the committee to whom was committed the sixth clause of the Enumeration [census] bill. It had been recommitted at the instant at urgent motion of Mr. Butler, and the committee, as if to insult him, reported the clause without alteration. The bill was passed, and ordered for the third reading tomorrow. Adjourned and went to hear the debates in the chamber of Representatives.

The paper containing the publication called The Budget Opened, was given by General Heister to Wynkoop, and never more heard of. I asked him for it this day, but he denied his knowing anything about it. Boudinot took up the whole time of the committee till the hour of adjournment. It was all dead loss, for nobody minded him. Wrote this evening to my brother. Paid this day one half Joe * for boarding; half for the week past and half of it in advance for next week.

February 18th.—We had a message this day from the President of the United States respecting the boundary between Nova Scotia and the State of Massachusetts. A committee was appointed some time ago to whom the business was referred. The report of the committee on the cession from North Carolina was called up. Some time was spent on it and it was postponed to Monday next. The Senate now adjourned, and we went into the lower House to hear the debates on Mr. Madison's motion.

---

* Contraction for Johannes, a Portuguese gold coin equal to about eight dollars.

Madison had been up most of the morning and was said to have spoken most ably indeed. He seemed rather jaded when I came in. He had, early in this business, been called on to show a single instance where anything like the present had been done. He produced an act of Parliament in point in the reign of Queen Anne. But now the gentleman quitted this ground and cried out for rigid right on law principles. Madison modestly put them in mind that they had challenged him on this ground, and he had met them agreeably to their wishes. Adjourned without question.

February 19th.—Attended at the Senate chamber. Here I found a packet from Mr. Nicholson. It contained two sets of his letters to me cut out of the newspapers. He apologizes for the delay of the prices I sent him for publication by the prior engagement of the press, meaning, as I take it, his letters to me. I believe I ought not to blame him; the priest will christen his own child first. They are all to appear on Saturday, as he expects.

This day we did nothing in the Senate but read the minutes, and adjourned over to Monday. Went to hear the debates in the House of Representatives, but they were dull and uninteresting, and yet the question was not put. All parties seemed tired, yet unwilling to give out. I am vexed with them. The real good and care of the country seem not to enter into all their thoughts. The very system of the Secretary's report seems to be to lay as much on the people as they can bear. Madison's [system] yields no relief as to the burden, but affords some alleviation as to the design the tax will be laid for; and is, perhaps, on that account more dangerous, as it will be readier submitted to.

There is an obstinacy, a perverse peevishness, a selfishness which shuts him up from all free communication. He will see Congress in no other light than as one party. He seems to prescribe to them to follow laws already made, as if they were an executive body; whereas the fact is, that the majority of the people, say three millions (the tax-payers), and the holders of certificates, a few thousand (the receivers), are the parties, and the business of Congress is to legislate on the principles of justice between them. A funding system will be the consequence—that political gout of every government which has

objected; expected some resolutions would be sent in from the
House of Representatives, to wait on the President, with compliments on his birthday, etc. I took my hat and came down-
stairs. Those who stayed were disappointed. Madison's matter
was over before I came down, and a poor show his party made.
The obstinacy of this man has ruined the opposition. The
Secretary's report will now pass through, perhaps unaltered. I
could not help observing that now both Fitzsimons and Clymer
spoke, and they were [the] Secretary all over. Fitzsimons gave
me notice of a meeting of the Pennsylvania delegation at his
lodgings at six o'clock. I went. The ostensible reason was to
consult on the adoption of the State debts, but the fact to tell
us that they were predetermined to do it. Morris swore "By
G— it must be done!" and Clymer, strange to tell, expatiated
on the growing grandeur of Pennsylvania if it was done. Our
roads would all be made and our communications all opened
by land and water, etc. These appeared strange words to me
coming from that quarter.

Fitzsimons was much more argumentative, but they were
all predetermined, and only called on our complaisance to assent
to their better judgment. I chose to mention publicly that I
thought we scarce did justice to the State we represented that
we did not meet oftener and consult on her interest. This met
with an echo of applause. Fitzsimons proposed his lodgings as
a rendezvous weekly. Mr. Morris directly spoke of wine and
oysters, and it was agreed to meet every Monday evening at
Simons'. I took, however, care to bear my unequivocal testimony
against the adoption now proposed, and, in fact, made the above
proposition to obviate any suspicion of obstinacy or unsociability.

February 23d.—The Senate sat more than an hour doing
nothing at all but looking at each other. Elsworth and Strong
got together at a time when we had all got in chatting parties
about the fires and stoves. We were suddenly called to order,
and Elsworth was up. It was a most formal motion, indeed,
which he made, and then read a resolution, stating that a mistake had been made yesterday in a communication which had
been sent to the House of Representatives, and desiring them
to return the paper. It was about the North Carolina session,
and I suspected all was not very right; but, indeed, as much

through pastime as otherwise, I opposed him. He grew serious and solemn and I grew rather sportive, but with a grave face on, and we made a noble debate of it. It would be idle to blot an inch of paper with it. The question was at length put, and Elsworth lost it. Greatly was he mortified indeed, and sat down in a visible chagrin.

Dr. Johnson, who had not spoken before, now got up and said angry things. He did not move absolutely for a reconsideration, but Elsworth followed him and urged a reconsideration. It was seconded by Strong. I got up and opposed the reconsideration as out of order, and another most important debate ensued. The Chair was called on, and he declared the question out of order. *Mirabile dictu!* I turned to Mr. Morris. Had he decided so in the case of the Susquehanna bill, said I, we should have had Congress on the banks of that river. Mr. Morris said yes.*

Mr. Morris got on the subject of the difficulties he labored under in the settlement of his account. Told me that he had to send again to Philadelphia for a receipt-book in which were some trifling accounts for money paid to the extent of forty [shillings] and such small sums; but concluded I will have everything settled and the most ample receipt and certificate of the account being closed.

February 24th.—Attended this day in Senate. No business of any consequence done. Was much afflicted with a violent headache; came home and bathed my feet; but my head was so bad I had to lie down. This was a day of company at our house. Madison was in the invitation, and came early and asked for me, but I could not come down-stairs. I was sorry for this, but, as the saying is, "There is no help for sickness." Drank tea and felt better after it, but kept my bed.

February 25th.—Feel almost well of my headache, but I thought best to stay at home, more especially as I expected nothing of consequence to be done at the Senate. Was agreeably surprised with the arrival of Mr. Richardson, who brought letters to me from my family; received also letters from Phila-

---

* Mr. Adams had decided that a motion to reconsider, made by one of the minority, was in order. In the last session a motion was reconsidered, and the Susquehanna bill lost.

delphia containing some newspapers, in one of which were two pieces which I forwarded some time ago for publication. Those from my family were, however, to me the most agreeable. Wrote back letters by Mr. Richardson, who goes to-morrow.

February 26th.—Attended at the Hall; showed it [the Hall] to Mr. Richardson; then went to the bank with him to get some money changed. Took leave of him. Visited Bobby Harris. Attended at the Hall, where no business was done. Received an agreeable letter from Dr. Logan. Went in the evening and drank tea with Mr. Wynkoop, who has got his wife with him. Finished the evening in reading.

February 27th.—No Senate this day. Went with the Speaker to buy books. I bought Peter Pindar, whose sarcastic and satirical vein will write monarchy into disrepute in Britain. His shafts are aimed personally at his present Majesty, but many of them hit the throne, and will contribute to demolish the absurdity of royal government. Thus, even Peter, who I guess to be a servile creature paying court to the heir-apparent and the rising royal family, may be a useful instrument in opening the eyes of mankind to the absurdity of human worship and the adulation, nay, almost adoration, paid to work of their own hands. Kings and governors originally were meant for the use and advantage of the governed, but the folly of men has puffed them out of their places and made them not only useless but burdensome.

General Heister called this evening. The Pennsylvania newspapers spoke, particularly Oswald's, of the 20th. It [the paper] had been in the House of Representatives, but the Speaker said Fitzsimons got his hands on it, and he saw no more of it. I reminded him that I had left one of those papers in his and the General's room, and that also was mislaid. I, however, got one of them for Heister, as two were inclosed to me. Wrote this day to George Logan, *vide* letter-book. Paid for the Speaker at the book-store £2 0s. 0d. Paid.

February 28th.—Being Sunday, stayed at home all day. Read and wrote letters to my family. Lent General Muhlenberg two half Johannes. Paid.

March 1st.—Visited Mr. Harris, whom I find mending fast. Returned to the Hall; sat for some time; nothing done. Re-

ceived a note to dine with the President of the United States.
Went into the Chamber of Representatives and heard the debates till three o'clock, which I thought unimportant. Ames,
however, read in his place a string of resolutions touching the
manner in which the States were to bring forward their claims,
which I thought alarming.

March 2d.—Just nothing done this day in Senate save receiving Bailey's bill for certain inventions from the Representatives. Some spiteful remarks made on it. To-morrow
assigned for a second reading. Visited Mr. Harris, whom I
find recovering fast. Did not attend in the House of Representatives. Our Vice-President goes every day, and the members
spend their time in lampooning him before his face and in
communicating the abortions of their Muses, and embryo wit-
tings resound the room. Perhaps they may have got and dressed
the buntings of their brains at their lodgings in order to pop
them on the company to the greater advantage. A resolve passed
the Representatives this day that seems to show that they begin
to *think*. It is a call on the Secretary to ascertain the resources,
that they may be applied to the payment of the State debts if
they should be adopted. The Speaker was at the levee to-day.
When he came home, he said the *State debts must be adopted.*
This, I suppose, is the language of the court.

March 3d.—This day Bailey's bill taken up for the second
reading. Five members rose to oppose it. I was up three times,
and I am convinced we should have carried it. Mr. Morris
rose, however, and proposed that it should be committed to the
very men who opposed it. Langdon made a formal motion to
this purpose, and was seconded by Bassett. Such a committee
was accordingly appointed. It is a new way, to commit a bill to
its enemies. We will see what will come of it.

CHAPTER VI

March 4th.—Visited Mr. Harris this morning. Found him recovering fast. I have an interest in everything that happened to him, of which he is little aware; indeed, nobody knows my feelings on this subject but myself. He will, I trust, be well in a few days, and if his complaint should be completely removed it may tempt me to advise a person, in whose welfare I feel myself deeply interested, to submit to the same operation. But of this hereafter.

My bodings of yesterday, were not ill founded with respect to Bailey's bill. A man ought not to put his hand in a dog's mouth, and trust to his generosity not to bite it; commit the bill to its declared enemies, and trust' to their generosity to report in favor of it! My conjectures were right, and they have reported dead against it.

Dined with the President of the United States. It was a dinner of dignity. All the Senators were present, and the Vice-President. I looked often around the company to find the happiest faces. Wisdom, forgive me if I wrong thee, but I thought folly and happiness most nearly allied. The President seemed to bear in his countenance a settled aspect of melancholy. No cheering ray of convivial sunshine broke through the cloudy gloom of settled seriousness. At every interval of eating or drinking he played on the table with a fork or knife, like a drumstick. Next to him, on his right, sat Bonny Johnny Adams, ever and anon mantling his visage with the most unmeaning simper that ever dimpled the face of folly. Goddess of Nature, forgive me if I censure thee for that thou madest him not a tailor, so full of small attentions is he, and so well qualified does he seem to adjust the etiquette of loops and buttons. But stay, perhaps I wrong thee. So miserably doth he measure politics, and so unmercifully and unskillfully would he play the shears of government in cutting out royal robes and habiliments, that it may justly be doubted whether the measure of his understanding be adequate to the adjusting the proportions of the back, belly, and breeches of the human form agreeably to the rules of an experienced habit-maker. Thus, goddess, among the savage tribes of the lazy, lying, lumpish Indian, who can neither hunt, fish, nor hoe corn, makest thou the dreaming, smoking, pretended prophet, priest, and politician. Goddess, we acknowledge thy power and submit to thy sway, but humbly pray we may never have another similar example of it.

March 5th.—Just after I entered the Senate chamber, I received from my brother a letter, which made me considerably uneasy, about some rascally carryings on at the Pennsylvania Land-Office. It has occasioned me to write sundry letters, and really has fretted me a good deal. But away with it! This day gave a fresh instance of the rascality of Otis. The committee on Bailey's bill reported yesterday, and said not one word more, nor was another word said in the Senate, but Otis had on the minutes ordered that the report be accepted. I did not immediately observe it, but I called on him about it. His excuse was Mr. Adams had ordered him to do so. Visited Mr. Harris; found him getting much better.

March 6th.—Stayed at home. In the evening visited Mr. Harris, whom I found recovering. I wrote this day to the Secretary and Receiving-General of the Land-Office respecting the affair of which my brother wrote to me. Read the account of the Pelew Islands by Keale, a catchpenny thing, perhaps true enough, but stretched and swelled as if it had been puffed by Hawksworth. Paid my barber for two months, and 1*s.* 6*d.* for a ribbon.

March 7th.—Devoted this day to writing to my family. Wrote to every one, even little Billy. I, however, crowded the girls into one letter. This is hardly fair, but I must be more liberal to them next time. Called to see Mr. Harris, and found him quite cheerful. He will be about in a few days, if nothing happens amiss to him.

March 8th.—This is the important week, and perhaps the important day, when the question will be put on the assumption of State debts. I suspect this from the rendezvousing of the crew of the Hamilton galley. It seems all hands are piped to quarters.

Four o'clock.—I was rather deceived, as the adoption party do not yet consider themselves strong enough to risk the putting of the question, for it seems the day has passed and nothing is done. The Naturalization bill was taken up. The debates were exceedingly lengthy and a great number of amendments moved. Mr. Morris stood by me in one, that was to enable aliens to hold lands in the United States. 'Tis said he has an agent in Europe now selling lands. I am wrong to minute this circumstance. He is, however, very seldom with me. I know not how it came, but I was engaged, on one side or the other, warmly on every question. The truth of the matter is, it is a vile bill, illiberal and void of philanthropy, and needed mending much. We complained [to the Representatives from Pennsylvania] that such an ungenerous bill should be sent to us—at least I did. They answered, "You have little to do," and they sent us employment.

This night the Pennsylvanians supped together at Simons. 'Twas freely talked of that the question was to have been taken this day on the assumption of the State debts, but Vining, from the Delaware State, is come in, and it was put off until he would be prepared by the Secretary [Hamilton], I suppose, so that my morning creed was a well-founded belief. The language of the Philadelphia gentlemen is still for adoption. The great reason formerly urged for it was that Pennsylvania would draw a great revenue from the Union. I brought forward the case of Amsterdam, to which the United Provinces owed great balances, which were not paid a century after the Revolution. Mr. Fitzsimons said they were not paid yet nor never would be; but then, with one voice, all the three citizens [Morris, Fitzsimons, and Scott] said little, if anything, would be due to Pennsylvania, and declared that settling old accounts was misspent time. Burn all old accounts, said Mr. Morris, and pay only the people who now hold certificates. I wished for harmony and declined argument, but said the citizens of Philadelphia would not abandon the State securities. This was admitted, but Mr. Morris said that the State might subscribe for the amount of them. This would be sinking two per cent to the State, as they would subscribe in at four per cent, and pay six to their own citizens. But I forbore entering into argument. Colonel Hartley kept shuffling about, still repeating all depends on the adoption of the State debts. "If this is not done, New England and Carolina will fly off, and the Secretary's scheme is ruined. We must, we must adopt it." Hartley is lucky, but this, in fact, is the court lesson.

March 9th.—In the Senate chamber this morning Butler said he heard a man say he would give Vining one thousand guineas for his vote, but added, "I question whether he would do so in fact." So do I, too, for he might get it for a tenth part of the sum. I do not know that pecuniary influence has actually been used, but I am certain that every other kind of management has been practiced and every tool at work that could be thought of. Officers of Government, clergy, citizens, [Order of] Cincinnati, and every person under the influence of the Treasury; Bland and Huger carried to the chamber of Representatives—the one lame, the other sick. Clymer stopped from going away, though he had leave, and at length they risked the question and carried it, thirty-one votes to twenty-six. And all this after having tampered with the members since the 22d of last month [February], and this only in committee, with many doubts that some will fly off and great fears that the North Carolina members will be in before a bill can be matured or a report gone through. Mr. Morris received a note signed J. C., communicating the news. He only said, "I am sorry it is by so small a majority." General Muhlenberg and Heister, of the Pennsylvania delegation, only, were in the negative.

I had to wrangle with the New England men alone on the Naturalization bill till near one o'clock. Johnston, of North Carolina, took in some degree a part with me. I held my own, or at least I thought so, with tolerable success, but such shuffling and want of candor I really scarce ever before was witness to. I certainly, however, gained greatly. Twice yesterday did we attempt, without success, to throw out the two years' residence. The amendments which I offered went to cure this defect with respect to the power of holding lands. Numbers of gentlemen now declared their dislike of the two years, and wished the bill committed for the purpose of having this part rejected. I agreed, but we were very unlucky in our committee. We Pennsylvanians act as if we believed that God made of one blood all families of the earth; but the Eastern people seem to think that he made none but New England folks. It is strange that men born and educated under republican forms of government should be so contracted on the subject of general philanthropy. In Pennsylvania, used as we are to the reception and adoption of strangers, we receive no class of men with such diffidence as the Eastern people. They really have the worst characters of any people who offer themselves for citizens. Yet these are the men who affect the greatest fear of being contaminated with foreign manners, customs, or vices. Perhaps it is with justice that they fear an adoption of any of the latter, for they surely have enough already.

March 10th.—Was the first at the Hall this morning. However, it was not long before some of the Secretary's [Hamilton] gladiators came in. What an abject thing a man becomes when he makes himself a tool to any one! I ventured to predict to one of them that the Secretary's system would fail. "Why, but the assumption of the State debts is carried already." I ventured to tell how. From me, distant as the room would let him, did he fly off. Bassett has this day declared in the most unequivocal manner against the adoption of the State debts; says if they are adopted he will move for two per cent. I asked him how Mr. Read would be on this question. He said against assumption. But both of them acted a weak part in the affair of the residence. The business of this day does not merit a minute. The Senate adjourned early and I came home, as I did not feel very well.

We had company this day. The greater part were New England men, who soon went away. Burke and Tucker both voted for the assumption of the State debts. Tucker declared his views in the most unequivocal manner; after the State [debts] were discharged by the Federal assumption, to sponge the whole. Burke reprobated the whole of the Secretary's report and declared it would blow up. He was not so explicit, but seemed in unison with Tucker. What must come of the report if these men are sincere? They have been among the supporters of it; but, alas! what poor, supple things men are, bending down before every dinner and floated away with every flask of liquor! Paid my boarding off this day.

March 11th.—Snowed all last night and a snowy morning. Attended at the Hall. Two bills came up from the Representatives—the bill for inventions and one to give additional salaries to clerks. Read for the first time. A bill for the mitigation of fines and forfeitures was taken up for a second reading. Opposed by Bassett and Few. A commitment was early moved and seemed generally agreed to, but the members popped up and down talkng about it and about it for above an hour. Something occurred to me which none of them touched; but I thought it useless to rise; besides, I had been almost constantly on my legs on the 8th and 9th, and a man, even a good speaker, loses all weight if he makes himself troublesome. Patterson, I find, belongs to the gladiatorial band. I ever thought since I knew him that he was a loaf-and-fish man. He talks of resigning, and I suppose we will hear of his being a judge or something better than a Senator.

March 12th.—Attended this day at the Hall. No business of consequence done. The committee on the Naturalization bill reported, but far short of the points which I wished established in it. There really seems a spirit of malevolence against Pennsylvania in this business. We have been very liberal on the subject of admitting strangers to citizenship. We have benefited by it and still do benefit. Some characters seem disposed to deprive us of it. I moved a postponement of a day that we might consider of this amendment. It was easily carried; but Izard snapped, ill-natured as a cur, and said "No" alone. Mr. Morris turned toward me this day and seemed to invite a *tête-à-tête*. He said Mr. Wilson is coming over. I asked if on any court business. He did not know; believed not. We spoke of who would be Governor [of Pennsylvania]. He declared in favor of St. Clair; spoke against Mifflin and Bingham. I said I had heard Miles spoken of. He objected to Miles as wanting knowledge. I never made mention of any of the Muhlenbergs. He objected to Mifflin; said, "See what sort of people he has put in office." The S. G. was mentioned. He said, "You should have had that office." I went into some details of the duties of that office, showed it was one in which a drone might slumber, but if filled well was a most laborious office, and pointed out how.

March 13th.—Being Saturday, the Senate did not meet. Stayed at home all day; read and looked over the journals of Congress. A day perfectly unimportant. The streets were very sloppy with the melting of the snow.

March 14th.—There was a considerable fire in the neighborhood last night; it, of course, raised me by daylight. After breakfast the day seemed so delightful I could not help walking. I went to Mr. Scott's lodgings. I got at him on the subject of the Secretary's report. He declared to me that he was altogether against it. I asked him if he had any correspondence with Pennsylvania. He declared no. I put Nicholson's piece into his hand; I put Mr. Findley's letter into his hand. I told him there were some people discontented in Pennsylvania. I read Dr. Logan's letter to him as proof of it. He called it anti-Federalism. I took out Dr. Rush's—call him anti-Federal if you will. It was worse. He went into the allegations against Nicholson with regard to the State accounts. To say all of him [Scott] in one word, he has thrown himself into Fitzsimons' wake more from the principles of indolence than anything else. He will not give himself the trouble of acting independently. I found a woman in the room with him with a young child in her arms. He appeared to be fondling on the child.

I called in the afternoon on a Mr. Ryerson, a member of the Assembly from Pennsylvania, at the City Tavern. I expected he had letters from my brother; but he had none, nor did my brother * know of his coming. I asked him what was doing in the Pennsylvania Assembly. He said not much. He had dined out with Mr. Morris. I spoke to him of the adoption of the State debts. Oh, yes, he believed people were generally for it. On speaking a little further, I found him absolutely ignorant of every ray of information about them. He owned it after some time, and desired me to put some state of the matter on paper, and that he would pay particular attention to it when he returned.

March 15th.—I complied with Mr. Ryerson's request, and

---

* Samuel Maclay, afterward United States Senator, 1803-1809.

furnished him with an abstract of the State debt of Pennsylvania, and a number of remarks on it. I read it very deliberately to him, and he seemed to understand it.

The only debate of any consequence this day in the Senate was on the Naturalization bill. The same illiberality as was apparent on other occasions possessed the New England men. Immigration is a source of population to us, and they wish to deprive us of it. I was up several times, but always endeavored to be concise and to the point as much as I possibly could. Mr. Morris was up once. I thought he lost himself, and, by way of getting out, said he was of the same opinion as the member from New York (Mr. King). Mr. King is as much against us as any of them, but he does it in an indirect manner. We spent to three o'clock on it.

I dined this day at Elsworth's by invitation from General Heister. Madison, Bishop Prevost, and a considerable number at dinner, the Speaker and General Muhlenberg. Nothing remarkable.

I called on Ryerson and put into his hands a number of remarks pointedly against the Assumption bill, etc. He talked of great intimacy with my brother. My brother had mentioned him to me in terms of respect in some of his letters. I therefore treated him with unbounded confidence. This was imprudent and I ought not to have done it, nor would I had it not been for some of my brother's letters, in which he mentions Ryerson as connected with him in some political points.

March 16th.—Mr. Morris looked with a strange degree of shyness at me for some time after we met in the Hall. I had heard that Ryerson came from Philadelphia to do business with Mr. Morris. It occurred in a moment to me that he had betrayed to Mr. Morris all that had passed between him and me, and likewise my remarks in manuscript on the assumption of the State debt. In this moment *mens conscia recti* was a treasure to me. I had told Ryerson that there were no hopes of Mr. Morris being with me on this question, but that I had passed no censure on him for it. I determined to avow all I had done, as I did nothing with any view of concealment. I had hinted to Ryerson that I rather wished than otherwise that the General Assembly [of Pennsylvania] should declare their sense on this

question of assumption, and the more so as Carolina had instructed her members for it.

Mr. Morris, after sitting serious a good while, turned to me
and began a familiar chat. At last he asked me to walk on one
side from our seats, and asked me if back lands could still be
taken up. I told him yes. He immediately proposed to me to
join him in a speculation in lands which he said he thought that
he, from his connections in Europe, could sell at a dollar an
acre. I paused a moment; said, as our waste lands were totally
unproductive, such a thing might be beneficial to the public as
well as ourselves; that in these points of view I saw no objection. I stated some affairs of our Land-Office briefly, and he
concluded we would make up our estimates at the first leisure
moment. If he is in earnest in this matter, he will be favorable
to the lowering of the terms of the Land-Office. I have, however, the most unequivocal proofs of the baseness of Ryerson,
who, notwithstanding his promises, has communicated everything to Mr. Morris. The principal debates this day were on the
Naturalization bill, and were characterized with the same
illiberality as those before mentioned.

We had company this day, mostly Virginians. Colonel Bland
was of the number. He is an assumer on the subject of the State
debts. He avowed his design to be a demonstration to the world
that our present Constitu. n aimed directly at consolidation,
and the sooner everybody knew it the better; so that, in fact, he
supported the Secretary on anti-Federal principles. This, I believe, is the design of Gerry and many more. The New England
men, however, want to get their debts shook off before they
declare themselves completely. In their former attempts to sink
them they raised Shays' insurrection. After dark I received a
letter from my brother, calling Ryerson a *scoundrel* in direct
terms. He is a mere tool to the Philadelphians, and has deceived
my brother.

March 17th.—The Appropriation bill was just read, and the
President passed to and took up the Mitigation bill [of fines,
forfeitures]. It was on the third reading, and Elsworth offered
an amendment and the bill was committed.

Now the Naturalization bill was taken up, and all our old
arguments went over and over again. The fact is, the adop-

tion of strangers has set Pennsylvania far ahead of her sister States. They are spiteful and envious, and wish to deprive her of this source of population; but it will scarcely do to avow openly such ungenerous conduct. It therefore must be done under various pretenses and legal distinctions. Two years' residence was insisted on in the bill. We cared not for this, but let the stranger hold land the moment he comes, etc., etc. Two law opinions were supported in the debates of the day: one, that of the power of holding lands was a feature of naturalization; that lands, etc., could not be held without it. This doctrine was pushed so far by Elsworth as to declare that the rights of electors, being elected, etc., should attend and be described in the act of naturalization. All that could be said would not support this doctrine. Elsworth was even so absurd as to suppose, if a man acquired the right of suffrage in one State, he had it in all, etc. This doctrine it was seen would not carry, and now one more conformable to the common law was set up.

It was alleged that the disability of an alien to hold lands arose from the common law, and was separable from the rights of naturalization, as in the case of denization in England, where the Crown could confer the right of giving, receiving, and holding real property. When an alien, therefore, was enabled to hold real estate, it was in reality by repealing part of the common law with respect to him; not by giving a power, but taking away a disability. It, therefore, strictly speaking, rested with the respective States whether they would repeal the common law with respect to aliens touching the point of holding property, and, being a pure State concern, had no occasion to be made any mention of in the Naturalization act, but must remain to be settled by the different States by law, as well as the rights of elections, etc. We of Pennsylvania contended hard to have a clause for empowering aliens to hold, etc., but the above reasoning prevailed, and we lost it.

Before the Senate was formed this morning, Mr. Carrol, of Carrolton, happened to be sitting next to me. We were chatting on some common subject. The Vice-President was in the chair, which he had taken on the performance of prayer. He hastily descended, and came and took the chair next to Mr.

Carrol's. He began abruptly: "How have you arranged your empire on your departure? Your revenues must suffer in your absence. What kind of administration have you established for the regulation of your finances? Is your government intrusted to a viceroy, nuncio, legate, plenipotentiary, or *chargé d'affaires?*" etc., etc. Carrol endeavored to get him down from his imperial language by telling him he had a son-in-law who paid attention to his affairs, etc. 'Twas in vain. Adams would not dismount his hobby. At it again; nor was there an officer, in the household, civil, or military departments of royal or imperial government that he had not an allusion to. I pared my nails and thought he would soon have done, but it is no such easy thing to go through the detail of an empire. Guardian goddess of America, canst thou not order it so, that when thy sons cross the Atlantic they may return with something else besides European forms and follies? But I found this prayer ruffled me a little, so I left them before Adams had half settled the empire.

Mr. Morris had some further chat on the proposal of yesterday. I told him that, if I thought it possible that disadvantage could flow either to the public or individuals, I never would hear of it. He said advantage would probably flow to the public from it. It would be the means of bringing us both money and people. I now touched him on the subject of lowering back lands of Pennsylvania. It was a cold scent. I find he is for what the speculators call *dodging:* selling the land in Europe before he buys it here. He repeated that a dollar an acre could be got for it.

March 18th.—The burden of this day's debate was the Naturalization bill over again. From the most accurate observation I have been able to make the conduct of the members has been influenced by the following motives: As Pennsylvania is supposed likely to derive most benefit by migrations, the Eastern members are disposed to check it as much as they can. Jersey nearly indifferent; Delaware absolutely so; Maryland as Jersey; Virginia unrepresented; North Carolina favorable; South Carolina and Georgia want people much, but they fear the migrations, and will check them rather than run the chance of importing people who may be averse to slavery. Hence the bill passed the House [Senate] nearly as it came up from the Representatives.

The governing ideas, however, seem to be the following: That the holding property was separable from and not absolutely connected with naturalization; that laws and regulations relating to property, not being among the powers granted to Congress, remained with the different States. Therefore, Congress would be guilty of an assumption of power if they touched it; that the holding of property was a common law right, and the disability of aliens to hold property from that quarter. King, Patterson, Bassett, Read, Henry, and Johnson, all finally settled in this way. Elsworth dead against this; the holding property (real) a feature inseparable from naturalization, etc. Strong rather inclined to Elsworth. Dr. Johnson said about as much on one side as the other. Few, too, is said to be a lawyer; but, though he spoke a great deal, he did not seem to enter into the distinctions. For our parts we wished the Naturalization bill to be in exact conformity as possible to the existing laws relating to aliens in Pennsylvania; and this, I am convinced, would have been the case had it not been for that low spirit which contaminates public characters as well as private life.

March 19th.—The Naturalization bill again taken up. Now Butler, too proud to have lent his aid to any motion that was not his own, came forward with two motions. They were, in fact, nearly the same which had been negatived three or four times before. It was alleged they were out of order; but he was indulged, and lost them both. Now Few must be a great man, and he must bring forward his motion, too. It was equally out of order; but he was indulged in the loss of it. It appears that all over Europe, where the civil law prevails, aliens hold property. It is the common law of England that deprives them of holding real estate. The common law has been received by us, and with it this consequence. However, since we can not get the rights of property fully acknowledged, it is best that the Naturalization bill say nothing about it.

Mr. Morris got warmly at me this day about the affair of land. Repeated he thought even more than a dollar per acre could be got, and requested me to write him an account of the

kind of land, distance to market, etc. I wrote him as follows:
New York, *March 20, 1790.*

Sir: The lands concerning which you have made inquiry are
situated in the county of Northumberland, on the head of the
Lycoming, Pine Creek, and Tioga branches of the river Susquehanna. Their distance from Philadelphia, as the roads now go,
is from one hundred and eighty to two hundred miles, but it
may be shortened by opening a more direct communication. The
county of Northumberland, in which the first settlements were
made about the year 1770, was totally desolated by the incur-
sions of the Indians during the Revolution, a misfortune it can
never experience a second time, as the late settlement of the
State of New York [being extended north of it] and Luzerne
County form a complete barrier, and the savages have greatly
diminished—must soon be totally excluded by the increasing
settlements from the Atlantic side of the great lakes Ontario
and Erie. Northumberland County now contains between two
and three thousand families. Provision of all kinds can be had
in abundance. The average price of wheat, rye, Indian corn,
barley, buckwheat, and speltz, when compounded, has seldom
been equaled, to a half a Spanish dollar per bushel. The present
year it is higher, not owing to any failure of crops, but the uncommon demand for exportation. The country in which these
lands are situated is mountainous, but the high ridges are never
included in the surveys. It is covered with an immense forest of
timber—maple-sugar tree, birch, beech, oak of all kinds, pine,
mostly of the white and spruce kinds, white walnut, wild cherry,
hickory, ash, etc. These forests, some time ago, seemed to set
husbandry at defiance; but we now know that, independent of
the advantages of clearing the ground, they can be converted to
useful purposes in the manufacture of potash. The different
streams of the Susquehanna offer the means of conveying any
produce whatever to market. This country has been observed to
be particularly favorable to grass, and perhaps the raising of
cattle may be the most profitable object of husbandry, as stock
carries itself to market. These parts enjoy in an eminent degree
the advantage and security of double crops.

The snows, which fall regularly at their proper season in
winter, insure a plentiful harvest of the fall grain, wheat and

rye, with tolerable husbandry seldom yielding less than twenty bushels per acre. The length of the summer is well adapted to Indian corn, flax, oats, spring barley, summer wheat, tobacco, and vegetables of all kinds. Buckwheat is often sowed with success in the same summer on the ground from whence wheat, rye, or winter barley had been reaped. Perhaps, so far as respects seasons, the interests of husbandry are nowhere better secured than in Pennsylvania. The abundant exports of flour, grain, etc., from the port of Philadelphia afford full proof of this. It is certain that as you advance southward and diminish the rigors of winter, you lessen the certainty of the winter crop; while ascending to the north, the contracted and chilly season seldom brings to maturity the summer produce, which is often blasted or perished by early frosts.

Yet such is the rage of migrations that lands with all the advantages of soil and climate in the bosom of society are neglected for fancied elysiums in Yazoo or Kentucky. I can not state with precision the quantity of these lands, having no actual surveys before me, but I know that they are no less than fifty thousand acres. If I can render you any further information, I shall be happy in doing so.

                    I am, sir, your most, etc.,   W. M.
Honorable R. Morris, Esq.

Writing the foregoing letter was all I did this forenoon. The Speaker took me in his carriage and we rode in the afternoon.

March 21st, Sunday.—Wrote letters to my family this forenoon. Dated a piece of intelligence from Hamiltonople, etc. After dinner walked alone, up and down, back and forward on the island. The Speaker told me the report was not to be taken up until Fitzsimons came back, which was to be on Thursday. He knows all the motions of the janizaries and gladiators.

March 22d.—Visited Mr. Wilson's lodgings with the Speaker. I then went with Mr. Wynkoop to visit Mr. Carrol, of Carrolton. We got on the subject of the State of Carolina having instructed their representation. Could any hints have gone from here, said he, to set them on this measure? He is a Roman Catholic, and the intimate friend of Mr. Fitzsimons.

This question raised the following train of ideas in my mind:

Fitzsimons is gone to prevent a similar measure in Pennsylvania, and I am suspected of having given hints to set such a measure going. Perhaps something of this kind may be alleged against me with justice. The doctrine of instruction may certainly be carried so far as to be in effect the tribunitial veto of the Romans, and reduce us to the state of a Polish Diet. But it is introduced. Perhaps the best way is for all the States to use it, and the general evil, if it really should be one, will call for a remedy. But here is a subject worthy of inquiry: Is it to be expected that a Federal law passed directly against the sense of a whole State will ever be executed in that State? If the answer is in the negative, it is clearly better to give the State an early legislative negative than finally let her use a practical one which would go to the dissolution of the Union.

A memorial of one Tracy was read, praying a bankrupt law to be passed under the authority of the United States. A motion for the appointment of a committee to bring in a bill for such a purpose. There was a great deal of speaking on this subject, and, really, I thought the subject had not justice done to it. I got up and was listened to with attention while I explained the difference between the common law for the discharge of insolvent debtors and the laws respecting commission of bankruptcy, and confined the latter to its proper field, the trading part of the community; and this part only belonged to Congress to take up, and I doubted whether they had done most harm or good, etc. I was led into a detail of the laws of England on this head. Much was said on all hands, but we negatived the motion.

The appropriation bill was now reported, with a very trifling amendment indeed; to divide a sum of about a hundred and ninety dollars between our doorkeeper and the doorkeeper of the Representatives. The momentum of a spittle would have been as effectual to stop the flowing of the sea as any effort to check this bill. The appropriations were all in gross, and to the amount of upward of half a million. I could not get a copy of it. I wished to have seen the particulars specified, but such a hurry I never saw before. I did not see the bill in the hands of any of the members, but they might have had it for aught I know. I really fear the committee gave themselves little trouble about it. The moment it was through, General Schuyler and Mr. Morris called for it on the third and last reading, for they said the Secretary wanted to make remittances to Europe. They got what they wanted, and thus we had done with it.

This mode of doing business can not last long. All evils, it is said, cure themselves. Here is a general appropriation of above half a million dollars—the particulars not mentioned—the estimate on which it is founded may be mislaid or changed; in fact, it is giving the Secretary the money for him to account for as he pleases. This certainly is all wrong. The estimate should have formed part of the bill, or should have been recited in it.

Am I too sharp-sighted, or have I observed some shyness in some people? I believe it is the former. Mr. Morris this day asked if I had prepared anything on the subject we had been conversing about [buying lands]. I put the letter into his hands. He read it with apparent satisfaction; put it into his pocket. He asked me if some kind of houses could not be raised and covered with bark at a small expense on these lands. I told him they might, if honest men were employed who would not make a job of it.

The Senate adjourned about two o'clock. I was told there was warmth in the House of Representatives on the Quaker memorial, and went in. The House have certainly greatly debased their dignity, using base, invective, indecorous language; three or four up at a time, manifesting signs of passion, the most disorderly wanderings in their speeches, telling stories, private anecdotes, etc. I know not what may come of it, but there seems to be a general discontent among the members, and many of them do not hesitate to declare that the Union must fall to pieces at the rate we go on. Indeed, many seem to wish it.

March 23d.—Went with a party to wait on Mr. Jefferson. He was out. We left our names. Sat a long time in the Senate chamber without doing anything whatever. At last up came the appropriation bill. The original bill gave Gifford Dally, the doorkeeper of the Representatives, one hundred and ninety-two dollars for services during the vacancy. We divided the sum, and gave ninety-six dollars to Dally and ninety-six dollars to Mathers, our doorkeeper. This they [the Representatives] would not agree to; continued the one hundred and ninety-two dollars to Dally, and put in ninety-six dollars for Mathers. Pretty amusement for the governors of a great empire to play at cross-purposes! King, Elsworth, and Morris were all up, and "Adhere!" "Adhere!" was heard from every quarter of the House. Our Vice-President put some questions, but whether it was for "non-concurrence," "insisting," or "adhering," I do not remember. It was, however, carried; no one thinking it worth while to say no.

Mr. Morris chatted with great freedom with me to-day on his private affairs. Explained some of the difficulties he had met with in the settlement of his accounts. Says the balance will be in his favor. Declares he will soon have done and put to silence his adversaries. Justice says plainly this ought to be the case, if he has been injured. He is very full of the affair between him and me. His countenance speaks the appearance of sincerity and candor. Interest, however, the grand anchor to secure any man, lies at the bottom.

March 24th.—This day little of consequence done in the Senate. The appropriation bill was sent up. The Representatives withdrew their amendments, after having showed a spirit of petulance to no purpose. I was called out of the Senate. When I came in, the report of the committee on the difference of boundary between the United States and Nova Scotia was under consideration. I said a few words, which appeared to be well received, on the subject. Izard and Butler both manifested a most insulting spirit this day, when there was not the least occasion for it nor the smallest affront offered. These men have a most settled antipathy to Pennsylvania, owing to the doctrines patronized in that State on the subject of slavery. Pride makes fools of them, or rather completes what Nature began.

This day the Speaker entertained. The company was not numerous; the discourse not entertaining, or at least nothing remarkable.

March 25th.—The Speaker told me last night that Mr. Clymer wished to see us this morning at his lodgings. As I always embrace the smallest hint to meet the delegation, I was early ready, but the "Friends," who had been in town on the abolition business, called in two parties to take leave of us. I, however, hastened to Mr. Clymer's lodgings. Found Scott, Heister, and Wynkoop at the door. I asked what had happened. Scott, with a great laugh, said Clymer had read them a letter to the Speaker, and was dreadfully afraid all the people would fly to the Western world. I replied, "Scott, I told you some time ago that all this would happen if you taxed the Atlantic States too high, and you gave me a great Monongahela laugh in answer." "Aye," says he, "and I will give you many more." I went up-stairs, and had a letter of Clymer's composing put into my hands; the amount of it was that every man was worth two hundred pounds sterling; that every man that went to the Western country was lost to the United States, and therefore every tract of land we sold to a settler would be attended with the loss of a man or his equivalent, two hundred pounds sterling, deducting the trifle the United States would get for the land.

All this fine reason falls dead to the ground should it appear that the man is not lost to the United States. It is, however, a fact that by an impolitic oppression of taxes we may detach the whole country from us and connect them with New Orleans; and in that case we will get nothing for the lands. Clymer came in, and said on the principle of that letter he would vote against paying any of the public debt with back lands. What a deal of pains he has been at to fish up some kind of reason to accommodate his vote to the wish of the *public creditors, alias* speculators! They are a powerful body in Philadelphia, and therefore are not to be neglected. I asked what our friends in Philadelphia thought, particularly on the assumption of the State debt. He said they were divided, but there were more *against it* than *for it*. He now said some fine things on the improvement of the State, etc. I walked with him and Colonel Hartley. All the way to the Hall did his tongue run on the subject of going to the Potomac. I bore my testimony in the plainest language against all this; regretted our not having tried an adjournment to Philadelphia a year ago; said, if we would go to Philadelphia with the promise of the permanent residence on the Potomac, we could without it. He was peevish and fretful.

No business of consequence done in the Senate. Two bills came up to be signed. Our Vice-President used these words from the chair before he signed them: "Is there any objection, gentlemen, to the signing of these bills?" He seems a tone lower than he used to be. The amendment on the mitigation bill was non-concurred in, and managers for a conference appointed.

March 26th.—The bill for augmenting the military to sixteen hundred men came up. Read, and Monday appointed for a second reading. A petition read from Captain Barry and others for communication. Nothing else done in the Senate. Spent some time on the bill for the encouragement of inventions, etc. The Speaker had company this day—all Pennsylvanians. Mr. Morris took pains to make himself agreeable. The Speaker told him they had determined to risk the revenue business, as they now found Williamson and Ash would be for the assumption, as they had changed their minds. How true is the observation made by Henry, of Maryland: "All great governments resolve themselves into cabals"! Ours is a mere system of jockeying opinions. Vote this way for me, and I will vote that way for you.

March 27th.—Being Saturday, read in my room. After dinner walked and caught cold. In the evening received a few lines from Dr. Rush, in which he tells me I am complained of for my correspondence with the Comptroller-General. This, I well know, comes from Fitzsimons. He would wish that no man but himself should know anything of the finances of Pennsylvania. I have made advances to the Philadelphians repeatedly, but they shake us off, and, when meetings had been settled for the communication of knowledge, they have broken them up. But I am found to possess knowledge of the finances of Pennsylvania. The presumption is that I correspond with Nicholson. [I] am become independent of them, and therefore criminal. I had written to the Doctor, but inclosed a note to him on this subject, for which see my letter-book.

Mr. Morris has made no agreement with me about lands. He said he would draw up something on this subject in writing. Nothing of this has happened, and perhaps never will. I thought such a thing might happen, and was careful in my letter. But I will make no rash conclusions. Time will settle all matters, and we, with all our little bristlings, will soon be as quiet as the trodden sod.

March 28th.—Being Sunday, was a day devoted to the thoughts of my family. Wrote letters, as usual. I have been

upward of three months from them. This is really disagreeable. The time may come when I would give anything in my
power to be one day with them, and now I am absent with my
own consent. I wish I was honorably off with this same business of the Senate. If Congress continues to sit in New York,
I can not pretend to continue a member of it. Circumstances
may direct me to what is best. God has, however, given to
every man his talent for the express purpose of making use of
it; or, in other words, that he may conduct himself on the
principles of right reason. May he enable me to keep my lamp
trimmed always! Stayed at home all day.

March 29th.—Committee on the bill for the progress of writs,
etc., reported. Three other bills came up to us: one for treaty
with Indians; for extending the effect of the State inspection
laws; and the North Carolina session. The last amended by
striking out the word "Honorable" from before the names of
the Senators. Butler bounced, and Izard made frightful faces
at it. They were opposed by King, Elsworth, and Patterson. I
was pleased to see the Yorkers and the Southern people at it.
The business was got rid of by a new clause altogether in the
beginning of the bill, from which a clear inference in practice
follows, viz.: That the whole of a bill is in the power of the
Senate, notwithstanding their former agreement, and the concurrence of the other House to any part or parts of it; and
their deliberations are not confined to the parts only respecting
which the disagreement subsists. I have spoken to Otis to copy
all the papers that I may plead this precedent, if necessary;
for this doctrine was pointedly denied in the disputes respecting the permanent bill, viz., my papers for the copies made out
by Otis.

This day the House of Representatives took up the report
of the Committee of the Whole House on the Secretary's report; and, after adopting the first three clauses, recommitted
the one on the assumption of the State debts—twenty-nine to
twenty-seven; so that I hope this will be rejected at last. The
Speaker has declared that he will vote against it if there should
be a tie in the House. This was my opinion, which he early
adopted and which he has so often subscribed to, that it will be
impossible for him to recede from it upon this principle—that

a matter of moment, not absolutely necessary, had better be omitted than carried by so small a majority vote as one vote. This opinion has met with much approbation from many members of the Senate, and I have taken care to let the Speaker know it.

March 30th.—The bill for additional pay to the clerks of the accounts between the United States and individual States was called up and lost. Third reading of the bill for the progress of useful arts produced a debate by the New England members in favor of a man from their country, but by being joined by the Southern men we defeated them. Read the law for giving effect to the inspection laws of the States. Message from the Representatives with Cession bill agreed to. Message from the President with nominations to vacant offices. The bill for the military establishment took up the rest of the day in desultory debate, and was finally committed to seven members. This bill seems laying the foundation of a standing army. The justifiable reasons for using force seem to be the enforcing of laws, quelling insurrections, and repelling invasions. The Constitution directs all these to be done by militia. Should the United States, unfortunately, be involved in war, an army for the annoyance of an enemy in their own country (as the most effective mode of keeping the calamity at a distance and enforcing an adversary to terms) will be necessary. This seems the meaning of the Constitution, and that no troops should be kept up in peace. This bill certainly aims at different objects. The first error seems to have been the appointing of a Secretary of War when we were at peace, and now we must find troops lest his office should run out of employment.

Dressed and attended the levee. I generally used to leave this part of duty to Mr. Morris; but now he is gone, and, lest there should be any complaints, I will discharge this piece of etiquette. The day was fine and the levee large.

March 31st.—A call of the gladiators this morning. Therefore expect it will be a day of some importance in the House of Representatives. In the Senate the bill for enforcing the inspection law of the State had a third reading. The appointment of Rufus Putnam, a Judge of the Western Territory; James Brown, Attorney for Kentucky; and Henry Bogart,

Surveyor for Albany, were consented to. Senate adjourned.
Went early to hear the event of this day's debates in the
House of Representatives. Nothing remarkable, save a violent
personal attack on Hamilton by Judge Burke, of South Carolina,
which the men of the blade say must produce a duel. The question was not taken, on the assumption. Mr. Wynkoop spoke to
me in the chamber of Representatives, to have a meeting of the
delegation. I supported this idea, and we agreed to meet at the
Speaker's. But I first went and drank tea with Mr. Wynkoop
and Mrs. Wynkoop. There was a great deal of desultory discourse at the meeting. Mr. Clymer took on him to assert that
the State of Pennsylvania was in debt to the Union, and dis-
believed all Mr. Nicholson's statements, and declared unequivocally for burning all old accounts. I mentioned Nicholson's statements as being made from authority, and that they
neither ought nor could be invalidated on supposition; that the
old Confederation had proceeded every step on the grounds of
a final settlement; that to annihilate the old accounts was contrary to the new Constitution, which had sanctified every act
of the old Congress; nor could I see how any State could call
on the Union to assume any debt of theirs until she showed
by a settlement that she had exceeded her requisitions. Both
Clymer and Wynkoop are seeking for some plausible excuse
to change their ground. I have endeavored to humor them, but
their pride and obstinacy are hard to subdue.

April 1st.—This day in Senate two bills were signed, the
Carolina Cession act and the bill for giving effect to the State
inspection laws. A committee was also appointed to settle the
pay of the Senators up to this time.

The Senate adjourned, and I went into the chamber of
Representatives to hear the debates. It was a dull scene. Gerry
took up the time of the committee to the hour of adjournment.
He is a tedious and most disagreeable speaker. The committee
rose and no question was taken. Soon after I came in I took
an opportunity of speaking to Mr. Wynkoop. I was pointing
out some inconveniences of the assumption. I found he seemed
much embarrassed. Lawrence and Benson had got him away
from his usual seat to near where they commonly sat. He paused
a little; got up rather hastily; said, "God bless you!" went out

of the chamber, and actually took his wife and proceeded home to Pennsylvania. The way in which this good man can best serve his country is in superintending his farm. Perhaps there is no method more acceptable to Nature; he certainly is wanting in political fortitude. Benson, Lawrence, the Secretary, and others have paid attention to him, and he has not firmness of mind to refuse them his vote. But he has done what equally offends them and subjects himself to ridicule: he has abandoned the whole business and deserted the cause of his country at a time when an honest vote is inestimable. To-morrow being Good Friday, we adjourned over to Saturday.

April 2d.—The House of Representatives met, but adjourned on account of the holiday. I conversed this day at the Hall with George Gray. He declares the people of Pennsylvania are universally opposed to assumption, now the matter is understood. This is the effect of the publications which I have labored hard indeed to get into the prints. The Speaker is now firm against the assumption, and so is Scott. Clymer is so, too, I believe, but I am not quite certain whether his wish of popularity has as yet been able to subdue his pride and obstinacy. Hartley is too giddy and unsettled for any one to determine how he will vote, and, as his judgment has no share in it, the presumption is that he will vote with Smith, of Carolina, and those whose company he always keeps. I have put my political life in my hand in starting this opposition in the teeth of the Philadelphians. If I fail, my seat in Congress and disgrace in the public eye will follow. But I am conscious of rectitude of intention, and *hic murus aheneus esto, nil conscire sibi, nulla pallescere culpa.*

I was this day to have dined with the Secretary [Hamilton], but a violent storm of wind and rain came on, and I could not get a hackney. The Speaker offered me his carriage, but then his servants were all gone to church.

April 3d.—Called in the morning at Mr. Hamilton's office to make an apology for not dining with him. Could not see him. He was closeted with the Secretary of War. Was desired to stay until he was disengaged. The importance of my business would not justify this. Gave my name and compliments to Colonel Hamilton, and information that the badness of the weather prevented my dining with him yesterday, as I happened to be so unfortunate as not to be able to procure a carriage; and now, this momentous affair being settled, went to the Hall. The minutes were read. A message was received from the President of the United States. A report was handed to the Chair. We looked and laughed at each other for half an hour, and adjourned. The report was the pay due to each member. Dr. Elmer and Mr. Bassett whispered me, after the report was handed in, that King and Schuyler were allowed full pay, notwithstanding they had not been much with us, and that Dr. Johnson was allowed full pay and mileage to Connecticut, though he lives here, while the time Dr. Elmer was absent was deducted. Honesty thrives but badly east of the Hudson.

I went into the Representative chamber, expecting the assumption would be taken up. A listless apathy seemed to pervade the whole. Two motions were negatived touching some appointment of a foreign nature that did not seem to have been well digested. Somebody said adjourn, and they adjourned accordingly. This really seems like the mockery of business. The New England men despair of being able to saddle us with their debts, and now they care not whether they do any business or not. Mr. George Gray, of the Lower Ferry, Mr. Luper, his son-in-law, Colonel Oswald, and another gentleman, dined with us. We had much free conversation after dinner. Mr. Luper had waited on Mr. Fitzsimons before he came away. Fitzsimons advised him not to come, and told him a year hence would be time enough; *that nothing would be done in the business until he returned to New York.* They sat till late. I was happy to have a company of Pennsylvanians.

April 4th.—I wrote my letters early. The day was inviting and I could not avoid the temptation of walking out. I went to Scott's lodgings and he walked with me. The town is much agitated about a duel between Burke and Hamilton. So many people concerned in the business may really make the fools fight.

When I was called down to dinner, the Speaker and General Muhlenberg were closeted with Clymer and Jackson. All was profound mystery. We had half finished our dinner before they joined us, I saw they were filled with thoughts of

importance, but I scorned to be inquisitive. I retired to my
chamber. The Speaker soon came to me and unfolded the
mystery. Clymer had a proposal to barter away the Pennsylvania votes for an assumption for the Carolina and Massachusetts votes for an adjournment to Philadelphia. He and Fitzsimons are now squirming like eels in a basket to regain the
popularity which they have or are likely to lose on this business by bringing forward a plausible pretext to justify their
last vote. The Speaker, however, openly avowed to me the
reason of the vote for assumption, viz., consolidation and uniting in one Government. I told him plainly Hamilton had no
ability for such work, and the thing would miscarry in his or
any other hands. I determined to go and call on Clymer about
this business. I did so, but he had Jackson (of the President's
family) with him.*

I sat till I was tired and rose with the first of the company
to come away. Clymer asked me to walk on the Battery, and
we roamed almost the whole length of the town, up the East
River and back again, without his giving me an opportunity
of speaking to him. I felt hurt at his distant treatment. I went
with him home. He called Jackson in. Jackson made a florid
harangue on the golden opportunity of bartering the votes of
Pennsylvania with South Carolina and Massachusetts to give
the assumption, and get the residence of Congress. Whatever
I might have done in other company, I would not commit myself
to Jackson. I spoke my sentiments sincerely on the villainy of
bartering votes; declared my opinion that Pennsylvania need
make no sacrifice to obtain Congress; that matters were working as favorably as could be wished; that I entertained no
doubt of adjourning to Philadelphia; that assuming the State
debts in the proposed manner was so radically wrong that nothing could justify the act, and that the postponement of it ought
to take place at any rate.

Clymer said it would not be postponed; it would be carried.
I said the Pennsylvanians might see each other before that time.
He said they could not. I told him if the Pennsylvanians were
able to postpone it after a contract was made they were able to
do it without any contract; and if they really meant to sell their

---

* Meaning a voter for Hamilton.

votes, it was idle to talk of giving them without and before a contract was made. Make a present of a thing, and you need not demand the price afterward. I concluded with saying I would have time enough to make up my mind before the business appeared before the Senate, but had no objection to deliver my sentiments at any time, and had given them now with freedom. The cold, distant, stiff, and, let me add, stinking manner of this man is really painful to be submitted to. I never will go into any company with design to give offense, but I really think out of respect to myself I ought to avoid his company; at least I need not go into it without necessity. Jackson's interfering in this business is far from proper.

Hence appears plainly how much the assumption of the State debts was made a point of by the court party. In fact, the reduction of the State governments was the object in theory in framing both the Constitution and Judiciary and in as many laws of the United States as were capable of taking a tincture of that kind. But it won't do.

April 5th, Monday.—The bill for the progress of the useful arts was concurred with after considerable debate. The report of the Senators from the joint committee on the Mitigation bill was that the disagreement continued. A communication was received from the President of the United States of three acts of the Legislature of New York. The whole paper was read. The act of transmission from the government of New York was pomposity itself. They, however, often reiterated the words "free and independent," which I thought done designedly. I had some discourse with Colonel Hartley, and he has promised to withhold his vote for the assumption for some time at least.

I went this afternoon to hear a negro preach. I can only say it would be in favor of religion in general if preachers manifested the same fervor and sincerity that were apparent in his manner. He declared himself untutored, but he seemed to have the Bible by heart. *Tempora mutantur et nos mutamur in illis.*

April 6th.—The Senate seemed likely to have no business before them this day; but all at once up rose Few, and offered a report of the bill for the military establishment. Some trifling amendments were made in the compensation to the officers, but the bill was materially the same. It was agreed to, as the sense of the Senate, that no report should be offered until the bill for regulating the intercourse with the Indians and the treaty bill should be put into the hands of the same committee; but whatever is, is best. It is out of the hands of the committee and postponed. I spoke against the whole bill as an egg from which a standing army would be hatched, as it is a standing army in fact, for the smallness of the number does not diminish the principle. But I foresee I will have much to say under this head at a future day.

Carrol, of Carrolton, edged near me in the Senate chamber and asked me if I had seen the King of France's speech and the acts of the "Tiers États," by which the distinctions of the nobility were broken down. I told him I had, and I considered it by no means dishonorable to us that our efforts against titles and distinctic... were now seconded by the representative voice of twenty-four millions. A flash of joy lightened from his countenance. How fatal to our fame as lovers of liberty would it have been had we adopted the shackles of servility which enlightened nations are now rejecting with detestation!

April 7th.—A committee was appointed in the Senate to bring in a bill for the territory of the United States south of the Ohio. I did not oppose the appointment of a committee, but told some of them that they must make it stand alone, as I wished to avoid all expense. I had no notion of salaries to the Governor, judges, etc. I considered the motion brought forward by way of making some entry on the journals as much as anything else. A short bill, however, came up and had a first reading.

The Speaker had company this day. I was wanting in spirits, and did not seem to enjoy it. The table was, however, filled well, and there was a good flow of conviviality. After dinner the Speaker told me that Fitzsimons and Clymer wanted to see the delegation at their quarters. I was not well. It was late, and a tempest of wind and cold. But I went. Fitzsimons [spoke as if he] had been hired to extol the political merit of Massachusetts and South Carolina and deprecate that of Pennsylvania. It was in vain that I told him everything in a pecuniary point of view must remain in doubt until the accounts were settled; that the only man who had it in his power to give an opinion on the subject (the Comptroller-General) had taught us to think differently. I said that the State, Navy, and defense of the river Delaware had cost vast sums. I could not see that the defense of the Delaware, etc., was any more charged against Pennsylvania than the expense of the American arms before Boston was a demand against Massachusetts, or the charges at Yorktown against Virginia. If Pennsylvania advanced the money, it was in the general defense, as well as her own, and the charge lay well against the Union.

The business of the meeting was to consult about an adjournment to Philadelphia, and, as the votes of Pennsylvania would determine for or against assumption, whether they could not be so managed as to affect that measure. I will only set down what I said on the matter as opinion, that to barter votes was unjustifiable; that the risk of losing votes was as great as the chance of gaining by making a bargain with the other side, for Philadelphia had friends on both sides; that the best mode was to postpone the assumption and push the adjournment to Philadelphia while both parties feared and both courted the Pennsylvania vote.

April 8th.—A bill which came up yesterday for suspending part of the revenue law with respect to the port of Yeomus in Virginia was read a second time. Now Elsworth moved some alteration of the law with regard to some ports in Connecticut. Langdon wanted an alteration in New Hampshire, and Dalton one for Massachusetts. It was committed to these three members. God forgive me if I wrong them, but I fear they want to make loopholes in the impost law to suit their private purposes, or rather the purposes of State smuggling.

I never observed so drooping an aspect, so turbid and forlorn an appearance as overspread the partisans of the Secretary [Hamilton] in our House this forenoon. If I had chosen to use the language of political scandal, I would call them "Senatorial Gladiators." Elsworth and Izard in particular walked almost all the morning back and forward. Strong and Patterson seemed moved, but not so much agitated. King looked like a boy that had been whipped, and General Schuyler's hair stood on end as if the Indians had fired at him. I accounted for the appearance of King and Schuyler from the publications that have appeared against them in the papers for two days past.

Just before dinner Andrew Brown, the printer, called. It seems there had been a meeting of the citizens of Philadelphia on Saturday last to consider on the subject of General Knox's report, and a committee is appointed to draw up something. Brown has refused to print for them, and has flown off to this place for the purpose of giving notice of the event and claiming his reward; and perhaps a third motive has had weight with him, for I really never saw any man have more the appearance of fright upon him. I know him to have been a spy and tool for Hamilton for some time past. He told us of some man having offered some violent pieces to him for publication, which he said were written well; but he refused to print them, and the author took them away. He said they were addressed to the yeomanry of Pennsylvania. I suspect this may be my friend George Logan. He ought to beware of A. Brown; he does not know him. Brown owned to us that Hamilton had written to Jefferson in his favor after publishing his recantation, and refused to print anything against the Secretary's report.

April 9th.—The committee of yesterday reported the bill with Elsworth's amendment only. Said Mr. Hamilton was of opinion, when the new impost law was enacted, the other amendments could be introduced. This is art in him to make friends to his new bill, and shows that he is either still confident of success or affects it. There was no objection and the bill had all its readings.

Elsworth reported a bill for the government south of the Ohio. It was to be the same as the government of the Western Territory, *mutatis mutandis.* I had some previous discourse with Elsworth on this subject. I can with truth pronounce him the most uncandid man I ever knew possessing such abilities. I am often led to doubt whether he has a particle of integrity; perhaps such a quality is useless in Connecticut.

In Senate this day the gladiators seemed more than commonly busy. As I came out from the Hall, all the President's family were there—Humphreys, Jackson, Nelson, etc. They had Vining with them, and, as I took it, were a standing committee to catch the members as they went in or came out. The crisis is at hand. At dinner the Speaker told me there had been a call of the Secretary's party last night. Fitzsimons, he said, had been sent for, and they had determined to risk an action to-morrow.

April 10th.—Busy to near eleven writing letters to my family. Dressed and attended to see the event of the day, but it was put off by consent. The Treasurer told me the reason of it afterward. Sherman, who is against the assumption, is expected to go away, and thus the other party will be less strong, or at least more so, by one vote. The Secretary's people scarce disguise their design, which is to create a mass of debts which will justify them in seizing all the sources of Government, thus annihilating the State Legislatures and creating an empire on the basis of consolidation.

April 11th, Sunday.—Stayed at my lodgings almost all day, a few minutes excepted, when I went to the lodgings of General Irwin, who is this day to set off on his journey to Carlisle. Wrote sundry letters, read, etc. I charged General Irwin with letters for Harrisburg and Sunbury. Wrote a few lines to Eleazer Oswald, editor of the Independent Gazetteer, to inclose his paper and forward it to my son Johnny, to be left at Adam Zantzinger's in Market Street, Philadelphia.

April 12th, Monday.—The business done in the Senate was trifling. A bill for establishing the government of the North Carolina cession was taken up. I had occasion to speak to it, and moved a postponement until the bill be printed and put into the members' hands. It was carried. Elsworth was fretted, and I cared not. Two amended bills came up from the other House and were postponed. We adjourned between twelve and one o'clock.

I went into the House of Representatives to hear the question of assumption taken up. Clymer got up; said the assumption was two and a quarter millions against his State; more than she ought to pay; but, for confirming the Government and for national purposes, he would vote for it. I could not hear all he said, but the above was the amount of it.

Fitzsimons hoped to have a great many conditions obtained, such as that the interest of the State debt should be paid in the respective States; that no improper charges should be brought forward. But he would vote for it now in expectation that these conditions would be obtained afterward. Certainly this could not be called the conduct of a wise man; he voted as well as Clymer for it formerly and took all the Pennsylvania delegation with him except Heister and General Muhlenberg without any condition whatever, unless it might be private ones known only to himself and the Treasury. The question was, however, taken and lost: thirty-one against it and twenty-nine for it.* Fitzsimons, Clymer, and Hartley voted for it.

Sedgwick, from Boston, pronounced a funeral oration over it. He was called to order; some confusion ensued; he took his hat and went out. When he returned, his visage, to me, bore the visible marks of weeping. Fitzsimons reddened like scarlet; his eyes were brimful. Clymer's color, always pale, now verged to a deadly white; his lips quivered, and his nether jaw shook with convulsive motions; his head, neck, and breast contracted with gesticulations resembling those of a turkey or goose nearly strangled in the act of deglutition. Benson bungled like a shoe-maker who had lost his end. Ames's aspect was truly hippocratic —a total change of face and features; he sat torpid, as if his faculties had been benumbed. Gerry exhibited the advantages of a cadaverous appearance, at all times placid and far from pleasing; he ran no risk of deterioration. Through an interruption of hectic lines and consumptive coughs he delivered himself of a declaration that the delegates of Massachusetts would proceed no further, but send to their State for instructions.

Happy impudence sat enthroned on Lawrence's brow. He rose in puffing pump and moved that the committee should rise, and assigned the agitation of the House as a reason. Wadsworth hid his grief under the rim of a round hat. Boudinot's wrinkles rose in ridges and the angles of his mouth were depressed and assumed a curve resembling a horse's shoe. Fitzsimons first recovered recollection, and endeavored to rally the discomfited and disheartened heroes. He hoped the good sense of the House would still predominate and lead them to reconsider the vote which had been now taken; and he doubted not but

---

* This, of course, greatly reduced the value of certificates.

what it would yet be adopted under proper modifications. The Secretary's group pricked up their ears, and Speculation wiped the tear from either eye. Goddess of description, paint the gallery; here's the paper, find fancy quills or crayons yourself.

April 13th, Tuesday.—Nothing of moment done this day in the Senate. The bill for the Territory south of the Ohio passed a second reading. Some trifling debate on the amendments of the bill defining crimes and punishments. The day was clear, though somewhat cold, but I felt a desire of being abroad, and walked out almost all day with Mr. R. Harris, who is now abroad again.

April 14th, Wednesday.—There was nothing of importance transacted this day in the Senate, no debate worth minuting. The Senate adjourned, and we, or at least I, went into the House of Representatives. But even there everything seemed equally unimportant. The House adjourned, and as I was to dine this day with Mr. Izard, the Speaker, and General [Muhlenberg] being likewise engaged at the same place, we had an hour on hand to saunter away before dinner. It began to rain as we got to Izard's. There was of the company Count von Berkel, the Speaker of the New York House of Representatives, members of Congress, etc. Among our wine I mentioned the expected death of Dr. Franklin. Izard knew him as well as any man in the world. Dr. Johnson would yield to no man on intimate acquaintance with his [Franklin's] character, and at him they both went. I really never was much of an admirer of the Doctor, but I could hardly find it in my heart to paint the devil so bad. He had every fault of vanity, ambition, want of sincerity, etc. Lee's rascally virtue of prudence was all they would leave him.

I must note it down that Clymer called me out of the Senate chamber this day. It was on no business of any consequence. He talked with me a considerable time. After I came into the Representative chamber he came and took a chair beside me. I must declare that, be his motives what they may, I never saw him so condescending. I will not balk him in his advances to me; my heart tells me that peace with all the world is the most acceptable and desirable object to be pursued. I will not shun her, but place myself in her paths. What is it that whispers in my ear that, if any dirty trick is played me that has its date about this time, I need not be at a loss to guess the author? No, no. I will give it no such meaning. I will not suppose him to have worn a cloak, but that he came clothed in candor.

April 15th, Thursday.—The bill for regulating the military establishment was called up. The friends of this bill seem to be chiefly Butler, King, and Schuyler. I have opposed this bill hitherto as often as it has been before the House as the foundation, the corner-stone of a standing army. The troops are augmented one half. The reasons hitherto given have been the distressed state of Georgia. Butler has blazed away on this subject at a great rate; declared over and over that Georgia would seek protection elsewhere if troops were not sent to support her, etc., etc., and said fifty Indians had penetrated into that State, of which he had authentic information, etc. Carrol joined him. King, Schuyler, Elsworth, and Lee opposed them. Lee made a set speech against standing armies. He really spoke well. King at last got up and rather upbraided the Georgia members for their silence on this question. This brought up Colonel Gunn. He declared he knew nothing of fifty Indians making any inroads into Georgia. He was just from there, and had the latest accounts. Georgia was in peace, and never had a better prospect of continuing so. There existed no cause in Georgia for augmenting the troops; and since that was the reason assigned for it, he should vote against it.

Infatuated people that we are! The first thing done under our new Government was the creation of a vast number of offices and officers. A treasury delated into as many branches as interest could frame. A Secretary of War with a host of clerks; and above all a Secretary of State, and all these men labor in their several vocations. Hence we must have a mass of national debt to employ the Treasury, an army for fear the Department of War should lack employment. Foreign engagements, too, must be attended to to keep up the consequences of that Secretary. The next cry will be for an Admiralty. Give Knox his army, and he will soon have a war on hand; indeed, I am clearly of opinion that he is aiming at this even now, and that, few as the troops are that he now has under his direction, he will have a war in less than six months with the Southern Indians.

Lent the Speaker fifty dollars.

April 16th.—And now again for the augmentation of the troops. I took a minute view of all the papers forwarded by General Knox. They were copies of letters which he had received from different places and carried, evidently, management on the face of them. Thus, for instance, General Knox writes to General Wayne in Georgia to inform him whether the Spaniards had not lately supplied the Indians with arms and ammunition. General Wayne answers that his inquiries on this head resolved themselves into the affirmative, and adds his opinion that it is highly probable hostile uses may be made of those supplies by the savages. In this manner leading letters procure favorable answers from men who expect to be employed in case troops are raised. Before Colonel Gunn came, the dangers and distress of Georgia were magnified as far as fancy could from frightful pictures. Colonel Gunn contradicts all this.

New phantoms for the day must be created. Now a dangerous and dreadful conspiracy is discovered to be carrying on between the people of Kentucky and the Spaniards. King unfolded this mysterious business, adding that he conceived his fears were well founded. He firmly believed there was a conspiracy; that it was dangerous to put arms into the hands of the frontier people for their defense, lest they should use them against the United States.

I really could scarce keep my seat and hear such base subterfuges made use of one after another. I rose, demanded what right gentlemen had to monopolize information. If they had it, let them come forward with it and give other people an opportunity of judging of the authenticity of the information, as well as the persons in possession of it; declared that I could not tamely sit and hear the characters of the people on the Western waters traduced by the lump. This day was the first ever I heard of the word "conspiracy" being applied to the inhabitants of the Western waters. I had a right to doubt it until authentic proof was brought forward of the fact. I felt myself disposed to wipe King hard, and certainly did so. It was moved and seconded very fairly to reduce the number to one thousand, and carried, eleven to nine. Elsworth, though he spoke for the reduction, voted against us. Mr. Morris desired to be excused from voting, as he had come but lately. Elsworth said he voted against one thousand because he wanted twelve hundred; and, though it was certainly out of all order, got a question put on this number and carried it by one vote. No man ever had a more complete knack of putting his foot in a business than this same Elsworth. At one thousand we should have had but one regiment. Now the committee to whom it is recommitted will try to continue them in two. And yet economy is all his cry.

I gave notice that, when the title of the bill came to be considered, I would move to strike out "for regulating the military establishment of the United States," and mentioned particularly what I took the intention of the troops to be agreeably to the old acts of Congress, viz., *protection of the frontiers of the United States; facilitating the surveying and selling the public lands and preventing unwarrantable encroachments on the same.* The man must be blind who does not see a most unwarrantable management respecting our military affairs. The Constitution certainly never contemplated a standing army in time of peace. A well-regulated militia to execute the laws of the Union, quell insurrections, and repel invasions, is the very language of the Constitution. General Knox offers a most exceptional bill for a general militia law which excites (as it is most probably he expected) a general opposition. Thus the business of the militia stands still, and the Military Establishment bill, which increases the standing troops one half, is pushed with all the art and address of ministerial management.

April 17th.—Being Saturday, a party was formed to go to Haerlem. Long cooped up in the city, I joyfully joined them, but the wind soon blew cold and raw from the east, and we could not stay out of doors. Like most other human expectations, our hopes vanished in disappointment. I got some cold, and felt slight complaints of the rheumatic kind. The ramble has, however, had its uses, and may cure me on the subject of excursions in the future.

April 18th, Sunday.—This is the most tempestuous day which I remember. Snow, torrents of rain, high winds. Kept the house all day; read and wrote to my family. The Speaker received letters by which it appears the Philadelphians, or at least the aristocrats, will support Mifflin rather than him [Muhlenberg] for Governor. He recapitulated the return they had always made to him for his engaging the Germans to support their measures. He had a share of the profits of the vendue office from Paton, but it amounted to little. They deserted him on the appointment of vendue-master. For the Northern Liberties he got the office in Montgomery by a constitutional vote, and it never paid him for the paper he spent for the Republican party.

April 19th, Monday.—The journals of the Senate can scarce designate a day of less importance than the present. The yeas and nays had been fairly taken on reducing the troop from sixteen hundred to one thousand, but the way the minutes read the question was for the striking out of every man, viz., the whole sixteen hundred. Elsworth moved to strike out the whole of the yeas and nays, etc. This certainly was against all rule: the reading of the minutes is for correction, not altering them. Wyngate and Langdon spoke a good deal, but it was in vain. They carried it.

I bought two little pocket-books for Betsey and Nelly, to be sent home by Bobby Harris. On the vellum in one of them I wrote:

> A daddy to a daughter dear
> This little present sends:
> May she to him, far off or near,
> By duty make amends!

In the other one I wrote the following:

> A father to a favorite child
> Presents this little toy:
> May she through life a sunshine mild
> And happiness enjoy!

Wretched man that I am, who do not break loose from this disagreeable place and stay, live and die with my family!

April 20th, Tuesday.—Dressed this day to go with Bobby Harris to the levee, but the President was gone to Long Island. We sat a long time in the Senate, without doing anything. At last the committee on the military bill reported. The report was a mere matter of detail, only the clause limiting the bill to two years was struck out. I had given notice that I would move to alter the title of the bill so as to express the use and intention of raising the troops, but our Vice-President, in order to jockey me, was for putting the question on the bill, without saying anything about the title at all. Elsworth, who can not bear that anybody should move anything but himself, and to whom I showed the title I had proposed to offer, pushed himself before me with a title different and much shorter. He was not seconded. I offered mine, and was seconded by Lee. A long debate ensued. Elsworth now gave all the opposition in his power. It was really painful to hear the servile sentiments that were advanced. The spirit of the whole was, that we had nothing to do with the troops; had no right to know what the President did with them or applied them to; it was interfering with his command, etc. I thought they were well answered. But what of that? We lost it. Elsworth now showed plainly that he cared little about his motion, and that he had only started his to draw off the Senate from mine. Butler had declared he would second him during the debate on mine. I, therefore, called for it. He now moved it differently, viz., "An act to raise the troops for the service of the United States." His first motion was "for the defense of the frontiers and for other purposes." All we could do was to get a question on it, such as it was. The Senate divided, ten to ten. The Vice-President made a remarkable speech. He said to raise troops for the service of the United States was as much a standing army as a military establishment, and voted for the old title. I thought I confirmed every argument I advanced, either from the old or new Constitution of Pennsylvania, or from the Constitution of the United States. But a sentence from the Secretary [Knox] is of more avail than all the Constitutions in the United States with many people.

The limiting clause at the end of the bill confining it to two years being lost, I moved that three years in the first clause should be struck out and two inserted. I brought forward the "appropriation" clause in the Constitution to support me in this motion, but, as it was known where the majority was, I could not obtain a second.

We had a meeting last night of our delegation on the subject of removing Congress. The avowed language of the Philadelphians [was] to make a Potomac contract. I insisted we should lose as much on one hand as we could gain on the other, and infamy was certain; that the business could be better done without it, etc.

April 21st.—The bill for regulating the military establishment was taken up for a third reading. Being in the Senate, and of course in order, I moved to restore the seventeenth section, which had been struck out yesterday, in the following words: "And be it further enacted that this act shall continue and be in force until the 26th day of March, 1792." I went over the Constitutions of Pennsylvania, old and new; that they were abhorrent of a standing army in time of peace inferred, as I thought, clearly the same doctrine from the Constitution of the United States. I then showed that this bill established a standing army. I was for regulating the military establishments of the United States. It carried a permanent establishment on the face of it, as it was unlimited in point of time. It clearly carried with it a permanent standing army. I compared it to the Mutiny bill of Great Britain. All the world knew that Great Britain had a standing army, and her soldiers were enlisted generally for life; and yet the jealousy of the nation was such that the boldest minister dared not propose the extending of the Mutiny bill to more than one year. In the legislative theory, the English had no standing army. It was but an annual one. But if the bill passed in its present form we should not have even a theory to oppose to a standing army, etc.

Elsworth got up and said the reason the clause was struck out was that it contradicted the terms of enlistment, and he made a distinction between enlisting men for three years and appropriating pay for them for three years. We could do the one. We could not do the other without breaking the Constitution. He wished they were enlisted for seven or ten years, etc. I answered that it seemed as if men strained their ingenuity to try how near they could approach an infraction of the Constitution without breaking it. There could be no doubt but what the clause limiting the appropriation to two years was meant as a bar against a standing army, and yet gentlemen seemed to strain their faculties to accomplish the very end prohibited, without being chargeable with a direct breach of commandments, etc.

Elsworth declared, both yesterday and this day, that military establishment meant and could mean nothing short of a standing army. Carrol used the same language, and expressly said that, though the Constitution of Pennsylvania might forbid it, we were not to be governed by any State Constitution. But of all the flamers, none blazed like Izard. He wished for a standing army of ten thousand men. He feared nothing from them. No nation ever lost its liberty by a standing army, etc. The Romans lost their liberty, but it was not by the army under Julius Cæsar. He was well answered by Lee, but it was in vain. A standing army was the avowed doctrine, and on the question Lee, Wyngate, and myself rose. I openly declared my regret that there were not enough of us to call the yeas and nays. Mr. Morris was not in at the taking of the question.

I find in some conversation which I have had with the Speaker that Hartley is very dependent in his circumstances. A mere borrower and discounter of notes at the Philadelphia bank. It is much against him in point of prudence that he should be the most extravagant member of the Pennsylvania delegation.

April 22d.—The morning looked so tempting I could not resist the impulse I felt for walking out. The Speaker joined me at the door. We called on Mr. Wynkoop, who is confined with his sore leg. We got on the assumption of State debts. I find the Speaker rather wavers of late. Wynkoop seemed all Secretary [Hamilton]. I embarked, as I generally do, and I endeavored to speak so plain that I scarce think it possible I could be misunderstood; and I could not help thinking that to understand and obtain consent were inseparable. He waved what I said as if he would push all by in the lump. But if I had talked to a mute camel, or addressed myself to a dead horse, my speech would have had the same effect; and yet he seemed to have neither opinion nor system of his own.

Attended at the Hall. A bill was committed, a message was received, and the Senate adjourned. Wrote a short piece against the assumption of State debts; sent a copy to Bailey for publication. This day there were accounts published of the death of Dr. Franklin, and the House of Representatives voted to drape their arms for a month. When I consider how much the Doctor has been celebrated, and when I compare his public fame with his private character, I am tempted to doubt whether any man was as perfect. Yet it is, perhaps, for the good of society that patterns of perfection should be held up for men to copy after. I will, therefore, give him my vote of praise, and, if any Senator moves crape for his memory, I shall have no objection to it; yet we suffered Grayson to die without any attention to his memory, though he belonged to our body, and perhaps had some claim to a mark of sorrow.

April 23d.—Felt rheumatic pains over a considerable part of me, and really have some fear that I shall have a fit of it. A bill had been committed yesterday "for the relief of a certain description of officers." I believe it came from the Secretary of War. It was absolutely unintelligible, and it really struck me it was meant as the stock to ingraft some mischief on with respect to the commutation pensions and half-pay of the old army, everything relating to which we had generally considered as settled. I spoke freely of it yesterday and this day, though I was not of the committee. The committee, however, reported against the whole of it, and it was rejected.

It really seems as if a listlessness or spirit of laziness pervaded the House of Representatives. Anything which comes from a Secretary is adopted almost without any examination. The military establishment bill came up—concurred in. Strange that not a Pennsylvanian should object to this bill. As it now stands, it flatly contradicts the Constitution of Pennsylvania, both old and new.

Carrol rose and made a motion that the Senate should wear crape for a month for the loss of Dr. Franklin. Before he was seconded, Elsworth got up and opposed it; said, as it would not be carried in the Senate, he trusted it would not be seconded. I rose and seconded Carrol. Izard and Butler hated Dr. Franklin, and I well knew that this opposition of Elsworth aimed at their gratification. Perhaps my supporting Carrol had something of a tincture of the same kind. King and Dr. Johnson joined Elsworth. Elsworth addressed Carrol and told him (through the Chair) that he might as well withdraw his motion, as it would be lost. This was really insulting. But as the matter, strictly speaking, was not senatorial or such as belonged to us in our capacity as a public body, and as it was opposed, Carrol looked at me and I nodded assent, and it was withdrawn.

April 24th.—A party was formed by General Muhlenberg to go to Long Island, but, recollecting the disappointment of last Saturday, I declined going with them. Stayed at home and spent the day rather in a lounging manner. Wrote some letters. The Speaker proposed a ride in his carriage. I was all passive. He took a lady who was indisposed. I went in the evening and sat awhile with Mr. Wynkoop. In the afternoon Henry Stone and some other members of Congress called on me to go and see some cattle of enormous size. I went. Two bullocks of great bulk indeed were shown to us. I was sorry for my walk. They were in the yard of the slaughter-house. I now learned some secrets of the butcher business which I never knew before. The ox is emptied by repeated bleedings of almost all his veins before he is killed. A place is fitted up to which their heads are drawn up by a rope, and the jugular veins are opened. The blood falls down on the boards, inclined so that it runs into a trough fixed in the ground; and hogs are kept to feed on it. All this preparation is made to make the beef white. Then the great, harmless creatures had undergone several of their bleedings, and were moving about faint and languid, with looks of dumb despair. O man, what a monster art thou! I can not get rid of the impression this sight has left me.

April 25th, Sunday.—I wrote letters as usual to my family this morning. At ten o'clock went to Mr. Wynkoop's lodgings, in order to go to the meeting. It blew up cold and began to rain. The clergyman we intended to hear (Dr. Lynn) was sick, so we did not go out, but I sat with him a considerable time. Our chat was on various and trifling subjects: weather, home, farming, and what not. After a pause he broke out with a laugh, saying how fine and quietly we got over the military establishment; all smooth—not a word of opposition. He expressed great satisfaction, and seemed to manifest that kind of triumph which would follow the performance of an arduous task with unexpected facility. Surely the ministerial gentry must have looked for opposition and prepared themselves

accordingly; and my worthy friend must have been of their
council, which seems a hard thought, but what am I to believe?
I, however, soon undeceived him with regard to the part I had
acted in the Senate, and he looked like a man who unexpectedly
finds himself in strange company.

April 26th, Monday.—Attended the Hall. Mr. Walker, from
Virginia, the gentleman elected in the room of Mr. Grayson,
took his seat. The Progress bill, which in fact consisted only
of one clause continuing the old one to another session, had
a second reading. We did not continue in our seats for more
than three quarters of an hour, till King moved an adjournment. Modesty by degrees begins to leave. We used to stay in
the Senate chamber till about two o'clock, whether we did
anything or not, by way of keeping up the appearance of business. But even this we seem to be got over.

Dr. Elmer asked me to walk with him. I saw cards handed
about the Senate, but this happens so often that I took no
notice of it. When we were in the street the doctor asked me
if I had not a card to dine with the President. I told him,
with all the indifference I could put on, no, and immediately
took up some other subject, which I entered upon with eagerness, as if I had hardly noticed his question. This is the second
time the Doctor has asked me the same question, so that the
President's neglect of me can be no secret. How unworthy
of a great character is such littleness! He [Washington] is
not aware, however, that he is paying me a compliment that
none of his guests can claim. He places me above the influence
of a dinner, even in his own opinion. Perhaps he means it as
a punishment for my opposition to court measures. Either way,
I care not a fig for it. I certainly feel a pride arising from a
consciousness that the greatest man in the world has not credit
enough with me to influence my conduct in the least. This
pride, however, or perhaps I should call it self-approbation, is
the result of my conduct and by no means the motive of it.
This I am clear in.

I am so very intent on getting Congress away from this
place that I went to see the Philadelphians and concert what
was further to be done. I wished to communicate to them the
result of my inquiries, and receive their stock of information

on the subject of removal. I had some time ago determined never to call on them any more, but my anxiety on this point made me break through this rule. But the result has made me re-enact my former resolution. I think it best to respect myself. Let this resolution be as a ring on my finger or the shirt on my back; let me never be without it.

This morning we had snow near two inches deep. It melted as it fell during the fore part of the day, and turned at last to rain.

This day Mr. Clymer made his famous speech for throwing away the Western world. A noble sacrifice, truly, to gratify the public creditors of Philadelphia! Reject territory of an extent of an empire so that it may be out of the power of Congress to oblige the public creditors to take any part of it. This, added to the confiscation of the seventeen shillings six-pence in every pound of alienated certificates, which virtually belonged to the person who performed the original service and bestowing on it a base speculation, completes the counterpart of villainy to the meritorious soldier on the one hand, and defrauded and betrayed country on the other, whose resources are rejected that the debt may become irredeemable and permanent.

April 27th.—This is a day of no business in the Senate. Before the House formed, Mr. Adams, our Vice-President, came to where I was sitting and told how many late pamphlets he had received from England; how the subject of the French Revolution agitated the English politics; that for his part he despised them all but the production of Mr. Burke, and this same Mr. Burke despised the French Revolution. Bravo, Mr. Adams! I did not need this trait of your character to know you.

In the evening I called at the post-office on a business of Mr. Zantzingers. Langdon, who lodges nearly opposite, called to me from a window. I went over and had a long discourse with him on the subject of removing Congress. He wants to make the assumption of State debts the condition of it. I was guarded as to any concessions on this subject. He avowed in the most unequivocal manner that *consolidation* of the different governments was his object in the matter; that perhaps it was against the interests of his State in particular, etc.

This morning was snowy and remarkably cold. I have used the cold bath for two mornings past, and, I think, with good effect. I certainly am in better health, and feel a very great improvement of appetite. Perhaps I must be guarded as to this point. The flesh-brush I never omit. The party who went on Long Island Saturday week have most of them repented of it.

April 28th.—This was really a snowy day. The distant hills in the evening were still white. Even in the town the houses were white till in the afternoon. Three successive snowy days at this time of the year appears extraordinary, indeed.

Childs this day published a piece which I contrived to get into his hands. Neither he nor any of the printers here know me to be a writer; nor will they know it unless the Speaker or General Muhlenberg should blow me; but even then they do not know me to be the author of more than two or three pieces.

As we had nothing to do in the Senate, Carrol moved for a committee to consider what was to be done about Rhode Island, etc. One was accordingly appointed. The Senate adjourned early, on pretense of doing business in committees. I went for a while into the House of Representatives, but, finding the debates unimportant, I went to settle some private business, and soon came home, where I remained the rest of the day. In the evening had the satisfaction to receive letters from home up to the 15th instant. All well.

April 29th.—Called to see Colonel Gunn. He was willing to talk, and I had no mind to interrupt him. He spoke freely relating to the barefaced conduct of King and Elsworth in supporting any measure proposed by the Secretaries. Indeed, their toolism is sufficiently evident to everybody. He says the agitating the affair of Rhode Island is only to furnish a pretext to raise more troops. Be this as it may, that Carrol was only a tool in bringing it forward yesterday was sufficiently evident. Gunn is going to Philadelphia, and I have arranged matters so that he will be taken notice of there.

No business was done in the Senate but consenting to some nominations sent down yesterday, and the Senators from Virginia laid a resolution on the table for opening the doors of the Senate on the discussion of legislative subjects.

April 30th.—A flood of business came up from the Representatives, but none of it was acted on save the first reading of bills and appointing a committee to confer with them on some point of order or etiquette. Mr. Morris spoke to me as to repealing the law or that part of the judiciary about holding a District and Circuit Court at Yorktown. I gave as my opinion that it was best to let the other House do it, as they had introduced Yorktown; and I find Boudinot has this day carried in a bill for this purpose. I hate the whole of the judiciary, and, indeed, made no place at first but Philadelphia for holding the courts. I shall not therefore give them my opposition. If a place is hereafter appointed for holding any Circuit Court, it, perhaps, should be Harrisburg.

Senate adjourned over to Monday.

May 1st, Saturday.—This is a day of general moving in New York, being the day on which their leases chiefly expire. It was a finer day than yesterday. I could not forbear the impulse of walking out. I went for Mr. Scott, but he had changed his lodgings and was not to be found. Fell in with Walker and Parker, of Virginia. They were coming to visit our house. They pressed us so hard for dinner that we consented. I had not, however, walked far enough, and went to see Mr. Wynkoop. We got again on the subject of State debt. I never saw a man take so much pains *not* to see a subject. It is, however, now disposed of, at least for this session.

I have a letter from Dr. Rush. He praises the piece I sent him. Calls it sensible; owns himself convinced. His words [were], "I have erred through ignorance on this subject" [State debts].

With less prudence than integrity I attacked the Secretary's [Hamilton's] report the moment it appeared. When the leading feature in it, the assumption of State debts, was carried by a majority of five in the committee of the whole Representatives, I redoubled my efforts against it; and I really believe that by my endeavors it was finally rejected. I am fully sensible that I staked every particle of credit [popularity] I had in the world on this business, and have been successful. But let me lay my account, never to be thought of for it. Be it so. I have made enemies of all the Secretaries, and all their tools, perhaps of the

President of the United States, and Bonny Johnny Adams for the many pieces I have written. With all the pains I have taken to conceal myself [the pieces] must have betrayed me in one shape or other. But I have no enemy in my own bosom.

Williamson's coming in, and one of his colleagues, had a considerable effect. When the whole of the North Carolina delegation appeared, it settled the business. The assumption would have completed the pretext for seizing every resource of government and subject of taxation in the Union, so that even the civil list of the respective governments would have to depend on the Federal Treasury. This was the common talk of the Secretary's tools.

We could not resist the pressing invitation of Parker and some Virginians to dine with them on turtle. All this is not worth a note, but on the next page are some anecdotes of General Washington.

No Virginian can talk on any subject, but the perfection of General Washington interweaves itself into every conversation. Walker had called at his farm [Washington's] as he came through Virginia. It consists of three divisions. The whole contains some ten or fifteen thousand acres. It is under different overseers, who may be styled generals, under whom are grades of subordinate appointments descending down through whites, mulattoes, negroes, horses, cows, sheep, hogs, etc.; it was hinted all were named. The crops to be put into the different fields, etc., and the hands, horned-cattle, etc., to be used in tillage, pasturing, etc., are arranged in a roster calculated for ten years. The Friday of every week is appointed for the overseers, or we will say the brigadier-generals, to make up their returns. Not a day's work but is noted; what, by whom, and where done; not a cow calves or a ewe drops a lamb but it is registered; deaths, etc., whether accidental or by the hands of the butcher, all minuted. Thus the etiquette and arrangement of an army are preserved on his farm. This may truly be called sham-care; but is it not nature? When once the human mind is penetrated by any system, no matter what, it can never disengage itself. Query: Did not the Roman poet understand nature to perfection who makes his heroes marshal their armies of ghosts in the

Elysian fields; and spirits imitate in shadows the copies of their former occupation?

May 2d, Sunday.—The fore part of this day was very pleasant. An east wind blew up and deformed the afternoon. I, however, walked a good deal. I have drunk wine with the Speaker at the rate of about three glasses a day, and I really consider myself worse for it. May be I am mistaken. I will observe for a day or two longer. I bore this day with more impatience and have thought more about my family than any other day since I have been in New York. I wrote as usual to them and sundry other acquaintances.

CHAPTER VII

May 3d, Monday.—There really was a considerable deal of business done in the Senate this day, and would have been much more had it not been for an appeal that was made to the Chair for information respecting the salary necessary for an ambassador. Full one half of our time was taken up in two speeches on the subject of etiquette and expense attending and necessary to constitute the very essence of an ambassador. The lowest farthing should be three thousand pounds sterling, besides a year's salary at setting out. Much of what he [Adams] said bore the air of the traveler; in fact, I did not believe him, and, of course, voted in the face of all his information. A commitment of the bill was called for, and I was, contrary to my expectations, put on it. Another short bill was committed, which I really suspect is a base job, calculated to make a nest for an individual. The spirit of the last session really was to make offices for men, to provide for individuals without regarding the public or sparing expense. I fear this spirit is not yet laid.

For some time past the Philadelphians had been proposing a weekly dinner. Our former meetings sank into disuse, but they are now very urgent, and this day we began the business. Judge Wilson, being a Pennsylvanian, was, of course, invited. We soon relaxed into conviviality, and, indeed, something more. We expected something political would be proposed by Fitzsimons, and out it came: "Gentlemen, it is expected of us that we should fix the Governor of Pennsylvania." I introduced some trivial remarks of the weather, etc., and the thing was checked for a time. Scott, General Heister, and General Muhlenberg went away. It was now broached seriously by Fitzsimons. Morris made a public declaration that he was fully sensible of the honor done him in the present appointment, but if the chair of the Governor fell to him he would discharge it

248

with impartiality, etc.; that he considered the present Governor as a very improper man, and hoped they would create opposition to him. The Speaker declared himself in terms of a similar nature. The result was this, that their friends should determine and that their utmost should be united to keep out Mifflin. Mr. Morris, by way of finishing the business, addressed himself to the Speaker. "May you or I be Governor." There is a prospect of Tench Coxe succeeding Duer in the assistancy of the Treasury. His character was spoken of with great asperity by Fitzsimons, Morris, and Wilson. Clymer rather supported him.

We got on the subject of the finances of Pennsylvania. Fitzsimons asserted that our State had drawn between two and three millions of dollars from the Continental Treasury, and that we had not more than four millions substantiated against the Union. I hinted to him that from anything I had seen we had not drawn more than about a million from the Continental Treasury, that Nicholson had rendered accounts to the amount of ten millions, and had stated an unliquidated charge of five millions; but, I added, let the account be fairly settled, and if we are really in debt let us pay it. We sat too long and drank too much; but we seemed happy, and parted in good humor.

May 4th, Tuesday.—I felt in some degree the effects of the bad wine I had drunk, for I had a headache. Dressed, however, for the levee. I had a card yesterday to dine with the President of the United States on Thursday. The pet, if he had any on him, has gone off.*

A great deal of business was done this day in the Senate in the way of passing and reading bills, but no debate of any consequence. Elsworth manifested some strong traits of obstinacy.

Went to the levee, made my bows, walked about, turned about, and came out.

May 5th, Wednesday.—A great deal of business was done in the Senate, but no debate was entered on. The Rhode Island committee reported. The amount of it was to put that State in a kind of commercial coventry, to prevent all intercourse

---

* Referring to his [Maclay's] not receiving a similar invitation a month before when the President gave a dinner, to which many Senators were invited.

with them by the way of trade. I think the whole business premature. We adjourned early.

I went to call on R. H. Lee and Mr. Langdon, both of whom are sick. Mr. Hazard, whom I met in the street, told me Mr. Langdon could not be seen. I called on Lee. Found him better. I now addressed myself to suit the merits of a bill, referred to myself and others, for the allowance of forty-five dollars per month to a Colonel Ely, which, by attending to his accounts in the office of the commissioner for army accounts, I find to be a most groundless and unjust charge. A petition of his was referred to the Secretary of War, and the Secretary of War reported in his favor—the great Pin on which so much hung.

The assumption of the State debts having failed, every other thing that can be thought of will be brought forward to increase the volume of the national debt. We already rejected in the Senate a bill which appeared to me of mischievous consequences touching the communication and half pay and pensions of officers. It is renewed and sent up to us. Baron Steuben is supported in a demand of near six hundred guineas a year. In fact, to overwhelm us with debt is the endeavor of every creature in office, for fear, as there is likely to be no war, that if there should be no debt to be provided for there would be no business for the general government with all their train of officers. Henry, of Maryland, expressed himself in words full up to the foregoing ideas to me a few days ago, but I spoiled his communications by expressing a wish of *the sooner the better*. It is remarkable to me at least that he has since that time left his usual seat, which used to be near, and commonly rambles from one empty seat to another on the opposite side of the House. The Secretaries have had a clear majority in the House of Representatives on every question save the adoption of State debts. They carried this at first, but some publications reminded the gentlemen that there was an election approaching.

May 6th.—Little was done in the Senate this day. Two bills came up from the House of Representatives. Agreed to. The Rhode Island committee requested that they might have back their report to amend it. This was complied with. Their amendment amounted to an adjournment, and I joined the committee on the bill for the salaries of ministers plenipotentiary, *chargé d'affaires,* etc. I bore my most pointed testimony against all this kind of gentry; declared I wished no political connection whatever with any other country whatever. Our commercial intercourse would be well regulated by consuls, who would cost us nothing. All my discourse availed nothing. The whole committee agreed with me that they were unnecessary. Why, then, appoint any or make provision for the appointment of any, for so sure as we make a nest for one the President will be plagued till he fills it? We agreed to the bill as it stood, but I proposed twice to strike out all about ministers plenipotentiary.

Went to dine with the President agreeably to invitation. He seemed in more good humor than I ever saw him, though he was so deaf that I believe he heard little of the conversation. We had ladies, Mrs. Smith, Mrs. Page, and Mrs. White. Their husbands all with them.

May 7th, Friday.—The ailment called the influenza rages to a great degree all over the city. I feel a dryness and sourness of my throat, and a pain and heaviness in my head and flying pains all over my body, so that I had better be as attentive as possible to my health.

No business of consequence done in the Senate. The members began to straggle about after the minutes were read. I called on the committee who had Ely's bill. We sent for Ely, and heard a peck of stuff from him, too flimsy to impose even on children. He may have rendered service to the sick on Long Island, but it appears that his own emolument was his object, and he has had this pretty completely answered already by a generous settlement with the State of Connecticut.

On my return into the Senate chamber one member of it only remained, sitting in a state of *ennui.* I have remarked him for some weeks past, and he really affords a striking proof of the inconveniency of being fashionable. He set up in a coach about a month ago, and of course must have it come for him to the Hall. But behold how he gets hobbled: the stated hour for the Senate to break up is three, but it often happens that the Senate adjourns a little after twelve, and here a healthy man must sit two or three hours for his coach to take him three or four hundred yards. This is highly embarrassing, and some excuse must be found for his staying for the carriage, and he is now lame and stays alone till the carriage comes for him. Thus Folly often fixes her friends.

Tench Coxe came this day to town in order (as he said) to enter on the assistancy of the Treasury. He was deeply affected with the literary itch, the *cacoethes scribendi*. He has persevering industry in an eminent degree. These are the qualities that have recommended him to this appointment. Hamilton sees that the campaign will open against him in the field of publication, and he is providing himself with gladiators of the quill, not only for defense but attack.

May 8th.—I felt myself rather indisposed, and stayed at home all this day. Drew a report on the affair of Colonel Ely. Read and lounged away the day.

May 9th, Sunday.—This day I employed, as usual, in writing to my family. I spend my time but miserably in absence from them. I will, however, endeavor to make out of this lesson. Colonel Hartley returned to town this day. What a strange piece of pomposity this thing is grown! He is, if possible, more affected and disgusting than ever. He called to see us, but took the Speaker twice out and kept him out with him almost the whole of the time he was on his visit. The State [Pennsylvania] has really a poor bargain of him, and if she can dispose of him at the October sales [elections] she need not care at how low a rate.

May 10th, Monday.—Attended the Hall at ten o'clock to hear Colonel Ely's witnesses. He failed in proving the points he had alleged in his favor. We spent some time while the Senate was engaged in business. When we came in we found them on the Rhode Island resolves. The committee had been called on to give reasons on which they founded their resolutions. Elsworth spoke with great deliberation, often and long, and yet I was not convinced by him. I saw I must, if I followed my judgment, vote against both resolutions. It was, therefore, incumbent on me to give some reasons for my vote. I observed that the business was under deliberation in Rhode Island; that the resolves carried on the face of them a punishment for rejection, on the supposition that they would ruin our revenue. Let us first establish the fact against them that an intercourse with them had injured our revenue before we punish them with a prohibition of all intercourse. This resolution I considered premature.

The other, for the demand of twenty-seven thousand dollars, I considered as equally so. Let the accounts be settled, and Rhode Island has a right to be charged with and has a right to pay her proportion of the price of independence. By the present resolutions the attack comes visibly from us. She is furnished with an apology, and will stand justified to all the world if we should enter into any foreign engagements.

This was a day of company at our mess. The strangers were Captain Barry, Colonel Moylan, and Mr. Tench Coxe, now succeeded to the assistancy of the Treasury. I could not help thinking of last Monday, as he sat in one of the seats, whence censure had been thrown on him a week ago. I was too sick to enjoy the company. I could eat but little and drink nothing.

May 11th.—The morning, or part of it, spent on the troublesome affair of Colonel Ely. The Rhode Island resolutions were taken up. I was twice up against these resolutions. They admitted on all hands that Rhode Island was independent, and did not deny that the measures now taken were meant to force her into an adoption of the Constitution of the United States; and founded their arguments in our strength and her weakness. I could not help telling them plainly that this was playing the tyrant to all intents and purposes. I was twice up; said a good deal, but it answered no purpose whatever.

May 12th.—This day, as chairman of the committee on Colonel Ely's bill, I handed in a report which was dead against Colonel Ely. The report stated that Colonel Ely had submitted his case to the Legislature in Connecticut; that they had made him what they considered as ample allowance. We had the whole fire of New England on us for this step, but we supported the attack, and finally carried the business hollow. I would now remark, if I had not done it before, that there is very little candor in New England men. Mr. Morris was in most of the time, and showed a disposition to make away from my side of the question. Surely, I had better keep myself to myself with regard to him. Wingate, though of the committee, behaved dirty on one point; at least I thought so at the time. It is vain to be wasting paper with this subject. Dr. Johnson certainly gave a most improper certificate on this subject, and one part of it was not true, viz., that the reason Colonel Ely had not an allowance in the old Congress was this, not having nine States when there were eleven at the time alluded to. I can not keep some other strange opinions out of my head about him and the report, which can not be found now by Alden, his son-in-law. The money saved by rejecting this bill [is] $2,025, or thereabout.

This day exhibited a grotesque scene in the streets of New York. Being the old 1st of May, the Sons of St. Tammany had a grand parade through the town in Indian dresses. Delivered a talk at one of their meeting-houses, and went away to dinner. There seems to be some kind of scheme laid of erecting some kind of order or society under this denomination, but it does not seem well digested as yet. The expense of the dresses must have been considerable, and the money laid out on clothing might have dressed a number of their ragged beggars. But the weather is now warm.

Joseph Thomas is the name of the man that has the statistics at large—an unsalable book. It is found we may occasionally want such a one. It is true that heretofore we used to be supplied with this book when we wanted it from Jay's or some other library, but it was soon found to be convenient (for the Yorkers) that we should take everything off their hands, that they can not otherwise dispose of, even to their insolvent debts.

May 13th.—This day was remarkably busy with me, and some singular occurrences happened. As chairman of the committee on the Baron Steuben's bill, I had called on the Commissioner of Army Accounts. He had furnished me with all [the information] in his power. Finding that a resolve had passed the old Congress on the 27th of September, 1785, giving him [Baron Steuben] seven thousand dollars in full, I called on Mr. Nousee, the register, for the receipts given by the baron for this sum, which were indorsed on the warrants or warrant given for it. I had first transacted some business of my own. Mr. Nousee was extremely polite and attentive; took the note or memorandum which I gave him, assured me my request should be complied with, asked when I would have the papers; followed me to the head of the stairs. As I came down-stairs

I told him I wished for them this day. He said I should have them.

This was ten o'clock. I received between eleven and twelve, at the Hall, a few lines from Mr. Nousee, stating the resolves of Congress: that three warrants had passed for the payments —one four thousand, the other for two, and the last for one thousand dollars; that the warrants themselves were deposited at the bank for the Secretary among the papers of the late Treasurer until a settlement could take place. I thought there was evasion on the face of this business, but I concluded that, if Mr. Hilligas had lodged his papers at the bank, the key and the care of them must be with some person; and off I went to the bank. I received for answer that some books, papers, or property of that kind, were lodged at the bank by Mr. Hamilton, who had the keys and the care of them.

I should have minuted that, as I left the Hall in Wall Street. I passed the Baron; he on one side and I on the other. I wished to make him a bow, as usual, but such an aspect he wore! nay, if he had brought all the gloom of the Black Forest from Germany he could not have carried a more somber countenance. Just as I came out of the bank-door I met Hamilton, and told him what I wanted. He refused me in pretty stiff terms; he could not answer for it, to open any gentlemen's papers. I told him I would take unexceptional characters with me—the Speaker of the Representatives. The papers I wanted belonged to the public and to no private gentleman whatever, nor would it do for him to refuse information to a committee of Congress. He then said if there was a vote of a committee for it he would get the papers. I told him any member of Congress had a right to any papers in any office whatever; that as chairman of the committee I had promised to procure what papers were necessary. I deemed this necessary, and of course called for it. He begged for half an hour to consider of it, and he would write me a note on the subject.

I parted with him, telling him I should expect to hear from him in half an hour. He said I should. This was before twelve; the Senate adjourned at one. I sat half an hour longer waiting for my note, but it came not. I went directly to the Treasury. The warrant to draw my indents was delivered to me with all the pomp of official ceremony. I told young Kuhn that I had further business with the Secretary [Hamilton] ; that he had promised me a note, which was not come to my hands. He returned to me, and desired me to walk into the inner room, or rather to enter the entry into a room in the other end of the house. I did so, and after being admitted into the *sanctum sanctorum* I told his Holiness [Hamilton] that he had been good enough to promise me a note which was not come to my hands. He got up, went out, and left me alone for a considerable time. Came in with young Kuhn with him.

But now a new scene opened. Before he went out he said the papers I wanted were here. I said, "What, here in the office?" He said yes. He now asked Kuhn, before me, "Do you know of any box, desk, or any place where Mr. Hilligas kept the warrants?" The young man said yes, the desk in the other room had them in it ; he added, "If I had them, there was no receipt on them, only 'received the contents.' " Hamilton said the desk was locked and bound around with tape, and Mr. Hilligas had the key in Philadelphia. I expressed great surprise that Mr. Hilligas should lock public papers belonging to the Treasury in his private desk. Hamilton affected to believe I must [have] some censure on his conduct. I repeated what I said, and declared I thought it very strange of Mr. Hilligas to do so, and concluded, "I suppose, then, I must write to Mr. Hilligas for to send over the key before I could see the papers." He said I could not get them otherwise ; and by way, I believe, of getting me out of the room, told me to come and see the desk. I walked into the room of the Assistant Secretary, and he there showed me the desk as he said contained the warrants.

I need make no comment on all this. I think I have his history complete. A schoolboy should be whipped for such pitiful evasions.

I went to see Mr. Meredith, but he was out. Fell in with Mr. Fitzsimons. He talked familiarly with me. I am tired of minuting any more for this day, but I must note part of Mr. Fitzsimons' discourse. These Southern people have a matter much at heart, and it is *my power to oblige them*. They fear settlement ; they can not bear it ; they have been negligent of their accounts, and the Eastern people have kept exact accounts of everything (perhaps, and more than everything added). This moment Hartley, fine as a lord, met us and broke off our discourse. Some trifling chat engaged us for a few moments, and Hartley parted from us. I waited for him [Fitzsimons] to take up the discourse again, but he did not.

We were approaching the Hall, where I knew we would part. I began: "They will want you to support them on the discrimination of tonnage, too, against the New England men; but as they are the people who keep us here, by joining the New England and York votes, I have no objection to see them whipped with their own rod." He seemed to enjoy this thought and laughed heartily, but the Hall was at hand and the old subject lost.

May 14th.—The business of most importance agitated this day was the Rhode Island bill, which must have had a first reading yesterday when I was out. I contented myself with giving my negative to every particle of it. I knew I could gain no proselytes, and that, as the bill could not be justified on the principles of freedom, law, the Constitution, or any other mode whatever, argument could only end in anger. Mr. Morris was one of the warmest men for it, although he knows well that the only views of the Yorkers are to get two Senators more into the House on whose votes they can reckon on the question of residence. But he must think the getting [of] Rhode Island is superior to all other considerations. The yeas and nays were called, and now, after the question was taken, there seemed to be a disposition for argument, and some very remarkable expressions were used. Izard said, *"If gentlemen will show us how we can accomplish our end by any means less arbitrary and tyrannical, I will agree with them."*

When we came to the clause for demanding twenty-five thousand dollars, Mr. Morris said, "This is the most arbitrary of the whole of it." The nays were Butler, Elmer, Gunn, Henry, Maclay, Walker, Wyngate—seven. Yeas: Bassett, Carrol, Dalton, Elsworth, Johnson, Izard, King, Langdon, Morris, Strong, Schuyler, Read—twelve.

This day, to my great joy, a statement of the Pennsylvania accounts came forward—$10,642,403.43 specie and $47,010,138 Continental money, liquidated and charged against the United

States by our State, and delivered to Mr. White, the general agent, and receipt taken for it in due time, besides an unliquidated claim of five millions specie. I understood this to be the state of our accounts at the beginning of the session; and so it seems to be considered by all of us; for Mr. Morris, Mr. Clymer, and Fitzsimons used to harangue on this subject, and cry up that so large an annual interest would be due to Pennsylvania that she would draw money from the continent to pay her whole civil list, make her roads, build her bridges, and open her canal. I knew that Hamilton was fool enough, at one time, to think that he could make the State governments dependent on the General Government for every shilling. I used to oppose all this dream of folly, but all at once the State debts must be assumed. It was demonstrable that this measure would defeat all settlement.

Now the very gentlemen who had promised us such revenues from the Union cried out: "Burn the books"; "No settlement"; "Pennsylvania is in debt; she had drawn from the continent between two and three millions of good dollars and had not substantiated but between four and five millions against the Union." A mutilated account of but about this sum was actually exhibited and handed about by Clymer and Fitzsimons, and an attack begun on the Comptroller about the same time, as if to annihilate his reputation, and turn him out of all employment; as if it had been foreseen that he was the only one who could detect this management or obtain justice for the State.

15th May, Saturday.—Devoted this day, although I was sick, to the matter of removing to Philadelphia. Mr. Morris entertained me with a long detail of the difficulties he met with in the settlement of his accounts. I believe the clamors against him make the officers inspect everything with a jealous eye.

I really acted rather improperly in ranging about so much this day in my bad state of health. Should the effects of my influenza increase, and I fall a victim to my zeal for serving the city of Philadelphia, my character would only suffer ridicule, and my dear family the loss of their head. I will, however, do what I think my duty.

Called to see the President. Every eye full of tears. His

life despaired of. Dr. MacKnight told me he would trifle neither with his own character nor the public expectation; his danger was imminent, and every reason to expect that the event of his disorder would be unfortunate.

May 16th, Sunday.—I called on Mr. Morris to advise with him in some points the little scheme we laid. Did not succeed in bringing in Lee, of Virginia, to make our motion. Mr. Morris proposed to me to call on him and walk out of town and catch a dinner. We did so, and the day was lost. I had written to my family in the forenoon. I considered the day as lost. Not a sentiment nor an expression that touched the heart or warmed the bosom with philanthropic feelings or vibrated on the strings of domestic joy. We dined at one Brannon's, where there were a greenhouse and some elegant improvements, but all was a mere flutter.

May 17th, Monday.—I was engaged this morning getting documents and papers respecting the bill for the granting the Baron Steuben seven thousand dollars and an annuity of two thousand dollars. I really never saw so villainous an attempt to rob the public as the system which has been brought forward by the Secretary of the Treasury. The baron's whole accounts have been settled on a liberal scale indeed. An office was created, in addition to his rank as a major-general, for which he had additional pay and emoluments. Seven thousand dollars over and above were granted to him. All these payments he has received. A mountain has been tortured to put money into his hands. The Secretary [Hamilton] has, however, framed a system which has as the basis of it the allowing him of five hundred and eighty guineas a year * over and above all his emoluments, both as a major-general and inspector-general of the army, and interest calculated up to a compound ratio on all the balances. And, after all, he is not able to raise a balance of more than about seven thousand for the baron. But all this without the shadow of proof of the baron ever having had any such office or salaries. However, if he had ever been possessed of them, he could not have held them and served

---

* Allowing twenty-one English shillings to a guinea, this would be $3,045.

us at the same time, and, since he chose our service and our pay, we are obliged to him, but we have no right to pay him for what he did not hold.

The baron's papers kept us of the committee until after three o'clock, and, this being club day,* I went to dine with the Pennsylvania mess. We sat down to dinner half after three. Eating stopped our mouths until about four, and from that to near nine I never heard such a scene of bestial badney † kept up in my life. Mr. Morris is certainly the greatest blackguard in that way I ever heard open a mouth. But let me shut out the remembrance of it forever.

May 18th.—No debate of any consequence arose this day until the Rhode Island bill, which had been recommitted, was reported. Mr. Lee opposed it in a long and sensible speech. Butler blustered away, but in a loose and desultory manner. King, Elsworth, Strong, and Izard spouted out for it. It was long before there was a slack. As this was to be the last reading, and as the yeas and nays would, in my opinion, be called, I took what I thought was new ground. The bill had been assigned to various motives, self-defense, self-preservation, self-interest, etc. I began with observing that the Convention of Rhode Island met in a week; that the design of this bill was evidently to impress the people of Rhode Island with terror. It was an application to their fears, hoping to obtain from them an adoption of the Constitution, a thing despaired of from their own free-will or their judgment. It was meant to be used in the same way that a robber does a dagger or a highwayman a pistol, and to obtain the end desired by putting the party in fear; that where independence was the property of both sides, no end whatever could justify the use of such means in the aggressors. I therefore was against the bill in every point of view, etc. The debate was long. I was up a second time, but to no avail. The question was put at about three o'clock and carried. The yeas and nays were called and stood nearly as before, with the addition of Mr. Lee in the negative.

I labored hard to arrange our affairs for bringing on our

---

* Meaning the day when the Pennsylvania delegation had agreed to dine at one house once every week.

† A word, no doubt, in common use at that time.

question of removing to Philadelphia, and can not help remarking that the Philadelphians seemed the slackest of any people concerned in the business. I appointed, warned, or I know not what well to call it, a meeting of the delegation at Clymer and Fitzsimons' lodgings. Mr. Morris and the Speaker were all that met. The Philadelphians really threw cold water on the business. Mr. Morris twice proposed that it should be the new Congress that was to meet in March next that should assemble in Philadelphia. Once he got on the subject of Trenton. Here he and I rather clipped. I proposed that we should all be busy in the morning among the members. I engaged to call on Gunn, Langdon, and Bassett, and set them to work on others. The form of the resolution was agreed to, but it all seemed uphill or like a cold drag with the Philadelphians. I hope one day to be independent of them, but this is a matter I must consult them in now.

May 19th.—I ran this morning like a foot-boy from post to pillar—now to Gunn, then to Langdon, Bassett, etc. Langdon refused to bring forward our motion, and I then called on Bassett. He excused himself. With much ado I got them to keep the motion, which I put into their hands. Neither of them would make the motion. Mr. Morris did not come near the Senate chamber until after twelve o'clock. I called him out. He said it must be omitted this day. I found I need not oppose him, and we came into the Senate chamber. Langdon soon after came and told us that Dalton objected to going to Philadelphia until March next, and that we must alter the resolution. Mr. Morris and Dalton went together, and Mr. Morris returned and told me he had agreed with Dalton that it should be the first of March next. Thus it is that all our measures are broken in upon, and, after all the pains I have taken, this business will end in smoke.

The most villainous and abandoned speculation took place last winter from the Treasury. Some resolutions have passed the House of Representatives, and are come up to us. King and Dr. Johnson and Strong, with many others, opposed these resolutions. In an abandoned and shameless manner this engaged the House [Senate] to three o'clock. They were committed, and the House adjourned.

General Heister and Mr. Buckley called on us this evening. We talked over the affair of the day. Mr. Wynkoop came in, and a kind of an agreement was made that the Pennsylvanians should meet to-morrow at Clymer's.

May 20th.—I could not attend at Clymer's this morning. I, however, saw the Speaker at the Hall. Some strange manœuvres have taken place. Jackson, of the President's family, * has been with both Morris and Langdon. Morris is set right, and Dalton will agree with us, but new mischief has happened. Dr. Elmer has crossed to the Jerseys; Patterson is not yet come; Few and Gunn are both absent, so that two States are this day unrepresented. I offered to make the motion. Mr. Morris, however, now makes a point of doing it; but the thinness of the Senate seems a good reason for putting it off for this day. I can not account for Jackson having meddled in this business, or his knowing anything of it by any other means than through Buckley. However, we have got the errors of yesterday corrected. Mr. Morris was called out, and came in with a most joyous countenance. "I was called out by Boudinot," said he, "to make proposals to me from the New England men in favor of Trenton." I immediately told him [Morris]: "You can not possibly make any bargain by which you will not lose as much as you can gain. A bargain with the Eastern people is to lose Maryland, Virginia, and all southward. A Southern bargain will, on the contrary, lose all the Eastern interest. We must be able to declare upon honor that we have no bargain."

He was a little hurt and said, "Leave that all to me." "No, sir, I will make no bargain! If it is but suspected that we have a bargain, we are ruined." I was called out and took the opportunity of calling out Mr. Fitzsimons, and told him of Boudinot's being in treaty with Mr. Morris, and begged him to counteract everything of this kind. He promised that he would.

The Senate got into a long debate on the resolves relating to arrears due to the Virginia and North Carolina lines of the army in 1782-'83, which have been made the subject of an abandoned speculation. The report had an addition of Els-

---

* Meaning one of the avowed supporters of the Administration measures.

worth's, calculated as much as possible to favor the speculation. It was debated to three o'clock, and adjourned.

Elsworth is really a man of ability, and it is truly surprising to me the pains that he will display to varnish over villainy and to give roguery effect without avowed license. I can see him warping over in the case of the baron [Steuben's extra pension case] to get a sum of money on his account, or rather only in his name, which would sink immediately into the jaws of Hamilton and his crew.

May 21st.—And now again Elmer is absent, and Patterson is not returned; and Mr. Morris thinks the motion had not best be made until they return, so one day more is lost.

I spent a good deal of time on the affair of the Baron Steuben, got the report agreed to, and now the debate of the day came on respecting the resolutions,* or rather the amendment offered to the last one. The amendment was supported by King, Elsworth, Dr. Johnson, Izard, and others. Lee answered them. Toward the end of all the debate I rose and explained the reason of the resolves, that they regarded the sums due, the places in which the payments were to be made, and what kind of transfers were to be considered as valid. All this was directory to our own officer, and had nothing to do with the proceedings of courts. Soldiers had entered into contracts, the resolves before the Chair defaced writings or tore the seals from obligations, and the law was open. The directions were, moreover, in conformity with the laws of North Carolina, one of the States whose citizens were concerned; that the present amendment was a modification of the resolution to protect the interest of the late speculation. The reason offered for it was that probably some innocent person might suffer. I did not believe this was possible. I would cheerfully agree that it was better ten guilty should escape than one innocent suffer, but no innocent man was privy to this business. The soldiers knew nothing of the matter. The speculators know, and they only know, in whose hands the lists were lodged, for the soldiers, having received their final settlements since the service was performed, concluded that nothing more could remain due, etc.

* Relative to the troops of Virginia, North and South Carolina, who were entitled to arrears of pay.

The question was put and the amendment lost—ten for, twelve against. The question was now put on the third resolution and carried—thirteen and nine. King, however, and a number of gentlemen called for the yeas and nays. Yeas: Bassett, *Butler*, Carrol, Few, Gunn, Hawkins, Johnson, Henry, Lee, Maclay, Read, Walker, Wyngate. Nays: Dalton, Elsworth, Johnston, Izard, King, Langdon, Morris, Strong, Schuyler.

Now a new whim came into their heads, and they would have the yeas and nays on the former question. They were told that it was out of order. However, they had them, and now Mr. Butler voted for the amendment, lest he should lose his interest at the Treasury, and of course we were tied, eleven and eleven. But for once, in my opinion, our Vice-President voted right, and gave it against the amendment.

May 22d.—Being Saturday, and no Congress, I got a horse and rode out. Came home about noon, prodigiously tired, indeed. The little exercise I have taken for the last three or four months makes me almost sink under it. I went to bed and slept about an hour, and rose much refreshed.

In the evening a large number of gentlemen called at our house. My barber had disappointed me in the morning. I was rather in *déshabille,* but came down-stairs. Although I am not in the least given to dress, yet I found that I was on this occasion below par; and to know that any point about one is deranged or improperly adjusted, imparts an awkward air to one. It is on this account, more than any other, that a propriety of dress should be attended to. To suspect that your company believes anything wrong about you distresses a modest man. Of the company was Mr. Fitzsimons. He took me by the hand and said:

"To-morrow, at nine o'clock, I wish to meet you and the Speaker."

May 23d.—It was near ten when I was called down on the coming of Fitzsimons. He had been some time with the Speaker. We had considerable loose talk on the subject of the removal of Congress. But Fitzsimons, after some time, declared that was not the business on which he came. It was to settle something as to the government of Pennsylvania. Who should be run for the Chair of it at the next election? He spoke of the dignity of the Speaker's present place, and the certainty of his continuance in it. It was evident that he wished the Speaker to decline.* The Speaker said, "Very well, I will give you an answer to-morrow morning."

Nothing remarkable happened this day. I wrote to my dear family, as usual.

May 24th.—I dressed and went early to work. Called on R. H. Lee, of Virginia, on Walker, and Dr. Elmer. After Senate met I reported the amendment on the Baron Steuben bill. It was the opinion of the committee that he should have an annuity of one thousand dollars. There never was so vile and barefaced a business as this. It is well known that all he would get would immediately sink into the hands of Hamilton. It lay, however, over for to-morrow. Some business came up from the Representatives.

And now Mr. Morris rose and made the long-expected motion in the following words: *"Resolved,* That Congress shall meet and hold their next session in the city of Philadelphia." Langdon seconded the motion. A dead pause ensued. Our Vice-President asked if we were ready for the question. General Schuyler got up and hoped not, as it was a matter of great importance to move the seat of government. He moved a postponement. Mr. Morris said, "If the gentleman will name to-morrow, he had no objection," and to-morrow was accordingly named for it. The Senate soon after adjourned, and now Izard, Butler, Dr. Johnson, Schuyler, and King flew about. The people they mostly attacked were Governor Johnston, Hawkins, and Gunn. I soon left them and came home.

But this was mess-day, and I went at half-past three and found the company already seated and the dinner almost eaten up. I could not stay long, as we had an appointment with Jefferson, the Secretary of State, at six o'clock. When I came to the Hall, Jefferson and the rest of the committee were there. Jefferson is a slender man; has rather the air of stiffness in his manner; his clothes seem too small for him; he sits in a lounging manner, on one hip commonly, and with one of his shoulders elevated much above the other; his face has a sunny

---

* The nomination for Governor of Pennsylvania.

aspect; his whole figure has a loose, shackling air. He had a rambling, vacant look, and nothing of that firm, collected deportment which I expected would dignify the presence of a secretary or minister. I looked for gravity, but a laxity of manner seemed shed about him. He spoke almost without ceasing. But even his discourse partook of his personal demeanor. It was loose and rambling, and yet he scattered information wherever he went, and some even brilliant sentiments sparkled from him. The information which he gave us respecting foreign ministers, etc., was all high-spiced. He had been long enough abroad to catch the tone of European folly. He gave us a sentiment which seemed rather to savor of quaintness: "It is better to take the highest of the lowest than the lowest of the highest." Translation: "It is better to appoint a *chargé* with a handsome salary than a minister plenipotentiary with a small one." He took his leave, and the committee agreed to strike out the specific sum to be given to any foreign appointment, leaving it to the President to account, and appropriated thirty thousand dollars generally for that purpose.

May 25th.—This day again I was engaged in the main business. Called on sundry of the members. The Yorkers are now busy in the scheme of bargaining with the Virginians, offering the permanent seat on the Potomac for the temporary one in New York. Butler is their chief agent in this business. Walker, a weak man, seems taken off by it. Patterson, however, is not yet come.

Baron Steuben's business was taken up. The committee were called on to give the reasons of their report. As I was chairman, I had to take the lead. I knew there was blame ready to fall on us. I, however, did not decline the business, but laid down the outlines in as strong colors as I thought consistent with truth: that those who came after me might not be bashful, and thus taking scope enough for them to act in. I thought I took many of the Senate with me; some I knew it was impossible. In fine, I thought demonstration was on our side; that the baron could demand nothing. Izard is certainly a bad man in grain. He drew conclusions that were obviously wrong, indeed, to his own party. Even Butler disowned his reasons; but he was for doing the same thing without a reason. Elsworth got up and spoke exceedingly well for more than an hour. He was severe in some of his strictures but I was pleased to hear him. The debate lasted until past three o'clock, and an adjournment took place without any question. One object of the delay was to put off our question on the residence.

May 26th, Wednesday.—This day may be considered by me as an unlucky one. Last night I rested but poorly, owing, I believe, to a rheumatic fever. My short slumbers were much interrupted by fanciful appearances of warriors passing by in flights or gliding along. I really have no faith in dreams, but, ever since I was plagued with this kind of fabling during my distress on board the sloop Swallow, I can not help considering such illusions as unfortunate.

The baron's [Steuben] bill, as it was called, was taken up. Perversion of reason, perversion of principle. The world turned upside down only could justify the determinations. But the cabals of the Secretary [Hamilton] were successful, and the baron's bill was triumphant. I put a question to myself whether there was on the face of the earth a deliberative body that could possibly depart further from the principles of justice and a regard to the public welfare. None, none, answered every faculty about me. But the fact is, that every officer of the Treasury has embarked in this business with the warmth of solicitors. John Adams gave twice the casting vote in this business. I really felt a disposition to take a lamentation over human frailties.

But after this was done, Mr. Morris called for his motion. If he really intended to lose it, he could not possibly have taken a more certain method. He rose, laughing heartily every time he got up. King laughed at him, and he laughed back at King, and a number more joined in the laugh. This was truly ridiculous. Few, Butler, and King rose, and the amount of all they said was that a removal was inconvenient; that Philadelphia was not central; if we once got into it we would be accommodated in such a manner that we would never leave it, etc.

I replied that a removal was not called for immediately by the resolution; that the next session of Congress was to meet in Philadelphia; that, although it was not central, it was more so than the place where we were now. The universal consent of the provinces, before we were States, and the States since, was in favor of Philadelphia. This was verified by every public assembly which had been called, from the meeting of the first Congress down to the late meeting of the Cincinnati; that the arguments drawn from the conveniences of Philadelphia, and the insinuations that if we were once there nobody would ever think of going away from it, I thought were reasons which should induce us to embrace this place, which would come so completely up to our wishes. I begged gentlemen, however, to be easy on that subject. Philadelphia was a place they never could get as a permanent residence. The government [of Pennsylvania] neither would nor could part with it. It was nearly equal to one third of the State in wealth and population. It was the only port belonging to the State. It was excepted by the Government in her offers to the Congress; that in such a place the deliberations of Congress on the subject of the permanent residence could be carried on to the greatest advantage, etc., etc.

I was up a second time, but to no purpose. A postponement was moved by Butler and seconded by Gunn. For the question of postponement: Strong, Dalton, Johnson, Elsworth, King, Schuyler, *Patterson,* Hawkins, Johnston, Butler, Izard, Few, Gunn—thirteen. Our side: Langdon, Wyngate, Elmer, Morris, Maclay, Read, Bassett, Carrol, Henry, Lee, Walker—eleven.

May 27th.—Mr. Morris went off yesterday in company with King, and I really thought there was too much levity in his conduct all through. I really suspected that he did not treat the matter with sufficient seriousness. This day he showed a violent disposition of anger, cursed and swore that he would go anywhere, but insisted on withdrawing the motion. I could not readily agree with him as to the propriety of withdrawing the motion, but he swore he would. Butler rose and said he gave notice that he would bring in a bill on Monday next to establish the permanent residence. Mr. Morris jumped up in haste and moved for leave to withdraw his motion. Langdon agreed. There was some demur, but the question was carried.

Now the baron's [Steuben's] bill, as we have called it, was taken up. If the fate of the Union had depended on it, it could not have been more pertinaciously adhered to. Elsworth persevered and cut King in argument more severely than ever I heard any member of the Senate heretofore. King felt it, and I confess I enjoyed it. Butler, by one of those eccentric motions for which he is remarkable, flew his party and voted on our side. Good God, what a consternation! I observed him rising, and said aloud, "It is carried."

The whole day was spent in a contest between the Secretary's [Hamilton] tools and the independent part of the House. As the arguments were nearly the same on every question, it is in vain to repeat them. Bonny Johnny Adams took uncommon pains to bias us, without effect. I voted uniformly against allowing him [Baron Steuben] one farthing, as I was convinced nothing was due him. I can not help noting John Adams' foolish speech. In extolling the baron he told us that he (the baron) had imparted to us the arts and principles of war, learned by him in the only school in the world where they were taught, by the great King of Prussia, who had copied them from the ancient Greek and Roman lessons; and that, in fine, to these arts and principles we owed our independence. Childish man to tell us this, when many of our sharpest conflicts and most bloody engagements had terminated fortunately before ever we heard of the baron.

CHAPTER VIII

THE PERMANENT RESIDENCE

May 28th.—This day we had expectations that the House of Representatives would have brought on the vote for adjournment to Philadelphia, but the day passed without anything being done. No debate of any consequence in the Senate. I felt exceedingly indisposed in the fore part of the day, and dreaded going into company. The Speaker entertained. I, however, joined them and drank a few glasses, and felt much better; but I must note how my feelings will be to-morrow.

May 29th, Saturday.—Can not complain of my health. I stayed in all day. It was raw and inclining to rain; almost too cold to be without fire. I was dull and heavy. In the evening received a note to dine with Colonel Gunn to-morrow.

May 30th, Sunday.—I rested but badly last night; had ugly dreams. Am to dine out this day. I had best be careful and attentive. How idle this idea! Dreams are but fallacious things. I have dined out and have met with no disaster. I had one strange dream of seeing a man fall from a place like a sawmill. I thought the mill was mine, yet it differed from my mill at Sunbury. What a heap of idleness! My head ached, hence I suppose my dreams. The man was not killed. A dead child plagued me at another time. I have really little to do, or I would not note all this down.

Last night Fitzsimons and Clymer called on us. They agreed to call on Goodhue, Gilman, Huntingdon, and some other of the New England men, and tell them calmly that the Pennsylvanians would not stay in New York; that if they of New England would persist in voting for New York, the Pennsylvanians would agree to any other place whatever; and from here they would go. Fitzsimons and Clymer were appointed for this service. I readily agreed to join Mr. Morris in a similar service with respect to the Senate.

May 31st, Monday.—Went early out to call on sundry members, and try to prepare them for the grand question. Came to the Hall at the usual time. The bill for intercourse with foreign nations came up from the Representatives with an insistence. Both Houses having insisted, it remained for us to recede or call for a conference. It ended in a conference. A considerable debate, however, or rather delivery of sentiments, took place. Elsworth, in a slow, languid manner, said it was easy to see that the Representatives had in view some old regulations by their insisting on the nine thousand dollars; that formerly the business had been done by some gentlemen for about six thousand dollars per annum.

Mr. Adams jumped up; said that could not be; that he had kept the accounts with his own hand at Paris, and they amounted to about three thousand guineas yearly. He had now a vast deal to say. When he had done, Elsworth took a small paper out of his pocket; said he was very willing to show the document from which he had spoken. Here was an abstract of the accounts of the honorable Vice-President while he was in Paris, and all the particulars for twenty months, amounting to ninety-eight hundred dollars, which was not more than at the rate of six thousand dollars per annum. Adams appeared cut. The fact was, that he was found lying, as they all have been on that subject.

Now Butler rose and had a good deal to say on the merits of the permanent residence, and concluded with asking leave to bring in a bill for a permanent and temporary residence. Lee made a long speech. I felt so much interested that I could not help rising. I observed that fixing the permanent residence to a future period would work no relief of present inconveniences; that the complaints were felt and well founded as to the place in which we now were; that the gentleman had given notice some days ago that he would offer a bill for the permanent residence. He now added the temporary residence, etc. The end of the matter was, that he delivered us his bill. I could almost curse Mr. Morris for having left me at such a time.

June 1st.—I called early this morning on Fitzsimons and Clymer. I told them that, all things considered, I thought it best in me to endeavor to postpone Butler's bill. They both approved of it.

I went to the Hall to observe the members as they came in. Langdon was there. He certainly manifested something which I thought singular in his manner. If I had not had such strong proofs of him heretofore, I would have suspected him. He desired me to assure the two members of Massachusetts that there was no bargain with the Virginians. I told him I would do anything he requested, and I did so.

The Senate met. I considered myself as among wolves, with only neutral characters to support me. The Vice-President was hasty enough to take up Butler's bill. Butler absolutely spoke against taking it up at all, as he said he was afraid of a difference arising between the two Houses. The word "agreed!" "agreed!" was heard from different parts of the House. I really felt happy.

A message was received from the President, and some other trifling business done. There was some small talk and communications which I did not mind. But all at once the Vice-President began to read the bill [as to the temporary and permanent residence of Congress]. I wished much for somebody else to begin an opposition, and was determined to throw myself along with them, let them mold their attack as they would. Mr. Read spoke against proceeding on the bill, but made no motion. Butler got up and moved that the bill should be committed. Gunn seconded. Mr. Carrol said there could be no use in committing it. I said that the honorable gentleman had set out with declaring that he wished to avoid any differences with the other House. None of us could affect ignorance of what had passed in the House of Representatives yesterday. A vote had passed for the meeting of the next session at Philadelphia; that we might every moment expect our door to be opened for the receipt of such a communication. For us, therefore, to adopt a different mode of treating the same subject would have the appearance of courting a difference, etc.

Butler got up in reply and said every insulting thing in his power. I had concluded that I thought it best that the bill should lie on the table until the resolution came up [i. e., from the House of Representatives], and that they should be considered at the same time. This took place, after a good deal of talk. It was remarkable that the resolution came up just as Butler began to rail at me. The Senate adjourned early, and soon after in came Mr. Morris, covered with sweat and dust.

June 2d.—I went early this morning to meet our delegation and to inculcate this doctrine on our Representatives: that in all cases we should be prepared for the worst, and that we should now think of the next step to be taken in case of the worst happening in our House [Senate]; that a conduct of this kind would keep the matter alive; keep the party in spirits and collected. They admitted the principle, but seemed at loss for the means. I hinted the propriety of bringing forward a resolution naming the day of adjournment and the time of meeting. Fitzsimons and Morris (all that were present) seemed to carp at it. However, I told them, "I only urge you to think of and provide your next step." In the course of this short chat with them I had room to remark that I can not be on terms of confidence with these people. A hint was dropped that I had better be at the Hall. I readily agreed, and went there. I could see, as the members came in, that we had nothing to expect from North Carolina, South Carolina, Georgia, nor Massachusetts.

The Senate met, and waited and waited for Mr. Morris. I never wished for him more in my life. I saw now that Butler's bill would be committed, and I wished to arrange something of a ticket for the committee. Several of the Senate asked why I did not send for him [Morris]. I went out and desired the doorkeeper to go for him. Mather [the doorkeeper] answered, "I have sent for him long ago." It was past twelve before he came, and we now went at the business. (I can not help asking myself in this parenthesis what Mr. Morris could possibly mean by this conduct. Indeed, I ask how he can account for his going away last week, or many other parts of his conduct. It is most certainly his interest to take Congress to Philadelphia. Is it possible that Hamilton can have an influence with him on this subject?)

I could remark something of a partiality in Adams at the setting out—the first question for commitment of Mr. Butler's bill. It was moved to postpone this, and take up the resolution for holding the next session in Philadelphia. Senate divided, twelve and twelve. J. Adams gave it [the casting vote] against postponement. Now on the commitment twelve and twelve. J. Adams gave it for it. This division was by States, on both these questions, or at least they divided so. We had New Hampshire, Jersey, Pennsylvania, Delaware, Maryland, Virginia. The others against us. Now it was that I regretted Mr. Morris' absence. Had he been there in time, I could have settled with him who should have been the committee. Now we could communicate only with our friends on one side of the House. The committee rather unfavorable—Butler, Dalton, Lee, Johnston, and Henry.

Now it was moved to refer the resolution [from the House] to the same committee. The Senate divided equally, but Dalton was against it and Patterson for it. As they sat next each other, I believe this was settled between them, and shows that Patterson is not to be depended upon, and, indeed, I have long considered him as a most despicable character.

June 3d.—Attended the Hall at the usual time. I determined to behave in personal deportment as nearly as I possibly could to my former habits, and I believe I effected it. Of this, however, I could not judge as well as, perhaps, others. Mr. Morris came the last of any of the members this day, but nothing remarkably so; much earlier than yesterday. I got into chat with him, and after some time remarked how unfortunate we had been yesterday in not prearranging a ticket for the committee. I said his absence had been unlucky, but could not now be helped. He said *his accounts had engaged him so closely he could not come.* I thought this stranger than ever, that he should stay away on no other excuse than his daily business. Wyngate, Elmer, almost the whole Senate, have taken notice of it. How can I avoid observing it, for I have smarted under it?

No business of consequence took place this day. The nominations for the officers of the army had come in yesterday and were taken up this day. I had made some objections a few days ago to giving my advice and consent to the appointment of men of whom I knew nothing. Izard got on to the same subject and bounced a good deal. However, the thing was got over by the members rising and giving an account of the officers appointed from the different States, and all were agreed to.

The Funding bill, which has engaged the Representatives

almost the whole session, came up yesterday; was taken up this day and Monday assigned for it.

June 4th.—This is a day of small consequence in the Senate. I had busied myself much last night and this morning in arranging and disposing of matters, but sundry pages would not contain the whole of it, so I will minute only what happened in the Senate.

We called on the committee to report. Butler excused himself, and the burden of the excuse was that Governor Johnston, one of the committee, had fallen sick. Mr. Morris moved, and was seconded by Lee, to add another member in his room. This occasioned considerable debate. Read, however, declared against us, and we lost the question. Izard manifested the most illiberal spirit; asserted in opposition to Lee things that even his own party were ashamed of. I left the Senate chamber this day completely sickened at the uncandid and ungentlemanly conduct of the South Carolina men. Few, of Georgia, said some improper things, but I this day was almost altogether a hearer. There really was no serious debate. It was nothing but snip-snap and contradiction.

June 5th.—This was a slack day. I had promised Mrs. Bell to go with her to the Hall [Senate], and I called about ten for that purpose. Mrs. Bell, however, could not go this day, and I found her as finicking and fickle as the finest lady among them, with a bunch of bosom and bulk of cotton that never was warranted by any feminine appearance in nature. She had learned the New York walk to a tittle; bent forward at the middle, she walked, as they all do, just as if some disagreeable disorder prevented them from standing erect. Is it ill nature or what that inclines me to assign this fashion to a cause of this kind?

I went from her, called on sundry people; went and sat a long time with Mr. Morris, and repeated to him all the arguments I had made use of on Monday and Tuesday last, when he was absent. One in particular he seemed pleased with, drawn from the difference of mileage which would arise to the Treasury of about eleven hundred dollars in favor of a residence in Philadelphia. I desired him to get from the Treasury an account of the expense of removing Congress from Princeton to New

York. He said he would do it. There seemed really to be more of cordiality in this *tête-à-tête* which I had with him than any ever I had. I then called on Mr. Wynkoop. I chatted a good while with him, and had again occasion to observe the blind obedience which he pays to the opinions of his Philadelphia colleagues.

Came home, read, and lounged away the day.

June 6th, Sunday.—Five months have I been in town this day. Devoted my time to thinking of my family. Wrote letters, read, etc., but did not stir out all day. Remarked something this day: General Muhlenberg talks of visiting Sunbury, etc. I received a letter yesterday from George Logan. He is greatly displeased about the grant to Baron Steuben. This is really a worthy man. I think he holds the first place in point of integrity. He has invited me strongly to call and see him. I believe I must do so.

This old man, the baron, it seems, talks in the most insulting manner of the grant which has been made to him, and tells that he must and will have more when a new Congress meets, etc. Being at the head of the Cincinnati makes him assume those arrogant airs. 'Tis probable the whole body of them will soon be demanding pensions to support their titles and dignity.

The Funding bill, the basis on which speculation has built all her castles, is now to come before us; and woe to him who says a word in favor of the country. Load the ass; make the beast of burden bear to the utmost of his abilities. I am really convinced that many a man has gone into the martial field and acquitted himself with gallantry and honor, with less courage and firmness than is necessary to attack this disposition in our Senate.

June 7th, Monday.—The Funding law underwent some debate this day. We adopted, by a kind of common consent, a mode somewhat different from former practice respecting it. Supposing ourselves in Committee of the Whole, a paragraph is read, and the members generally express their sentiments on it. After every one has given his sentiments, it is passed by postponement, with a design to commit it to a special committee. We proceeded about half-way with the bill in this way.

The committee on the bill for the permanent residence and

the resolution sent up from the Representatives were called on to report, and Butler, their chairman, did so. He read the report, which was a sleeveless thing for the Potomac to be the permanent residence, but alleged that the ground was too narrow to fix the temporary residence. Many desultory things were said, and all went off until to-morrow.

This was Pennsylvania mess-day. I was so unwell that I first told Mr. Morris that I could not attend, but I afterward went. We here agreed to send for all the Senators who were friends of moving to Philadelphia. Eleven attended—Virginia, Maryland, Delaware, Pennsylvana, Dr. Elmer, from New Jersey, and New Hampshire. Much desultory discourse was held. Virginia and Maryland manifested a predilection for the Potomac; but the final resolutions, in which Virginia led the way, were as follows: "That as the business of a permanent residence was brought forward by our enemies evidently with a design of dividing us, we would uniformly vote against every plan named for the permanent residence." The Virginians and Marylanders declared they would vote against the Potomac. Mr. Morris declared he would vote against Germantown and the Falls of the Delaware. The Susquehanna was not publicly named, but of course implied, for Mr. Morris, in enumerating the places to be voted against, named the Potomac, Germantown, and the Falls of Trenton. The line of proceeding for to-morrow was agreed to: Mr. Lee to move and Langdon to second the postponement of the permanent seat in order to take up the resolution for the next session being held in Philadelphia. If all was lost, let it go down to the House of Representatives for them to originate new measures on it.

June 8th, Tuesday.—How shall I describe this day of confusion in the Senate? Mr. Lee laid on the table a report of some additional rules relative to the intercourse between the two Houses. After this he moved that the bill for the permanent residence of Congress shall be postponed to take up the resolution of the Representatives for adjourning to Philadelphia.

Now it was that Izard flamed and Butler bounced, and both seemed to rage with madness. Mr. Lee's motion was in writing, and they moved a postponement of it. The division was eleven, and the Vice-President gave it against the postponement. Now all was hurry and confusion. Izard and Butler actually went and brought Governor Johnston with his night-cap on, out of bed, and a bed with him. The bed was deposited in the committee-room. Johnson was brought in a sedan [chair]. Few was well enough to come without being carried, and we waited half an hour. The vote was taken. We had our eleven and they had thirteen against the resolution. I thought all was over now; but no such thing. They must carry their conquest further.

In the mean time a mob and noise was about the Hall [Senate] as if it had been a fish-market. The postponed bill and the report of the committee on it were called for. The report was read. The first clause of the report was a resolution that the permanent residence should be now fixed. The question was taken on it and it was negatived. This threw them all in the dumps. The report was, however, lost. But now they would have the bill. They accordingly had it, for they had the most votes, and, although the Senate had decided by a most unequivocal vote that the permanent residence should not be taken into consideration, yet they moved to fill the blank with the Potomac. This was lost—fifteen and nine.

Much desultory discourse was now engaged in, and many motions were made of postponement of the bill. Some of them were actually carried, and yet they still made new motions for the blank to be filled. Baltimore was named. This was lost— seventeen to seven. Wilmington was named. It had only three or four. A motion was made to adjourn. The first was lost. A motion was even made to pass the first clause of the bill with a blank, notwithstanding the absurdity of it, even in the face of a vote that this was an improper time to fix the permanent residence. All, in fact, was confusion and irregularity. A second vote of adjournment was called for and carried. So ended the uproar of the day.

John Adams has neither judgment, firmness of mind, nor respectability of deportment to fill the chair of such an assembly. Gunn had scolded out a good deal of stuff; "were we forever to be plagued with a removal, etc.?" This, I thought, deserved some answer. I went over all the disadvantages of New York, contrasted it with Philadelphia, and concluded that such inconveniences would always produce such complaints and un-easiness, and could not be removed but by taking away the cause. I was listened to, but made no converts. I was up a good while, as I went largely into the business, but I took the same ground which I had before traveled over, the notes of which I sent to Dr. Rush.

Just before I rose, I asked Mr. Morris for an estimate of re-moving Congress from Trenton, which he had promised to pro-cure. He had nothing of it. I really communicated this matter to him to enable him to make some figure in the debate, and if possible to bind him to me by this kind of confidential communi-cation. But I have another proof that all advances on my part are in vain. I walked this evening with Mr. Wynkoop. Fell in company with several of the Representatives, exhorted them all, as much as I possibly could, to unanimity and firmness, and did not fail to recommend to steady perseverance under the assur-ance that we would be successful.

June 9th.—Attended the Hall at the usual time. The Rhode Island bill had a third reading. And now the Funding bill was taken up. We had passed the clause funding the old Continental money, and left a blank on Monday. I then called it the resur-rection of a dead demand against the public. Mr. Morris seemed in sentiment with me. King spoke against the clause altogether. But now the Secretary's report was the text-book, and it must be funded at forty for one. I called the attention of the Senate to the characters who now had this money. Many meritorious persons received it as gold and silver, and still kept it as the monuments of the sacrifices which they made in the cause of America. Would seventy-five for one, forty for one, or one hundred for one, indemnify such characters? Would it not be a mockery of their demands? A time might come, a manner might be thought of for their relief, but this was not, perhaps, the time, nor was it the manner. The other class of individuals who were possessed of it had collected it from the holes and corners after it had ceased to be an object of speculation when it was really worth nothing, and who neither gave value for it nor had any merit in the act of collection. For these humble speculators in-finitely too much was done. They had no claims in justice. The whole of the Continental money was sunk by depreciation, a most unequal mode of taxation truly, but an effectual one. He that touched it was taxed by it. This was creating a claim. A defunct demand was conjured up against the Union, as if they feared the mass of debt would be too small, though I fear they would find it much larger than we could discharge, etc. The clause was passed, and we went to the fourth.

Mr. Morris moved, in a moment, to strike out the first two alternatives, and blazed away for six per cent on the nominal amount of all public securities. Elsworth answered, want of ability. Mr. Morris made nothing of the whole of it. The broadside of America was able enough for it all. We had property enough, and he was for a land-tax, and if a land-tax were laid there would be money enough. He said many weak things, and was handled closely for them by Elsworth. The debate, loose indeed, and desultory, continued until three o'clock. Adjourned.

June 10th.—Attended at nine o'clock at the Hall on the bill for making compensation to one John McCord. It was a painful business. His claims do not seem over well founded in point of law or any act of Congress. He is seventy-nine years old, and appears to have suffered deeply in the American cause. We spent a considerable time on his business.

When we came into the House of Representatives, the Funding bill was under consideration. It was passed over without much debate in our cursory way. But now rose Elsworth, and in a long, elaborate discourse recommended the assumption of the State debts. He concluded that he would read his motion, which he said had the approbation of the Secretary of the Treasury. It was verbatim one of Gerry's papers, which had been moved and laid on the Speaker's table in the House of Representatives about a week ago. We had speakers enough now. Dr. Johnson was somewhat singular in his assertions. He denied there was any such thing as a State debt; they were all equally the debts of the United States.

The day was mostly spent in this business. I rose and took the field which I had several times labored in with my pen. The old acts of Congress settle and assume the balances, etc. A short publication which I wrote, and which by one means or other got into almost all the newspapers, was the basis of it. The Boston men and King talked much of their fears of the consequences, etc. I objected Hancock's speech to one and the divided votes of their Representatives to the other. One of the Massachusetts men now produced instructions from their government authorizing their voting for the measure. I alleged that, if one State instructed, all should instruct, and perhaps this should be considered as a good reason of postponement until all instructed on the subject, etc. The consideration was postponed until to-morrow.

June 11th.—Attended at the Hall on Mr. McCord's bill early. Mr. Morris joined us. Went in and attended the Funding bill; the clause for the assumption of the State debts. Mr. Gerry's amendment was negatived. Nine only rose for it. The bill was now committed. The only debate of any consequence was between Elsworth and myself. He set forth in a curious argument that the debts contracted near the seat of Congress were made Federal; that those at a distance were made State debts, supposing that the authority of Congress was less efficacious.

There really was not a shadow of truth in this. He only adapted his argument to an accidental fact, South Carolina and Massachusetts having the largest State debts. I rose and showed that there really was nothing at all in this matter; that the origin of some State debts was their adopting the debts due to individuals, which they did by way of paying their requisitions, and got credit for them accordingly. This was the origin of the large State debt of one of them at least. King was obliging enough to get up and tell the House I meant South Carolina, etc. This brought up Butler and Izard, with some degree of warmth.

It was a good while before I could say anything. I, however, avowed and supported all I had said; that the fact was indubitably so; that no censure was implied in anything I had said; that South Carolina had assumed debts due to her citizens to the amount of $186,799, and had credit in full of her quota of the requisitions of the 10th of September, 1782. On that account Pennsylvania had paid at the same time $346,632, and Massachusetts a large sum of the said requisition; that Pennsylvania might have brought forward her State debt and had credit for it in the requisition, but she did not do so, but remained burdened with both her State debt and requisitions, and had done much toward paying both, while South Carolina had paid nothing to either. The committee were: Mr. Lee, Elsworth, Maclay, King, and Patterson. Some little council business was done, and we adjourned. Just as we had adjourned, Butler wished Carrol joy of a vote being carried in the Representative chamber for the temporary residence to be in Baltimore.

There was some kind of entertainment to which I heard Fitzsimons a few days ago inviting the Speaker. I thought he took him to the door to do it. The Speaker asked me to go with him. I declined it, as well I might. After the Speaker came home I asked him what *he had heard* Mr. Morris say of the Baltimore vote. *He had not made up his mind.* I can find he is now scheming and will not vote for Baltimore. I have had a spell of fishing, of which I was the subject, to know whether I would not oppose the Baltimore vote. I saw clearly the person who was set on to do it, and will report to his employers. I, in all probability, am come to the point that will be seized to turn the whole city of Philadelphia against me, but I trust no taint of dishonor will ever stain my conduct. As to consequences, I care not.

June 12th.—A day of storm and rain. I attended at the Hall at eleven on the Funding bill. The alternatives, as they were called, were the chief subjects of discussion until near three o'clock. Candor, sit by me while I describe the committee:

R. H. Lee, the man who gave independence (in one sense) to America. A man of a clear head and great experience in public business; certainly ambitious and vainglorious, but his passions seek gratification in serving the public.

Elsworth, a man of great faculties and eloquent in debate, but he has taken too much on himself; he wishes to reconcile the Secretary's [Hamilton's] system to the public opinion and welfare; but it is too much; he can not retain the confidence of the people and remain in the good graces of the Secretary. He may lose both.

King, plausible and florid.

Patterson, more taciturn and lurking in his manner, and yet when he speaks commits himself hastily. A *summum jus* man.

Both lawyers and both equally retained by the Secretary [Hamilton].

And now, Billy, what say you of yourself? Not overburdened either with knowledge or experience, but disposed to make the best of your tools.

I objected in general to the bill, disliking funding at all; was willing to pay as an interim three per cent, and place it on the footing of disability to do more. I objected to funding the interest; proposed to establish a land-office to sink the interest now due, and that indents should be given to all persons entitled to them, receivable in that office; declared that even prodigals abhorred compound interest; that the bill went on this principle, though not in an annual ratio. It was, however, in vain, although I could perceive that I made an impression.

There were three alternatives in the Secretary's report. The last was by much the most favorable to the public. This, however, really meant only to try the disposition of Congress, and Fitzsimons, when he took in his resolutions, contrived to have this rejected and one substituted vastly more favorable to the subscribers. A good man could not have done this.

I found I could not effect anything on my own plan. I therefore watched and promoted every favorable sentence that fell from Lee and Elsworth. The result of all was, that we struck out all the alternatives and voted a general fund of four per cent.

In the evening came Mr. Wynkoop heyday all wrong; to go to Baltimore, etc., full charged with the permanent seat, etc. I know he had not this of himself. I, however, delivered myself with firmness on the subject, recapitulated the conduct of the Yorkers, etc., showed him (as I thought) that to concur with Baltimore vote was politically right. He found he could make no impression. It was nearly dark when he went away. I followed to the door. He took the way of Queen Street, and the Speaker, who was with me, said he was going to Fitzsimons'.

This day changed my last bank bill of fifty dollars.

June 13th, Sunday.—This day was very wet. I stayed at

home all day in my usual occupation of writing to my dear family, reading, etc.

June 14th, Monday.—I left home early and called on the Assistant of the Treasury on McCord's affair. He would not let me tell my business, so keen was he on the subject of proposing a bargain with me. Pennsylvania to have the permanent residence on the *Susquehanna,* and her delegation to vote for the assumption [of State debts]. I constrained my indignation at this proposal with much difficulty within the bounds of decency, and the more so as I knew that, however it might be with him, Hamilton, the principal in this business, was not sincere. I gave him such looks and answers as put an end to this business. I then got my errand settled. Went to Mr. Jefferson's office on Mr. Bailey's affair. Arranged this affair and went down Broad Street. Here I met Mr. Lee. Spoke a few words with him, and passed on to the lodgings of Mr. Carrol. My only business with him was to forewarn him that an objection would be made to Baltimore that there were no public buildings, and that he should be prepared on this subject.

From here I went to Mr. Morris' lodgings. I found him somewhat engaged, but the moment he disposed of a small matter of business he dismissed his clerk; told me he was just going to look for me, and was fortunate in my coming in. Said he had much to say, but some part of it must be in the most entire confidence; that on Friday Jackson, of the President's family,* in whom he said he could not have some confidence, had been at Clymer's and Fitzsimons' lodgings; that [Tench] Coxe, of the Treasury, had been there; that their business was to negotiate a bargain: the permanent residence in Pennsylvania for her votes for the assumption, or at least as many votes as would be needful. The burden of their business seemed to be to open the conference with Mr. Hamilton on this subject. Mr. Morris continued: "I did not choose to trust them, but wrote a note to Colonel Hamilton that I would be walking early in the morning on the Battery, and if Colonel Hamilton had anything to propose to him [Morris] he might meet him there, as if by accident. I went in the morning there, and found him *on the sod before me.*" Mr. Hamilton said he

* Meaning a supporter of the measures adopted by the Administration.

wanted one vote in the Senate and five in the House of Representatives; that he was willing and would agree to place the permanent residence of Congress at Germantown or Falls of the Delaware, if he would procure him these votes.

Mr. Morris owned that he complied on his part so far as that he agreed to consult some of the Pennsylvanian delegation (I abruptly said, "You need not consult me"), but proposed that the temporary residence of Congress in Philadelphia should be the price. They parted on this, but were to communicate on the subject again.

Mr. Morris and Mr. Fitzsimons made a party out of town and took Mr. Read with them, yesterday, as the man whose vote they would engage. (Let me here recollect the application made to me on Saturday night by Mr. Wynkoop. I now know that he was trying me on that subject, and the Speaker was not much out when he said Wynkoop was gone to Fitzsimons. He should have added, "and Morris.")

Mr. Read's answer was what Mr. Morris called polite: "Gentlemen, I am disposed to facilitate your wishes." But now, this morning, says Mr. Morris, I have received a note from Colonel Hamilton that he can not think about negotiating about the temporary residence; that his friends will not hear of it. Mr. Morris added: "I know he has been able to manage the destruction of the Baltimore vote without me, but I can not yet tell how. I sent for Mr. Read. He says they have accounts that the Senators from Rhode Island are appointed and expected every moment." But Mr. Morris added, "I think he has some other assurances." I now parted with Mr. Morris and joined the Committee on the Funding bill.

The Senate were formed some time before we joined them, and after some of the routine business of the day was done, and the Baltimore resolution handed in, it was called for. Schuyler moved it should be postponed a fortnight. Governor Johnston, of North Carolina, seconded him. Elsworth got up; said this matter mixed itself with all our affairs. There was a secret understanding, a bargaining, that run through all our proceedings, and therefore it ought to be postponed.

I retorted his secret understanding, bargaining, etc., on himself. As he knew there were such things, he knew where they arose, and, if they "mixed" with and polluted our proceedings, it was time to put an end to them, which could only be done by deciding the matter, etc. The question was put, and it was the old eleven and thirteen.

This was mess-day. I did not join the company until about five o'clock, and stayed until after eight. But, oh, such noise and nonsense! Fitzsimons railed out at one time against Pennsylvania interferences about the assumption of the State debts. Had it not been for these, the funding system would have been completed months ago. He had received letters that stones would be thrown at him in the streets of Philadelphia if he were there, etc.

June 15th.—We finished our observations on the Funding bill, and reported. The whole day was spent in debate on it. I had so often expressed my sentiments respecting the subject of this bill, that I need not set any of them down here. I was not often up. I took at one time some pains to explain the nature of facilities and indents, but no question was taken on any point. All was postponed.

Dr. Elmer told me as I left the Hall that he had something to impart to me. Mr. Morris, however, called me aside and told me that he had a communication from Mr. Jefferson of a disposition of having the temporary residence fifteen years in Philadelphia and the permanent residence at Georgetown on the Potomac, and that he (Mr. Morris) had called a meeting of the delegation at six o'clock this evening at our lodging on the business. I was really unwell, and had to lie down the most of the afternoon. The delegation met at six. I was called out. However, when I came in, what passed was repeated to me. Hamilton proposed to give the permanent residence to Pennsylvania at Germantown or the Falls of the Delaware, on condition of their voting for the assumption. In fact, it was the confidential story of yesterday all over again. Mr. Morris also repeated Mr. Jefferson's story, but I certainly had misunderstood Mr. Morris at the Hall, for Jefferson vouched for nothing.

I have seen no prospect of fixing the permanent residence of Congress at the present session, and whenever it is gone into will be involved in much difficulty. I have, therefore, declared against everything of the kind; but to continue the temporary residence here, under the promise of the permanent residence being in any part of Pennsylvania, I consider as madness. It was giving them time to fortify and intrench themselves with such systematic arrangements that we never should get away while the law acted as a tie on us and bound us hand and foot, but gave them all the power and all the opportunity of fixing us permanently in this place. I would rather be under no obligation and keep up an unremitted effort to get away, which I had no doubt would be crowned with success.

I know not whether what I said was the reason of it, but these sentiments seemed to be adopted. As to the bargain proposed by Hamilton, I spoke of it with detestation. Mr. Morris now proposed that a paper should be drawn up, with reasons for our conduct, that they might not be able to brand us with any neglect of the interests of Pennsylvania; and a committee for this purpose was appointed—Mr. Morris, Mr. Fitzsimons, and Mr. Hartley.

CHAPTER IX

THE FUNDING BILL

June 16th.—I early called this morning at Colonel Hartley's lodgings in order to give him a sketch of what I thought might be well enough for us to sign. He was gone, but I fell in with him at the Hall and delivered it to him.

I sauntered about till Congress formed, and now we got at the Funding bill. Here we had all the stuff over again of public credit, etc. The great question was whether the report of the committee for four per cent should be adopted. I soon committed myself in such sort that I must expect all the public creditors to be my enemies. The great ground that I took was, that I did not believe we could impose any direct taxes on our constituents for a purpose which they knew as well as I did; that the holders of certificates in Pennsylvania had them funded when they were but 2s. 6d. on the pound; that £100 purchased £800; that they had drawn interest on the nominal amount for four years, equal to £192. Justice and law allowed them but £124; hence they had £68 clear already, and the certificates into the bargain, etc.

I was up a long time. Mr. Morris rose against the report. His collar fairly choked him. He apologized to the House that his agitation had deprived him of his recollection on the subject, and he sat down. He rose again some little time before the Senate adjourned, mentioned his late confusion, but declared it did not arise from the personal interest he had in public securities; that, although he was possessed of some, he was no speculator, etc. I wish he had not made this last apology, for I fear it fixed the matter deeper on him.

We spent until past three o'clock, but took no question; and, indeed, it seemed almost agreed that we would not proceed without the other bill.

June 17th.—Spent this morning, before the meeting of the Senate, in calling on Mr. Coxe for the papers in the case of McCord, and at the office of the Secretary of State on Mr. Bailey's affair.

The Senate met, and until near two o'clock we were engaged on the subject of consuls and vice-consuls. The grand question was, whether foreigners were eligible to those offices. It was admitted that they were, and a number accordingly appointed. When I came home to dinner, the Speaker told me that a bill was proposed in the House of Representatives for giving them salaries. Thus it is that we are led on, little by little, to increase the civil list; to increase the mass of public debt, and, of course, the taxes of the public. This, however, is all of a piece with former management from the offices.

The Funding bill was now called for. Butler repeated the same things he had said yesterday. But now up rose Patterson with a load of notes before him. To follow him would be to write a pamphlet, for he was up near an hour. Near the beginning he put a question: "What principle shall we adopt to settle this business? If we follow Justice, *she says three per cent or even two is as much as the holders of certificates can demand.* But what says law?—six per cent," and he was a *summum jus* man to the end of the chapter. It was near three when he had done.

I felt an impatience to attack him, and up I got. At first exploded a doctrine which he had stated of Congress being a party and the claimants another. I stated the people at large as being the debtors and the holders the creditors, and Congress the umpire—the Legislature between them. I then stated his two principles of justice and law; declared myself an adherent of the former. Law was the rule for courts and magistrates in the execution of their offices, but justice was our guide, and had been the guide of all just legislation from the Jewish jubilee to the present day; that even in law it was a maxim that rigid law was rigid injustice. Hence the necessity of courts of chancery expressly for mitigating the severity of unjust contracts. I repeated his own words of "three per cent—perhaps two per cent" being the voice of Justice. If, then, the point of justice stands at three per cent, or if at two per cent, all beyond that

point is injustice to whom? To the very people whose interests
it is our bounden duty to support and protect. I reprobated his
position even with acrimony as the Shylock doctrine of "my
bond, my bond."

June 18th.—We went early to the Hall, as I was on two
committees this morning—the one the case of one Twining,
the other McCord's. We spent a considerable space of time
on Twining's affair, which to me did not seem a just subject of
legislation. I then joined the committee on McCord's case.

This was truly one in which Compassion mingled herself
with Justice. The generals, Thomson, Irvine, and others, had
received effects from him in Canada in the year 1776. They
gave him a bill which was never paid. The Auditor and Comptroller settled the sum due on this bill, $809.71. He had suffered
greatly in Canada: had his house burned; took our Continental
money to a considerable amount as specie, which he produced
to us to the amount of $1,200 or $1,300; advanced money and
goods to many people who now refuse to pay him, and many
of them he can not find. All these things are indubitable. I
had no difficulty in allowing him the $809.71 in ready money,
in lieu of a certificate, but anything more I seemed to feel a
difficulty in. Lands had been set apart by the old Congress to
make compensation for Canadian sufferers. We reported the
$809.71, and left a blank for the value of his lands. The Senate
filled the blank with $500. My heart would not let me rise against
the motion. Though it is a trifle to his sufferings, yet how many
hundreds of our own people suffer equal distress!

Up now came the Funding bill. Butler railed at Elsworth.
Elsworth talked back. There really was no entertainment. No
man ever rambled or talked more at random than Butler. He is
ever quoting authors on trade, finance, etc., ever repeating what
he has seen in Europe. This day he asserted that the circulating
coin of Great Britain was three hundred millions. Authors (if
I remember right) place it at about sixteen. There really was
nothing new. Some were pressing for the question, but it was
postponed generally.

I received a letter from Dr. Rush and a newspaper containing a mutilated publication of the piece which I had sent
to him on the subject of Federal residence. He has left out

many of what I consider as the best arguments, and very improperly reduced the arguments drawn from the mileage one half by his miscalculations. But I really never was served otherwise.

This evening Mr. Morris and Mr. Fitzsimons called on us. Hamilton had been with them again. Never had a man a greater propensity for bargaining than Mr. Morris. Hamilton knows this, and is laboring to make a tool of him. He affects to tell Mr. Morris that the New England men will bargain to fix the permanent seat at the Potomac or at Baltimore. Mr. Fitzsimons counted all the members who it was likely would vote for such a measure, and the conclusion was that no such measure could be carried by them.

June 19th.—Attended at ten o'clock at the Hall on Mr. Twining's bill. The committee heard all the witnesses produced.

We then walked to view the demolitions of Fort George; the leaden coffins and remains of Lady and Lord Bellamont, now exposed to the sun after an interment of about ninety years. They and many more had been deposited in vaults in a chapel which once stood in the fort. The chapel was burned down about fifty years ago and never rebuilt. The leveling of the fort and digging away the foundations have uncovered the vaults.

The talk of the day is the death of one Tilfair, from Georgia, who this morning cut his throat with a razor. A negro boy who waited on him has manifested marks of astonishing attachment. 'Tis said he was separated from the dead body by force, and restrained with difficulty from committing violence on himself.

June 20th, Sunday.—I spent the most of this day at home, finishing some letters; read occasionally. In the evening I went to see Mrs. Bell. She proposed to walk, and offered to come and see Mrs. Muhlenberg. I set out with her, but she knew almost everybody we met. A Mrs. Somebody joined us and made us gad over almost the whole town to visit somebody else. We, however, parted with our adventitious comrade and performed our first tour. This does not deserve notice only for what Mrs. Bell mentioned, as the subject of the removal of Congress from this place was her constant theme.

She took occasion to tell me that Mr. Morris was not sincerely attached to the Pennsylvania interest on that subject; that his commercial arrangements were calculated for this place [New York]; that the Yorkers depended on him, but were lately staggered by an oath which it was said he had sworn that he would have Congress away. I endeavored to persuade myself that Mr. Morris was now in earnest, and the Yorkers would find him so, etc. Yet I had my own thoughts on the subject. Mrs. Bell replied that he may have good reasons now to wish for popularity in Pennsylvania.

June 21st.—Attended at the Hall early on the bill for remitting certain penalties to one N. Twining. The Senate met. I observed a strangeness of disposition in the House the moment, or rather a few moments, after the minutes were read. Patterson moved to adjourn. Schuyler seconded. This was lost. It was now moved to take up the vote of the House of Representatives for fixing the time of adjournment. This was agreed to, and King, Bassett, and Walker appointed on our part to confer. Izard now rose; said there was something to put on the minutes, and renewed the motion for adjournment. Seconded by Patterson. This was lost.

And now the Funding bill was taken up. We had a great deal of the old ground gone over again. King received a note; rose and moved that the Funding bill should be postponed, as the House of Representatives had negatived the bill for the ways and means. He was seconded by Schuyler. We had now a long, desultory kind of debate whether the bill should be postponed. It was not postponed. Now the debates on the merits of the bill. The question was whether all the alternatives should be struck out and a fund of four per cent adopted. Adopted; thirteen for, ten against. Now the question on the striking out of the indents. Elsworth and the New England men knew that Pennsylvania has a number of indents, and the invention of all of them is at work to turn it to her disadvantage. The vote was, however, carried to keep the indents, since the other back interest was to be funded. I bore my testimony in the strongest terms against funding any interest, and proposed to open a land-office as a sinking fund for the whole of the back interest, including the indents, but I found no second. The interest of the whole was placed on one footing, almost without a division. Now a long debate ensued about the Jersey payments and a proviso which had been inserted to favor them. No other question was, however, taken, and the House adjourned a quarter after three.

This was mess or club day.* I went and stayed till the fumigation began, *alias* smoking of cigars, a thing I never could bear. Elsworth made a long speech, amounting to this: that since a general system of funding could not be obtained, gentlemen would be against all funding whatever. I placed his speech in as strong colors as I could; that since a party in Congress could not build as they pleased, they would turn and pull all down. There was a majority against the assumption of the State debts and the minority, indignant at being controlled, since they could not rule, would join the discontented part of Congress and stop all business.

Adams affects to treat me with all the neglect he can while I am speaking, by turning his head a different way, looking sidewise, etc. But I care not. I will endeavor to bear it.

June 22d.—I called this morning on General Irwin, who is one of the commissioners for settling accounts between the United States and the individual States, for the amount of the Jersey claims for interest paid by the State on the Continental certificates. Found it to be about half a million. Now attended the committee on Twining's case. Mr. Morris called me aside. (I had yesterday expressed my indignation of the New England attempt upon Pennsylvania, in excluding, or trying to exclude, those indents, which would pass into her hands in consequence of the late funding law, from being funded; had endeavored to possess him of the facts to obtain his assistance, and indeed expressed unguarded solicitude on that subject.)

He told me this is an important affair respecting the indents to Pennsylvania. "I would have you think well of it. The New England men are determined to carry it against us. The assumption is the only way we can rid ourselves of this thing. I would have you think of it—think of it."

I had to say I will think of it. I felt a little disturbed: not

---

* Meaning the day set aside by the Pennsylvanian delegation for dining together.

if I knew my own mind with regard to the part I should act, but to think that everything should be set to sale, and that even just measures could not be pursued by contract, and that men should be hunted into measures. I have often thought myself deficient in readiness of judgment or quickness of determination. Perhaps any man can think more and better too at twice than at once. I, however, in a few minutes took my seat beside Mr. Morris; told him that I considered the assumption so politically wrong and productive of so much injustice, that no offer could be made which would induce me to change my mind. I had, however means of another nature. I could depend nothing on the promises of the New England men; but, further, had calculated that the State of New York was circumstanced nearly in the same way as Pennsylvania with respect to the indents; and I consider this as the sure pledge that we should not be pushed to extremities on that ground. The result showed that I was right; for, after a great deal of debate in the House, affairs settled as I would have them.

There is a lesson in the matter, and I must be on my guard with respect to my colleague. Hamilton unhappily has him in his power with respect to these old accounts, which are still before the Treasury. The bill for establishing the post-office was read the first time. We adjourned early.

Mr. Fitzsimons called this afternoon. We had much loose conversation on the subject of adjournment. I expressed a wish, the sooner the better. Fitzsimons said it never would do to go away without funding the debt. Pennsylvania was too deeply interested. She would draw *three millions of dollars* annually from the funds. I stared, as well I might, for at four per cent she must possess more than the whole of the Continental debt to do it, viz., seventy-five millions. He corrected himself, and said above fifteen millions would belong to her and her citizens. I said this might be. He now got on the subject of Pennsylvania paying her civil list, etc., with Continental revenue. In fact, this man has no rule of conduct but convenience, and he shifts opinions and sentiments to answer occasions.

The Speaker walked away with Mr. Fitzsimons. When he returned, I asked him to repeat what Mr. Fitzsimons had said. He [the Speaker] said Mr. Fitzsimons had explained himself in their walk, that the State of Pennsylvania possessed three millions on which she would draw interest, and that the citizens of the State possessed fifteen millions on which they would draw interest. There are more turners than dish-makers; but in fact none of these things deserve noting down.

CHAPTER X

June 23d, Wednesday.—This day could not be considered as very important in the Senate. The Funding bill was called for and postponed.

The Intercourse bill, or that for appointing ambassadors, had been referred to a committee of conference so long ago that I had forgotten it, but the thing was neither dead nor sleeping. It was only dressing and friends-making. The report increased the salaries and added ten thousand dollars to the appropriations. I concluded they had secured friends enough to support it before they committed it to the House. This turned out to be the case. The whole appropriation was forty thousand dollars, and they were voted with an air of perfect indifference by the affirmants, although I consider the money as worse than thrown away, for I know not a single thing that we have for a minister to do at a single court in Europe. Indeed, the less we have to do with them the better. Our business is to pay them what we owe, and the less political connection the better with any European power. It was well spoken against. I voted against every part of it.

We received also a bill for the East Indian trade. Read for the first time. Mr. Morris was often called out. He at last came in and whispered me: "The business is settled at last. Hamilton gives up the temporary residence." I wrote on a slip of paper (as we could not converse freely), *"If Hamilton has his hand in the residence now, he will have his foot in it before the end of the session."* I afterward told Mr. Morris that this seeming willingness of Hamilton proceeded from his knowledge that the North Carolina Senators and Colonel Gunn could not be restrained from voting for Baltimore, and that the present proposal and bill (for a bill was shown to me by Mr. Morris) were meant to divert the Southern members from Baltimore, and they would finally destroy the bill.

I got Henry, of Maryland, into the audience-room and gave him a detail of what was going on, and made the same reflections on it to him. I saw he believed the North Carolina men would vote for Baltimore. I find there is a ferment among them, and good may come of it.

Paid my lodgings.

There are jockeying and bargaining going on respecting which I am not consulted and which I hear of only by-the-by: the temporary residence in Philadelphia for fifteen years and the permanent residence on the Potomac. A solemn engagement has been entered into by eleven Senators to push the temporary residence only. On this ground we of Pennsylvania are perfectly safe, and our interest is to keep this contract alive. If we go from this the temporary residence may remain in New York and the permanent residence to the Potomac. It is a species of robbery to deprive Pennsylvania of the residence. How can a delegate reconcile himself to such a vote unless he confide in future contingency to repair his errors, which is neither safe nor honorable?

June 24th.—This was a day of small business in the Senate. The report on a bill for remitting fines to one Twining was rejected and the bill confirmed; contrary, in my opinion, to every idea of justice, for this man had got already from the public upward of two thousand dollars without consideration.

Though little business was done in the Senate, yet I ought never to forget this day. In the Senate chamber, Mr. Walker told me that the Pennsylvania delegation had, in a general meeting, agreed to place the permanent residence on the Potomac and the temporary residence to remain ten years in Philadelphia. I answered, I know nothing of any such agreement. No truth was ever better founded. He said Scott had come from the meeting to him. He seemed willing I should take a lead in the business. I heard nothing further on the business. Dr. Elmer and I called on Mr. Morris, and here for the first time I heard him declare he was satisfied with ten years. He did not say much to me, but the moment I came home the Speaker attacked me: "Here you have been doing fine things; you have broken the bargain," etc.

I denied that I had broken any bargain; that I never knew

of any bargain for ten years being made. Did not General Muhlenberg speak to you? Yes, on Monday last he bid me tell Mr. Morris that he thought Matthews could not make them agree to more than ten years. I forgot to mention it to him then, but mentioned it to him afterward. He said if we agreed to ten they would propose seven, etc., and declared himself against listening to any such proposals, We, however, met in the evening. Bassett and Read, of the Delaware State, came in with Mr. Morris. Dr. Elmer came some time after. I now did the most foolish thing I ever did in my life. I declared that I considered the permanent residence as a matter that ought to belong to Pennsylvania, in whatever point of view it was considered, geographically or politically; that to deprive her of it was, in my opinion, a species of robbery; *but, since we came there to consult the public good, I was willing to be governed by republican ideas, and would stand by the vote of the majority, as a house divided against itself could not stand.*

Mr. Morris now said my arguments were too late. I should have made these objections when the contract was made for fifteen years' residence at Philadelphia. I very freely declared I never entered into any such contract. Morris, Fitzsimons, and the Speaker declared that I did, and the Speaker reminded me that a committee was appointed. I agreed that a committee was appointed, but it was to draw up our reasons for rejecting Hamilton's proposals; and that I understood them so would be evident from my sentiments, which I had committed to paper at the time, and which were now in the hands of Colonel Hartley. They all three persisted in the charge. Hartley, however, had spirit enough to say there was no such contract. This seemed to cool them a little. But after some time Scott came in. The matter was repeated to him. He declared there was no number of years mentioned at all as any bargain, and, of course, no contract. This made them look a little blue.

I must note that I read the sketch which I gave to Hartley to the Speaker, and he approved of it; and I expressly mentioned both to him and Colonel Hartley that all that we did respected only what was past. But now the Speaker put the question, "Shall we vote for a bill giving the temporary residence, ten years, to Philadelphia and the permanent residence to the Potomac?" They all said yes but myself. I said no, but, unluckily, am bound by my foolish declaration. Good God, deliver me this once! Fate, familiar as her garter, ended the difficulty. But the tale is long, and I had better begin the business of the day on the next page.

June 25th, Friday.—A day of excessive rain. I went to the Hall in the Speaker's carriage at an early hour to attend the committee on the post-office business. I found Mr. Carrol there. We had much loose talk. He told me his plan, which was to take Butler's bill, amended so that the residence should be ten years in Philadelphia, at the end of which the permanent residence should be on the Potomac.

The first business was the report on what was called Stephen Moore's bill. This man is the owner of the land on which the old fort of West Point stands. He is got in debt in town to the amount of two thousand or some such sum. He has nothing but the rocks of West Point. The Secretaries of War and Treasury and other influential characters have interested themselves in getting this bill passed to buy the land from him, to pay his debts, under the notion that the ground is necessary for a fortress. Barefaced as this business is, it was carried in the Senate by a great majority. Am I mistaken, or is it the spirit of prodigality broke loose since Rhode Island came in? Yesterday Twining's base business; this day Moore's case, and a bill for a claim for one Gould came up. The yeas and nays are on the journals, and, strange to tell, Mr. Morris for once was with me.

Mr. Carrol now rose and was seconded by Lee. Izard, Few, King, on one side, Carrol and Lee on the other. Butler bounced between both, but declared for the bill and he would be for it. The motion was made to take up the bill. The Vice-President said: "There has been a motion for postponement. I do not know whether it has been seconded." No such thing had happened, but the hint was soon after taken.

And now all was consternation and commotion. Out ran King, Schuyler, Izard, and sundry of the Eastern gentry, and in were ushered the Senators from Rhode Island. And now the hinted-for postponement was called for of the bill, which, in fact, had not been taken up. But the new members, just sworn and seated, did not get up. Signs and motions were ineffectual; they kept their seats, and the bill, of course, was taken up, or, in parliamentary style, not postponed.

Izard begged leave to explain, or, in other words, to tell the new-come gentlemen, that they ought to have voted for the postponement. Mr. Adams without any ceremony put the same question over again. King got on one side and Elsworth on the other of the new members and got up with them. Butler, too, after all his declarations, voted for the postponement. It was thirteen and thirteen, and Bonny Johnny voted for the postponement; and thus the business of the day was got over without much difficulty so far, or at least the knotty parts of it, and thus my neck got out of the noose.

Adjourned until Monday.

I must note here that a number of our own people were duped in pushing the Rhode Island bill. They are now paid for it. I told them at the time what was intended. They must take what follows.

June 26th, Saturday.—Attended this day on the Committee on the Post-Office bill. The bill came up from the Representatives with every post-road described, both main and cross-roads. Carrol and Strong were for blotting out every word of description, and leaving all to the Postmaster-General and the President of the United States. I proposed a different plan: that one great post-road should be described by law from Portland, in New Hampshire, to Augusta, in Georgia, passing through the seats of the different governments, and that two cross-roads only should be described from New York to Canada, and from Philadelphia or some other improper place to Fort Pitt, for the accommodation of the Western country. The other or block system prevailed, but we are to meet again on Monday, at ten o'clock.

June 27th, Sunday.—Called on Scott this morning. Went to walk, but the heat was insupportable. Returned to my lodgings. Spent the residue of the day in writing letters, reading, etc.

June 28th, Monday.—Met at ten on the Post-Office Committee, but such running and caballing of the Senators nothing could be done. Stephen Moore's bill the first business. Izard made a long speech, telling *how injurious it would be for this man if the bill did not pass,* etc., and would now let the question be put until the Senate was full. It was carried.

Now the Baltimore vote was read. Carrol and Lee moved to postpone it. It was postponed. Carrol now moved to read some representations from Baltimore and Georgetown. This was complied with. Carrol surprised me by taking me out and requesting me to move the insertion of Baltimore for the permanent residence. Said he wished to be put and negatived. This had a crooked aspect. I declined it. Izard, however, moved this very thing, and Walker told me it was expected that he would do it. I called for the amendment proposed on Friday, but Carrol got up and wished the vote on Baltimore. It was negatived.

Carrol now got up with the amendments. He surprised us with his slowness. We wrangled on till nearly three o'clock, calling yeas and nays on almost every question—but for these *vide* the minutes. When we came to the blank for the place of temporary residence—and by-the-by there was no blank in the amendment which Carrol read on Friday, but he was now suffered by Adams to proceed on the original bill. He evidently waited and paused until Izard moved to fill the blank with New York. Now we had the warmest debates of the day. Mr. Morris took no part whatever. Langdon and myself were the warmest. The question was put at three o'clock and carried for New York—thirteen to twelve. Colonel Gunn has been absent all day—designedly, it is supposed.

This day the [Pennsylvania] delegation had invited the Vice-President and the other officers of the General Government to dinner. The Chief-Justice and the Vice-President did not attend. The three Secretaries were with us. The discourse before dinner turned on the manner of doing business in the Senate. It was remarked that, as every question of moment was carried only by one majority, or for the most part by the casting vote of the Vice-President, it might be as well to vest the whole senatorial power in the President of the Senate. The fact really is as it was stated. But they did not mention the fact that Hamilton and his New York *junto* do business on the principles of economy, and do not put themselves to the expense of hiring more than just the number necessary to carry their point. This is a deplorable truth with respect to our Senate, and certainly is a foul evil at the root of our legislation.

I could not help making some remarks on our three Secretaries. Hamilton has a very boyish, giddy manner, and Scotch-Irish people could well call him a "skite." Jefferson transgresses on the extreme of stiff gentility or lofty gravity. Knox is the easiest man, and has the most dignity of presence. They retired at a decent time, one after another. Knox stayed the longest, as indeed suited his aspect best, being more of a Bacchanalian figure.

June 29th.—The Tonnage bill was taken up and committed. This bill uses the same rates of tonnage as the old bill, and why it was brought forward is more than I can say, unless it was solely to employ time. A bill to make compensation to one Gould was also committed.

And now the Residence bill was taken up. The joy of the Yorkers made them cry out for an adjournment when they had filled one of the blanks. Now the other was to be filled with the time of the temporary residence. It was carried for ten years, and Carrol voted for it : thirteen to twelve. But now the question was taken on the clause, and the whole was rejected : sixteen to nine. Now Izard and the adherents of New York showed visible perturbation and bounced at a strange rate. I looked at Carrol, and got him to rise with his clause, ten years for Philadelphia. Why he kept it back so long explains itself.

Schuyler and King offered to amend it by dividing the time, five years to each place. Long debate here. The question was lost : thirteen to thirteen, the Vice-President against. They now moved Baltimore. Lost it : ten to sixteen. Butler now moved to stay two years in New York : thirteen to thirteen, the Vice-President against. The question was put on the clause : thirteen to thirteen, Vice-President against. So the clause was lost. The question was now put, "Shall the bill pass to a third reading?" The noes certainly had it, but the House did not divide, and an adjournment obtained before anything more was finished.

In the course of King's speech, I noted down the following words, "convulse the Union," etc. This, as he stated it, would be the effect of removing from New York. In my reply I mentioned the words. He denied that he had used such words. Mr. Morris was the first to cry out that he did not use any such words. From the drift of chaff and feathers it is seen how the wind blows. Mr. Morris did not rise this day nor yesterday; I might speak or let it alone—he has never said one word except giving me the above contradiction. Mr. Wyngate and sundry other members declared he [King] did use them, but, as he chose to retract, I passed it by as words that had never been spoken.

June 30th.—I called early at the Hall. Langdon only there. Went and paid off my bill for Monday, twenty-eight shillings, the price of a two days' headache. When I came to the Hall, Dr. Elmer told me that Carrol & Co. were using every endeavor to pass the bill to a third reading without anything of the temporary residence. Here we certainly had every right to leave them, yet Walker said they would drop Philadelphia if we would not go with them. I am fully satisfied that they have had an under plot on hand all this time with the Yorkers. Carrol, finding the bill could not be carried to a third reading, moved a reconsideration of the Philadelphia clause. But he was out of order, not having been of the majority. I passed the word to get Butler to move, as he had been of that side. He did so, after talking almost half an hour. It was reconsidered and adopted, fourteen to twelve, Butler changing his ground. Before we could get a question on the paragraph, they moved the question of five years in New York and five in Philadelphia. Lost: twelve to fourteen. Then to stay two years in New York. This Butler joined them in, and the House stood thirteen and thirteen. The Vice-President gave us a long speech on the orderly conduct, decent behavior of the citizens of New York, especially in the gallery of the other House; said no people in the world could behave better. I really thought he meant this lavish praise as an indirect censure on the city of Philadelphia, for the papers have teemed with censorious charges of their rudeness to the members of public bodies. Be that, however, as it may, he declared he would go to Philadelphia without staying a single hour, and gave us his vote. I think it was well he did not know all, for, had he given this vote the other way, the whole would have been lost. The question on the passage to the third reading was carried: fourteen to twelve.

Mr. Langdon now moved a reconsideration to strike out the loan of the one hundred thousand dollars. A long debate ensued. It was evident his vote would turn it. This I mentioned to Walker. We told him, however, that we were with them. But they did what good policy directed. They gave the matter up, and the appropriation was struck out. The question on the bill passing to a third reading was now taken. Carried: fourteen to twelve.

I am fully convinced Pennsylvania could do no better. The matter could not be longer delayed. It is, in fact, the interest of the President of the United States that pushes the Potomac. He [Washington], by means of Jefferson, Madison, Carrol, and others, urged the business, and, if we had not closed with these terms, a bargain would have been made for the temporary residence in New York. They have offered to support the Potomac for three years' temporary residence (in New York, I presume), and I am very apprehensive they would have succeeded if it had not been for the Pennsylvania threats that were thrown out of stopping all business if an attempt was made to rob them of both temporary and permanent residence.

July 1st.—Knowing nothing of immediate consequence, I attended the Hall early. Took a seat in the committee-room. Began an examination of the journals of the old Congress touching some matters before us in committee. Had thus an opportunity at the members as they came in, but such rushing and caballing of the New England men and Yorkers!

When the minutes were read, King observed that the yeas and nays were not inserted on the motion for staying two years in New York. The Vice-President and Secretary of the Senate both denied that they were taken, but I believed they erred. This, however, I did not consider as much for them. We read the Rhode Island Enumeration [Census] bill. Committed the Settlement bill and one for the regulation of seamen.

And now came the residence. Elsworth moved that the extent of the Potomac should be thirty miles above and thirty below Hancocktown. Lost. Second motion, "To insert the first Monday in May, instead of first Monday in December, for removal." The yeas and nays equal. And now John Adams gave us one of his pretty speeches. He mentioned many of the arguments for removal, and concluded that justice, policy, and even necessity, called for it.

Now King took up his lamentations. He sobbed, wiped his eyes, and scolded and railed and accused, first everybody and then nobody, of bargaining, contracting arrangements and engagements that would dissolve the Union. He was called on sharply. He begged pardon, and, blackguard-like, railed again. Butler replied in a long, unmeaning talk; repeated that he was sure the honorable gentleman did not mean him; and yet, if there really was any person to whom King's mysterious hints would apply, Butler's strange conduct marked him as the most proper object for them. Talk followed talk. It was evident they meant to spend the day. Dr. Johnson cried, "Adjourn!" "Question! question!" re-echoed from different quarters of the House. Few begged leave to move an amendment. It was to restore the appropriation clause. It was lost, and at last we got the question on transmitting the bill to the Representatives— yeas, fourteen; nays, twelve.

As I came from the chamber [Senate], King gave me a look. I replied, "King's Lamentations." "That won't do," said he. When we were down-stairs he turned on me, and said, "Let us now go and receive the congratulations of the city for what we have done." I had heard so much and so many allusions to the hospitality, etc., I thought it no bad time to give both him and them a wipe. "King, for a session of near six months I have passed the threshold of no citizen of New York; I have no wish to commence acquaintance now." He muttered some ejaculation and went off. In truth, I never was in so inhospitable a place. The above declaration I thought it not amiss to make, that they may know that I am not insensible of their rudeness; and, further, that I am quite clear of any obligations to them.

July 2d.—Attended the committee on the affair of Gould's bill. There did not appear much animation in the House. That keenness of look and eagerness which marked all our former looks had departed with the residence. Elsworth moved a commitment of the resolution with regard to the State debts. I saw we were taken unawares on this subject. They carried the commitment and the committee both against us. Carrol joined them.

We got now at the Indian bill. It was committed, and now we have joined the Post-Office bill and debated on it to the adjournment.

Wyngate told me this day of a violent breach having happened between King and the Massachusetts men. They would not vote for the Potomac, as King wished them to do. Had they joined the Connecticut and York votes, we would have obtained the temporary residence on much worse terms. This is still further proof of what I knew before—that there was an under-plot and a negotiation still open between the Potomac and New York. The Speaker told me this day that the assumption [of State debts] would pass. I heard him with grief, and trust I may yet disbelieve him. He dined with the President yesterday.

July 3d.—General Irwin called early on me this morning. It was to tell me that King and Lawrence had been asserting with great confidence that we had bargained to give the assumption of State debts for the residence, etc.; that I was to go away, and Carrol to vote direct for it, etc.; that a very great hubbub was raised among the Southern gentlemen, etc. I could only tell him that it was false, and much, indeed, as I wished to see my family, that now home I would not go; that I would stay, and he was at liberty to say so. I called on Williamson as I went to the Hall, and on Hawkins, and told them so.

These Yorkers are the vilest of people. Their vices have not the palliation of being manly. They resemble bad schoolboys who are unfortunate at play: they revenge themselves by telling notorious thumpers. Even the New England men say that King's character is detestable—a perfect canvas for the devil to paint on; a groundwork void of every virtue.

Senate sat until three on the Post-Office bill, but the debates were unimportant.

When I came in, the Speaker told me that the York malevolence was showing itself in curious caricatures, in ridicule of the Pennsylvanians, etc.

July 4th.—Being Sunday, was celebrated only by the firing of cannon about noon. I walked to Scott's lodgings. He came home with me. He showed a disposition to go all over the

arguments which I had used in the Senate on that subject.
I did so with much cheerfulness. Spent the rest of the day in
writing letters to my family and others. I called this morning
on Mr. Lee, and showed him plainly, as I thought, how we
could, by a side-wind in the bill for the settlement of accounts,
give the assumption a decided stroke. I promised I would see
him to-morrow.

July 5th.—I was detained long before I could get to see Mr.
Lee. He had consulted Madison, as he said, and had altered
the amendment in point of form. But it certainly was much
more obscure. Said he would second the motion if I made it.

The Post-Office bill was taken up, and a long debate [fol-
lowed] whether the Postmaster should appoint the post-roads
or the Congress declare them so by law. It was carried in
favor of the Postmaster doing it.

A motion was made that Congress should adjourn to wait
on the President, with the compliments of the day. Negatived.

A second motion to adjourn one hour, for the above purpose, lost. Some business was done, and a second motion for
adjournment was called. All the town was in arms; grena-
diers, light infantry, and artillery passed the Hall, and the
firing of cannon and small-arms, with beating of drums, kept
all in uproar. This motion was carried, and now all of us
repaired to the President's. `` got some wine, punch, and
cakes. From hence we went to St. Paul's, and heard the anniversary of independence pronounced by a Mr. B. Livingston.
The church was crowded. I could not hear him well. Some
said it was fine. I could not contradict them. I was in the pew
next to General Washington. Part of his family and Senators
filled the seats with us. Was warm, and sweated a good deal.

Some say that the Yorkers will make a desperate resistance
to-morrow. Others say they will die soft. Jackson gave me this
day the President's compliments and an invitation to dinner
on Thursday.

CHAPTER XI

THE SETTLEMENT AND ASSUMPTION BILLS

July 6th.—Was called on early this morning by Mr. Hanna, of Harrisburg. A letter from Mr. Harris says my family are well. Attended at the Hall after having paid some visits. The Post-Office bill was passed after some debate. Gould's bill was rejected. I had occasion to be up on both these bills. Now came the Settlement bill. Mr. Lee had spoiled my amendment, or at least had greatly obscured it; but, if I stirred at all, I must use his motion, and, great man as he is, there really was misspelling in it. The ground I took was that the fifth section of the bill laid down a ratio in consequence of which there must, in the nature of things, be creditor and debtor States. The sixth section told us how the creditor States were to be paid, but not one word was said as to the debtor States. Paying one was as necessary as the other. Justice demanded it. *Vide* my amendment: "And those States against whom balances shall be found shall have a portion of their State debt, which shall have accrued as aforesaid, left charged upon them equal to such deficient balance; and if it should so happen that the whole State debt of any particular State shall fall short of such balance, such deficiency shall remain charged against such State on the books of the Treasury."

I attacked the Secretary's [Hamilton's] system of supposititious balances as not only unjust, and a total departure from acts and requisitions of Congress, but as going to lay great taxes and increase the volume of our debt.

Elsworth and Strong answered. King admitted every principle which I had laid down, but wavered. Lee seconded, and forsook me. The child was none of his. I really thought I had the best of the arguments, which grew bulky and by degrees spread over our fields of finance; but on the question I had a small division in favor of the motion.

The true history of the bill is that it has been fabricated by the Secretary's people, particularly Fitzsimons, and is meant as a mere delusion or to amuse the public, for they seriously never wish the accounts to be settled. But a show must be kept up of giving satisfaction on this point. As to myself, I may draw a lesson from Lee's conduct, to bring forward my own motions only. I spoiled the amendment to obtain his support, and he saw it perish with the indifference of a stranger.

July 7th.—Attended at the Hall. Every face bore the marks of anxious expectation. Schuyler came to me and owned the bill for the settlements of accounts was to the full as I had stated it yesterday, and showed me a long amendment; said the bill should be committed. Wished me to second him. I readily agreed to it, and now we went on the subject of debate. I was not alone, as yesterday. I supported my old system of ascertaining the expenses of the war; agreeing to the ratios and fixing the quotas; giving certificates to the creditor States and leaving the State debts on the debtors, respectively, so far as to equalize the accounts. Elsworth certainly confused himself. He wished to equalize the accounts by credits only, taking the lowest exertion as the basis and setting off to each State in proportion to it and funding all over it, as the exertions of some of the States stood nearly at o. This, in fact, would be funding nearly the whole expenses of the war.

Butler had a third system, viz., take no notice of anything bygone, but divide the existing debt among the States. I thought it strange to hear my colleague declare for the last opinion. After some very long debate, the bill was committed.

The Secretary's [Hamilton's] people got the advantage of us again. A bill which had disappeared a long while, of the most futile nature, with regard to relieving certain officers from what they considered as a grievance, was reported on favorably, but rejected. This same bill, or at least one verbatim the same, had been rejected by us formerly. Some other trifling business was done, and we adjourned.

Sundry questions were taken in the House of Representatives on the Residence bill. The decisions hitherto have been favorable, but the question on the bill has not yet been taken.

July 8th.—This day was slack in the Senate until the report came in on the bill for the settlement of the accounts. As might be expected, their amendments followed the Secretary's report, or nearly so. It amounted to this: That the net advances of the States should be made an aggregate, and this aggregate divided by the ratio of population which would fix the quotas. Then the quotas, compared with their respective advances, would determine the balances or credit, or turn out just equal. And here it was agreed to leave the matter for the present, as the bill respected the ascertaining the balances only, and left the payment to the creditor States and the payment from the debtor States to the future operation of the Legislature. All this was far short of what I wanted, and indeed the bill will turn out, as I fear, a mere delusion. But under its present form the State debts must be embraced in the accounts, if the commissioners do their duty; and if so, this will operate as a reason why they should not be assumed.

I was called out by Mr. Hanna, who was just setting off home. I wrote a hasty line by him to Charles Biddle that the votes stood this day twenty-eight to thirty-three on the residence.

Stayed at the Hall until four o'clock, and went to dine with the President. It was a great dinner, in the usual style, without any remarkable occurrences. Mrs. Washington was the only woman present.

I walked from the President's with Mr. Fitzsimons part of the way to his lodgings. He really seemed good-humored and as if he wished to be on good terms with me. Clymer called at our lodgings in the evening, and seemed condescending and good-humored in a remarkable degree, but all in the dumps again about the residence; only thirty real friends to the bill in the House of Representatives, etc.

It is time, indeed, that this business should be settled, for all our affairs are poisoned by it.

Nothing can be plainer than the simple mode of debtor and creditor for the settlement of the public accounts of the Union. But the State of South Carolina is most miserably in arrears, and wishes to avoid all settlement, or to have such a partial one as will screen her defects. She has been devoted to New York on the subject of the residence. Therefore New

York (or I should rather write, Hamilton) labors incessantly to confuse, embarrass, and confound all settlement. The thing can not be openly denied, but they will involve it in so many difficulties as will either prevent it altogether, or render it useless if it should take place.

July 9th.—Attended at the Hall at the usual time. There was much whispering of the members—Elsworth, Strong, and Izard. We had a bill for regulating the intercourse with the Indians, which has passed—a vile thing which may be made the basis of much expense. Superintendents are to be appointed, although the superintendence of the Indians in the government northwest of the Ohio is already vested in the Governor, and so south of the Ohio. By and by we shall have a call for their salaries. It really seems as if we were to go on making offices until all the Cincinnati are provided for.

The Settlement bill engaged us warmly for the most of the day. The object was to find the balances due to the creditor States and how. Ingenuity itself is tortured to find ways and means of increasing the public demands and passing by and rendering the State governments insignificant. I declared what I thought plainly on the subject—that the bill was one for the settlement but not the payment of the respective balances; that the old Confederation clearly contemplated the payment of the balances from the delinquent States to the creditor States; that every act of the old Government carried this on the face of it; that, although we could not lay unequal taxes, yet the adoption of the new Constitution did not go to the discharge of just debts due from the States which might be hereafter found debtors, and that Congress certainly had the power of liquidating the balances and making the demands from the debtor States.

The bill, after a long debate, passed on the principle of a Settlement bill only.

I find, by letters which I have received, that the public creditors are to be the body who are to rise in judgment against me and try to expel me from the Senate. This is only what I expected. Nor are they the only ones. The adoption of the new Constitution raised a singular ferment in the minds of men. Every one ill at ease in his finances; every one out at elbows in his circumstances; every ambitious man, every one desirous of a short cut to wealth and honors, cast their eyes on the new Constitution as the machine which could be wrought to their purposes, either in the funds of speculation it would afford, the offices it would create, or the jobs to be obtained under it. Not one of these has found a patron in me. In fact, I have generally set my face against such pretensions. As such men are generally wanting in virtue, their displeasure—nay, their resentment—may be expected. *"Why, you want nothing neither for yourself nor friends!"* said a Senator one day to me in some surprise. It was somewhat selfish, but I could not help uttering a wish *that he could say so with truth of every one.*

July 10th.—Being Saturday, the Senate did not meet, but I went to the Hall by a kind of instinct created by custom, somewhat like a stage-coach which always performs its tour whether full or empty.

I met King and Langdon here. We spent an hour or two in very familiar chat. Nothing worth noting unless it was the declaration of King that a bargain was certainly made on the subject of the residence to obtain at least one vote in the room of his [King's], as it was most likely he would vote against the assumption if the residence went to Philadelphia. I was astonished at King's owning this, which, in fact, amounted to this: that he had engaged his vote for the assumption if the residence stayed in New York.

July 11th, Sunday.—This was with me a very dull day. I read at home; wrote the usual letters to my family and other correspondents. After dinner, walked alone out on the commons beyond the Bowery wherever I could find any green grass or get out of the dust, which was very troublesome on the roads.

July 12th, Monday.—Attended at the Hall at the usual time. We received two messages from the Representatives, one of them containing the Residence bill. We had considerable debate on the Post-Office bill. Insisted on our amendments and appointed a committee to confer. Insisted on our amendment to the Indian Intercourse bill, and passed the tonnage. This bill deserves a remark.

This bill is in every respect the same as the old one, bating the remission of some unintentional severities which had fallen on some fishermen and coasters, which were remitted. The taking all the time and passing all the forms of a new bill, would perhaps bear an interpretation as if we feared running out of work.

A motion was made for taking up the Funding bill, but withdrawn. No other serious business was gone on. The House adjourned.

A number of us gathered in a knot and got on the subject of the assumption, the report of which had just been handed in by Mr. Carrol. It was in favor of it. And now from every appearance Hamilton has got his number made up. He wanted but one vote long ago. The flexible Read was bent for this purpose some time ago, and Carrol having joined to make up the defection of King. The mine is ready to be sprung. Since I am obliged to give up Carrol's political character, I am ready to say, "Who is the just man that doeth right and sinneth not?"

The sum they have reported to be assumed is twenty-one million dollars. This is most indubitably to cover the speculations that have been made in the State debts. The assumption will immediately raise the value of State securities and enable those people who have plunged themselves over head and ears in those speculations to emerge from impending ruin and secure them the wages of speculation. The report is ordered to be printed. After dismissing this subject, we got on the prospect of an approaching war between Spain and England. Here was a large field for conjecture, and we indulged our fancies on the subject until near three o'clock.

Here I will note down an observation which I wonder never made an impression on the Pennsylvanians. Every State is charged with having local views, designs, etc. Could any motive of this kind be justly chargeable on our State in adopting the Constitution? By our imposts we laid many of the neighboring States under contribution—part of Jersey, Delaware, part of Virginia, and almost the whole of the Western country. It appears one fourth of the whole impost is received at Philadelphia. This was a great sacrifice. Query: Did our politicians ever think of this advantage?

July 13th.—I attended this day at the Hall at the usual time, or rather sooner. General Schuyler only was before me. Our

Vice-President came next. They sat opposite me, and had a long chat on various subjects, but nothing very interesting. Mr. Morris came at last.

The resolution for the assumption of twenty-one millions of the State debt was taken up. This was perhaps the most disorderly day we ever had in the Senate. Butler was irregular beyond all bearing. Mr. Morris said openly before the Senate was formed, "I am for a six-per-cent fund on the whole, and, if gentlemen will not vote for that, I will vote against the assumption." I thought him only in sport. But he three times in Senate openly avowed the same thing, declaring he was in judgment for the asumption, but, if gentlemen would not vote for six per cent, he would vote against the assumption and the whole Funding bill. His adding the Funding bill along with it in the last instance operated as some kind of palliation. But I really was struck with astonishment to hear him offer his vote for sale in so unreserved a manner. Izard got up and attacked him with asperity. Mr. Morris rose in opposition. Then Izard declared he did not mean Mr. Morris, so much did he fear the loss of his vote. But his invective was inapplicable to anybody else. I was twice up and bore my most pointed testimony against the assumption. It was insuring a certain debt on uncertain principles. The certain effect was the incurring and increasing our debt by twenty-one millions by mere conjecture.

This debt was already funded by the States, and was in train of payment. Why not settle and let us see how the account stands before the States are discharged of their State debts? I alleged the funds on which these debts were charged by the States were those which these States could pay with the greatest facility, as every State had facilities of this kind. The transferring the debt to any general fund would lose these local advantages. It was dealing in the dark; we had no authentic evidence of these debts. If it was meant as an experiment how far people would bear taxation, it was a dangerous one. I had no notion of drilling the people to a service of this kind, etc. But I can not pretend to write all I said.

Mr. Morris has twice this day told me what great disturbances there would be in Pennsylvania if six per cent was not carried. I considered these things as threats thrown out against my reappointment [to the Senate]. But, be it so; so help me God, I mean not to alter one tittle! I am firmly determined to act without any regard to consequences of this kind. Every legislator ought to regard himself as immortal.

July 14th.—This day the resolutions on the assumption were taken up. I am so sick and so vexed with this angry subject that I hate to commit anything to writing respecting it. I will, however, seal one of the copies of it in this book as a monument of political absurdity.*

---

* [THE ASSUMPTION BILL—COPY.]
Congress of the United States—in Senate, July the 12th, 1790

The committee appointed July the 2d, 1790, reported as follows:

Whereas, A provision for the debt of the respective States by the United States would be greatly conducive to an orderly, economical, and effectual arrangement of the public finances; would tend to an equal distribution of burthens among the citizens of the several States; would promote more general justice to the different classes of public creditors, and would serve to give stability to public credit; and

Whereas, The said debts having been effectually contracted in the prosecution of the late war, it is just that such provision should be made:

Resolved, That a loan be proposed to the amount of twenty-one millions of dollars, and that the subscriptions to the said loan be received at the same time and places, by the same persons, and upon the same terms as in respect to the loans which may be possessed concerning the domestic debt of the United States, subject to the exceptions and qualifications hereafter mentioned. And the sums which shall be subscribed to the said loan shall be payable in the principal and interest of the certificates or notes which, prior to the first day of January last, were issued by the respective States as acknowledgments or evidences of debts by them respectively owing, and which shall appear by oath or affirmation (as the case may be) to have been the property of an individual or individuals or body politic, other than a State, on the said first day of January last. Provided, that no greater sum shall be received in the certificates of any State than as follows. That is to say:

In those of New Hampshire	$ 300,000
In those of Massachusetts	4,000,000
In those of Rhode Island and Providence Plantations..	200,000
In those of Connecticut	1,600,000
In those of New York	1,200,000
In those of New Jersey	800,000
In those of Pennsylvania	2,200,000
In those of Delaware	200,000
In those of Maryland	800,000
In those of Virginia	3,200,000

It has friends enough—fourteen to twelve—so far, but I am not without hopes of destroying it to-morrow. I am now convinced that there must have been something in the way of the bargain, as King alleged on Saturday. It must have been managed with Butler. Elsworth at one time this day used the following words: "No man contemplated a final liquidation of the accounts between the United States and the individual States as practicable or probable." I took them down and showed them to Mr. Morris and Mr. Walker. He observed me, and after some time got up and, in the course of speaking, said, "A settlement was practicable, and we must have it." He will absolutely say anything, nor can I believe that he has a particle of principle in his composition.

Mr. Morris, Langdon, and others, moved to strike out the third section. We of the opposition joined Elsworth and kept it in. The State of Pennsylvania has not but about one million of existing State debt. This clause, if the vile bill must pass, may

In those of North Carolina	2,200,000
In those of South Carolina	4,000,000
In those of Georgia	300,000

$21,000,000

And provided that no such certificate shall be received which, from the tenor thereof or from any public record, act, or document, shall appear or can be ascertained to have been issued for any purpose other than compensations and expenditures for service or supplies toward the prosecution of the late war, and the defense of the United States or some part thereof during the same.

Resolved, That the interest upon the certificates which shall be received in payment of the sums subscribed toward the said loans shall be computed to the last day of the year one thousand seven hundred and ninety-one inclusively, and the interest upon the stock, which shall be created by virtue of the said loan, shall commence or begin to accrue on the first day of the year one thousand seven hundred and ninety-two, and shall be payable quarter-yearly, at the same time and in like manner as the interest on the stock to be created by virtue of the loan that they may possess in the domestic debt of the United States.

Resolved, That if the whole sum allowed to be subscribed in the debt or certificates of any State as aforesaid shall not be subscribed within the time for that purpose limited, such State shall be entitled to receive, and shall receive from the United States, at the rate of four per cent per annum upon so much of the said sum as shall not have been subscribed, in trust for the non-subscribing creditors of such State, to be paid in like manner as the interest on the stock which may be created by virtue of the said loan, and to continue until there shall be a settlement of accounts between the United States and the individual States, be considered as in her favor, more especially if they prevail and prevent a settlement of the accounts.

I saw Mr. Pettit yesterday at the levee, and, as I was advised by letter that he was appointed agent for the settlement of the Pennsylvania accounts with the Union, I waited on him with great joy, hoping for much information on the subject. But what disappointment! He could tell me nothing about them, but came here to gain information and return back again; seemed to speak rather unfriendly of the Comptroller as to what he had done about the accounts. This surprised me. He quitted the subject with impatience, and attacked me rather with rudeness on the subject of the public debts. I have heard him spoken of as smooth, artful, and insinuating. He certainly displayed none of these qualities, and, as to the public accounts, he seems rather as an agent for the public creditors, and talked of the settlement as a very distant object. He teased me to tell him who were the principal holders of certificates in Boston, Newport, New York, etc., declaring that he wished to correspond with them, and unite with them in the common cause. I can not help regarding him as the curse of Pennsylvania.

For some time after the war certificates were sold as low as ninepence on the pound. John Ray, my old servant, told me that he sold one of eighty pounds for three pounds, and could get no more. But it appears, by a remonstrance of the Executive

---

and in case a balance shall then appear in favor of such State, until provision shall be made for the said balance.

But as certain States have respectively issued their own certificates, in exchange for those of the United States, whereby it might happen that interest might be twice payable on the same sums:

Resolved, That the payment of interest, whether to States or to individuals, in respect to the debt of any State, by which such exchange shall have been made, shall be suspended until it shall appear to the satisfaction of the Secretary of the Treasury that certificates issued for that purpose, by such State, have been re-exchanged or redeemed, or until those which shall not have been exchanged or redeemed shall be surrendered to the United States. And it is further

Resolved, That the faith of the United States be, and the same is hereby pledged to make like provision for the payment of interest on the account of the stock arising from subscriptions to the said loan, with the provision which shall be made touching the loan that may be proposed in the domestic debt of the United States; and so much of the debt of each State as shall be subscribed to the said fund shall be charged against such State, in account with the United States.

Council of the Legislature of Pennsylvania, entered on their minutes, that the market price was two shillings sixpence on the pound at the time of passing the funding law. Yet, by the instrumentality of this man on a weak (and in some cases interested) Legislature, six per cent was given on the certificates, or forty-eight per cent on the real specie value. This Pennsylvania paid for four years. As the certificates were generally below two shillings sixpence, it is no exaggeration to say every speculator doubled his money in four years, and still has the certificates on which he expects forty-eight per cent with respect to the original cost. Thus one hundred pounds specie bought eight hundred pounds in certificates (perhaps much more). These certificates brought forty-eight pounds per annum for four years, equaling one hundred and ninety-two pounds, and the holders of certificates remain as clamorous as ever.

July 15th.—The business of the Senate was soon done this day. The Vice-President took up the Funding bill without any call for it. Mr. Morris appeared in high good humor; asked me if anybody had taken me aside to communicate anything to me. I told him no. But it was easy to observe that something was going on. He said there was, but did not tell me what it was, nor did he affect to know. I saw Carrol writing a ticket with a number of names on it, sand,* and put it by. In the mean time up rose Elsworth and moved that both the Funding bill and the resolutions for the assumption should be referred to a committee. He was seconded soon. Lee rose; said we knew no good could come from a commitment. Mr. Morris rose; said he was for the commitment; that they might be made in one law, and the rate of interest fixed at six per cent. I rose; said I knew of but two ends generally proposed by commitment—the one was to gain information, the other to arrange principles agreed on. The first was out of the question; the second only could be the object; but what was the material to be arranged? A bill originated in the other House, and resolves on the assumption which had originated in this. I knew the opinion of many of the Representatives was opposed to our power of originating anything relating to the subject of the public debts. Taking two so dissimilar objects together, more especially if our powers were called

---

* They used sand in those days instead of blotting-paper.

in question, was the way to lose both. Gentlemen hoped much good from this measure. I wish they might not be disappointed; but I was not certain of anything but delay, which, in our present circumstances, I considered as an evil, etc.

The Vice-President, who was to appearance in the secret, seemed impatient until I had done, and putting the question it was carried. The R—— were all six-per-cent men and all the assumption men. They carried the committee, all of their own number. This done, the Senate adjourned.

Henry came and sat beside me a good while. He told me that Carrol wrote his ticket with the seven names (that being the number of the committee) before any business whatever was done. This I had observed in part myself. We did not need this demonstration to prove that the whole business was prearranged, nor can any person be now at a loss to discover that all three subjects—residence, assumption, and the funds equivalent to six per cent—were all bargained and contracted for on the principle of mutual accommodation for private interest.

The President of the United States has (in my opinion) had a great influence in this business. The game was played by him and his adherents of Virginia and Maryland, between New York and Philadelphia, to give one of those places the temporary residence, but the permanent residence on the Potomac. I found a demonstration that this was the case, and that [New] York would have accepted of the temporary residence if we did not. But I did not then see so clearly that the abominations of the funding system and the assumption were so intimately connected with it. Alas, that the affection—nay, almost adoration—of the people should meet so unworthy a return! Here are their best interests sacrificed to the vain whim of fixing Congress and a great commercial town (so opposite to the genius of the Southern planter) on the Potomac, and the President has become, in the hands of Hamilton, the dishclout of every dirty speculation, as his name goes to wipe away blame and silence all murmuring.

July 16th.—Senate had not been formed but a few minutes when a message from the President of the United States was announced. It was Lear, and the signature of the President to the Residence bill was the communication.

The Pension bill came up from the House of Representatives. The committee on the Indian bill reported that twenty thousand dollars, in addition to seven thousand in the hands of the Secretary of War and six thousand in Georgia, in goods, should be granted for the holding treaties with the Indians; and all this when there does not appear a shadow of reason for holding a treaty at all with any Indians whatever. Opposition was in vain. It was carried.

Now Mr. Morris came, raving angry; said and swore he would vote against everything. The committee had agreed to the Secretary's third alternative for the principal and three per cent on the interest due, and he had left them. The report came in after some time and it was proceeded on. I whispered to Mr. Morris, now he had got the residence, it was our province to guard the Union and promote the strength of the Union by every means in our power, otherwise our prize would be a blank. I told him I would move a postponement of the business and I would wish a meeting of the delegation this evening. He assented.

A vast deal was said on the subject of the contract and breach of obligation. Then I rose and stated that I had no difficulty on that head; that we stood here as legislators. Judges and executive officers were bound to observe laws and contracts; but justice was the great rule which we should govern our conduct by. The holder of the certificate called, "Do me justice." But the original performer of the service, who sold it for one eighth part of the nominal value, and on whom the tax to make it good is about to fall, cries, "Do me justice also."

Both sides of this picture ought to be viewed and their relative numbers to each other. No guess can be made in this matter, but by comparing the number of speculators with the number of those who had sold, and perhaps the ratio would not be one to one hundred. It was also true there was a class of men, the original holders, who were not embraced in the above description; but if we cast our eye over the calamities of the late war they would appear to be the fortunate characters. All the others who touched Continental money were taxed by it, and it finally sunk in their hands. The original holders have, if not the whole value, at least something to show, etc. I hoped for the progress of the public business, and that a short postponement would perhaps bring us nearer together and moved for to-morrow; but it was not carried.

The report was pushed with violence and all carried, twenty members rising for it, four only sat, two going out. The Vice-President said twenty for, four against. When they came to the part for ingrafting the assumption resolves on the bill, Mr. Lee, with what assistance I gave him, retarded the business a little. When I spoke I endeavored to narrow the ground a little, and spoke solely to the question of combining the assumption with the Funding bill. The Funding bill was to provide for the domestic debt which floated at large, and was at this time in no train of payment.

The propriety of paying the foreign and domestic debt was admitted by every person. It was really the business which brought us together. But here we must not pass it, unless we tack it to another, which we considered as a political absurdity. This was contradicting the spirit of free legislation. Every subject ought to hang on its own merits. It was offering violence to our understandings. I said a good deal on the subject, and could not restrain myself from going into the merits of the assumption. But I might as well have poured out speech on senseless stocks or stones. It was carried against us, fifteen to eleven. A committee was immediately appointed to make the arrangements. We adjourned.

I came down-stairs, and all the speculators, both of the Representatives and city, were about the iron rails. Ames and Sedgwick were conspicuous among them. The Secretary [Hamilton] and his group of speculators are at last, in a degree, triumphant. His gladiators, with the influence that has arisen from six dollars per day,* have wasted us months in this place. But I can not see that I can do any further good here, and I think I had better go home. Everything, even to the naming of a committee, is prearranged by Hamilton and his group of speculators. I can not even find a single member to condole in sincerity with me over the political calamities of my country.

---

* The pay of Congressmen and Senators,

Let me deliver myself from the society of such men, for I verily believe the sun never shone on a more abandoned composition of political characters.

July 17th.—Having some leisure this morning, I called on Dr. Williamson and told him my intention of going home. He got into a long tale of his settling his children in Philadelphia and taking a more Northern position for his family than North Carolina, etc. By the way, I would only remark he has one child only born, but he has begotten another, as he says. But no gray-headed man ever was fuller of future arrangements for a numerous progeny.

He went into the Hall and everybody soon had it that I was going home, etc. I went from here and called on Fitzsimons and Clymer; told them I wished to go home, but had no objection to take the sense of the delegation on the measure. Fitzsimons said nothing, but looked *Go to the devil,* as I thought. Clymer spoke most pointedly against my going; said we would lose nine votes south of Virginia on a postponement bill which was going to be brought forward. By the by, we never had but seven from that quarter. I told him the delegation were to dine together to-morrow; if it was their opinion that I should stay, I would do so.

Attended at the Hall. Little was done, and we sat waiting an hour for the committee to report the bill with amendments. It was done. An attempt was made to pass it immediately by a third reading down to the House of Representatives. It was moved that it should be printed. This was opposed. The Vice-President gave the history of both the bill and the resolutions. With respect to order, he made this out to be the third reading; and of course the question would be, the sending of it to the Representatives.

It was now proposed, as an expedient, that the Secretary [of the Senate] should read the bill from the desk for information of the members. This obtained, and now behold, to a great many innovations and amendments a whole new clause was added! There was something of unfairness in this. It was, however, ordered to be printed for Monday.

When I came down-stairs, Mr. Clymer came to where I stood

with General Irwin. We talked over the general belief that the assumption was forced on us to favor the views of speculation. Mr. Clymer mentioned one contract on which about eight shillings in the pound had been cleared on eighty thousand pounds. General Irwin seemed to scruple eight shillings in the pound! Mr. Clymer said he was not so sure of the rate cleared, but the sum speculated on was eighty thousand pounds. Much of this business was done in the 'Change alleyway. Constable, however, is known in the beginning of the session to have cleared thirty-five thousand dollars on a contract for seventy thousand dollars. The whole town almost has been busy at it; and, of course, all engaged in influencing the measures of Congress. Nor have the members [of Congress] themselves kept their hands clean from this dirty work; from Wadsworth, with his boat-load of money, down to the daily six dollars, have they generally been at it. The unexampled success has obliterated every mark of reproach, and from henceforth we may consider speculation as a congressional employment. Nay, all the abominations of the South Sea bubble are outdone in this vile business. In wrath, I wish the same fate may attend the projectors of both!

July 18th, Sunday.—This day the [Pennsylvanian] delegation dined at Brandon's. Mr. Morris stated to the Representatives the train of business was in the Senate. Mentioned the importance of completing the Funding law, particularly to us who now had the residence of Congress before us; that the rising of Congress without funding might go to shake and injure the Government itself, etc. We had much talk, but nothing was concluded or any agreement entered into. Mr. Fitzsimons averred, in the most unequivocal manner, the grand object of the assumption to be *the collecting all the resources of the United States into one treasury.* Speaking of the State of Pennsylvania, he avowed she would be a debtor State to a large amount on the settlement of the accounts, and the next moment said she would draw interest on three million dollars annually. It is not easy to reconcile his assertions on this subject. A great deal of loose talk passed among us. As I had the delegation together, I mentioned my intention of going home, and desired to know if any of them had any objection. The discourse soon took a ludicrous turn; but no objection was made, and I believe I will set off to-morrow afternoon.

July 19th.—Have made up my mind on the subject of going home. I can not serve my country anything by my staying here longer. I will certainly feel ashamed to meet the face of any Pennsylvanian who shall put to me the question, "What have you done for the public good?" I can answer with truth, "I have tried the best in my power."

Settled with the Speaker. He would have me pay nothing for any liquors, but said his boy had cost him fifty dollars, which he desired me to pay one half of. I agreed. He had about forty dollars of my money in his hands. I owe him four shillings and sixpence, Pennsylvania. I well recollect the service of the boy was mentioned, or at least all the services which I wanted in that way when I settled for my boarding at four dollars per week. I have drunk, occasionally, some of his wine—he said, not amounting to more than a bottle or two. I am convinced it would not amount to gallons. But I most cheerfully agreed to pay what he proposed.

I attended the Hall at the usual time. And now the material business of the day, the Consolidated Funding bill and assumption, were taken up. Mr. Morris showed a vindictive and ireful disposition from the very start, and declared he would have the yeas and nays on every question. This, in fact, is declaring war against me only, as it is me only whom they can effect in Pennsylvania. I know they mean to slay me with the sword of the public creditors. He was as good as his word, and moved every point to increase the demand against the public, and uniformly called the yeas and nays. All the motions were made for augmentations by him, Schuyler, and King, *vide* the minutes for the yeas and nays.

When he moved that six per cent should be paid on the back interest, as there were but four of them for it, and enough did not rise for the yeas and nays, I told him I was sorry to see him in distress, and jumped up. If I can turn these yeas and nays against him, the act will be a righteous one.

In the language and calculations of the Treasury, the third alternative is actually six per cent, without taking in the advantage of the quarterly over annual payments, grounded on the irredeemable quality of the debt. But I really question if we shall ever see that 'Change-Alley doctrine established here, which makes debt valuable in proportion to that qualification. It never can happen without a gradual fall of interest, which, in this country, may be rather considered as improbable.

Before Congress met I walked awhile across the [Senate] chamber with Mr. Lee. He lamented equally with me the baneful effects of the funding disease. No nation ever has adopted it without having either actually suffered shipwreck or being on a voyage that must inevitably end in it. The separation from Great Britain seemed to assign us to a long run of political existence; but the management of the Secretary [Hamilton] will soon overwhelm us with political rule. Schuyler assigned a new kind of reason this day for taxation. Three millions and a half of dollars annually would be only one dollar per head on the average. It was nothing, etc. It is true it is not a heavy tax, but it ought not to be imposed without necessity.

This wretch is emaciated in person, slovenly in dress, and rather awkward in address. No Jew ever had a more cent-per-cent aspect. He seems the prototype of covetousness. Nor is it possible to assign to his appearance any passion, property, or affection but the love of money and the concomitant character of a miser.

I can not help noting something which may be void of design. Yesterday two letters were shown at dinner: one by Mr. Morris to the Governor and Council [of Pennsylvania], another by Clymer to the mayor and corporation [of Philadelphia]. It was agreed that the Senators should sign the one to the Governor and Council, and the Speaker, in behalf of the delegation, should sign the one to the corporation. I was much pleased with this arrangement, for there was a clause in Clymer's letter of advice to erect a new building for Congress, for the giving the State-House to Congress would furnish a reason for removing the seat of Government elsewhere. This day in Senate, Mr. Morris produced this last letter to me, desiring me to sign it. I declined it, telling him the Speaker was to sign that letter. I could not help concluding there was design in this business.

There was a dinner this day which I had no notice of, and

never thought of such a thing. In the evening Mr. Rees, clerk to Mr. Morris, called on me with the letter to the Government. This I readily signed; but here comes the Speaker with the other letter for me to sign. All this does not look like candor. I told the Speaker my objections. There is a subject in that letter which I never have touched. I will not touch it now. I have already written fully to the mayor on the subject.

July 20th.—We went this day at the funding system and pursued it with nearly the same temper that we did yesterday. Mr. Morris had often declared himself that he would be for an assumption equal to the representation, and had calculated a schedule for the purpose; but, all I could say to him, he would not gratify me in moving it. I knew there was no chance of carrying it. But he leveled his whole force against the nineteenth section, which, in fact, is the only favorable one to our State, for our existing State debt can not be much more than one million. I will refer to the minutes for the proceedings of the day. Mr. Morris having often threatened that he would vote against the bill, at last made this remarkable speech: "Half a loaf is better than no bread. I will consent to the bill on behalf of the public creditors, for whom I am interested" (I looked up at him, and he added), "as well as for the rest of the Union." This last shed some palliation over his expressions.

I contended that the speculators generally had dealt on the face of the certificates; or, if they had dealt on the amount, it was always at an abated rate—clear proof they never expected the back interest to be funded. By the bill, every hundred of principal draws four annually, and as the back interest is about on the average equal to half the principal (at least it is so by the Secretary's [Hamilton's] report), this, at three per cent, adds one and a half more—equal to five and one half per cent per annum for ten years; and then the other third (or what is equal to it in 'Change-Alley calculation) comes at six per cent, which, added, gives about seven and a half per cent on the face of the original certificate.

I have turned the leaf to note that I may consider myself as now having passed the Rubicon with the Philadelphians. I saw Clymer through the window of the Senate chamber. Morris was sent for and went out. He came in with the same letter which I had refused to sign yesterday, and asked me to sign it. I refused, and told him plainly it touched a subject which I never had touched, nor would now. He said no more.

Mr. Morris told me this day I must allow myself to get the lands of which he had spoken to me. I told him all on my part was ready; only put the warrants into my hands. I, however, added, we have ruined our land-office by the assumption. The State certificates were the materials to buy the lands with. The offices will now be shut, for neither State money nor specie can be got or spared for it. He was silent, and I really thought he looked as if he feared that his conduct would be turned against him in the public eye.

After dinner this day I read a letter to the Speaker from John Montgomery, of Carlisle, not much in favor of Mr. Morris. He then gave me the following intelligence: That Fitzsimons' and Mr. Morris' adherents, fearful that he could not be carried by a popular election, were determined to change the mode to electors. But all the difficulty was to know how Wilson could save his credit in convention and carry his party over with him after what had already happened, this being one of the pillars on which his late popularity was supported. It is easy to see the reason of all this. The mode of electors admits of more cabal, intrigue, etc.

July 21st.—King's motion of yesterday for postponement and sundry other matters which I had observed made me fearful that some storm was gathering. I called on Mr. Morris and expressed my apprehension and proposed to him that if any unexpected manœuvre should display itself we should, with the utmost coolness, call for a concurrence of the resolution for the adjournment on the 27th.

Attended at the Hall on the affair of Donald Campbell; the most impudent and ill-founded set of claims ever I was witness to. The first business in the Senate was the new bill of ways and means. Committed.

A message, with a bill, respecting consuls and vice-consuls.

The bill for the military grants of lands to the Virginia officers. Committed.

The Senate was now full, and the Funding bill was taken up for the last time. I made a despairing effort. Having almost uniformly opposed the measures of Congress during the present session, some general declaration of my principles or motives may be necessary to prevent any suspicion of a disposition inimical to the Government itself.

First, then, I am totally opposed to the practice of funding, upon republican as well as economical principles. I deny the power as well as the justice of the present generation charging debts, more especially irredeemable ones, upon posterity; and I am convinced that they will one day negative the legacy. I will suppose (suppositions are common in this House) that not one member of Congress has been influenced by any personal motive whatever in arranging the American funding system, which now spins on the doubtful point of pass or not pass; and, as it falls, may turn up happiness or misery for centuries to come. No; I will take gentlemen at their word, and believe that it is the glare of British grandeur, supposed to follow from her funds, that has influenced their conduct, and that their intentions are pure, wishing to render America great and happy by a similar system. This will lead to an inquiry into the actual state of Britain; and here, I trust, we shall find all is not gold that glitters.

It is, if I mistake not, about a century since the commencement of the English funds, or, in other words, since that nation began to mortgage the industry of posterity to gratify the ambition and avarice of the then Government. Since that period wars have been almost continual. The pretexts have been ridiculous—balances of power, balance of trade, honor of the flag, sovereignty at sea, etc., but the real object was to fill the Treasury, to furnish opportunity for royal peculation, jobs and contracts for needy courtiers, to increase the power of the crown by the multiplication of revenue and military appointments and the servility of the funds, for every stockholder is, of course, a courtier. The effect of these wars has been the commotion of almost the whole world; the loss of millions of lives; and the English nation stands at this day charged with a debt of about two hundred and fifty millions sterling, the annual interest of which and charges of collecting in that country is above eleven millions annually, and would be above fifteen in this.

It has been said that this is nothing in a national point of view, as the nation owes it to individuals among themselves. This is true only in part, as foreigners draw great sums. Yet it is believed that near half a million of the inhabitants of Great Britain, including army, navy, revenue, and stockholders, are supported from the Treasury. The whole of them, be the number what it may, must be considered as unproductive drones, who are ever ready to support the administration, be it ever so oppressive to their fellow-citizens.

There is another calculation said to be more exact, viz., that near a million of paupers, reduced by exorbitant taxes below the power of housekeeping, are dependent on national charity and poor-rates. Great cry has been made about Mr. Pitt as the political savior of his country—that he has paid part, and will finally discharge the whole, of the national debt. This is a vile deception. By some management between him and the stock-jobbers, as he buys they raise the price of the remaining stock, the aggregate value of which is now greater, at the market price, than when he began to purchase, so that the nation, instead of gaining, is a loser to the amount of the new duties. It is not likely that the trading of Government in stock or certificates ever will have a different effect.

There is another part of his conduct for which I am ready to give him proper credit. He seems by his sham armaments, to have hit on an expedient to plunder the nation without bloodshed. Let him enjoy this praise in common with other English robbers, who, unlike those of other nations, seldom accompany their depredations with murder. It is in vain to expect the payment of the British debt in any other way than by a national bankruptcy and revolution. Is this the precipice to which we would reduce the rising nation of North America? It may be said none of us will live to see it. Let us at least guard our memories from the approach of such misconduct.

It may be here asked, What, then, is to be done? Just what the public expectation called for. The Western lands have been considered from the beginning of the late contest as the fund for discharging the expenses of the war. The old Congress made laudable advances in this way. The present session has not passed without applications on that subject as well from companies among ourselves as persons from Europe. We have now a revenue far exceeding the limit, five per cent, which the desideratum of the old Congress and the want of which occasioned the formation of our present Constitution, and fully sufficient to discharge a reasonable interest, proportionate price of the public debt until the whole is extinguished by the Western sales. Thus no one will sustain loss. Substantial justice will be done, and the public expectation will be fully satisfied. But to bind down the public by an irredeemable debt with such sources of payment in our power, is equally absurd as shackling the hands and feet with fetters rather than walking at liberty.

The friends of the bill paid no attention whatever to me, and were but too successful in engaging the attention of others by nods, whispers, engaging in conversation, etc. Morris, Dalton, and some others went out and stayed for an hour. They carried the bill against us—fourteen to twelve. It is in vain to dissemble the chagrin which I have felt on this occasion.

We had a resolution relating to Howell's committee. I am of the committee. Report of joint committee on Settlement bill read for information, but could not be acted on, as the bill is in the power of the Lower House. I find I need be under no uneasiness about the Residence bill.

July 22d.—Attended at the Hall this day, as much to take the wrinkles out of my face, which my yesterday's disappointment had placed on it, as for anything else. It is in vain to think of changing a vote anyway; a majority are sold, and Hamilton has bought them. I can be of no further use, and will absolutely leave them. It is certainly a defect in my political character that I can not help embarking my passions and considering the interest of the public as my own. It was so while I was at the bar, in respect of my clients, when I thought their cause just. Well, be it so. It has its inconvenience, and hurts my health, but I declare I never will endeavor to amend it.

Attended all the committees on which I was, and gave my opinion as to the reports, etc. In Senate the Collection bill was reported. Almost an entire new system, or the old one so renovated as to make a volume of new work for Congress. I listened an hour to the reading of it. Rose, bade a silent and lasting farewell to the Hall, and went to my lodgings for the purpose of packing.

And now, at last, we have taken leave of New York. It is natural to look at the prospect before me. The citizens of Philadelphia (such is the strange infatuation of self-love) believe that ten years is eternity to them with respect to the residence, and that Congress will in that time be so enamored of them as never to leave them; and all this with the recent example of New York before their eyes, whose allurements are more than ten to two compared with Philadelphia. To tell the truth, I know no such unsocial city as Philadelphia. The gloomy severity of the Quakers has proscribed all fashionable dress and amusement. Denying themselves these enjoyments, they, as much as in them lies, endeavor to deprive others of them also; while at the same time there are not in the world more scornful or insolent characters than the wealthy among them. Witness the Wartons, Pembertons, etc. No, these feeble expectations will fail. Go they [Congress] must.

Nay, taking another point of view. Political necessity urges them and a disruption of the Union would be the consequence of a refusal. There is, however, a further and more latent danger which attends their going. Fixed, as Congress will be, among men of other minds on the Potomac, a new influence will, in all probability, take place, and the men of New England, who have hitherto been held in check by the patronage and loaves and fishes of the President, combined with a firm expectation that his resignation (which is expected) will throw all the power into their hands, may become refractory and endeavor to unhinge the Government. For my knowledge of the Eastern character warrants me in drawing this conclusion, that they will cabal against and endeavor to subvert any government which they have not the management of.

The effect must be sensibly felt in Philadelphia, should a great commercial town arise on the Potomac, She now supplies all the over-hill country, and even the frontiers of Virginia and other Southern States with importations. This must cease; nor need she expect a single article of country produce in return from the west side of Susquehanna.

It is true that the genius of Virginia and Maryland is rather averse to exclusive commerce. The Southern planter is situated on his extensive domain, surrounded with his slaves and dependents, feels diminution and loses his consequence by being jumbled among brokers and factors. And yet we have seen what Baltimore has become in a few years from the small beginnings of a few Pennsylvanians at first, and afterward by the accession of other strangers, for wherever the carcass of commerce is thither will the eagles of traffic be gathered. For my own part, I would rather wish that the residence of Congress should not be subject to commercial influence.

Too much has that influence, conducted by the interest of New England, whose naval connections throw them into that scale, governed—nay, tyrannized—in the councils of the Union. My consolation for going to the Potomac is, that it may give a preponderance to the agricultural interest. Dire, indeed, will be the contest, but I hope it will prevail. I can not, however, help concluding that all these things would have been better on the Susquehanna. But, query, is not this selfish, too? Ay, but it may, nevertheless, be just.

PART THREE:

THIRD SESSION

OF THE FIRST CONGRESS

CHAPTER XII

AS TO RE-ELECTION

Philadelphia, December 1, 1790.—Late in the afternoon I arrived in Philadelphia in order to attend Congress, which is to meet on Monday next. Saw nobody this afternoon nor evening.

December 2d.—Dressed and called first on General Mifflin. He was abroad. Then on Mr. Morris, who received me with frankness. Called on the President, Clymer, and at Fitzsimons'. The day soon became rainy. Came home. Heard from my brother in the evening that some attempt was making on the Sunbury lands by one Sewell and Hurst. This has cut out work for me in the morning.

December 3d.—Dressed and went early to the Governor's. He was at breakfast, and had four school-boys about him making them show him their Latin exercises, repeat their lessons, tell what books they were reading, etc. So much does he love to be the cock of the school that he seems actually to court the company of children, where he is sure he will meet with no contradiction. His tongue ran like a whirligig. There was no getting a word in among the children. I had, however, considerable attention paid to me by two dogs, who pawed me over. I learned that no decision had been given by the Board of Property in the case of the Sunbury lands. Took the first opportunity I possibly could of withdrawing. No public character ever appeared to me more disgusting.

Called on David Kenedy, of the Land-Office, and made what we thought the best arrangement respecting the affair of Sunbury.

Met with Mr. Langdon and went a-visiting, in which we spent the forenoon. Called in the evening at Mr. McConnell's, the broker. He told me the public creditors were very busy under their chairman, Petitt, preparing petitions, memorials, etc., for Congress. I made some remarks tending to show that they were well enough for the purpose intended. He readily joined me; said it was carried on to answer electioneering purposes; that Petitt wanted to be in Congress, etc. Petitt is my old enemy, and will supplant me if he can. Agreed.

December 4th, Saturday.—I have deliberated much on the subject whether I will call to see Bingham, Powell, and others. I have called on Morris, Clymer, and Fitzsimons. Why not on them? By the rules of etiquette, perhaps, they should call on me. I have resolved all over in my mind. *Jacta est alea,* and I will go. But as I went I fell in with Mr. Clymer, and away we went a-visiting. Clymer certainly means to be on good terms with me. We had two long visits. I called at Bingham's. Found him at home and had a long chat. Took leave and left a card at Mr. Powell's. Called at Mr. Chew's, who urged me to stay for dinner. I accepted his invitation for two o'clock, and the rest of the day was accordingly disposed of, for it was past three before we sat down.

I called twice this day at Dr. Rush's, but saw him not. Saw the Speaker. The Speaker said, on the authority of Dr. Rush, that we would all be re-elected. Believe it not.

December 5th, Sunday.—Was sent for early by Mr. Morris on the subject of taking up the frontier lands. I agreed to procure him a draft of such parts of the State as had vacant lands in them. No contract with him. I mean to have such a draft made for the use of the members of the Assembly, or at least for their information. Pressed me to dine with him. Did so.

Mr. Powell returned my visit. Visited Langdon in the evening.

December 6th, Monday.—My brother informed me this morning that Charles Thompson had applied to one Collins, a member from Berks County, for his interest to obtain my place as Senator. It comes very direct, and was talked over yesterday at Blair McClenachan's, where Matthew Irwin dined, from whom my brother [Samuel Maclay] had it. Out some of the citizens would have me, if they should put the devil in my place. This is what I must expect of them.

Attended at the Hall at eleven. Senate was formed, but no

business done save the sending a message by our Secretary to the Representatives that the Senate was ready to proceed to business.

Spent the rest of the day in visits, etc.

December 7th.—Went early this morning to see if Mr. Montgomery, of our county, or Mr. White were come in. Found none of them. Called at Mr. Findley's lodgings on my way home. He said he would call on me in the evening. Colonel Curtis spent some time this forenoon with me.

Attended at eleven at the Hall. A House was formed by the Representatives. On the 7th of January last King had introduced a new record altogether on the minutes, the intention of which was to secure the delivery of the President's speech in the Senate chamber. A resolution verbatim, with the entry of last January, was moved, carried, and sent down for concurrence. While this was done with us, a resolution passed to the Representatives for a joint committee waiting on the President with information that quorums were formed in both Houses. Our Secretary and the Clerk of the Representatives passed each other on the stairs with their respective resolutions. Each House appointed committees under their own resolutions, and the committees met. The Representatives urged that it was idle to name any place to do business in until it was known whether any business would de done. The President was in our favor.

This silly thing kept us talking an hour and a half. The Clerk of the Representatives announced the non-concurrence of our resolution. This had like to have raised a flame, but a motion was at length made and carried for the concurrence of the resolution which came up. The joint committee now waited on the President, who charged them with information that he would to-morrow at twelve o'clock deliver his speech to both Houses in the Senate Chamber, and so ended this arduous affair. The Senate adjourned.

The first levee was held this day, at which I attended.

At about seven o'clock Mr. Findley called on me. We had a long conversation, or at least a busy one, for about an hour. I must be blind, indeed, if I did not see that he is doing everything in his power to supplant me by way of preparing me for

the part which he was about to act. He first told me that
Gurney and he had some conversation, which would seem to
impart that John Montgomery, of Carlisle, was the man to supplant me. I mentioned it as a matter that would savor too
strongly of cabal to take one of the electing members. This
threw him off his guard, and he spoke rather tartly of my remark, and alleged there could be nothing in it; said *"if I am
elected I will serve,* but I will take no part in the matter, and
I will give you leave to blame me if I do."* This sentiment he
reiterated more than once. He kept looking at his watch incessantly and was in evident perturbation from the time I hinted
the impropriety of one of the electing members being chosen.
When I hinted that some complaints had been raised against
my brother, he alleged it was so; that I likewise had made proposals to Colonel Smith, which he insinuated had not been adhered to. I told him what I recollected of the discourse between
Colonel Smith and myself, and said I had entered into no engagements with him or any other one on the occasion.

December 8th.—This was the day assigned for the President
to deliver his speech, and was attended with all the bustle
and hurry usual on such occasions. The President was dressed
in black, and read his speech well enough, or at least tolerably.
After he was gone, and the Senate only remained, our Vice-
President seemed to take great pains to read it [the speech]
better. If he had such a view, he succeeded; but the difference
between them amounted to this: one might be considered as
at home and the other in a strange company. The speech was
committed.

I could not help taking some pains to counteract Mr. Findley. But my situation is a critical one. I must stand with open
breast to receive the wound inflicted by my adversaries, while
the smallest endeavors on my part, either to obtain favor or
to remove misrepresentation, is called begging of votes by
pretended though false friends. I will, however, do what I
think proper, for to attempt pleasing every one would be to
carry the ass, indeed.

Findley drew away my mind for a moment. Let me return
to the President. Does he really look like a man who enters
into the spirit of his appointment? Does he show that he re-

ceives it in trust for the happiness of the people, and not as a fee simple for his own emolument? Time and practice will, perhaps, best elucidate this point.

December 9th.—This day the Senate afforded neither motion nor debate. The communications hinted at in the President's speech were delivered to us, and continued to be read till past two o'clock, when the Senate adjourned. A war has actually been undertaken against the Wabash Indians without any authority of Congress, and, what is worse, so far as intelligence has come to hand, we have reason to believe it is unsuccessful. Mind what comes of it.

The Vice-President, Mr. Wyngate, and some more of us, stood by the fire. When the affairs of France were talked, I said the National Assembly had attacked royalty, nobility, hierarchy, and the Bastille altogether, and seemed likely to demolish the whole. The Vice-President said it was impossible to destroy nobility; it was founded in nature. Wyngate engaged. The Vice-President's arguments were drawn from the respect shown to the sons of eminent men, although vicious and undeserving. When the parties had nearly exhausted themselves, I asked whether our Indians might not be considered as having devised an excellent method of getting rid of this prejudice by ranking all the children after the mother. This sent off the whole matter in a smile; Adams, however, never was cured, or is relapsed into his *nobilimania.* After we were seated and a slack moment happened, Mr. Morris drew his chair near mine and hinted to me that Bingham's unamimous vote for the Speaker's chair was the price of his influence in favor of Findley. I said I thought likely. But Bingham had obtained his end, and might now be on the other tack.

December 10th.—This day was unimportant in the Senate. The committee reported an answer to the President's speech. The echo was a good one, and was adopted without material amendment.

A packet had arrived a few days ago from France, directed to the President and members of Congress. The President, from motives of delicacy, would not open it. It came to the Senate, and was sent back to the President, and now returned opened. It contained a number of copies of the eulogiums delivered on Dr. Franklin by order of the National Assembly. Our Vice-President looked over the letter some time and then began reading the additions that followed the President's name. He was Doctor of the Sorbonne, etc., to the number of fifteen (as our Vice-President said). These appellations of office he chose to call "titles," and then said some sarcastic things against the National Assembly for abolishing titles. I could not help remarking that this whole matter was received and transacted with a coldness and apathy that astonished me; and the letter and all the pamphlets were *sent* down to the Representatives as if unworthy the attention of our body. I deliberated with myself whether I should not rise and claim one of the copies in right of my being a member. I would, however, only have got into a wrangle by so doing without working any change on my fellow-members. There might be others who indulged the same sentiments, but 'twas silence all.

December 13th.—The Senate having adjourned over from Friday to this day [Monday], nothing of public nature has taken place. I was engaged Saturday and this morning in negotiating the sale of some certificates, which I completed, and placed the money in the bank.

The minutes were read about half after eleven, and the committee on the business reported that the President had appointed twelve to receive our address. Twelve soon came, and we went on this formality, which finished the senatorial business of the day.

This day completed the sale of Mr. Harris's certificates at the most either Bobby or myself could make of them. Got a check on the bank and put the whole in part notes.

December 14th.—Attended the Senate, but no business of moment was transacted. Official information was communicated to the Senate of General Harmer's expedition. The ill-fortune of the affair breaks through all the coloring that was given to it. 'Tis said one hundred Indians have been killed. But two hundred of our own people have certainly perished in the expedition.

This was levee day, and I accordingly dressed and did the needful. It is an idle thing, but what is the life of men but folly? —and this is perhaps as innocent as any of them, so far as respects the persons acting. The practice, however, considered as a feature of royalty, is certainly anti-republican. This certainly escapes nobody. The royalists glory in it as a point gained. Republicans are borne down by fashion and a fear of being charged with a want of respect to General Washington. If there is treason in the wish I retract it, but would to God this same General Washington were in heaven! We would not then have him brought forward as the constant cover to every unconstitutional and irrepublican act.

December 15th.—This day was really a blank in the Senate. Two petitions were presented which, being only counterparts of what were expected to be acted upon in the Lower House, were laid on our table. Mr. Morris was called often out by our own citizens. The doorkeeper named the people who sent in for him. Peter Muhlenberg was one, Colonel Hartley was another. This day certificates raised fourpence in the pound.

December 16th.—I, this day, attended the Board of Property. There never was a more groundless persecution than has been set on foot against me, and is now supported by one Rowls, the same with whom my brother quartered last winter. He seems determined to injure my reputation if possible. I had to oppose him, and there certainly never was a clearer case. It was, however, agreed that my brother's deposition should be taken, and the Board to meet to-morrow. I was taken away the whole day by this vile business.

December 17th.—Got my brother's deposition and attended at the Board, having first heard prayers and sat a half hour at the Hall. Rowls was at the Board, and displayed every pettifogging shift and evasion. He is really a rascal, and all this matter is pushed by him to injure me at my ensuing election. I have letters from my dear child Johnny, telling me that he had information of this kind.

I spent the residue of the day in various other pieces of business.

December 18th.—Being Saturday and excessively cold, stayed at home all day. Was visited by Madison, Bishop, and White, and many other respectable characters.

Settled with Mr. Ogden. His bill in full for the coupé carriage, horse, and lodging for two weeks, ending the 15th at night, and all the washing heretofore done, £4 7s. 7d. Paid off, and he has ten dollars in his hands to stand opposite firewood. The rate of boarding, three dollars per week, exclusive of firewood, at least it is so by this bill.

This night it is reported that the six-per-cents were at par.

December 19th, Sunday.—The cold continued. Dined out with Mr. Powel. Spent the most of the day in writing letters to home.

December 20th, Monday.—Paid some visits. Attended at the Hall. Congress were engaged until almost three with the reading of a long and most impudent memorial from the public creditors. Paid visits, etc. The weather abated, and prospect of a thaw.

December 21st, Tuesday.—The memorial and remonstrance of the public creditors engaged us some time. I saw, or at least I thought I saw, a storm gathering in the countenances of the Senators yesterday, and moved an adjournment. I told Mr. Morris of it, and he agreed it was so, and for fear of this same storm he moved an adjournment this day. But Schuyler had a long motion. It concluded with the "danger" and "inexpediency" of any innovation in the funding. A variety of opinions were now offered as to the time of proceeding to-morrow. Monday, Friday, and Thursday were all spoken of, and Thursday agreed to take it up.

This day the Governor of our State was proclaimed. Mr. Morris spoke early to me. His words were, "I expect every moment to hear from the delegation who are now meeting to fix a time to wait on the Governor, and I will let you know of it." I waited, but heard nothing from him.

December 22d.—I called this morning on the Comptroller, and he was obliging enough to send for Mr. Smilie, and did my character justice in respect to sundry aspersions cast on it by Mr. Findley and Smilie.

I came home; was dressed and went out to visit about ten. Came to the Hall about eleven. Here Mr. Langdon told me that Mr. Morris and the delegation were just gone to wait on the Governor. I posted after and thought to overtake them. Called on the Governor; was sure I would find them there. It was not so. Was sure they would come in every moment.

They did not come in. I returned to the Hall; found Mr. Morris there. He apologized: said he got the notification yesterday in company; the time was half after ten. He had sent his servant up with the note to me. I asked at my lodgings. No note was there, nor had anybody seen the servant. From the drift of dust and feathers you see how the wind blows.

Paid my boarding up to last night; three dollars.

I can not help wishing myself honorably quit of the enviable station. What a host of enemies has it not raised about me, with calumny and detraction in every corner! Fate but grant me this, that their dissensions and cabals may protect the election until my period be expired, and if you find me in this city twenty-four hours longer, inflict what insult you please on me. Placed on an eminence, slander and defamation are the hooks applied to pull me down. It is natural to make some efforts to disengage one's self from such grapplings, yet even the slightest endeavor of this kind is reprobated as an attempt to procure votes. What a set of vipers!

December 23d.—Visited this morning to near eleven. Attended at the Hall. Mr. Morris was late in coming. And now the resolution respecting the public creditors, or rather in answer to their memorial, was taken up. Every mode was tried to let them down easy, as the phrase is. Great accommodation was tried to get Mr. Morris to come into the measure, and it really seemed that more than once he was satisfied with Elsworth's modification of the resolution. King offered a second one, or, perhaps, I might say, a fourth one, which was adopted. Mr. M. told me he would agree to it. But a number rose for the yeas and nays. Mr. Monroe, of Virginia, desired to be excused, and was so. Mr. Morris was the only nay. I was in good humor myself, although I considered the vote of this day as waging a war with the public creditors, in which I will most probably lose my re-election, and was sorry to see my colleague manifest such a degree of obstinacy and peevishness. He left the Senate chamber immediately after the vote.

A vote for the inexpediency of altering the funding system at this time, from a person who uniformly opposed the system in its passage into a law, may seem to require some apology. My vote proceeds not from an approbation of the funding system, but from a total disapprobation of the memorial now before us. Upon republican principles, I hold the voice of the majority to be sacred. That the funding law has obtained that majority is undeniable, and acquiescence is our duty; but I never will subscribe to a blind and unalterable one. The making debts irredeemable and perpetual is a power that I am convinced posterity will spurn at. The Western lands are the natural fund for the redemption of our national debt. It is now unproductive. Perhaps the fault is ours that it is so. As soon as it is otherwise, I would be happy to see all stock made strictly personal, unalienable, and incapable of descent or any negotiation, save commutation in lands; and let it die with the obstinate speculator who refuses such commutation. The stockholder, to any amount, is an unproductive character—worse, he is the tool of a bad administration. A good one needs none. It is enough that we have seen one generation of them. Let us not perpetuate the breed; their children, cut off from such expectations, will be restored to industry.

It is a fact that the six-per-cents are now nearly at par, or at least this appearance is kept up among the speculators. An act passed hastily just at the close of the last session directed the borrowing two millions of dollars with design of buying in the public debt and lessening it. The real object was the increasing it by raising the value. Three millions of florins have been borrowed in pursuance of this law. The Board of Purchase named in the law completed their purchase of November at about 12s. 4d. on the face and 7s. 3d. arrears. It was natural to expect this would be about the standing value, but, by one effort of impudence, par was demanded in three days on the appearance of the Treasurer's advertisements.

December 24th.—The papers full of the advertisements this day of stock of every kind for sale, and there is no doubt but the show of sales nearly at par will be kept up in order to save appearances and cover the advance prices which are daily given by the Board of Purchase through the medium of the Treasury. This whole matter of purchasing in stock to sink the debt, ostensibly, has really no other object but to raise the value of it, and so to make immense fortunes to the speculators who have amassed vast quantities of certificates for little or nothing. I did not think it possible that mankind could be so easily duped, and yet there never was a vainer task than to attempt to undeceive them.

Very little was done in the Senate to-day. Sundry communications were made from the Representatives relating to the settlement on Port St. Vincennes, on the Wabash. Which was laid on our table.

Yesterday the Secretary's [Hamilton's] report on the subject of a national bank was handed to us, and I can readily find that a bank will be the consequence. Considered as an aristocratic engine, I have no great predilection for banks. They may be considered, in some measure, as operating like a tax in favor of the rich, against the poor, tending to the accumulating in a few hands; and under this view may be regarded as opposed to republicanism. And yet stock, wealth, money, or property of any kind whatever accumulated, has a similar effect. The power of incorporating may be inquired into. But the old Congress enjoyed it. Bank bills are promissory notes, and, of course, not money. I see no objection in this quarter. The great point is, if possible, to prevent the making of it a machine for the mischievous purposes of bad ministers; and this must depend more on the vigilance of future legislators than on either the virtue or foresight of the present ones.

December 25th.—This, being Christmas-day, dined with Parson Ewing, and had the task of hearing him rail almost all the time I was with him against Congress. He talked of demonstration and mathematical proof of the impositions which he had sustained. But he really did not understand the laws. I waived all altercation with him as much as I could. He had the terms rogue and cheat very familiarly at his finger' ends, or, I should rather say, at his tongue's end. He, however, talked of selling out.

I was this day assured that the six-per-cents were above par. The law for purchases allows the overplus money in the Treasury, after satisfying the appropriations, to be laid out in the purchase of certificates as well as the two million dollars to be borrowed abroad. It was originated and passed after I left New York, and is certainly the most impudent transaction that I ever knew in the political world. I regret my being absent when it passed, although my presence could have had no effect whatever on the progress of it further than I would have borne my testimony against it. This nominal reduction is a virtual raising of the whole value of the debt. Something of this kind, I have heard, is common in England. When governments attempt a purchase of any kind of stock, the holders of that kind of stock never fail to raise the residue. Hamilton must have known this well. Our speculators knew all this. They have a general communication with each other. They are actuated by one spirit, or, I should rather say, by Hamilton. Nobody, generally speaking, but them buy. It is easy for them, by preconcert, to settle what proposals they will give in; and, these being filled, the commissioners are justified in taking the lowest. I can not, however, help predicting that when the florins are out there will be a crash and the stocks will fall.

December 26th.—Being Sunday, my brother agreed with me that we would visit Dr. Logan. This man has every testimony, both of practice and profession, in favor of his republicanism. He has been in the Assembly of Pennsylvania, and there had it in his power to have formed a coalition with the city interest. He has, however, continued firmly attached to the rural plans and arrangements of life and the democratic system of government. His motto is, *"Vox populi vox Dei."* But mottoes and professions nowadays are as the idle wind which no one ought to regard unless supported by practice; and scarce can you depend on practice unless you see it embracing interest. This has been in some degree his case. We had been but a little while with him when we were joined by Judge Burke, of South Carolina. This was the very man who, while in New York, railed so tremendously against the Quakers, and against Pennsylvania for having Quakers. Behold a wonder! Now he rails against slavery, extols Quakers, and blazes against the attentions showed to General Washington, which he calls idolatry; and that a party wish as much to make him a king as ever the flatterers of Cromwell wished to raise him to that dignity.

Dr. Logan has Oswald's [news] paper at his devotion, and I can see that Burke will discharge many of his sentiments through this channel. Burke said many just things, but he is too new a convert to merit confidence. I find, however, on examination, that this is the same man who wrote against the Cincinnati.

December 27th, Monday.—I received just after breakfast a letter from Mr. Harris, and spent the day mostly in buying things which were to go by the man who brought the letter, he being a wagoner. Just as I came out of the door of the Hall, Hartley had fallen and broke his arm. I was among the first to show him every attention that his situation required, and the more especially as I have reason to consider him as inimical to my reappointment to the Senate of the United States. This day produced nothing of importance in the Senate. My attention to Hartley prevented my returning into the Senate chamber.

December 28th, Tuesday.—Attended the Senate as usual. A slight debate took place respecting a law for containing permission to the States of Rhode Island, Maryland, and Georgia the power to levy certain duties of tonnage for the purposes of repairs on their respective ports. The bill was recommitted, with two additional members added to the committee.

This being levee day, I attended in a new suit. This piece of duty I have not omitted since I came to town, and if there is little harm in it there can not be much good. Jackson looked shyly at me this day. I observed his eye upon me, and it had, in my opinion, something of the malignant in it. But I never cared less for court favor. I really feel a thirst to return to my family, and, although I will feel the pang which the insult of being rejected will inflict, yet, perhaps, a re-election might be among my misfortunes.

December 29th.—This day a blank in the Senate with respect to any business of importance. Mr. Morris told me I was blamed for not going among the members and speaking to them, etc. What a set of vipers I have to deal with! One party watches and ridicules me if I am seen speaking a word to a member. In order to avoid the censure of them I have rather secreted myself from the members, and the fault is fixed on it.

William Montgomery called this evening to tell me that he must go home on account of the indisposition of his wife. This is, perhaps, a vote out of pocket, but can not be helped.

I called this evening at the lodgings of some of the members who were out. Fitzsimons had often said he was at home in the evening, and desired me to call. I drank tea with him and the family. Sat a good while. The chat was various. He did not touch the subject of my re-election. He did not come with me to the door when I took my leave—as much as to say, I want no private communication. Be it so. If I want help, I need not look to him for it. Whatever is, is best, and I have little doubt that my rejection, if it takes place, will be best.

The character of Brackenridge was introduced. Fitzsimons said he came down in the State Legislature once. We took notice of him, and he embarked for us like a barrister through thick and thin. But he sold himself by it, lost his popularity, and we have never seen him since. He accompanied this with a loud laugh, which is uncommon with him, as his risibility seldom exceeds a dry smile or a sarcastic grin. Mrs. Fitzsimons cried out: "How insufferably cruel is that, my dear! You first mislead the man, and now ridicule him for the consequences of his mistakes." She did not just say the devil does so, but something not unlike it. It gave my friend Thomas Fitzsimons the flats, for he hardly said a word afterward.

December 30th.—I called this day on sundry members of the Assembly. As I came home I called at Boyd's, the place where all the plots are laid against me. Findley talked confidently. Smiley and Boyd rather seemed to oppose him. But I have a right to consider myself as among a den of thieves. I need never cross this threshold again. Advances to them are idle.

Attended the Hall at the usual time. A communication from the President respecting the prisoners at Algiers, fourteen of whom only are alive, was delivered to the Senate. Read and committed to the Committee on the Mediterranean Navigation. Did some business about the offices. Called and sat a good part of the evening with White, who had two of the Lancaster members with him—Carpenter and Brickbell. I need say nothing more to them. They now know me. From White I had much information of the malignant whispers, innuendoes, and malevolent remarks made respecting me. It was painful, and I could not refrain demanding of him what or whether any charge was made against me. No, no; nothing in particular, but everybody says: "The people don't like you; the people won't hear of your re-election." Who are they that say so? "The leading members of the Assembly, officers of the Land-Office, citizens of Philadelphia, and others." Query: Is not the same spirit that dictated the ostracism at Athens, the petalism at Syracuse, and similar measures in other places, still prevalent in the human mind and character? The true cause of these banishments, whether by the oyster-shell or the olive-leaf, was really to remove a blameless rival out of the way of less deserving competitors for office by the name and clamor of the people when no other cause could be alleged against him. In this way is there not in every free country, where the competition for office is laid open, a constant ostracism at work on the character of every man eminent for worth or talents? These arts will, no doubt, prevail on many occasions, but they will now be universally successful. When they do, we must submit to them as in some measure inseparable from republicanism.

December 31st.—Attended at the Senate this day, where nothing was done of any consequence. Sundry papers relating to the inhabitants of Port Vincennes, or Vincent, on the Wabash, were committed. I was one of the committee.

I went a-visiting with Mr. Langdon. Dined this day with Mr. Morris. I can observe in general rather a coolness of the citizens toward me. Be it so. I will endeavor not to vex myself much with them.

This is the last day of the year, and I have faithfully noted every political transaction that has happened to me in it. And of what avail had it been? I thought it possible that I would be called on with respect to the part I had acted in the Senate by the Legislature of Pennsylvania, or at least by some of them; but is there a man of them who has thought it worth while to ask a single question? No. Are they not, every man of them, straining after offices, posts, and preferments? At least, every one of them who has the smallest chance of success? Yes, verily. Nor is there a man who seems to care a farthing how I acted, but wished me out, to make a vacancy. Reward from men it is in vain to look for. It is, however, of some consequence to me that I have nothing to charge myself with.

Having some leisure on hand, I have looked over my minutes for the last month. It is with shame and contrition that

I find the subject of my re-election has engaged so much or any of my thoughts. Blessed with affluence, domestic in my habits and manners, rather rigid and uncomplying in my temper, generally opposed in sentiments to the prevailing politics of the times; no placeman, speculator, pensioner, or courtier —it is equally absurd for me to wish a continuance in Congress as to desire to walk among briers and thorns rather than on the beaten road. It may be said a love for the good of my country should influence my wishes. Let those care to whom the trust is committed; but never beg for that trust when, in my own opinion, I have been of so little service, and have sacificed both health and domestic happiness at the shrine of my country. Nothing that I could do, either by conversation or writing, has been wanting to let men see the danger which is before them. But seeing is not the sense that will give them the alarm; feeling only will have this effect, and it is hard to say how callous even this may be. Yet when the seeds of the funding system ripen into taxation of every kind and upon every article; when the general judiciary, like an enforcing machine, follows them up, seizing and carrying men from one corner of a State to another, and perhaps, in time, through different States, I should not be at all disappointed if a commotion, like a popular fever, should be excited, and, at least, attempt to throw off these political disorders. Ill, however, will the Government be, under which an old man can not eke out ten or a dozen years of an unimportant life in quiet; and may God grant peace in my day!

But as to the point in hand, let me now mark down some rules for my future conduct.

First, then, let me avoid anything that may seem to savor of singularity or innovation; call and speak to my acquaintances as formerly, but avoid with the utmost care the subject of senatorial election and everything connected with it. If any other person introduces it, he must either be a real or a pretended friend. Hear him, therefore, with complacence, and even with a thankful air; avoid every wish or opinion of my own, especially of the negative kind, for everything of the sort will hazard my sincerity.

Should an election come on while I am in town, stay in my

place during the time of it; and if it should be adverse, a thing I can scarce doubt of, immediately send in my resignation, as the appointment of another person must be considered as equivocal proof of my having lost the confidence of the State. For this purpose let my letter of resignation be ready, all to filling the date; and revise it while I am cool, for it is not unlikely that with so many eyes upon me I may undergo some perturbation at the time.

Lastly, have my mare in readiness, and let the first day of my liberty be employed in my journey homeward. A determination of this kind is certainly right, for I have tried and feel my own insignificance and total inability to give the smallest check to the torrent which is pouring down on us. A system is daily developing itself which must gradually undermine and finally destroy our so much boasted equality, liberty, and republicanism—high wages, ample compensations, great salaries to every person connected with the Government of the United States. The desired effect is already produced; the frugal and parsimonious appointments of the individual States are held in contempt. Men of pride, ambition, talents, all press forward to exhibit their abilities on the theatre of the General Government. This, I think, may be termed grade first; and to a miracle it has succeeded.

The second grade or stage is to create and multiply officers and appointments under the General Government by every possible means in the diplomacy, judiciary, and military. This is called giving the President a respectable patronage—a term, I confess, new to me in the present sense of it, which I take to mean neither more nor less than that the President should always have a number of lucrative places in his gift to reward those members of Congress who may promote his views or support his measures; more especially if by such conduct they should forfeit the esteem of their constituents. We talk of corruption in Great Britain. I pray we may not have occasion for complaints of a similar nature here. *Respice finem* as to the third.

CHAPTER XIII

January 1, 1791.—Neither Congress nor the Legislature of the State met this day. I went to settle some business with the Comptroller of the State, but he was equally complaisant to the day as the Government. I determined to do something since I was out, and called on my tailor, who took the amount of his bill. I then visited Hartley, who lies ill with his broken arm. Just as I passed the President's house, Griffin called to me and asked whether I would not pay my respects to the President. I was in boots and had on my worst clothes. I could not prevail on myself to go with him. I had, however, passed him but a little way when Osgood, Postmaster-General, attacked me warmly to go with him. I was pushed forward by him; bolted into the presence; made the President the compliments of the season; had a hearty shake by the hand. I was asked to partake of the punch and cakes, but declined. I sat down, and we had some chat. But the diplomatic gentry and foreigners coming in, I embraced the first vacancy to make my bow and wish him a good-morning.

I called next on the Governor of the State and paid my compliments, and so came home to my dinner; and thus have I commenced the year 1791.

January 2d.—Being Sunday, I stayed at home in the forenoon and attended at meeting in the afternoon. To worship once on the day devoted to the Deity is as small a compliment as decency can pay to the religion of any country, and a regard to health will prefer the after to the forenoon service at this season of the year, as the fire in the stoves has had then time to produce a greater effect in warming the house. I saw nobody this day, but received a letter from home by Colonel Cook.

January 3d.—Being Monday, I attended at the Hall early on a committee respecting the settlers on the Wabash and Mississippi. The business being tedious, the committee agreed to meet to-morrow morning at ten o'clock. We had a communication from the President with some nominations, and one from the Representatives respecting the Algerines. It was from Jefferson. It held out that we must either go to war with these piratical states, compound and pay them an annual stipend, and ransom our captives, or give up trade. The report seemed to breathe resentment, and abounded with martial estimates in a naval way. We have now fourteen unhappy men in captivity at Algiers. I wish we had them relieved, and the trade to the Mediterranean abandoned. There can be no chance of our wanting a market for our produce. At least, nothing of the kind has yet happened.

This day the Bank bill reported. It is totally in vain to oppose this bill. The only useful part I can act is to try to make it of some benefit to the public, which reaps none from the existing banks.

January 4th, Tuesday.—Attended early on the committee on the Wabash business. I could not help remarking the amazing predilection of the New England people for each other. There was no room for debate, but good sense and even Demonstration herself, if personified, would be disregarded by the wise men of the East if she did not come from a New England man.

The several bills were read this day, and business proceeded in the usual routine without any debate of consequence.

It was levee day. I dressed and did the duty of it. Handed a petition of Mr. Adlum's to Major Jackson. Nothing else of consequence happened. This petition business carried me there, and now I think, unless I am somehow called on, I will never see them more.

January 5th, Wednesday.—Attended early at the Hall to meet the committee, but they let me sit an hour without attending me. Strong had not made his draft of a report and was busy at it in the Secretary's office, and Elsworth would do nothing without him. But at last both drafts, Strong's and mine, were produced. I was ready to condemn my own when there was a shadow of objection, but even this conduct would not excite a particle of candor. I, however, cared but little, and was so well guarded that the smallest semblance of discontent did not escape me. General Dickenson came in. He took me to one side. "You have," said he, "enemies in this place. I dined yesterday with the Governor. He is your enemy. He said you will be hard run, and mentioned Smilie as being your competitor." I thanked him for the communication, nor could I do less, however indifferent I might be as to the event.

And now it is evident what plan has been chalked out at Boyd's. My brother overheard Matthew Irwin tell Findley that he (Findley) could command anything in the power of the people; that another man, whom my brother believed to be Smilie, could not do it so certainly; therefore, that Findley must depend on the people and the other one on the Legislature. Mr. Kenedy told my brother that Maclure wanted much to be in the Representatives, and the arrangement of districts which Findley read over at our lodgings plainly pointed out a nest for Mr. Lane—Franklin, Bedford, Mifflin, Huntington, and Northumberland Counties. Maclure is all-powerful in Franklin and Bedford, and has a son living and a considerable party attached to him in Huntington, so that the patriotism of all these three champions for liberty resolves itself into providing places for their accommodation.

I could add more names, evidently abstracted by the same principles, but the shortest way of completing the category is by determining the rule general, for I candidly confess I know not an exception among the present political figments of Pennsylvania. Avarice and ambition are the motives, while the cry of patriotism and the interest of the people are used as the ways and means of advancing their private ends. This peculiar malady is not peculiar to Pennsylvania. It is the disease of all popular governments. Nor does the fault seem to be in Nature. She certainly at all times produces stores of candid and ingenious characters; but these, generally modest and unassuming, are passed by in the ferment of popular elections, while the fiery and forward declaim on general grievances and pour forth their promises of redress. It is thus that ambitious men obtain the management of republics, and to this cause is, perhaps, owing their fall and declension throughout the world, for no selfish, ambitious man ever was a patriot.

January 6th, Thursday.—Nothing of consequence to the continent was transacted to-day, unless it was the report of the committee on the Algerine affair. The amount of it was:

First. The trade of the American States in the Mediterranean can not be supported without an armed force and going to war with them.

Secondly. This ought to be done as soon as the Treasury of the United States will admit of it. It is evident that war has been engaged in with the Indians on the frontiers in rather an unadvised manner, and it is also evident that there is a wish to engage us in this distant war with these pirates. All this goes to increase our burdens and taxes, and these in a debate of this day were called the only bonds of our Union. I will certainly oppose all this.

Dined this day with Mr. Bingham. I can not say that he affects to entertain in a style beyond everything in this place, or perhaps in America. He really does so. There is a propriety, a neatness, a cleanliness that adds to the splendor of his costly furniture and elegant apartments. I am told he is my enemy. I believe it. But let not malice harbor with me. It is not as William Maclay that he opposes me, but as the object that stands in the way of his wishes and the dictates of his ambitions, and on this principle he would oppose perfection itself.

January 7th.—Attended at the Senate as usual. We reported a bill for the Wabash and Illinois donation. Sundry other things were done in the usual routine of business. The Kentucky bill was taken up. I considered it so imperfectly drawn with respect to what were to be the boundaries of the new State that I opposed it, and there was much altercation on the subject, but entirely in the gentlemanly way. It ended in a postponement, with the consent of the Virginia member, Mr. Monroe.

Mr. Morris stayed out all the time of the debate. When the Senate adjourned he asked me to go and eat "pepper-pot" with him. I agreed, and accordingly dined with him *en famille*. I can not believe that he is my enemy with respect to my re-election; the thing is impossible. I chatted with the family till nearly dark, and came home, as I had an opportunity, with Mr. Hanna.

The human heart really is a strange machine. I certainly

have severely felt the inconvenience of being from home these two years past, and my judgment plainly tells me that I am wrong in having submitted to it. Further, I can not help knowing that my re-election, with no friends and many enemies, is impossible; and yet, under all these circumstances, the man who expresses favorable wishes is by far the most acceptable to me. But upon the whole this is right. Good ought to beget gratitude; but oh, what a recollection is it that under such circumstances I am independent, or, in other words, that my manner of living has always been within my means!

A letter to Mr. Harris [the founder of Harrisburg, Pennsylvania] :

PHILADELPHIA, *January 8, 1791.*

DEAR SIR: Agreeably to your request I send you by Mr. Hanna £61 : 14 : 6 in State money of 1785, and 3,200 dollars in post notes of 100 dollars each, being 1,200 pounds; the whole amount which I received for your certificates was 1,275 : 13 : 5. The present remittance leaves a balance of £75 : 13 : 5 in my hands, from which deduct £9 : 15 : 0 paid for carpet, and £10 : 15 : 11 paid for groceries :

$$£9 : 15 : 0 \atop 10 : 15 : 11 \Big\} \qquad £75 : 13 : 5 \atop 20 : 10 : 11$$

$$£55 : 2 : 6$$

This leaves a balance of £55 : 2 : 6 of your money in my hands, agreeably to an account current which I inclose. This balance I will pay you at any time.

As for newspapers and other occurrences I refer you to Mr. Hanna for them. The bills are all inclosed to you, and one which I paid to Edward Brooks, not put into my account, as you gave me four dollars for this purpose.

I am sir, with much regard, your most obedient servant,

W. M.

I added a considerable deal more to my letter, and sent the $3,200 and the State money, £61 : 14 : 6, along with Mr. Hanna, who set off on Sunday morning. I find that Mr. Hanna or I made a mistake, and he has a note of $1.70 instead of $100. I

have sent the note of $100 by Bobby Harris. This only lessens
the balance I owe Mr. Harris to the value of the small note
13*s*. 6*d*.

$$
\begin{array}{lr}
 & £55:\ 2:6 \\
\text{Less,} & 13:6 \\
\hline
\text{Balance,} & £54:\ 9:0
\end{array}
$$

January 9th, Sunday.—The most disagreeable of any day this
year. I, however, went to meeting, and the consequence was
a cold. Wrote letters to my family, and spent the after part of
the day at home.

January 10th, Monday.—Attended at the Hall as usual. The
Bank bill was the order of the day. I did not embark deeply,
but was up two or three times. The debates were conducted in
rather desultory manner. The objectors were Izard, Butler, and
Monroe. A postponement took place.

January 11th, Tuesday.—The Bank bill taken up, and the
debates became rather more close and interesting. I was up
several times, but the debates were rather on collateral points
than on the substance of the bill. The ostensible object held
out by Butler and Izard was that the public should have all
the advantages of the bank; but showed no foundation for
this, no system, no plan or calculation. They were called on to
show any, and were promised support if they could show any
practicability in their system. Till after three o'clock was the
matter agitated, and a postponement broke up the business of
the day.

January 12th, Wednesday.—The Bank bill was the business
of this day, but Monroe called for a postponement of the subject,
and succeeded. A bill was now called up respecting consuls and
vice-consuls. This bill was drawn and brought in by Elsworth,
and, of course, he hung like a bat to every particle of it. The
first clause was a mere chaos—style, preamble, and enacting
clause all jumbled together. It was really unamendable; at least,
the shortest way to amend it was to bring in a new one.

This same Elsworth is a striking instance how powerful a
man may be in some departments of the mind and defective in

others. All-powerful and eloquent in debate, he is, notwithstanding, a miserable draftsman. The habits of the bar and
the lists of litigation have formed him to the former; the latter
is in a degree the gift of Nature.

I dined this day with Mr. Nicholson. The company: Mr.
Montgomery, Smilie, B. McClenachan, T. Smith, Kittera, Hamilton, and others. Desultory conversation on a variety of subjects. I left them, for, from some hints, it seemed as if they
meant to discourse of the appointment of a Senator, etc. A
thought passed my mind that Nicholson, who has often expressed approbation of my conduct, had some hand in it. But
I will not disgrace myself in this business. Circumstanced as
I am, all the caballing and intrigue I could exercise would not
be effectual. And suppose me successful, what am I to gain?
Pain, remorse, vexation, and loss of health; for I verily believe that my political wrangles have affected my corporeal feelings so as to bring on, in a degree, my rheumatic indisposition.
It is a melancholy truth, but I see plainly that even the best
men will not emerge to office in republics without submitting,
either directly or indirectly, to a degree of intrigue. It is not,
perhaps, so much the case in monarchies, for even tyrants
wish to be served with fidelity. *Sed ubi plurima notent non ego
paucis offendar maculis.*

January 13th, Thursday.—This day the Bank bill was debated, but in so desultory a manner as not to merit the commitment of anything to paper.

This day I dined with General Dickinson. As I went there
I fell in with Mr. Morris. He told me that Bingham had informed him great discontents prevailed in the General Assembly,
and that they were about to instruct their Senators. He added
that he was sure that Bingham had a hand in it.

The dinner was a great one, and the ladies, only three of
whom attended, were richly or at least fashionably dressed.
Nothing remarkable. I sat between two merchants of considerable note. I broached the subject of the bank, and found them
magnetically drawn to the contemplation of the moneyed interest.

January 14th, Friday.—This day the bank engaged us to
the hour of adjournment. It was limited to twenty years. Mr.

Morris had yesterday declared that the public ought to subscribe on the same terms as other individuals. It was not so in the bill. I showed him an amendment to this purpose, and asked him to support me in it. He said Schuyler had told him that Hamilton said it must not be altered, but concluded, "I will speak to Hamilton. Adjourned over till Monday."

January 15th, Saturday.—This was a very disagreeable day. I stayed at home and read Price on Annuities. I find he establishes an opinion which I had long entertained that women are longer-lived than men. This I used to charge to accidents and intemperance. But he goes further, and seems to place it in nature, as more males than females die in infancy.

January 16th, Sunday.—Went to meeting and caught some cold, as usual. Spent the residue of the day in reading.

January 17th, Monday.—This day Mr. Morris stayed very late. Langdon came and complained of him. "This is always his way. He never will come when there is any debate." He, however, came. I asked him whether he had called on Hamilton. No. I said I had a mind to move a recommitment, that the Secretary of the Treasury might be consulted and furnish the committee with calculations on this subject, as I had no doubt but he had such. He said he would move such a thing, but did not. The question was put on the clause. Several said ay. I got up; spoke longer than I intended; and made such a motion, but my colleague did not second me. I was seconded by Butler.

And now such a scene of confused speeches followed as I have seldom heard before. Every one affected to understand the subject, and undervalue the capacities of those who differed from himself. If my mental faculties and organs of hearing do not both deceive me, I really never heard such conclusions attempted to be drawn. I wanted some advantage to the United States. They were to subscribe two millions specie. Elsworth repeatedly said they were to do this only as a deposit, and I am convinced he wanted to deprive the public of all advantage save that of safe keeping and convenience in collecting which they could derive from the banks in existence as well as from any new one. All other persons had the power of subscribing three fourths in public securities. It was contended that this was nothing against the public, although it was admitted on all hands that six-per-cents were now at sixteen shillings in the pound. King, Elsworth, and Strong all harped on this string with the most barefaced absurdity that I ever was witness to in my life.

I am now more fully convinced than ever before of the propriety of opening our doors. I am confident some gentlemen would have been ashamed to have seen their speeches of this day reflected in the newspapers of to-morrow. We sat till a quarter after three, and adjourned without any question being put.

I know not whether this fear of taking the question did not arise from some pointed expressions which fell from me. I told them plainly that I was no advocate of the banking systems; that I considered them as machines for promoting the profits of unproductive men; that the business of the United States, so far as respected deposits, could be done in the present banks; that the whole profit of the bank ought to belong to the public, provided it was possible to advance the whole stock on her account. I was sorry that this at present was not possible. I would, however, take half, or I should rather, in the present case, say one fifth of the loaf rather than no bread. But I must remark that the public was grossly imposed upon in the present instance. While she advanced all specie, individuals advanced three fourths in certificates, which were of no more value in the support of the bank than so much stubble. To make this plain: Suppose the vaults empty, and a note presented for payment: would the bearer take certificates as specie? No, verily. Besides, the certificates were all under interest already, and it was highly unjust that other paper should be issued on their credit which bore a premium and operated as a further tax on the country.

January 18th, Tuesday.—This day the Bank bill was taken up again. I feel much reluctance to minute anything on this subject. I never saw the spirit of speculation display itself in stronger colors. Indeed, the guise of regard for the interest of the public was not preserved. Two millions of specie is to be subscribed in by the public. This is to be the basis of the bank; and the other subscribers, who are to draw dividends according to their subscriptions, are to pay three fourths in certificates.

King evidently wanted, by a side-wind, to exclude the public from any dividend, under an idea which strangely inculcated that the subscription of the public was to be over and above the capital—ten millions—of the bank, and was to be considered as a deposit. A position which resolved itself into this: that the public should find the specie to support the bank while the speculators, who subscribe almost wholly in certificates, receive the profits of the dividends.

Morris gave me some marks of his malevolence. While I was up and speaking and saw well what I said, he said, loud enough to be heard over half the Chamber, "that I was mistaken." I varied the arguments a little; took a new ground, and after placing them in what I thought an incontrovertible light, I concluded, "Here I am not mistaken." The point on which my mistake was charged was my alleging that the Bank of North America wrought but seven hundred and fifty thousand dollars. General Dickenson sat by me and was willing to be called on that they wrought but seven hundred and forty thousand dollars—ten thousand dollars less than I had mentioned. He is, however, a very good-natured man, and I would not call on him. He [General Dickenson] whispered to me: "This day the Treasury will make another purchase, for Hamilton has drawn fifteen thousand dollars from the bank in order to buy, as I suppose." What a damnable villain!

January 19th.—My brother went with me last night to the lodgings of Mrs. Bell and communicated to her the news of the death of her father. She manifested the most unbounded grief, so as to give distress to the bystanders. Death, Death, thou art a solemn messenger, and will take us all in rotation! But let me pause. What art thou? I have been so ill that I would have swallowed thee in an anodyne. Yes, when our joys leave us, when pain possesses all our feelings, thou art the grand composer of all our miseries, the last portion in the cup of life; and surely it need not be called a bitter one, for none ever complained after swallowing the draught. How little of the sweet and how deeply dashed with gall is the diet of life! Passes there a day in which we taste not of it?

This day the Bank bill passed all through. The last clause was caviled at. I supported it on the principle that any law containing a grant of any kind should be irrepealable. Laws touching the *regulation* of morals, manners, or property, are all made on the principle of experiment and accommodation to time and place; but when legislators make grants the deed should remain inviolate. Three opinions prevailed in the Senate respecting this bill; or rather, I should say, three motives of action. The most prevalent seemed to be to accommodate it to the views of the stockholders who may subscribe. The Potomac interest seem to regard it as a machine which, in the hands of the Philadelphians, might retard the removal of Congress. The destruction of it, of course, was their object. I really wished to make it as subservient to the public as possible. Though all professed this, yet I thought few gave themselves any trouble to promote it. I can not help adding a sincere wish that the integrity of the directors may make amends for the want of it in many of the legislators who enacted it. For, in the hands of bad men, it may be made a most mischievous engine; but, indeed, so may even the best of human institutions.

January 20th.—The business of this day was the third reading of the Bank bill. The same questions were agitated over again, but without heat. It was moved to reduce the limitation to ten years. I at one time thought this long enough, but I conversed on the subject with every moneyed man I could find, and they uniformly declared that they would not subscribe on so short a period, and the consequence would be that they would all join in supporting the old banks and bearing down the national one. I sincerely wish to derive a benefit to the public from the bank; and considering that the public are, in this respect, in the hands of the moneyed interest, I thought it best to agree to such a bargain as we could make, and accordingly voted against this motion.* Accident threw me in the company with these men, but I abhor their design of destroying the bank altogether. Mr. Morris came very late this day—indeed, not until all the business was over—but he desired leave to have his vote inserted on the minutes, which was granted.

Dined with the President this day. Sundry gentlemen met me at the door, and, though I rather declined, they pushed me for-

---

* The motion to limit the term of the bank to the year 1801 instead of 1811.

ward. After I had made my bows and was inclining toward a vacant seat, the President, who rose to receive me, edged about on the sofa as he sat down, and said, "Here is room." But I had put myself in motion for another vacant seat. A true courtier would have changed, but I am not one, and sat on the opposite settee or sofa with some New England men. At dinner, after my second plate had been taken away, the President offered to help me to part of a dish which stood before him. Was ever anything so unlucky? I had just before declined being helped to anything more, with some expression that denoted my having made up my dinner. Had, of course, for the sake of consistency, to thank him negatively, but when the dessert came, and he was distributing a pudding, he gave me a look of interrogation, and I returned the thanks positive. He soon after asked me to drink a glass of wine with him. This was readily accorded to, and, what was remarkable, I did not observe him drink with any other person during dinner; but I think this must have been owing to my inattention.

Giles, the new member from Virginia, sat next to me but one. I saw a speech of his in the papers, which read very well, and they say he delivers himself handsomely. I was, therefore, very attentive to him. But the frothy manners of Virginia were ever uppermost. Canvas-back ducks, ham and chickens, old Madeira, the glories of the Ancient Dominion, all fine, were his constant themes. Boasted of personal prowess; *more manual exercise than any man in New England;* fast but fine living in his country, wine or cherry bounce from twelve o'clock to night every day. He seemed to practice on this principle, too, as often as the bottle passed him. Declared for the assumption and excise, etc. He is but a young man, and seems as if he always would be so.

But after this digression let me turn to the unexpected incident of dining with the President and his marked attention to me. He knows the weight of political odium under which I labor. He knows that my uniform opposition to funding systems (at least to ours), assumptions, high compensation, and expensive arrangements have drawn on me the resentment of all speculators, public creditors, expectants of office, and courtiers in the State. There is another point which, I presume, he does not know, viz., that I will receive no support from the Republican or opposition party, for there is not a man of them who is not aiming at a six-dollar * prize, and my place is the best chance in the wheel. But he knows enough to satisfy him that I will be no Senator after the 3d of March, and to the score of his good nature must I place these attentions. Be it so. It is, at least, one amiable trait in his character.

I have now, however, seen him for the last time, perhaps. Let me take a review of him as he really is. In stature about six feet, with an unexceptionable make, but lax appearance. His frame would seem to want filling up. His motions rather slow than lively, though he showed no signs of having suffered by gout or rheumatism. His complexion pale, nay, almost cadaverous. His voice hollow and indistinct, owing, as I believe, to artificial teeth before his upper jaw, which occasioned a flatness of—

[The following leaf, on which the rest of this description was written, has been torn out and is lost.]

January 21st, Friday.—This was a day of no great business in the Senate. Colonel Gunn, of Georgia, wanted copies of the secret journal. Much talk passed about his application. He was, however, gratified. In fact, we have never kept our journal agreeable to the Constitution. All the executive part has been kept secret without any vote for it. A committee is, however, appointed, and the matter will hereafter be under regulation.

We received some lengthy communications from Captain O'Brien and the prisoners at Algiers. A committee of the Senate some time ago recommended a war with them. War is often entered into to answer domestic, not foreign purposes. I fear such was the design of the present report. It was even talked how many ships should be fitted out and of what force. But O'Brien seems to show plainly that a peace may be obtained on easy terms by furnishing them naval stores. We have it plainly also from his letters that the French, Danes, and, above all, the British, have done us all the injury in their power with the Algerines. In fact, all who are at peace with them are decidedly

---

* The Senator's pay being six dollars per day.

against us, and have done us all the disservice they could. The former report was committed and these referred to them.

Mr. Morris came late and left us soon. We adjourned at about half after two o'clock. George Remsen, one of the clerks of the Treasury, returned from New York, where he had been sent by the Secretary [Hamilton]. Among his letters he pointed to a packet and said it contained ninety thousand dollars. How can I help believing that speculation was the object of his journey?

January 22d, Saturday.—The Speaker of the House of Representatives called on me yesterday; asked me to go and visit with him this day. I agreed, and called at his house about ten. He was, however, gone. His House sat this day, and this will be his excuse. I went to the Chamber of the State Representatives. The resolutions against the excise were the order of the day, and were passed by a great majority. The arguments were not important nor striking. Some ill-nature was expressed by Mr. Findley against a Mr. Evans.

I feel a sincere pleasure that so much independence has been manifested by the yeomanry of Pennsylvania. Indeed, I am fully satisfied that, if a spirit of this kind was not manifested from some quarter or another, our liberties would soon be swallowed up.

I trifled away the rest of the day. Much as was said in the Chamber of Representatives, they seemed totally ignorant of the principle that seems to actuate the adherents of Hamilton. Taxes originally flowed from necessity. Ways and means follow contracted or unavoidable expense. Here the system seems reversed. The ways and means are obvious to every reader of a registry of European taxes. We have heads, we have slaves and cattle, and every article of European or Asiatic convenience or luxury is used among us. The difficulty is to find plausible pretext for extending the arm of taxation and ways and means to consume the collected treasures, and the reigning party seem to consider themselves as wanting in duty if the fiscal rent-roll should fall short of the royal revenues of England.

January 23d, Sunday.—I had fairly devoted this day to my family in the way of writing letters, but, just as I had adopted the resolution, a message was brought me from Governor Langdon to go with him to meeting. This I could not refuse. Before I was half dressed I received a polite note from Mr. Morris to be one of his friends at a family dinner, and this I could not refuse; and, before I had quite dressed, Langdon called on me. We attended at Arch Street meeting.

Dined with Mr. Morris. The company: Judge Wilson, Governor St. Clair, General Butler. General Irwin was expected, but did not come. We were sociable, and I sat later than I usually do.

Mr. Wallis came into town this evening, but brought no letters, and now I hear that Charles Smith set off this day for Sunbury without giving me an opportunity of writing, or at least without my knowing of his departure. It is not handsomely done of either of them. But somebody else will do them a dirty trick; God forbid it should be my luck to do it!

I had told the Treasurer [Hamilton] some time ago that I wanted to sell him some stock. When I came home from meeting I found a note from him importing that he would buy to-morrow. This, in a great measure, confirms my former suspicions with respect to the Treasury.

CHAPTER XIV

January 24th, Monday.—This day voluminous communications were introduced by Secretary Lear. A volume of a letter from a Dr. O'Fallon to the President, avowing the raising of a vast body of men in the Kentucky country to force a settlement with the Yazoo country; the state of Indian affairs both in the southern and government northwest of the Ohio; the translation of all which was a want of more troops.

But the most singular of all was a proclamation for running lines of experiment for the ten-mile square. The message accompanying the proclamation calls for an amendatory law, permitting the President to locate lower down and to lay half of the square in Virginia. This seems like unsettling the whole affair. I really am surprised at the conduct of the President. To bring it back at any rate before Congress is certainly the most imprudent of all acts. To take on him to fix the spot by his own authority, when he might have placed the three commissioners in the post of responsibility, was a thoughtless act. I really think it not improbable that Opposition may find a nest to lay her eggs in from the unexpected manner of treating this subject. The general sense of Congress certainly was that the commissioners should fix on the spot, and it may be a query whether the words of the law will warrant a different construction. The commissioners are now only agents of demarkation, mere surveyors to run four lines of fixed courses and distances.

Sold my stock, six-per-cents at seventeen shillings fourpence, deferred, and three-per-cents at nine.

January 25th, Tuesday.—Had this day another hearing at the Board of Property. I really have suffered persecution on this affair. Rowls, my adversary, did not appear, and Daniel Rees called about dinner-time to tell me that Robert Vaux Coots had been told of my cheating a man out of a tract of land after it had been surveyed to him. I really have had my share of trouble with this business of Senator, and it would be well for me if I were fairly and honorably out of it.

Mr. Brown, of Northampton, called on me and told me that Muhlenberg was very busy in giving oyster-suppers, etc., and seemed to think that I should go more among the members, etc. I find I will offend him and some others if I do not. But it is a vile commerce, and I detest this beast-worshiping. How melancholy a thing it is that the liberties of men should be in the hands of such creatures! I can not call them men. But Brown seemed to think that Muhlenberg had made an impression on the Governor, or some of them. Be it so. Such arts have prevailed and will prevail, but the day of my deliverance draweth nigh. The 4th of March is not distant from the different schemes and parties that are formed and the want of any fixed form or mode of election. I can not think the choice will be made before that time; and let them affront me if they find me here afterward.

January 26th, Wednesday.—I never in my life had more distressing dreams than last night. But I received imaginary relief from my visionary perplexities, and the emotion was so great as to awaken me. The agitation I underwent was so extreme that my head ached for some time after I awoke. This I may charge to the vexation of yesterday.

I went and called on a number of the members of the Assembly and [State] Senators. All seemed fair and smooth. Some of them, indeed, expressly said that they would support me at the coming election, believing that to be the object of my visit, as in some measure it was. *Sed nulla fides fronti* may be applied to many of them.

The bill for regulating consuls and vice-consuls had the second reading this day. A letter from the National Assembly of France, on the death of Dr. Franklin, was communicated from them and received with coldness that was truly amazing. I can not help painting to myself the disappointment that awaits the French patriots, while their warm fancies are figuring the raptures that we will be thrown into on the receipt of their letter, and the information of the honors which they have bestowed on our countrymen, and anticipating the complimentary echoes of our answers, when we, cold as clay, care not a fig for

them, Franklin, or freedom. Well we deserve—what do we deserve? To be d——d!

CURES FOR RHEUMATISM

1. A teaspoonful of the flour of brimstone taken every morning before breakfast. General St. Clair and Mr. Milligan both relieved by it. NOTE.—They are both Scotchmen.

2. Asafœtida laid on burning coals and held to the nose. Mr. Todd greatly relieved by this.

3. Cider in which a hot iron has been quenched. This has relieved many, though cider is to many people very hurtful in that disorder.

January 27th.—This day communications were received from the President of the United States relating to the Indian depredations. A post on the Muskingum cut off. The wishes of many people are gratified to involve us in war. To involve us in expense, at any rate, seems to be the great object of their design. It, perhaps, would be unjust—perhaps cruel, too—to suppose it. But had a system been needed to involve us in the depth of difficulty with the Indians, none better could have been devised.

Last year, at New York, much altercation happened, whether a discrimination in the duties of tonnage should not be made in favor of foreign nations in treaty with us. This measure was lost, although, in my opinion, a just one. The court of France remonstrates against the duties, expecting favors as a nation in treaty. Some gentlemen, on receiving the communications, affected recantation publicly, and by these very means obtained themselves to be put on the committee. This day they reported against the claims of France.

I have hitherto attended only to the part acted by some persons whose conduct, from appearance, is not very consistent. I called on Otis for the papers. He said Butler got them and had given them to one of the Representatives. A minute after I saw them in the hands of Mr. Dalton. But Otis is really so stupid that I know not whether he lied or blundered.

When the matter of no discrimination was carried in Congress, in our first session, I could hardly suppress a thought, which I felt ready to spring up in my mind, that some person wished to destroy the confidence between us and France, and bring us back to the fish-pots of British dependence. This I charge to the influence of the city of New York, but Philadelphia has not altered the tenor of their political conduct.

Elsworth could not rest a moment all this day. He was out and in, in and out, all on the fidgets. Twice or thrice was an adjournment hinted at, and as often did he request that it might be withdrawn, expecting the Excise bill to be taken out. But he had to bear his impatience. Three o'clock came before the bill. I can see that he will stand foremost in the gladiatorial list.

January 28th, Friday.—Much crowded this morning with people with whom I had not much to do. Had to call at the Board of Property. 'Twas the usual time before I went to the Hall. The Excise bill came up; but oh, what a mistake! It is only a bill for discontinuing certain duties and laying others in their stead. The odious name is omitted, but the thing is the same. It was read and ordered to the press.

I went to the Senate of the State to hear the debates on the resolutions. But they were postponed. Returned to our Chamber, and the report of the committee on the difference with the court of France was taken up. Almost everybody gave it against the French demands. I differed from them on some points, but, as I could not obtain a sight of the papers, I joined in the motion for a postponement, which was carried.

January 29th, Saturday.—Called twice this day at the office of our Secretary to get the French papers. Otis says Carrol took them away, but there is no believing a word he says. Went to hear the debates in the State Senate. The resolutions for instructing the Senators had been postponed yesterday expressly for the purpose of obtaining a sight of the bill, which is in its passage through Congress. But the same men pushed for a decision this day. The State has now an opportunity of seeing the benefit of two Houses. The division was nine to eight. The yeas and nays were called. Graff, of Lancaster, was going home. This was the reason for pushing the vote this day. Assemblymen and Senators may be equally considered as representatives of the people. From the division of the two Houses the voice of the people appears to be unequivocally against an excise.

January 30th, Sunday.—Not very well this day, and stayed at home most of the day. Went in the evening to the funeral of Judge Bryan. This man rests from his labors, but the tongue of malevolence resteth not, so inhumane are many of the citizens of this place as to speak of his decease with joy. But the anodyne of death hath spread her mantle over him. He was said to be spiteful and revengeful; his enemies were not less so, and he had the qualities of industry and love of freedom. He was the father of the Abolition laws.

January 31st, Monday.—The Excise bill read a second time; but, the bill not being in our hands, it was made the order of the day for Wednesday.

The affair of the French discontents taken up. God forgive me if I wrong some people, but there certainly have been more censorious conclusions than to charge some people with a design of breaking our connection with France!

I called on Friday; I called twice on Saturday. Otis lied basely about the papers, and I have never got my eyes on them.

When or how will all these mad measures lead us? We have it ever in our ears that the present General Government (with respect to the persons who compose it) contains the collected wisdom and learning of the United States. It must be admitted that they have generally been selected on account of their reputation for knowledge, either legal, political, mercantile, historical, etc. Newspapers are printed in every corner. In every corner ambitious men abound, for ignorance or want of qualifications is no bar to this view. Thus, then, the Tylers and Jackstraws may come in play, and talents, experience, and learning be considered as disqualifications for office; and thus the Government be bandied about from one set of projectors to another, till some one man more artful than the rest, to perpetuate their power, slip the noose of despotism about our necks. 'Tis easy to say this never can happen among a virtuous people; ay, but we are not more virtuous than the nations that have gone before us.

February 1st, Tuesday.—This day I had much to say against the report of a committee which went to declare war against the Algerines. It is not suspicion that the designs of the court are to have a fleet and army. The Indian war is forced forward to justify our having a standing army, and eleven unfortunate men, now in slavery in Algiers, is the pretext for fitting out a fleet to go to war with them. While fourteen of these captives were alive, the barbarians asked about thirty-five thousand dollars for them; but it is urged that we should expend half a million dollars rather than redeem these unhappy men. I vociferated against the measure, and, I suppose, offended my colleague. This thing of a fleet has been working among our members all the session. I have heard it break out often.

February 2d, Wednesday.—The Excise bill read over and remarked on and committed to five members. I gave notice that I would endeavor to show that a much lower duty would answer the demand of the Secretary. I spoke to sundry of the members to second a general postponement for the session, but not a man approved of any such thing.

Dined this day with Mr. Burd. Lewis was there; Rowls was there; old Shippen was there. I endeavored to be easy, but could not be sprightly. From the circle of the universe could not be collected a group who have manifested equal malignity to me personally as I have received from the above characters. May they never have it in their power to do unto others as they have done unto me!

February 3d, Thursday.—This was an unimportant day in the Senate; no debate of consequence took place. I was called off the street to dine with a Quaker at about two o'clock. As he seemed very friendly, I went and ate heartily of a good dinner, and was perfectly easy; much more than I could say of the great dinners where the candles are ready to be brought in with the going out of the last dishes. This high life is really very distant from nature. All is artificial.

I neglected sundry small matters and went in the evening to the meeting of a society formed lately for promoting the improvement of roads and inland communications. Dr. Smith is at the bottom of this business. His object is to consolidate the report of the commissioners who have lately reviewed the communications on the Susquehanna, Juniata, etc., at least so far as to bring forward the Juniata only. In this business Findley is joined with him, and a dirty pair they are. I attacked the proceedings of the committee who drew up the memorial with perhaps more eagerness than prudence. I had, however, some success. My old friend showed some malignity. From the drift of chaff and feathers you know how the winds blow, says the proverb; much more so if you see ships sail or trees come down with the blast. Yesterday Ryerson, the devoted creature of Mr. Morris, put up a nomination of William Findley for Senator in my room. They will be easy when they get my place, and I trust I will be easier without it than with it.

What is the reason that I do not hear a single word from Harrisburg, not a word from Davy, not a word from Bob, not a word from the old man? I will give myself no trouble about them, or as little as I can help.

February 4th, Friday.—This day we had a large report from the Secretary of State transmitted to us from the House of Representatives respecting the fisheries of New England. The great object seems to be the making them a nursery for seamen, that we, like all the nations of the earth, may have a navy. We hear every day distant hints of such things as these; in fact, it seems we must soon forego our republican innocence, and, like all other nations, set apart a portion of our citizens for the purpose of inflicting misery on our fellow-mortals. This practice is felony to posterity. The men so devoted are not only cut off, but a proportionate share of women remain unmatched. Had the sums expended in war been laid out in meliorating the kingdom of England, or any other modern Government, what delightful abodes might they have been made; whereas war only leaves traces of desolation!

Dined this day with Charles Biddle. He has some point to carry with the State government, as I believe, and the dinner may be on account of my brother. The company were mostly members of the Legislature.

I must here note of our Vice-President that he this day hurried the adjournment for to-morrow at eleven o'clock. All this is plain. He is deep in the cabals of the Secretary [Hamilton]. The Secretary sat close with the committee on the Excise bill. Every moment it was expected they would report, but so anxious are the Secretary's party to have it passed that even John Adams, who used to show as much joy on an adjournment from Friday to Monday as ever a school-boy did at the sweet sound of play-time, fixed the House to meet to-morrow.

February 5th, Saturday.—The Senate met. I found Hamilton with the committee who had the Excise bill in their hands. We sat and sat and sat, but no report. I had busied myself in getting a return of the number of stills from the different members of the Assembly. I went to the door of the committee-room to use it in argument with them, but, finding Hamilton still with them, I returned. Mr. Morris took the paper and went in, and I suppose no further use was made of it. He, however, restored it again. The report on the fisheries by Jefferson was directed to be printed.

No report from the committee. It was agreed to, that powers of the inspectors should extend only to the importations and distillations, but I find Hamilton will have even to modify this to his mind. Nothing is done without him. I have been troublesome in my speeches against the excise. Upon general principles it is equally exceptionable as a poll-tax. Wealth is not its only object. The mouth of one individual may be supposed to consume as much liquor as another; any difference is rather in favor of the most costly imported liquors. It is a tax oral, and has only this advantage over the poll-tax, that you may refrain from using your mouth in drinking liquor. With some people this is as impossible as to do without a head.

February 6th, Sunday.—Attended meeting and wrote letters to Harrisburg and home to my family. On the 3d of March Congress will rise. I have written for my mare to be here against that day, and from deceit, dissimulation, and ambition; from mere artificial life, whence both truth and sincerity are banished, I will go and meet nature, love, affection, and sincerity, in the embraces of my wife and dear children.

February 7th.—Attended at the Hall. Mr. King made one of his curious stretches. He said the minutes were wrong and he wished to correct them. The report, which was ordered to be printed on Saturday, he wished to be postponed to the 28th of December next, and corrected the minutes of Saturday to read so. This same King is a singular man. Under the idea of correcting the minutes he introduces matter totally new. It is not correcting matter of form, but total alteration and adjection of new matter. I opposed him, and certainly he ought to be ashamed of the measure; and yet it was carried, but amended afterward and placed nearer the truth.

There certainly is a design of quarreling with France, and that Jefferson should seem to countenance this! What can this mean? I am really astonished at all this. I think I must be mistaken, and yet to think so is to disbelieve my senses. And what can I do? I have attempted everything and effected nothing, unless it be to render myself an object of aversion. For well indeed speaks the poet:

> Truths would you teach, or save a sinking land,
> All fear, none aid you, and few understand.

February 8th, Tuesday.—The Senate met. The Appropriation bill had the last reading. There was a pause about taking up the Excise bill, like people pausing on the brink of a precipice, afraid to take the dangerous leap. However, it was at length attempted, and we blundered to the fourth section. Objections had been made to this section, and it was expected the committee would alter it. They have done so with a vengeance. It now runs that there shall be an inspector-general over a district, the district to be divided into surveys, and an inspector to be set over each survey, who shall appoint people under him to do the business; as many of them to be appointed as the President shall think proper, and he shall pay them, too. It is the most execrable system that ever was framed against the liberty of a people. This abominable clause was postponed. The members by degrees stole away. The men who did it showed their disapprobation of it in their looks. It is in vain. Our Government can not stand. All my opposition has been considered as vain babbling. But to get quit of it in some degree this business of commitment has taken place, and now the majority have a kind of scapegoat in the committee, and a pretext for following them and disregarding opposition under the idle idea of their knowing best, having consulted Hamilton, etc., etc.

How abandoned is the conduct of these men! Abuse, rail at, vilify, and traduce the European systems of excise as much as you will; demonstrate their absurdity, villainy, and deplorable effect on society as much as you please. 'Tis all right.

They echo every sentence. "Ours" is no such thing in their language; quite innocent and harmless. Yet such is the indolence of Hamilton and his adherents that they will not even use the guise of different terms or words to conduct the copy. Nor will they stop till, perhaps, as in Britain, ten men may be employed to guard one distillery.

February 9th, Wednesday.—Attended at the Hall this day, and was, perhaps, never more vexed. Were Eloquence personified and reason flowed from her tongue, her talents would be in vain in our Assembly; or, in other words, when all the business is done in dark cabals, on the principle of interested management. The Excise bill is passed, and a pretty business it is. The ministry foresee opposition, and are preparing to resist it by a band, nay, a host of revenue officers. It is put into the power of the President to make as many districts, appoint as many general surveyors and as many inspectors of surveys as he pleases, and thus multiply force to bear down all before him. War and bloodshed are the most likely consequence of all this. Congress may go home. Mr. Hamilton is all-powerful, and fails in nothing he attempts. Little avail as I was sure it would be of, I nevertheless endeavored not to be wanting in my duty, and told them plainly of the precipice which I considered them as having approached; that the Legislature of Pennsylvania had been obliged to wink at the violation of her excise laws in the western parts of the State ever since the Revolution; that, in my opinion, it could not be enforced by collectors or civil officers of any kind, be they ever so numerous; and that nothing short of a permanent military force could effect it; that this, for aught I knew, might be acceptable to some characters. I could only answer for myself that I did not wish it, and would avoid every measure that tended to make it necessary.

February 10th, Thursday.—I returned home this day from the Senate chamber more fretted and really more off the center of good humor than ever I did in my life. I really was ready to pray, "Lord, deliver us from rascals!" I can not have charity enough to believe that the prevailing party in our Senate are honest men. Some letters, however, have come in since yesterday from New England, and Strong was willing to move the reductions which we wanted. After the bill was read over and ready for the question, Foster, from Rhode Island, moved a reduction of three cents on the distillations from molasses, etc. I rose and seconded him, on condition of his extending the motion through all the distillations in the United States and a reduction to forty cents on the contents of stills.

King objected to the lessening of the ratio, as productive of deficiencies in the revenue demanded. I showed, in answer, that the importation into the port of Philadelphia, and the sums expected from the stills in this State, would go in a great way toward raising one half of the eight hundred and twenty-six thousand dollars demanded by the Secretary.

Elsworth answered, with rudeness, that I was mistaken; that the Secretary demanded a million and a half. I replied by reading part of the Secretary's report, which confirmed the position I had made, and repeated my other arguments. He did not reply. This man has abilities, but abilities without candor and integrity are characteristics of the devil.

At half after three the question was ready to be put. Henry, of Maryland, told me he had a bet depending with Butler on the division of the House, and desired the yeas and nays. I needed not this excuse, and called sharply for the yeas and nays. With all their strength, they were startled; and up got King, and round and round and about and about; one while commit; then recommit; then postpone. Elsworth, too, had the world and all to say; and now, in fact, they are afraid of the figure they have raised; and the fourth section was recommitted. This whole day Mr. Morris was dead against me in the voting way; sat quite away back from me, but spoke none, either way.

February 11th.—I find this day that the reason for recommitting the Excise bill yesterday was to enable Hamilton to come forward with some new schemes. Three new clauses were brought forward, and all from the Treasury. The obnoxious one (to me at least) was the putting it in the power of the President to form districts by cutting up the States so as to pay no respect to their boundaries. This was curiously worded. For fear of the little States taking any alarm, it stood by adding "from the great to the lesser States." This they got adopted. And having been successful so far, King got up and talked about it and about it. He wanted the United States divided into a number of districts, independent of any of the State boundaries. Like an Indian at the war-post, he wrought himself into a passion; declared that we *"had no right to pay any more attention to the State boundaries than to the boundaries of the Cham of Tartary."*

When he had spent his froth on this subject, up got Elsworth and echoed most of what he said, but said he wished only three great districts, and the President might subdivide each into six. When he had done, up got Mr. Morris and declared himself in sentiment with King, and spoke against the conveniency of the State boundaries.

King arose again, repeated his old arguments, and wished for an opportunity for taking a question on the principle of dividing the United States without any regard to their boundaries. At length, pop out of his pocket comes a resolution. It imported that the United States should be divided into six districts: two east of the Hudson, two from that to the Potomac, and two from that southward, or words to that import; and that the President should subdivide these into surveys, etc. This pretty system was, after all, negatived.

Annihilation of State government is undoubtedly the object of these people. The late conduct of our State Legislature has provoked them beyond all bounds. They have created an Indian war, that an army may spring out of it; and the trifling affair of our having eleven captives at Algiers (who ought long ago to have been ransomed) is made the pretext for going to war with them, and fitting out a fleet. With these two engines, and the collateral aid derived from a host of revenue officers, farewell freedom in America. Gently, indeed, did I touch it in argument; but is not a motion for the destruction of the individuality of the States, treason against the duty of a Senator, who, from the nature of his appointment, ought to be guardian of the State right? The little I said, however, I believe raised a goblin that frightened them from the project, at least for this time.

February 12th.—This day we passed the excise law; a pretty piece of business it is. I found there was an unwillingness in many of the members to have the yeas and nays. I, however, called them sharply, and enough rose, and I had the pleasure of giving my decided negative against what I considered the box of Pandora with regard to the happiness of America.

The communications came in this morning respecting the Indian affairs, and the bill as ordered to be printed. As we came down-stairs, Dr. Johnson spoke with great joy. "No," said he, "all is over, and the business is complete. We have a revenue that will support the Government and every necessary measure of Government. We have now the necessary support for national measures," etc. I told him we might perhaps undo all; that the high demands we had made would raise opposition, and that opposition might endanger the Government. He seemed a little struck. I repeated that the Government might, and perhaps would, fall by her overexertion to obtain support.

I called this evening at Boyd's. I found Gallatin and Beard and James Findley. I told them I wished to hear them speak freely on the defense of the frontiers. Some desultory discourse passed. I sat awhile, and Dr. Hutchinson came in, greasy as a skin of oil and puffing like a porpoise. This must certainly be a dirty fellow if external appearances do not much belie mental management and internal intention. Fame fixes them on the same footing, and I fancy for once she has not sounded a false alarm. He had a pretty tale to tattle over, quite new, quite à la Doctor, quite medical. Is the town sickly, Doctor? No, no; yes, yes, for the season. Accident, accident; half a family struck down yesterday. They had fed on pheasant. All who had eaten affected; all the doctors called; discharged the offensive food; recovered: the craws of the pheasants examined; laurel-leaves found in them. The death of Judge Bryan explained; he and his wife ate pheasant; both felt torpid; she evacuated, he died. And thus we were entertained with the belchings of this bag of blubber for half an hour. I took my hat and left them.

I had come but a few steps when I met Mr. Findley; told him I had called to talk on the subject of the Western war with the Indians; that, although the management would be in different hands, yet, as the means must be furnished by us, it was in some measure necessary to contemplate the mode. He immediately quit the subject and got at the excise. It must be submitted to; great credit due to the General Government; very honorable management to raise the debts to their full value, etc. In short, I believe he forgot himself or the company he was in. I begged pardon for stopping him in the street and left him. He chose to let me know of his communications with General Knox and other great men, etc.

February 13th, Sunday.—I went to a meeting at Market Street. Came home. The day rather disagreeable in the afternoon, and I stayed at home the residue of the day. I had made a remark here which I think it best to erase. Spent the day mostly in reading. Went, however, down-stairs; found a large company; the subject was religion, and most unmercifully was it handled. The point which was attempted to be established was that the whole was craft and imposition; that all our objects were before us—believe what you see; observe the fraud and endless mischiefs of ecclesiastics in every age, etc. Few of the historic facts which they adduced could be refuted, but by way of opposition Luther's Reformation was mentioned. It was easily answered that, had there been no abuse, they needed no reformation. But a further remark was suggested—that Luther was a mere political machine in the hands of those German princes who could no longer bear to see their subjects pillaged by Roman rapacity. The doctrine was, pay for indulgences and purchase salvation with good works, *alias* money. The new doctrine was, faith is better than cash; only believe, and save your money. It need not be doubted but the new doctrine was on this account more acceptable to both prince and people. Luther, however, had the Scripture with him.

Another position I thought still less tenable; that man was but the first animal in nature, that he became so by the feelings of his fingers and hence all his faculties. Give, said they, only a hand to a horse, he would rival all the human powers. This I know to be groundless. The 'possum, from its feeble, harmless, and helpless faculties, is almost extinct in Pennsylvania, and yet one that I killed on the island at Juniata had as complete a hand, with four fingers and a thumb, as one of the human species.

February 14th.—'Tis done. I doubt no longer. This day came in a bulky communication from the President. The amount was the result of a negotiation carried on by his order with the court of Great Britain through the agency of Gouverneur Morris. From the letters from the President it appears that the vote against discrimination which had involved us in difficulties with France was the work of the President, avowedly procured by his influence; and that he did it to facilitate a connection with Great Britain, thus offering direct offense to France and incurring the contempt of Britain, for she has spurned every overture made to her. And now the result is, I suppose, a war with Great Britain; at least these troops are, as I suppose, meant to wrest the posts from her. She will resist. Reprisals at sea will take place, and all the calamities of war ensue.

It is with difficulty that I refrain from giving the most severe language to some of our Senators. King vapored this day at a most unaccountable rate. The opponents to the Constitution, said he, were blind; they did not see the ground to attack it on. I could have shown them how to defend it. The most popular ground against it never was touched. The business was now complete. We need not care for opposition. Henry, of Maryland, joined with him; said the Constitution of the United States implied everything; it was a most admirable system. Thus did these heroes vapor and boast of their address in having cheated the people and establishing a form of government over them which none of them expected.

I will here leave a blank to copy General Washington's letters in. Perhaps this is wrong, for I never can contemplate the insult offered to France, *to procure more agreeable arrangements,* without feeling resentment.

The system laid down by these gentlemen was avowedly as follows, or rather, the development of the designs of a certain party:

The general power to carry the Constitution into effect by a constructive interpretation would extend to every case that Congress may deem necessary or expedient. Should the very worst thing supposable happen, viz., the claim of any of the States to any of the powers exercised by the General Government, such claim will be treated with contempt. The laws of the United States will be held paramount to all their laws, claims, and even Constitutions. The supreme power is with the General Government to decide in this, as in everything else, for the States have neglected to secure any umpire or mode of decision in case of the differences between them. Nor is there any point in the Constitution for them to rally under. They may give an opinion, but the opinion of the General Government must prevail, etc. This open point, this unguarded pass, has rendered the General Government completely uncontrollable. With a fleet and army, which the first war must give us, all the future will be chimerical.

I ventured to dissent from these political heroes by declaring that the people themselves would guard this pass; that the right of judging with respect to encroachments still remained with the people; it was originally with them, and they never had divested themselves of it.

With all their art, however, since they now confess their views, I think they have made but a bungling hand of it. The old Congress had no power over individuals, and, of course, no system of consolidation could take place. Their legislative or recommendatory powers were over States only. The new Constitution, by the instrumentality of the judiciary, etc., aims at the government of individuals, and the States, unless as to the conceded points, and with regard to their individual sovereignty and independence, are left upon stronger ground than formerly, and it can only be by implication or inference that the General Government can exercise control over them as States. Any direct and open attack would be termed usurpation. But whether the gradual influence and encroachments of the General Government may not gradually swallow up the State governments is another matter.

February 15th.—This day was rather unimportant in the Senate. General Dickenson and I had a long discourse in the committee-room. The subject was the speculation of the Treasury, or, I should rather say, of Hamilton. Nobody can prove these things, but everybody knows them. Mr. Morris labored, in private, with me this day to get me to join in postponing the complaints of the French court. The President, although it is undeniable that it was through his instrumentality that the offense was given to France, yet now wishes all this done away; the breach made up with France, and the resentment shown to England. The measure is right, but his motives wrong. Never should the paths of rectitude be forsaken. Had the President left Congress to themselves the discrimination would have obtained, and as the discrimination had heretofore obtained by the State laws, England would have taken no umbrage, and we should have experienced no interruption of harmony with France. The crooked policy of the President has involved us in difficulty. Unless we repeal the law, we lose forever the friendship of France. And even after repealing it the confidence of France in us will be impaired, as she may attribute our first motives to ingratitude and our last to fear. Continuing the law will have no effect on Britain, as she has already treated General Washington's application with contempt, but a repeal of it will be followed with a burst of resentment. This we will have to submit to and ought not to regard.

King delivered an opinion that Executive papers should be delivered to the President's private secretary. It was evident he alluded to the communications of yesterday and to the strictures passed on them. No vote was taken on the subject, but I have hitherto been unsuccessful in endeavoring to lay my hands on them.

February 16th.—Engaged this morning in unimportant matters about the land-office and other places.

After the Senate met, Mr. Carrol moved for leave to bring in a bill supplementary to the Residence bill. The matter, I believe, stands thus, in fact: Virginia is not fully satisfied without having half of the ten miles square. She gives the one hundred and twenty thousand dollars, perhaps, on this very principle of having Alexandria included. This can not be done without the supplementary law, which is now applied for. I spoke to Mr. Morris and gave him my thoughts on the matter. He made a just observation: "There will be people enough to manage this affair without our taking a part in it." The rule demands one day's notice to be given for bringing in a bill. Carrol withdrew his motion on being told of this, but afterward hoped that the Senate would indulge him by common consent. Elsworth, however, said it had better lie over one day.

My friend, on the subject of resolution, told me that he had some conversation on that subject with the Speaker of the State Senate. The result was, that they would soon elect a new Senator; said he found him wavering, but on the whole considered him as friendly. I had business out, and called on Mr. Montgomery; told him that the agricultural interest of Pennsylvania ought to unite; that it was the policy of the city to disunite Findley and myself and run in Bingham; at least, this was the game he was playing. He agreed with me. Mr. Smilie soon after called on me. He spoke more harshly of Findley, particularly of his insufferable vanity, than ever I heard any one do before. He promised he would call on me.

I returned to the Senate. Found the drafts of General Harmer's expedition before the committee. They look finely on paper, but, were we to view the green bones and scattered fragments of our defeat on the actual field, it would leave very different ideas on our minds. This is a vile business, and must be much viler. I believe I ought not to vote for any of the new bill.

February 17th.—This day Mr. Carrol's motion for the amendatory act respecting the Potomac was to be taken up. Mr. Morris was very late in coming. It is remarkably singular that I never knew him otherwise when a debate was expected. I, however, wish he had stayed away, for he voted for leave to bring in the bill. I confess, to my astonishment, I saw him considerably embarrassed. How noble it is to be independent!

Leave was obtained, and the bill read. The Military bill was reported, with amendments much longer than itself. They were ordered to be printed. I shall most undoubtedly vote against the augumentation of the troops. The war is undertaken without the shadow of authority from Congress, and this war is the pretext for raising an army meant to awe our citizens into submission. Fitzsimons has been heard declaring that *one thousand men would avenge the insults offered to Congress.* Where are these things to end? By the "insult offered to Congress" is meant the State deliberations, etc., respecting the excise. But I can already plainly see that all this matter will vanish in air. Findley, Gallatin, Smilie, Montgomery, in fact all the conductors of the business, having nothing further in view than the securing themselves niches in the six-dollar temple of Congress,* and then popular measures are only meant as the

---

* The pay of Senators and Representatives being six dollars per day.

step-ladder to facilitate their ascent. I confess I have more than once been taken in with the sunshine of some of their speeches in my favor, but actions are louder than words. I have differed beyond the power of reconciliation with the citizens and high-flying Federalists, and genuine republicanism has been my motive. If the old constitutional party were really patriots, they would glory in taking me up. This, however, is not the case; and I am greatly mistaken if they do not lord it with as high a hand over the people, should they get into Congress, as the present majority, and perhaps even there we may not hear a word against the excise.

February 18th.—A number of communications were handed in respecting the appointment of David Humphreys, resident at the court of Portugal. The President sends first, and asks our advice and consent afterward.

Now Carrol's amendatory bill was called up. It was debated with temper, but a good deal of trifling discourse was had upon it. I had determined to say nothing upon the subject. I, however, changed my mind, and made the following remarks:

So far as I had an opportunity of knowing the public mind, the expectations of the people had been disappointed. A belief had obtained that the President would appoint three commissioners, who under his direction would lay out the ten miles square. I did not arraign his authority, and did not call it in question, but he had done himself what should have been done by others under his direction. I would neither pull down nor build up. Let the measure rest on the law. If all was right, it would support itself; if wrong, our mending it was improper, etc.

Mr. Morris followed me. I could not well collect his drift; but he said, with pretty strong emphasis, that if any one would move a postponement, he would be for it. This hint was laid hold on by Langdon and Schuyler, and a postponement moved, which was carried. Mr. Morris sustained a small attack from Gunn for this as an indirect way of getting rid of the measure. Twice, however, did Mr. Morris declare he would vote for the bill if the question was taken on it. I think this kind of conduct ill judged, for the court will think as ill of him as they do of me, who voted dead against the measure from the beginning.

Oh, I should note that Mr. Jefferson with more than Parisian politeness, waited on me at my chamber this morning. He talked politics, mostly the French difference and the whale-fishery; but he touched the Potomac, too, as much as to say, "There, oh, there."

Wednesday, 23d.—I have in general been so closely engaged that I have not had time to minute the daily transactions, and, indeed, unless I wish gratification to myself, there is no use in it, for no man has called on me for any information. On Friday the amendatory act was taken up and read, and postponed for a week. Mr. Morris, Langdon, and Schuyler voted for the postponement. They might as well have voted against the bill, for the postponement is equally ungrateful at court. Saturday we had communications from the President, etc.

A most villainous bill (in my opinion) was committed to General Dickenson, Wyngate, and myself. It was for paying off at par one hundred and eighty-six thousand dollars due to foreign officers. This was a domestic debt beyond a doubt. The bill went to pay it out of the funds appropriated to foreign debt. Strip it, however, of all coloring, it is to sanctify the most abandoned speculation. Some say the whole of it has already been bought up. I set myself to defeat it, and happily succeeded. The consequence is, that I have all the Secretary's [Hamilton's] gladiators upon me. I have already offended Knox and all his military arrangements; I have drowned Jefferson's regards in the Potomac. Hamilton with his host of speculators is upon me, and they are not idle; the city hates me, and I have offended Morris, and my place must go. My peace of mind, however, shall not go, and like a dying man I will endeavor that my last moments be well spent.

Tuesday my report was read, and Wednesday it was agreed to, or at least the resolution subjoined was adopted, that the bill should not pass to a third reading. Business crowded much, and I have almost determined to pass all. The difference, however, on the new impost law between the two Houses explains so fully the trim of the Senate that I must have a word or two on the subject.

The bill commonly called the excise law, though the term is carefully avoided in the law, puts it in the power of the

President to appoint as many inspectors as he chooses, and to pay them what he pleases, so that he does not exceed five per cent on the whole sum collected. This check is mere nullity, and depends on a point arising posterior to the appointments. The reason given for vesting the power in the President is the want of knowledge of the subject; how many, what duties, etc., they will have to discharge. The House of Representatives seem to say that experience will dispel this ignorance in two years, and therefore they amend, limiting this power of paying, etc., to two years. No, say our Senate, we will not trust the new Congress, etc. In fact, the object is to throw all possible power into the hands of the President, even to the stripping of the Senate. A conference appointed.

It is believed that any measure that can be fairly fixed on the President will be submitted to by the people, thus making him the scapegoat of unconstitutional measures and leading them, by their affection to him, into an acquiescence in these measures that flow from him. To break down the boundaries of the States has been a desideratum. This was attempted at the time of the impost. The geographical situation of Maryland, with respect to Chesapeake Bay, afforded a pretext to do something of this kind under plea of convenience, by adding the Eastern Shore to the State of Delaware and indemnifying Maryland out of Virginia. Clouds of letters reprobated the measure. It would not do. The President is now put upon something of this kind—to alter the lines of the States, by taking from the larger and adding to the smaller—in his arrangement for collecting the excise. Will he really become the tool of his own Administration?

February 24th, Thursday.—This day nothing of moment engaged the Senate in the way of debate until the Virginia Senators moved a resolution that the doors of the Senate chamber should be opened on the first day of the next session, etc. They mentioned their instructions. This brought the subject of instructions from the different Legislatures into view.

Elsworth said they amounted to no more than a wish, and ought to be no further regarded. Izard said no Legislature had any right to instruct at all, any more than the electors had a right to instruct the President of the United States. Mr. Morris followed; said Senators owed their existence to the Constitution; the Legislatures were only the machines to choose them; and was more violently opposed to instruction than any of them. We were Senators of the United States, and had nothing to do with one State more than another. Mr. Morris spoke with more violence than usual.

Perhaps I may be considered as imprudent, but I thought I would be wanting in the duty I owed the public if I sat silent and heard such doctrines without bearing my testimony against them. I declared I knew but two lines of conduct for legislators to move in—the one absolute volition, the other responsibility. The first was tyranny, the other inseparable from the idea of representation. Were we chosen with dictatorial powers, or were we sent forward as servants of the public, to do their business? The latter, clearly, in my opinion. The first question, then, which presented itself was, were my constituents here, what would they do? The answer, if known, was the rule of the Representatives. Our governments were avowedly republican. The question now before us had no respect to what was the best kind of government; but this I considered as genuine republicanism. As to the late conduct of the Legislature of Pennsylvania, I spoke with but few of them. I had no instruction from them, and, all things considered, I was happy that I had given my voice on a former occasion for it. The reasons which I gave them operated still, in full force on my mind.

The first was, that I knew of no reason for keeping the door of any legislative assembly open that did not apply with equal force to us. The second was, that I thought it a compliment due to the smallest State in the Union to indulge them in such request.

The objections against it, viz., that the members would make speeches for the gallery and for the public papers, would be the fault of the members. If they waged war in words and oral combats; if they pitted themselves like cocks, or played the gladiator, for the amusement of the idle and curious, the fault was theirs; that, let who would fill the chairs of the Senate, I hoped discretion would mark their deportment; that they would rise to impart knowledge, and listen to obtain information; that, while this line of conduct marked their debates, it was totally immaterial whether thousands attended, or there was not a single spectator.

This day Butler handed forward a resolution for augmenting the salaries of all Federal officers of the different departments one fourth. It is a great object to increase the Federal offices and salaries as much as possible, to make them marks for the ambitious to aim at. This single stratagem has carried the new Government on so far with increased rapidity.

February 25th, Friday.—This was a busy day in the Senate. We had a long communication from the President respecting the loan of three million florins, which, it seems, came at five and a fouth per cent, the expenses of the negotiation being between four and five per cent up. Now was taken a bill for altering the time of the meeting of Congress. The title was the same with that of a bill rejected the other day. But the former had the first Monday in November; this had the fourth Monday in October. The President declared that, as the day was different, the bill was a different bill. There might be as many different bills as days in the year. It passed, but I confess I thought him wrong. Mr. Morris' vote carried the bill. I spoke against it, but without effect.

Now we had the resolution for opening the doors. Nine votes were given for it, and it was lost.

And now came the Potomac amendatory act. A postponement was moved, but Langdon, Schuyler, Elmer, Morris, and Read voted against the postponement and finally for the bill. This is astonishing, indeed. It is plain the President has taught them. I know not their price, but that is immaterial. I had a good opinion of Elmer once; it is with pain I retract it. I think the city [Philadelphia] must see Morris in a new point of view. Were I to give such a vote, I certainly dared not walk the streets. Mr. Morris wishes his namesake, Gouverneur (now in Europe selling lands for him) placed in some conspicuous station abroad. He has acted in a strange kind of capacity, half pimp, half envoy, or perhaps more properly a kind of political eavesdropper about the British court, for some time past. Mark the end of it. As to Langdon I am at no loss; the appointment of his brother Woodbury is sufficient explanation.

Schuyler is the supple-jack of his son-in-law Hamilton. Of Elmer I know not what to say. I once thought him honest. As to Read I have heretofore known him to have been shaken by something else besides the wind.

February 26th, Saturday.—The third reading was given this day to the detestable bill of yesterday, and the last hand was put to the more detested excise law. All of these, however, were condemned as trifles in political iniquity.

For weeks has the report of the committee on the French complaints lain dormant. Shame! I believe some hand is keeping them back. But now a steady phalanx appeared to support the report. I opposed it what I could, and contended against the alternatives in the report of the Secretary of State as exceptional, and opposed the whole. But all in vain. The report, with some variation, was adopted. I was the only one who voted boldly and decidedly against it. I have annexed the alternatives proposed by Jefferson and the resolutions of the committee, and some of my observations in opposition to Elsworth. They may afford me some amusement at a future day. I will, however, call on Otis for a certificate of my having voted against the resolutions.

Resolved, as the opinion of the Senate, that the eighth article of the treaty of amity and commerce between the United States and his Most Christian Majesty is merely an illustration of the third and fourth articles of the same treaty by an application of the principles comprised in the last-mentioned articles to the case stated in the former.

Resolved, That the Senate do advise an answer to be given to the court of France defending this construction in opposition to that urged by the said court, and at the same time explaining in the most friendly terms the difficulties opposed to the exemptions they claim.

Second. If it be the opinion that it is advantageous for us to close with France in her interpretation of a reciprocal and perpetual exemption from tonnage, a repeal of so much of the tonnage law will be the answer.

That there has been a design to sacrifice French interest as a peace-offering to the British court I can not doubt; but that this should be persisted in after the disappointment attending Gouverneur Morris' management is strange indeed. They, however, hope, or affect to hope, to carry their point. Mr. Morris, a few days ago, asserted that we would, early this spring, have a minister from Great Britain, and the papers have many lying accounts to the same purpose.

There is a system pursuing, the depths of which I can not well fathom, but I clearly see that the poor goddess of liberty is likely to be hunted out of this quarter as well as the other quarters of the globe.

I deliberated much whether I should minute in any degree of accuracy the proceedings of this day. Hitherto delicacy has prevented me from keeping any memoranda of the executive or secret journal, but if I am ever to give any account of my conduct to the State government, there is perhaps no part to which they will turn their eyes with more attention. I have another reason for secrecy on this subject, for I certainly never behaved so badly in my life.

Elsworth opened: hoped this business would meet no further delay, as it had been long on the table, and hoped that the resolution would be adopted; that the members had full time to make up their minds, etc. I declared that opportunity as well as time was lacking, although the time had been long; some members had not had the opportunity; that I had called often for a sight of the papers, but always experienced disappointment; that I had indeed seen the alternatives offered by the Secretary of State, and no more; that eminent as the Secretary was for abilities, I could not truly approve of any of his alternatives (here I received a loud——), and, of course, must be opposed to the resolution which was ingrafted on the first. To suppose that, after having passed the third and fourth articles, they were so obscure as to require a fifth by way of illustration, is an absurdity that can not obtain belief. The framers must have had a separate object in view consistent with their reputation as men of understanding, and so it clearly appeared to me.

To justify the construction I will read the articles; here I read them the third: "Grants, certain rights, etc.," in trade, etc., to the subjects of the Christian king in the American ports with respect to duties and imposts. The fourth reciprocated these rights, etc., to the people of the United States in the French ports. Here I took the words "duties" and "imposts" in the strict and limited sense as applying to the impositions charged on the cargo, and to no other. The fifth article has an imposition of another kind for its object, which evidently was not considered as falling within the province of the third or fourth article, viz., tonnage, a port charge which is laid on in proportion to her burden, independent of cargo, and is charged whether she comes loaded or in ballast.

It is, in fact, the machine by which commercial nations encourage or discourage the shipping of their neighbors. I am ready to admit that the poverty or rather the want of preciseness in commercial terms often confuses and confounds them together, but with these ideas and with this view of the subject, which I am satisfied are correct, let us examine the fifth article. And the first feature that presents itself is a reciprocal design of augmenting and favoring the shipping of the contracting parties. Duties and imposts laid upon goods are taxes paid by the consumers. Tonnage is a tax on the ship. To lessen the tax on the shipping, or rather to do it away altogether, is in favor of naval property, and in this spirit ran the stipulation of the fifth article.

But if gentlemen will view them conjointly, what will be the effect? Exemptions are generally stipulated between the contracting parties in the third and fourth articles. What says the fifth? In the above exemption is particularly comprised the imposition of one hundred sols per ton, etc., with the exception of the coasting trade to French vessels between their own ports, which the Americans are allowed to balance with a similar tonnage on French vessels coasting in the American ports. And even this coasting-trade tonnage is not to continue longer than the most favored nations pay it. Will any man undertake to say, on seeing this article, that the French can legally charge the tonnage of one hundred sols or any greater or less tonnage on American vessels in their ports (unless they become coasters) consistent with treaty? I think not. If the French, then, can not on the principles of reciprocity, we can not.

What, then, is to be done? Repeal the law, but upon a different principle from that held out by the Secretary either in his second or third alternative. The second is sordid, as having advantage for its basis; the third carries something like an airy insult, as much as to say: We are right, you are wrong, but take it; our good nature shall yield to your peevishness. Second idea of compensation for favors is worse infinitely. This is a subject on which the American nation is and will be bankrupt, to compensate the political salvation of America. France ought to be placed in the deplorable position which afflicted America [was in] when rescued by her helping hand, and ought to be returned in turn. Statements that seem beyond human events. Where would have been our Washington and patriots of every grade had it not been for French interference? When the meekest and most gentlemanly of all the British commanders would not associate them with any other idea than that of a lord. Not the virtues of a Padilla would have saved one of them. No, let us do homage to the spirit and letter of [the] treaty, own our mistake, and repeal the law. I have ever thought that a liberal and manly policy, more conformable to the genius of the people, was the surest method of engaging and preserving the esteem of that magnanimous nation. And the alternative might be war and confusion.

A burst of abuse now flowed forth against the French by Elsworth in the most vituperative language that fancy could invent. Selfishness, interested views, their motive. To dismember the English empire; *"Divide et imperia"* their motto. Nay, slay the British subjects with the sword of their fellows. No gratitude in nations, no honor in politics. None but a fool would expect it. Serve yourself the first article is the creed of politics. No return due to them. Ridicule, not thanks, would attend acknowledgments. He [Elsworth] seemed to have mistaken the genius of the people, and said some sarcastic things about America which I could not very well comprehend. The term monkey was used; it was meant in ridicule of what I said. He fell on me with the most sarcastic severity. No confusion anywhere but in the speaker's head. Alas! how shall I write it? I almost lost my temper, and, finding no protection from the Chair, left the room.

A moment's reflection restored me. I recollected that I had the volume of Congress of 1783, which I had looked up for this occasion, before my seat, where the greatest encomiums were bestowed on the French. I returned. King was up, and, although he was in the same sentiment as Elsworth, he said Mr. Jay had given a similar construction with me, or at least I so understood him. I did not hear one of the statements which I made answered or attempted to be answered. I happened to turn round and the full-length portrait of the King and Queen of France caught my eye. I really seemed to think they would upbraid me if I was silent. I knew the disadvantage I labored under, but I got up.

Nations being composed of individuals, the virtue, character, and reputation of the nation must depend on the morals of the individual, and could have no other basis. Gratitude, generosity, sensibility of favors, benignity, and beneficence had not abandoned the human breast; in fact, these were the conditions on which the human race existed; that these passions, so far as they respected the French nation, were deeply engraved on the bosom of every American Revolutionist. I knew there were characters of a different kind in America; but for them we cared not; that I was convinced the sense of America had been fairly expressed by Congress on the resignation of General Washington, when the epithet of "magnanimous nation" was applied to them.

What were the expressions of Congress as reported by a committee, some of whom are now within my hearing, in the year 1783, with respect to that now vilified nation? "Exertions of arms," "succors of their treasury," "important loans," "liberal donations," "magnanimity," etc. Yes, all this and more, for I have the book before me. In fact, language labored and seemed to fail in expressions of gratitude to our ally. But here is a reverse indeed. If right then, we must be wrong now; and my heart tells me it is so. Vituperation and abuse, more especially in the national way, are of the reflective kind, and attach disgrace rather to the assailants than to the assailed. Who ever believed that the grins or dirty tricks of the baboon or monkey in the African or American wilds disgraced the traveler that walked below, although they attached contempt to the filthy animal above?

Elsworth took a great deal of snuff about this time. He mumped, and seemed to chew the cud of vexation. But he affected not to hear me, and, indeed, they were all in knots, talking and whispering. Mr. Adams talked with Otis, according to custom. The committee alluded to were: Madison, Elsworth, and Hamilton. I am too sparing; I should have read that part of the report with their names.

I can not help a remark or two. A war in some shape or other seems to have been the great object with Hamilton's people. At first they would have war with the Northern Indians. That failed. They have succeeded in involving us with the North-western Indians. Britain at one time seemed their object. Great efforts were made to get a war with Algiers. That failed. Now it seems to be made a point to differ with the French. That lively nation do not seem to have been aware that ours was a civil war with Britain, and that the similarity of language, manners, and customs will, in all probability, restore our old habits and intercourse, and that this intercourse will revive— indeed, I fear it has already revived—our ancient prejudices against France. Should we differ with France, we are thrown inevitably into the hands of Britain; and, should France give any occasion, we have thousands and tens of thousands of anti-Revolutionists ready to blow the coals of contention.

February 27th, Sunday.—This day made inquiries of George Remsen, one of the clerks of Hamilton's office, respecting a story which is circulating with respect to Bingham having got thirty-six thousand dollars of counterfeit certificates registered and a new certificate for them. He declares the fact is so. These certificates have been copied from genuine certificates, the counterfeits handed to the Auditor (Milligan), passed by him to the Register (Nourse), and a new certificate given for the amount. Thus the counterfeits being disposed of, there could be no danger of detection, as the genuine and counterfeit ones could never meet. Now, the genuine ones coming forward to be loaned, the fraud is found out.

I dined this day with Dr. Rushton. I mentioned this circumstance. A gentleman of the name of Curry came in while I talked of it. Without mentioning names, he said this must be Mr. Swanwick. He was asked how large a certificate Swanwick had founded in this way; he said only twenty thousand dollars. Hell surely must have emptied her rascals upon us, or we never could have been served thus! Remsen has promised to give me more information on this subject.

February 28th, Monday.—This day I fell in discourse with Mr. Morris, and mentioned the thirty-six thousand dollars in possession of Bingham. It seems it is the same which Swanwick had. A Charles Young owed Swanwick, and was arrested in New York for the debt on his return from Boston; paid these certificates to Swanwick; was discharged; they were registered. Swanwick sold to Bingham for twelve hundred pounds, knowing the state of the registered certificates. This cast an air of innocence over the transaction. Perhaps we shall hear more of it.

Schuyler's bill, which went to make debts due to the United States payable in certificates, etc., the object of which could not be observed, and which truly might be called a snake in the grass, was laid over to the next session.

I could not ascertain the point in the above conversation who obtained the registry of the above certificates, and therefore have endeavored to find from Mr. Morris who discovered the cheat; at what time with respect to the registry, viz., whether before or after. But he was guarded, and either knew not or would not tell; but he admitted that they were known to be counterfeits at the time of the sale. This, in my opinion, involves both in criminality. O deluded public, little do you know of what stuff the Federal debt is composed which you are daily discharging with sorrow!

March 1st.—Attended this morning the eulogium in honor of Dr. Franklin, pronounced by Dr. Smith. People say much of it; I thought little of it. It was trite and trifling. Perhaps I am censorious. I despise Smith. He certainly is a vile character.

Much business was hurried through the Senate this day. Now is the time for dark, designing men to carry in and hurry through, under some spurious pretense, the deep-laid plots of speculation. The immature resolve and ill-digested law often escape examination while nothing but home occupies the minds of departing members.

Few days happen in which I do not meet with something to fret my political temper, but this day I met with something that really roused every feeling of humanity about me. The President was directed some time ago to take measures to ransom eleven Americans who are slaves at Algiers. Money was appropriated for this purpose out of the Dutch loan in 1788. The President, however, sent us back a message to appropriate the money for the purpose; and now a committee, who had the African business committed to them, reported twenty thousand dollars to treat with the Emperor of Morocco, but not a cent for the poor slaves. Hard was the heart that could do it, and clay-cold was the conduct of the President even in the business. I said and did what I could, but all in vain; and we will not only confine to slavery, but murder with the plagues of that deleterious climate, these unhappy men.

Izard came over, and made a long complaint against Hamilton. Here, said he, have we been waiting, nobody knows how long, and Hamilton has promised to send us a bill for the Mint. And now at last he sends us a resolution to employ workmen. Two things are clear from this: that Hamilton prepares all matters for his tools (this I knew long ago) ; the other is that he has kept back this exceptionable business till there would be no time to investigate it.

Bassett this day laid on the table a resolution for a committee of both Houses to wait on the President to request him to take measures with the Indians, etc. A pretty pass of society we have already arrived at! It would be much more consonant to the dignity of Congress to establish a spirited inquiry how we came to be involved in a war without the authority of Congress, than to be begging our own servants to spare the effusion of human blood. Every account of this kind seems to be received with an air of satisfaction by the adherents of the Administration, as if our military defects were political virtues.

March 2d.—Oh, 'twas joyful news when I came home and found my man sent by Bob Murdock, and had the pleasure to hear of the welfare of my family. More business has been hurried through the Senate this day than has been done in a month of our former sessions at other periods. The Secretary [Hamilton] has bought the present House, and he wishes to have his money's worth out of them. The resolution of the Mint was foully smuggled through. I hope somebody will take notice of it in the other House. It is evident what a system has been adopted by the Secretary [Hamilton]. We used to canvass every subject and dispute every inch of his systems, and this sometimes detached some of his party from him and defeated him. To prevent this, all has been put off until this late moment, and now not a word will be heard. The plea of want of time prevails, and every one that attempts to speak is silenced with the cry of question and a mere insurrection of the members in support of the demand. I am at no loss now to ascertain the reason why the Mint business has been delayed and finally came forward under the form of a resolution rather than a bill. Bills can not be read out of order but by unanimous consent.

It was known that I had controverted sundry positions laid down by Hamilton in his report, and had prepared myself on the subject. It was easy to call the question and silence debate, but now the time was short and I still had a vote. By refusing consent to an irregular reading of a bill, this rule did not extend to a common resolution. King made a motion by a side-wind to bring in the principal of the bill for paying off the foreign officers, but being smoked he sneaked off. This great man is miserably deficient in candor. He is an active member of the smuggling committee. It was to a bill for the protection of the Treasury that he wished to detach his moved amendment. This bill seemed in a peculiar manner committed to his care. Two laws empowered [the] Government to borrow of Holland: one was to pay the interest on the foreign debt; the other was to reduce the domestic debt by buying in while it was under par (this the ostensible reason, but the real one was to make a machine of this money for raising the stocks). The first was a matter of necessity, as the interest fell due. The second loan was expressly confined to be done at an interest of five per cent; but it has been done at a charge of four and one half per cent; or, in other words, ninety-five and a half only is received, on which five is paid annually as interest. Now, a bill is silently passed along in the mass of business to sanctify this willful deviation. The thing is done, the money received, brought over, and in part, at least, expended. There was nobody to hear speeches or attend argument. I could not, however, help condemning the measure. The duty of the Government was to borrow at five per cent or let it alone; but if the Treasury could once establish the practice of acting without or contrary to law, the whole freedom of the Government might be sapped by fiscal arrangement, and the Congress of the United States might in time become, as in Great Britain, the mere tool of ministerial imposition and taxation.

It has been usual with declamatory gentlemen, in their praises of the present Government, by way of contrast, to paint the state of the country under the old Congress as if neither wood grew nor water ran in America before the happy adoption of the new Constitution. It would be well for the future, in such comparisons, to say nothing of national credit (which, by the by, I never considered as dependent on the prices current of certificates in the hands of speculators), for the loan of 1788 was done in Holland at five per cent, only postponed.

March 3d.—As well might I write the rambles of Harlequin Ranger or the vagaries of a pantomime as to attempt to minute the business of this morning. What with the exits and the entrances of our Otis, the announcings, the advancings, speechings, drawings, and withdrawings of Buckley and Lear, and the comings and goings of our committee of enrollment, etc., and the consequent running of doorkeepers, opening and slamming of doors, the House seemed in a continual hurricane. Speaking would have been idle, for nobody would or could hear. Had all the business been previously digested, matter or form would have been of little consequence. This, however, was not the case. It was patching, piecing, altering, and amending, and even originating new business. It was, however, only for Elsworth, King, or some of Hamilton's people to rise, and the thing was generally done. But they had overshot themselves; for, owing to little unforeseen impediments, there was no possibility of working all through, and there was to be a great dinner which must absolutely be attended to. Terrible, indeed, but no alternative—the House must meet at six o'clock.

In the evening by candle-light. When I saw the merry mood in which the Senate was assembled, I was ready to laugh. When I considered the occasion, I was almost disposed to give way to a very different emotion. I did, however, neither the one nor the other; and, feeling myself of as little importance as I had ever done in my life, I took pen and paper and determined, if possible, to keep pace with the hurry of business as it passed, which I expected would now be very rapid, as I had no doubt that Hamilton's clerks had put the last hand to everything:

1. Mr. Buckley announced that he brought a new resolve for the safe-keeping of prisoners, etc.

2. A bill for compensation to commissioners of loans for extra expenses.

3. A salary bill for the executive officers, their clerks, and assistants.

4. Resolve for the President to lay before Congress an estimate of lands not claimed by Indians.

5. The Mint resolve.

These obtained the signature of the President of the Senate and were sent off for the deliberation and approbation of the President. The prisoner resolve was agreed to and sent back to the Representatives by Otis.

6. Mr. Buckley: second message.

A new bill to carry into effect the convention with the French, etc. This business has been most shamefully neglected. I had often spoken on the subject, but my influence was gone. I had, however, spoken lately to sundry members of the House of Representatives, and even at this late hour was happy to see the bill. To speak in the present uproar of business was like letting off a pop-gun in a thunder-storm. But this was the merest matter of form possible. It was only giving the authority of law to a convention solemnly entered into with the French. My colleague cried "No!" on the second reading. I called for the yeas and nays, and not out of resentment, but merely with an exculpatory view, if this conduct should draw on us the resentment of France, for I consider it disrespectful (to say no worse) toward her and dishonorable in us.

7. Mr. Buckley: third message with the Pension, Invalid, and Lighthouse bills.

The committee reported the enrollment of the following acts:

8. For the continuance of the post-office.

9. For granting lands to the settlers at Vincennes, Illinois.

10. Supplementary act for the reduction of the public debt.

11. For granting compensation to judicial officers, witnesses, and jurymen.

These bills received the signature of the President of the

Senate after being brought up by Mr. Buckley in his fourth message.

12. Who brought at the same time a new bill for the relief of David Cook? Twice heretofore has there been an attempt to smuggle this bill through in the crowd. It happened, however, to be smoked and rejected.

13. Mr. Buckley's fifth message brought a bill for making further provision for collection of duties on teas, etc., which received the signature, etc.

14. An enrolled resolve, which also received the signature, etc.

There now was such confusion with Otis, Buckley, Lear, our committee of enrollment, etc., that I confess I lost their arrangement. Indeed, I am apt to believe if they had any they lost it themselves. They all agreed at last that the business was done. The President left the chair, and the members scampered downstairs. I stayed a moment to pack up my papers. Dalton alone came to me, and said he supposed we two would not see each other soon. We exchanged wishes for mutual welfare. As I left the Hall, I gave it a look with that kind of satisfaction which a man feels on leaving a place where he has been ill at ease, being fully satisfied that many a culprit has served two years at the wheelbarrow without feeling half the pain and mortification that I experienced in my honorable station.

THE RULES OF PROCEEDINGS FOR THE FIRST UNITED STATES SENATE

(From the cover of William Maclay's Journal.)

EACH House may determine the rules of its proceedings, punish its members for disorderly behavior, and, with the concurrence of two thirds, expel a member—(Second clause, fifth section, first article on the Constitution of the United States).

RULE 1. The President (of the Senate) should be in the chair within half an hour of the time to which the Senate stands adjourned; and the Senators shall immediately take their seats in a circular order; those from New Hampshire occupying the right of the Chair and those from Georgia the left.

RULE 2. The minutes of the preceding day shall be read before any other business is entered upon; inaccuracies or inelegancies may be corrected or amended; but no reconsideration as to matter of substance shall take place on such reading.

RULE 3. Every Senator presenting a petition, memorial, or other writing, shall briefly state the import of the same; and every such paper after being read shall be deemed to lie on the table, unless the same is dismissed upon special motion for impropriety or want of decency.

RULE 4. Every motion made and seconded shall be repeated from the Chair and then be open to discussion. The motion, if verbal, shall be put in writing at the request of the President (of the Senate) or any two Senators.

RULE 5. Adoption, rejection, amendment, commitment, or postponement, shall be considered as proper modes of treating business; and in all cases (treaties, returned bills, etc., and the expulsion of a member, excepted) a majority of votes shall govern.

RULE 6. Every Senator when speaking shall address himself to the Chair. No Senator shall be named in debate, but may be referred to by mentioning the State he represents or by alluding to his place in the House.

RULE 7. In case of a debate becoming tedious, four Senators may call for the question; or the same number may at any time move for the previous question, viz., "Shall the main question now be put?"

RULE 8. Priority of speaking and all questions of order shall be decided by the President (of the Senate); but either party may appeal to a vote of the House.

403

RULE 9. The name of the Senator making and of the one who seconds a motion shall be entered on the journals of the House.

RULE 10. No Senator shall speak more than twice on the same subject without leave obtained from the Chair.

RULE 11. Inviolable secrecy shall be observed with respect to all matters transacted in the Senate while the doors are shut, or as often as the same is enjoined from the Chair.

RULE 12. Every member of a committee shall attend the same at the time appointed by the chairman, who shall be the Senator of the most northerly State of those from whom the committee are taken.

RULE 13. When a commitment is agreed upon, the President (of the Senate) shall take the sense of the Senate as to the manner of appointing the committee, whether by motion from the Senators, nomination from the Chair, or by ballot; which shall take place accordingly.

RULE 14. The files of the House shall remain open for the inspection of all the Senators, etc., but no original paper shall be removed from the House without leave obtained for that purpose by the Senate.

RULE 15. The yeas and nays on any question shall be entered on the journals at the desire of one fifth of the Senators present.

RULE 16. These rules shall be engrossed on parchment and hung up in some conspicuous part of the Senate chamber. And every Senator who shall neglect attendance during a session, absent himself without leave or withdraw for more than a quarter of an hour without permission after a quorum is formed, shall be guilty of disorderly behavior, and his name, together with the nature of the transgression, shall be written on a slip of paper and annexed to the bottom of the rules; there to remain until the Senate, on his application or otherwise, shall take order on the same.

INDEX

Note.—As the diary of William Maclay covers a space of only two years, the public affairs of that period are treated very fully, and in detail. This threw peculiar difficulties in the way of the indexer. If the exceedingly numerous and oft-repeated references to the position of prominent individuals in various questions of public interest had all been separately indexed, the list would have been extended to too great a length for practical purposes. All such references have, therefore, been grouped together under appropriate titles in the list of references following each name, as: IZARD, on the impost,—on the tonnage act, etc. In this way nothing remains un-indexed, while the inconvenience of an endlessly minute system of reference is avoided.

405